Charles Brandon

About the Author

Dr Steven Gunn is Professor of Early Modern History and Tutor in History at Merton College, Oxford. He has taught Tudor history at Oxford University for over twenty years and is a regular commentator on the subject for BBC Radio and the broadsheet newspapers. His other books include *Arthur Tudor, Prince of Wales*, *Cardinal Wolsey: Church, State and Art* and *Early Tudor Government*.

Charles Brandon

Henry VIII's Closest Friend

STEVEN GUNN

AMBERLEY

For my parents

Amberley edition first published 2015
This edition first published 2016

Amberley Publishing
The Hill, Stroud
Gloucestershire, GL5 4EP

www.amberley-books.com

British Library Cataloguing in Publication Data.
A catalogue record for this book is available from the British Library.

ISBN 978 1 4456 6031 8 (paperback)
ISBN 978 1 4456 4194 2 (ebook)

Typesetting and Origination by Amberley Publishing.
Printed in the UK.

Contents

List of Illustrations, Maps and Tables

Illustrations

1. From a private collection.
2. Courtesy of British Library, flickr.
3. Courtesy of Rijksmuseum.
4. Courtesy of British Library, flickr.
5. Courtesy of Lee Hutchinson, flickr.
6. Courtesy of Mike Cox, flickr.
7. Courtesy of National Portrait Gallery.
8. Courtesy of Josephine Wilkinson and Amberley archive.
9. Courtesy of Jason Schultz, flickr.
10. Courtesy of Jonathan Reeve.
11. Courtesy of Rijksmuseum.
12. Courtesy of Rijksmuseum.
13. Courtesy of Jonathan Reeve JR1092b20fp89615001550.
14. Courtesy of Duncan H, flickr.
15. Courtesy of David Baldwin.
16. Courtesy of giborn_134, flickr.
17. Courtesy of Ashmolean Museum, Oxford.
18. Courtesy of British Library, Additional MS 19176, fo. 64, reproduced by courtesy of the Trustees of the British Library.
19. Courtesy of Victoria and Albert Museum, London.
20. Courtesy of British Library, flickr.
21. Courtesy of Library of Congress.

22. Courtesy of British Library, flickr.
23. Courtesy of British Library, flickr.
24. Courtesy of Library of Congress.
25. Courtesy of Jonathan Reeve JRCD2b20p76915501600.
26. Courtesy of PRO and reproduced by permission of the Controller of Her Majesty's Stationery Office.
27. Courtesy of Elizabeth Norton.
28. Courtesy of Rijksmuseum.
29. Courtesy of Jonathan Reeve JR968b42p40415001600.
30. Courtesy of Ian Patterson, flickr.
31. Courtesy of Barry Skeates, flickr.
32. Courtesy of Courtauld Institute of Art; reproduced by kind permission of Lady Willoughby de Eresby.
33. Courtesy of Jonathan Reeve.
34. Courtesy of Elliott Brown, flickr.
35. Courtesy of Yale Centre for British Art.
36. Courtesy of Elizabeth Norton.
37. Courtesy of Royal Collection, Windsor; reproduced by gracious permission of Her Majesty the Queen.
38. Courtesy of Royal Collection, Windsor; reproduced by gracious permission of Her Majesty the Queen.

Preface

Charles Brandon has been at times an elusive quarry. Not only are most of his thoughts and feelings lost to us, but even his itinerary, his finances, his landlordship, and the personnel of his household and administration can be reconstituted in far less detail than those of a number of his contemporaries. Yet he still seemed worth pursuing, if only in the attempt to produce a coherent picture of a man whose name has been fitted to so many conflicting stereotypes. More generally, he also has much to tell us about the possibilities open to the king's friends in early Tudor England.

The shape of this study was conditioned both by the limitations of the evidence – in a thematic, rather than a chronological, treatment, all too many sections could have reached only the most tentative of conclusions – and by the desire to show how the different aspects of Brandon's career fitted together in successive periods. Even so, the paucity and ambiguities of the evidence are sometimes such that I have tried to present that evidence where necessary, rather than supply conclusions which the records do not quite warrant. Clarity may have been lost in the determination not to over-simplify, but that seemed the lesser of two evils in dealing with a man who enjoys no modern biography, but was the central character in a 1953 Disney film.[1]

I have incurred many debts in the writing of this book and of the thesis on which it is based, not least to the Warden and Fellows of Merton College, Oxford, who have supported my research through a Senior Scholarship and a Junior Research Fellowship. I should like to thank the College of Arms, the Henry E. Huntington Library, and the Marquess of Bath for permission to cite material in their possession, and Drs M. L. Bush, G. Redworth, D. R. Starkey, and S. K. Walker for permission to use their unpublished theses. I am grateful for their help to the staffs of the libraries and record offices in which I have worked, especially to the staff of the Suffolk Record Office, who made uncatalogued material available to enable me to use it in this book. For profitable discussion and useful references I am indebted to Ian Archer, Gary Hill, Richard Hoyle, Henry James, Phillip Lindley, Diarmaid MacCulloch, Helen Miller, Jeremy Maule, Glyn Redworth, Rhys Robinson, Neil Samman, Susan Vokes, Anne Ward, and Andrew Wathey. I benefited greatly from the friendly and constructive comments of my examiners, Professor J. J. Scarisbrick and Dr P. H. Williams. George Bernard, Peter Gwyn, Roger Highfield, and Simon Payling have been particularly helpful and encouraging, as have Jacqueline Boyers and my parents. Lastly, I am grateful to Cliff Davies for his unfailingly stimulating and enthusiastic supervision of my research, and for enlightening discussions at every stage of this study's development.

Preface to the 2015 Edition
I thank Amberley Publishing for the opportunity to produce a new version of this book, not least since public interest in Charles Brandon has so much increased since the first edition. I remain grateful to those thanked above, and in particular Jacqueline Boyers, who became my wife not long after the book was first published and has been a source of cheerful encouragement and loving support ever since.

S. J. G.
Merton College, Oxford

Note on Conventions

In all quotations punctuation and capitalisation have been modernised, as has the use of u and v, i and j. Accents have been used in French quotations only when these appear in the original. Dates are old style, with the year taken to begin on 1 January.

1

The Rise of Charles Brandon:
c. 1484–1514

In spring 1509 Charles Brandon was one among ninety-three esquires of the body in the funeral procession of Henry VII.[1] By spring 1514 he was Charles, Duke of Suffolk, by Tudor rules of precedence Henry VIII's fifth most exalted subject; he wielded great power in domestic politics, and cut a figure in European affairs. Contemporaries accepted readily the king's duty to reward those who served him well, and acknowledged – sometimes reluctantly – that such benefits might be earned as the king's friend at court rather than in more obvious service to the commonwealth. But the speed of Brandon's rise and the heights that he attained shocked his own generation and tempted later writers to explanations founded in romantic myth. In a swashbuckling tale of 1676, Roger Boyle staged Brandon's first meeting with Henry deep in the forest, where the young king found the future duke defending a beautiful damsel against a furious stag.[2] Henry joined in the fight, and Brandon saved the king's life. They both paid court to the maiden, and to defuse their rivalry she made them swear to eternal friendship. The story's details were ludicrous, but Boyle's imagination had captured some of the themes that blended in the powerful friendship of Henry and Charles. Chivalrous rivalry and brotherhood in arms, courtly love and the chase combined in reality as in fiction. Boyle's depiction of Brandon as an errant squire, the son of a soldier disenchanted with civil war, and taught from his youth to avoid the court's vanity and danger, was much further from the truth. Charles Brandon's career was rather the product of two generations' efforts to back the winners in civil strife and claim a place at court.

The Brandon Inheritance

Charles Brandon's grandfather, Sir William Brandon, was the first of his line to emerge from the obscurity of minor merchant status in the Norfolk coastal ports.[3] He did so as the servant of the Mowbray dukes of Norfolk, rising to a leading place in their council and affinity, and making a good marriage to Elizabeth Wingfield, the daughter of another Mowbray officer. Local offices and a seat in parliament were the rewards he won through the duke's influence, but he aimed higher still and secured a place in royal service, first under Henry VI, then under Edward IV. When the last Mowbray duke died in 1476, Brandon remained the king's man, and unlike most of his colleagues in the Mowbray affinity, did not move on to serve the Howards.

Like many of Edward IV's household servants, Sir William and his three sons gambled on the overthrow of Richard III, first in the 1483 revolts and then at Bosworth. For Sir William the gamble paid off, and until his death in 1491 he enjoyed a trusted place in the government of Suffolk. His eldest son, another William and by all accounts an unsavoury character, died a hero's death at Bosworth, leaving a daughter and two sons: yet another William, who died in the later 1490s, and Charles. It was Sir William's second son, Sir Robert, who inherited his father's East Anglian estates and influence, but he proved to be a quarrelsome and untalented man who could offer little help to his nephew Charles besides an introduction to Suffolk gentry society. As he grew up Charles had virtually no lands – his mother was an heiress, but her inheritance passed to a son by a previous marriage, while in 1502–3 Charles was trying to recover his small shale of his grandmother's lands from his cousin John Loveday – and neither in 1504 nor in 1509 did he hold the £40 worth of estates which would have made him liable to distraint for knighthood.[4] As a country gentleman his prospects were dim, but fortunately the route lay open for advancement at court. Charles's younger uncle, Sir Thomas, inherited from old Sir William the family house in Southwark and the office that went with it, that of marshal of the king's bench prison. He followed Sir William's lead in building a career in the royal household, becoming an esquire of the body by 1489 and master of the horse by 1501, and in the 1490s he was among Henry VII's most active courtiers, jousting with distinction and often busy about the king's pleasures.[5]

Sir Thomas was well placed to bring Charles to court, but he was not just a courtier. He served Henry VII as a councillor, a naval and military commander, and an increasingly prominent diplomat. Meanwhile he established himself in the south-west and south Midlands. He married first the widow of William, Marquis of Berkeley, then the coheiress of John, Lord Dinham, who retained lands from previous marriages to Sir John Sapcote and Fulk, Lord Fitzwarin. He took a firm grip on these dower lands, and gained a further foothold in the area by obtaining the wardships of successive lords Saye.[6] At Henry VIII's accession he exploited his position at court, his friendship with the leading survivors of the old king's council, and his involvement with horses and the chase – half the warrants he counter-signed in later 1509 were issued from royal hunting lodges – to reap his share of the more bountiful patronage dispensed by the new king.[7] He seemed set for great things, and London political gossip named him as an influential figure; but in January 1510 he became fatally ill, making his will on the 11th and dying on the 27th.[8]

Sir Thomas Brandon's funeral demonstrated various aspects of his legacy to his nephew Charles. Sir Robert Brandon was chief mourner, and both uncles had remained in contact with their nephew.[9] William Sidney, Charles's cousin, bore the banner: he had lived in Sir Thomas's household and 'contynually waytid apon hym in the coort', and would be close to Charles.[10] The presence of a king-of-arms and a pursuivant witnessed to the knightly accomplishments which Charles was already emulating. The other leading mourners were Anthony and Humphrey Wingfield and John Brews, all relatives through Sir William's Wingfield marriage, a connection which would serve Charles well. Finally, Sir Thomas's coat of arms was delivered to Sir Edward Poynings and Sir Thomas Lovell, prominent members of the circle of knights who had passed from Henry VII's council into that of his son. Lovell in particular was close to Sir Thomas Brandon, as an executor and relative by marriage, and he must have been a useful friend to Charles, as he was to another ambitious man at court, Thomas Wolsey. Lovell's influence over the distribution of crown wardships, as Master of the Wards from 1513, was especially significant.[11]

The value of Charles's inheritance from his childless uncle lay more in such connections than in lands or goods. Thomas's gowns and the wardship of Lord Saye passed to Charles, but even the few lands he did eventually inherit were kept by Sir Thomas's widow until her death in 1516. His uncle's grants from Henry VII were in tail male, and so reverted to the crown; and Sir Thomas left his purchased lands, and the Southwark house, to Lady Jane Guildford, the widow of Sir Richard Guildford, a colleague in Henry VII's household who had died in 1506.[12] Charles had to rent back his uncle's house from her at £42 6s 8d a year, and she settled down in the London Blackfriars to live on this rent and her meagre dower until her death in 1538.[13] Sir Thomas had secured a long lease on the meadows from the house to the river, to make the Southwark residence potentially very grand, and this family seat was intimately connected with his most obvious legacy to Charles, the office of marshal of the king's bench. This had been in the family since 1457, and only a week after his uncle's death it was granted to Charles.[14]

The prison lay opposite the Brandons' house across Borough High Street.[15] The marshal enjoyed a free hand in running the gaol, and this could be profitable in various ways. Many prisoners, or their friends, would pay for a higher standard of comfort, and charitable individuals like the king would send money directly to the marshal to redeem poor prisoners.[16] The deputies who actually ran the prison had to be carefully supervised, since marshals frequently had to sue for pardon for escapes, or pay amercements for them.[17] Offering illegal bail could pay dividends, though, as could the threat of imprisonment in irons, and the household marshalsea prison, which Brandon was shortly also to control, was very well equipped for the latter.[18] The position carried certain specific rights within Southwark, but also a general influence there. Charles was named a Surrey justice of the peace in January 1511, over a year before he joined the Suffolk bench, and in March he was placed on a Surrey commission of gaol delivery, though he probably did not sit.[19] In 1512–13 he headed the list of Southwark subsidy commissioners, and his cousin John Glemham, who had no other link with the borough, was also named.[20]

First Years at Court

His uncle's position gave Charles the chance to begin a career in royal service. In 1501 he waited on Arthur, prince of Wales, on the morning after the prince's ill-fated wedding to Catherine of Aragon, but he did not accompany the young couple's household to Ludlow.[21] Nor is there any evidence that he served in the household of Prince Henry, either before or after Arthur's death, though he did have close links with some of Henry's servants. His uncle John Redyng, with whom Sir Thomas Brandon maintained close contact, was treasurer of the prince's household, and his aunt Mary Redyng, whose house Charles used often in 1508–9, was a gentlewoman to the prince.[22] Meanwhile Charles himself became, by about 1503, a sewer for the board's end, spending much time at court in the company of the young Walter Devereux, Lord Ferrers, who also waited on Henry VII at table.[23]

More significant for his future relationship with Henry VIII were two other positions Brandon held between 1505 and 1509. He was, towards the end of Henry VII's reign, master of the horse to the earl of Essex, and stayed at his house and travelled with him on occasion.[24] Doubtless this provided useful experience when Brandon came to be master of the king's horse, but Essex was also very prominent at court and as a military leader early in Henry VIII's reign, and Brandon's proximity to him must have been advantageous. Essex was appointed lieutenant of the company of king's spears established by Henry in October 1509, and Brandon, like almost every other young courtier, was a member.[25] But the company had its origin, in much smaller form, in Henry VII's reign. In 1505–6 at least there existed a small body, organised in lances as in Henry VIII's ordinances, and administered by a 'clerke of the cheke of the speres'.[26] Many of them took part in the court jousts of 1506, and of the five known members Brandon, John Carr and William Parr did well early in Henry VIII's reign, and Maurice St John had been close to Prince Arthur.[27]

Membership of Henry VIII's spears, despite the expense and effort devoted to them by the king, was a sign of belonging only to a very broad charmed circle.[28] The same was true of Brandon's position as an esquire of the body, first to Henry VII (by 1507) and then to Henry VIII, for he was not one of the attendant esquires with the fee, and even these posts no longer afforded truly intimate contact with the king.[29] What marked him out at court, presumably before 1509 and certainly soon afterwards, was a close personal friendship with the young Henry VIII.

The King's Companions

In the early years of Henry's reign Charles Brandon shared the king's favour with a small circle of his friends: Edward Howard, Thomas Knyvet, and Edward and Henry Guildford, the sons of Sir Richard. Edward Howard and Edward Guildford attended Brandon's secret marriage in 1508, and stood godfathers to his first two daughters.[30] Brandon and Knyvet owed money together to Henry VII in 1508, Brandon and Howard were granted a wardship together in 1509, and early in the new reign Brandon, Knyvet, and Howard joined with Edward Guildford twice in trading ventures.[31] From 1509 Henry showered them with patronage of all kinds, and Brandon and Henry Guildford in particular were frequently the recipients of gifts of clothing from the king.[32] Of this group only Henry Guildford had long been a member of Henry's household before 1509, but the others must have met him at court, for Henry VII's refusal to dispatch his second son to Wales made the king's and the prince's households almost indistinguishable.[33] Above all Prince Henry had been impressed by their feats of arms. When

Brandon, Knyvet, and others organised jousting at court in May and June 1507, Henry watched with enthusiasm,

> Syth our prynce moost comly of stature
> Is desyrous to the moost knyghtly ure
> Of armes to whiche marcyall aventure
> Is his courage.[34]

When Henry came to the throne, it was no surprise that this circle found a prominent place in the king's own pageants and tournaments. From 1509 to 1511, Brandon, Knyvet, and Howard took part in more masques and jousts, usually jousting on the king's side, than any other courtiers except Edward Nevill.[35] Henry Guildford was often master of the revels, and appeared in these more often than anyone except Nevill and the earl of Essex. Edward Guildford organised tournaments as master of the armoury, and acted as marshal of the jousts as his father had done.[36] Their political importance is hard to judge, all the more so because the politics of the years after 1509 remain highly obscure. They enjoyed no monopoly of the king's company – Nevill or Essex often danced or jousted with Henry and two or three of them – and thus presumably no overwhelming influence over him.[37] Though Howard and Knyvet, as son and son-in-law, were closely linked with Thomas Howard, Earl of Surrey and one of the leading councillors, they did little to help the policy, sometimes ascribed to the earl, of restraining Henry's aggression towards France.[38] Their round of tourneying must rather have inflamed the king's martial ardour, as contemporaries commented.[39]

When war began in 1512, the courtiers readily became captains, but Brandon's first taste of real warfare was bitter. In the naval campaign of that summer, he and Sir Henry Guildford were entrusted with elite troops in a large and newly refitted ship. Through misfortune or incompetence they failed to assist Sir Thomas Knyvet when he grappled with a French vessel, and had to watch him and most of his crew die when the French craft exploded and both ships burned. For his remaining weeks at sea Brandon carried among his crew an unpleasant reminder of this action, in three gunners 'remaining on lyve of them that were brent'.[40] It is probably significant that Brandon never served at sea again, but Sir Edward Howard's reaction to the death of their friend Knyvet was more remarkable. Perhaps in imitation of Sir Gawain, Howard vowed 'that he wyl nevyr se the kyng in the face tyl he hath revengyd the dethe of the nobyll and valyant knygth Sir Thomas Knyvet.'[41] He remained at sea, seeking battle with the French, until at length his infectious enthusiasm for combat, so much admired by the king, turned into foolhardy heroism and led Howard to his death in April 1513.[42]

Dominance at Court

In the short term, Howard's sudden demise opened up new military possibilities for Brandon, but its long-term effects were more important. In Sir Edward, Charles Brandon lost his closest friend. Brandon was Howard's only executor besides his widow, and he bequeathed to Brandon not only the chain on which his admiral's whistle used to hang, but also whichever of his two bastard sons the king did not choose to raise, for Charles had been his 'special trusty friend'.[43] With the death of Howard, Charles Brandon also lost the one rival who consistently outshone him in the court and in war. The eulogies at Sir Edward's death, and the king's reaction to it, left little doubt of the impact he had made.[44] But with Knyvet and Howard dead, only Brandon survived of the leaders of their circle: it was natural that he should become the king's closest friend. Where all three had shared with the king in jousts and pageants, and Howard had often performed more spectacularly than anyone,[45] from 1512 to 1514 Brandon played an increasingly distinctive role. Only Sir Henry Guildford masqued more than he did in these years, only Essex and Edward Nevill as often.[46] Where Brandon had been omitted from some earlier disguisings, or not taken a central part, he was now narrowly identified in dress with the king. At New Year 1512 only he and Henry wore one kind of hose, only they and Henry Guildford another variety. On 6 January 1513 Brandon and the king wore special jackets to differentiate them from the other four leading courtiers involved.[47] Charles would seem to have been growing especially close to the king even before his friends' deaths, but these placed him in a position of unique prominence: it was typical that he and Howard were both elected to the Garter on 23 April 1513, but Howard died before the installation ceremony.[48] In April and May 1513 Brandon secured various important grants, while at this time Howard's continued absence at sea seems to have strained his relationship with the king; but it was the fact that Howard would not be coming home in triumph that set the seal on Brandon's rise.[49]

It was in the joust above all that his increasing dominance was evident. He first entered the lists publicly in the splendid and innovative tournament of 1501, and he performed well.[50] In the last years of Henry VII's reign and the early years of Henry VIII's he was a leading figure in tournaments. He was the only esquire among the six challengers at the coronation jousts, in a completely gilt armour. He frequently featured in the teams of three or four challengers led by the king, and even when only an answerer he was at the centre of an opening allegorical display.[51] But on 1 June 1512 he and Henry challenged alone together for the first time, and this was the pattern for the next two years.[52]

Brandon had both the ability to perform consistently well in the lists, and the common sense not to outdo Henry (though both men seem to have been rather shown up by the Burgundian nobles in 1513).[53] It was quite possible to aim one's body at the opponent's lance and thus ensure his success, and Brandon seems to have done just this in February 1511. After three courses the king was only slightly ahead, in the fourth Brandon struck Henry on the body while the king broke his lance on Brandon, thus edging further into the lead; in the last two runs Brandon judiciously failed to score, Henry shattered two lances on Charles's body, and the king won a dashing, but apparently hard-fought, victory.[54] Brandon's usual success against every other opponent, of course, merely highlighted the king's own skill.

Charles Brandon's primacy in the king's jousts marked his growing friendship with the king, and paralleled in particular his increasing military responsibility. It also proclaimed these facts to all and sundry. Henry's court was used to the practicalities of the structure of the 'lance' (a small unit of horsemen used in the king's company of spears) and its reflection in tournament arrangements. The bond between the knights of romance was a familiar ideal, implying close ties of chivalric loyalty despite competition in the quest for honour. In particular, in an age of liveries and sumptuary legislation, identity in dress was a powerful symbol of attachment. By December 1513 the great wardrobe was producing batches of clothes of similar design not for the king and several courtiers, but for Henry and Charles exclusively.[55] In tournament dress this identification was far closer, and far nearer to the realities of kingship than was the masque. Henry as King of England would never dress as Robin Hood, but he did go to war in full armour and barded horse. In 1510–11 groups of challengers often dressed in the same coats as the king who led them.[56] In October 1513 at Tournai, only the king and Brandon dressed alike, and the message was obvious. Brandon, arrayed like Henry in 'the most sumptuous manner imaginable', in an outfit 'considered a remarkable thing', must be 'his favourite'.[57]

Their friendship was far more than a matter of tournament symbolism. It was evident, for example, in Henry's dispatch not only of his wife's Spanish doctor to attend on Brandon in the proposed Brittany expedition of 1513, but also of 'Blynde Dikke, our harper', a much-favoured royal musician.[58] The first five years of the reign established Brandon in a position in Henry's trust and affection which was to be the basis of his subsequent career.

Marshal of the Household and Master of the Horse

One sign of that trust was the collection of a growing number of lucrative and significant offices. In November 1511 Brandon was granted in survivorship with Sir John Carew the office of marshal of the king's household. Carew had held it since December 1507, but he died in the same disaster as Sir Thomas Knyvet, leaving Brandon to exercise the office alone.[59] Primarily this involved keeping a prison about 100 yards from the king's bench gaol in

Southwark, with high fees and the potential for profit, through refusal to release after bail and the employment of 'force and dures'.[60] Though the prisoners of the court of the marshalsea, whose jurisdiction covered the royal court, may not have been numerous, there were valuable sidelines. Despite statutory prohibition, the sheriff of Surrey and Sussex used the prison as a common gaol, and the royal council sometimes used it too.[61] Originally a deputy to the marshal of England, the marshal of the household could be a substitute for him in other roles. In Henry VII's reign the marshal, Sir John Digby, sat on commissions to try rebels, and took a part in the creation of Prince Henry as Duke of York. The jobs of the various knight marshals and marshals of the household were fluid, however, and appointments under Henry VII were erratic enough to make it unclear what Brandon's work involved.[62]

Certainly the office could be profitable, especially if Brandon, like Edward IV's marshal, received all the issues of the marshalsea court.[63] When combined with the king's bench marshalcy, it also made his influence in Southwark remarkably strong: in 1504 the first commissioner for the aid in Southwark had been Sir Thomas Brandon, the second Sir John Digby.[64] The post gave him the responsibility to imprison defaulting crown officials, and probably judicial experience on the bench of the marshalsea court.[65] More significantly, it also brought involvement in the important and personal matter of the king's safety.

Thus Brandon was presumably at the centre of the Newbolt affair in 1512, when a yeoman of the guard killed a man in Westminster Palace.[66] Henry was torn between his admiration for Richard Newbolt, a 'specyall archour', and the need to do justice (and preserve his own safety). Safety came first, and he resolved to have Newbolt hanged; perhaps it was for trustworthy service at moments like these that he increasingly rewarded Brandon.

Like his uncle, Charles was involved with the royal passion for the chase. In April 1512 he was created ranger or riding forester of the New Forest, a post he kept for life.[67] This entitled him to take a number of bucks and fell a quota of trees in the forest each year, and he capitalised on these rights by making Robert Hussey his deputy: Hussey was a local man perpetually in trouble for cutting down the king's woods, who probably paid well for the chance to do so legally.[68] Of more immediate relevance to Brandon was his patent of March 1512 as keeper of Wanstead, Essex. The previous keeper had been Hugh Denys, Henry VII's favoured groom of the stool, and much work had recently been carried out on the house and park.[69] Both kings hunted there, and, perhaps more important for Brandon, Mary Tudor, his future wife, was staying at the house in 1514. Brandon took an interest in Wanstead, leasing some land there. He also collected a fee of 2*d* a day, though how much went to deputies is incalculable.[70]

The mastership of the horse was of still greater practical and symbolic importance. This was his uncle's old office, filled by Sir Thomas Knyvet from 1510 to his death in 1512, and then from 6 October of that year by Brandon. It gave him complete control over the royal stable, and thus over the transport of the household and the king's own horses for hunting and war. Expenditure under Charles reached almost £1,500 a year and the total personnel 137, where under Edward IV these had been under £380 and forty-five respectively.[71] The bulk of this money went to feed the horses, and pay the wages of his proliferating subordinates, and preparations for war especially spread the stable's activity into many corners of the country.[72] The right to appoint all the stable's officers gave Brandon considerable patronage, but its exercise was limited, as the continuity in the department's personnel even over long periods was very high, and officials could survive changes of superior, and even of reigning dynasty, with ease.[73]

Deputies, especially the avener, of course did most of the day-to-day work. George Lovekyn, clerk of the stable, was very active as deputy to both Sir Thomas Brandon and Sir Thomas Knyvet.[74] It does seem that Charles Brandon took a greater personal interest in the stable than they had done, for where warrants had directed money or material to their subordinates, saddles and cash now passed directly to him.[75] Such attention was justifiable because of the importance Henry attached to his horses. Foreign observers in 1513 were struck by the care lavished on them. Henry's enthusiasm for those sent to him by the Marquis of Mantua in 1514 was wonderful to behold, and when he saw the Mantuan envoy's skill with horses he tried to recruit him into his own service.[76] Though the master of the horse was not ordinarily a very prominent household officer, under special circumstances the position became very important for Brandon. Henry was a dedicated horseman in hunt and tournament: the Mantuan who brought the horses, though misunderstanding Brandon's name, thought that the master of the horse was the first person about the king and had been charged with the dispatch of his business.[77] Brandon was not slow to exploit this, and asked the impressed envoy in secret what he could do for the marquis.

The master of the horse was also the king's esquire. With Henry, a king who jousted and rode in processions frequently, this was a significant role. When they challenged together in tournaments, Brandon was the loyal apprentice to Henry's knight. When the king rode out in 1513 to meet his ally, the Emperor Maximilian, and again to meet Maximilian's grandson Prince Charles, Brandon always rode immediately behind him, with his spare horse; in the latter procession Brandon's green velvet outfit was so thickly decorated with gold that the velvet was invisible.[78] The position thus proclaimed his proximity to the king. Especially in the Low Countries this led to a very high estimation of Brandon's importance, for in the Burgundian household the *escuier d'escuyrie* was a far more magnificent officer than his English equivalent.[79] It is noteworthy that Netherlanders like Philippe de Brégilles, the attaché at the English camp of Margaret of Austria, regent of the Low Countries, always referred to Brandon by this office when describing his influence over the king.[80]

The Brittany Raid

Brandon's military responsibilities grew in proportion to his prominence at court. His first major command was in the raid conceived by the king in May 1513 to avenge the death of Sir Edward Howard. Sir Edward's elder brother, Lord Thomas Howard, was designated to replace him as admiral, while Brandon was appointed to lead a landing force to co-operate with the fleet. The stratagem chosen was one of which Henry would remain fond: the fleet and army would execute 'a secret enterprice of our ennemyes' by destroying the French navy in its Breton ports.[81] Despite the disruption which it brought to the plans for the invasion of France that summer, the king was very enthusiastic about the raid. At one point he wished to travel secretly to Portsmouth, 'not only to see th'estate of your armye, but also to see the same spedely sette forthward'.[82] It seems, however, that the whole expedition was too impromptu to stand much chance of execution. From its inception, experienced administrators like Bishop Fox and John Dawtrey warned that its original timetable was impossible.[83] Requirements in weapons and tools were calculated, and Howard and Brandon were carefully instructed to plan their attack in a council of their captains and expert mariners.[84] But doubts were rife: Howard was shocked at the state of the fleet, and badly wanted advice from Fox.[85] Fox stressed the disruption to the summer's main project, Henry's personal invasion of France. He thought that the raid 'woll not be feneshed shortely'; he was also worried that Brandon's army of 4,000 was insufficient, and that 10,000 would be better.[86]

Arrangements did reach an advanced stage. German mercenaries arrived at Southampton where the army was to gather, and artillery was sent from London. Richmond herald was paid in advance for forty days' attendance on Brandon.[87] But the shortage of empty casks and the need to redirect supplies from Calais or London, where they were being sent for the summer's campaign, made victualling difficult. Brandon's servants tried to help solve these logistical problems, but the diversion of troops from the Kent ports to Southampton with as little as eight days' warning caused chaos.[88] Time continued to run against the expedition. By 21 May most of the troops were waiting two days' march outside the port to avoid exhausting the food there, and Brandon had arrived; but Howard was still pinned in Portsmouth by adverse winds, and the victuallers' ships from London and Sandwich were nowhere to be seen.[89] In any case, reports suggested that the French fleet had dispersed from Brest.[90] It had always been intended that Brandon should bring his army to Calais after the raid, so the scheme was abandoned and they were simply shipped from Southampton, instead of from Dover and Sandwich.

Unfortunately the abortion of the enterprise proved complicated. The victuallers were disgruntled over unused and decayed food and drink.[91] More significantly, Howard and Brandon apparently fell out. Brandon had always been far closer to Sir Edward Howard than to Lord Thomas. By 4 June Howard was still trying to attack Brittany in a purely naval raid, despite having 'had a great lette' by Brandon's 'maters'. He was having to disperse some of the troops by land, while hoping to use their weapons and supplies for an expedition with the fleet alone. Fox apparently sided with Howard, assuring Wolsey that, in contrast with Brandon, 'I warant you he woll not slepe his maters.'[92] Recriminations were more complex, though, for Howard complained that Fox and Brandon had overruled Henry's personal orders to him. Fox and Howard continued work until the fleet was ready to leave on 13 June, but the raid never took place.[93]

For Brandon the importance of the Brittany raid lay less in its failure than in its potential. The first initiated a decade of difficult relations with Lord Thomas Howard, soon earl of Surrey. The second, his appointment to a position of great military responsibility which neither his experience nor his rank merited, demonstrated his high favour. When the letters to raise troops were sent out he was only a knight, though on 15 May he was created a viscount, partly perhaps to facilitate his command.[94] He was to lead an army including three barons and numerous knights, like Sir William Sandys and Sir Maurice Berkeley, who were far wiser warriors than he.[95] In fact Brandon was reaping the benefits as much of their military misfortune as of his courtly success. For the senior captains appointed to serve under him had almost all shared in the previous summer's disastrous expedition to Guyenne, some had been personally humiliated by the king, and all were tainted by failure there.[96] Brittany would have given them a chance to redeem themselves under Brandon, whose reputation, if unestablished, was at least untarnished.

The Campaign of 1513

For the king's invasion of France Brandon was appointed high marshal of the army.[97] Many who met Henry and Brandon together on the continent were struck, like Margaret of Austria, by 'the greatt love and trust that the kynge baare and hadd' towards him.[98] But French heralds negotiating their masters' release, or Dutch nobles begging for their troops in English service to be paid, sought Brandon's help not only because he was the king's friend, but also because he was high marshal.[99] He did not command huge numbers of troops, leading the vanguard of the king's ward, a little over 3,000 men. He apparently took little part in the military decisions of the campaign, and saw no fighting in its earlier stages.[100] This was natural, as others were far more experienced. Yet as high marshal, and especially since the king commissioned him lieutenant of the whole army, he enjoyed powers of command over the duke, earls, and battle-hardened knights below him.[101]

His authority as marshal was proclaimed repeatedly throughout the army, first when his letters patent were read out in the market-place at Calais, and subsequently in the weekly or more frequent declarations of the statutes and ordinances of war.[102] His jurisdiction spread over all civil and criminal cases in the army and he could inflict the death penalty; as lieutenant he could create knights.[103] His activity reached most areas of the army's life, from supervising the guide-master's native guides and the provost-marshal's victuallers, to choosing campsites and taking the muster of foreign mercenaries with Essex and the Marquis of Dorset.[104] He was to imprison virtually all offenders against the statutes and ordinances of war, even those who failed to make proper sanitary arrangements at the siege of Thérouanne. In theory at least his court sat thrice a week, and was to arbitrate disputes between captains and their men.[105]

He seems to have performed well. Effective food supplies were more Wolsey's achievement, and the failure of Brandon's jurisdiction to cover German mercenary companies necessitated Henry's personal intervention. But the army's excellent discipline was noted by foreigners, and two hangings prevented any repetition of trouble-making with the local population.[106] Some of Henry's whims, like having 'all my ryche tentes sett up' on the expectation of battle, may have been awkward; but complex cases like that of the two Netherlandish captains who fought over a castle, each assuming the other to be French, were referred to Henry's whole council.[107] Brandon was helpless when a major riot developed between English and German soldiers on Ascension Day, but then even Henry and his ally Maximilian only just succeeded in preventing a full-scale battle.[108]

The marshal was also important in the administration of prisoners and their ransoms. The prisoners taken in 1513 were sufficiently elevated for many to belong to the king, and Henry and Maximilian appointed commissioners to deal with them. Yet Brandon was certainly involved in their distribution, presumably had to apply the complex rules for shares in their ransoms, and may well have mediated in early disputes between English and Netherlanders, over prisoners who had surrendered to the Flemings because they did not trust the English not to kill them.[109]

Brandon's power in the army was impressive. When he asked Margaret of Austria's agent at the siege of Thérouanne to recommend his services to her, the envoy reported to Margaret that he was a 'second king', who 'does and undoes'.[110] As the campaign went on, his military role also increased. At Toumai he controlled the main artillery battery against the 'tour Blandinoise et porte Coquerel'. When the time came he led an assault on this gate which forced the inhabitants to 'retirer es eglises et crier misericorde'.[111] His men were too few to proceed, but they held the gate, encouraging the citizens to emerge for negotiations next morning. Brandon was among the negotiators, and while experienced diplomats settled the details of the surrender, he too played an important role: he terrified the contingent of burghers into a rapid and generous conclusion.[112] Having 'fort le coeur a ladicte basterie' he was loath to cease it, constantly threatening to recommence it, and rabidly eager for an assault. Perhaps this was genuine, perhaps convincing bluff; it certainly had the effect desired by the king, for Henry had every reason to avoid taking

Tournai by storm and thus dispersing its wealth among his soldiers rather than keeping it for himself.[113]

Henry's prized conquest was shared with his friend. He handed the keys to Brandon, who occupied, searched and guarded the city, set up a gallows, and offered to Notre Dame de Tournai.[114] Though it was Sir Edward Poynings who was soon appointed lieutenant, it was Brandon's occupation that attracted attention. The diarist John Taylor thought he had been made governor, and news in Italy reported that the city was entrusted to the king's bastard brother, surely Brandon rather than the ageing Poynings.[115] Given the status of royal bastards around Europe, the latter was no mean compliment to Brandon.

Profit and Power

By the end of the 1513 campaign Charles Brandon was clearly Henry's leading courtier. He was a knight of the Garter and a viscount, and at last enjoyed some military laurels too. Yet he naturally faced problems in converting his influence with the king into the wealth, land-holding, and 'manred' which brought lasting power. Life at court was expensive, and Brandon seems always to have been short of money. He borrowed 10 marks in 1506 to be repaid on his wages as a spear, and he owed Henry VII over £70 at that king's death.[116] Under Henry VIII he took larger loans from the king, and various benefits in kind, like some of the splendid garments and horse furniture he used in court festivities.[117] His many offices also carried fees, though these were rarely pure profit. From 3s 4d a day as a spear he had to support the other members of his lance, while the Welsh offices granted to him in 1509, 1512, and 1513 paid well, perhaps £300 at best, but deputies took some of this.[118] As master of the horse he apparently received £60 13s 4d a year from the chamber, plus £40 a year from the exchequer.[119] Brandon also secured grants of various stewardships of royal manors and keeperships of royal parks in the southern midlands in April 1513.[120] These were near the lands of his ward Lady Lisle, and they paid useful fees. But a royal grant was insufficient to ensure a steady income. As far as the auditors were concerned, letters patent to Brandon on one set of manors, even when countersigned by Sir Robert Southwell, general surveyor of the king's lands, could not dislodge the existing steward.[121] Brandon tried again, jointly with Gerard Danett, an associate of the locally influential Edward Belknap. Their grant in survivorship of June 1513 promised a joint annuity of £6 13s 6d, but was to no avail.[122] Only after the act of resumption of 1515 could Brandon secure a patent which succeeded in bringing him his fees, which eventually totalled on all these offices £18 6s 10d.[123] Perhaps Brandon, unlike other office-holders in the area, could not rely on the support of the local empire-builder William Compton, groom of the stool to the king. Relations between Brandon and Compton were always strained, apparently more by a clash of personalities than by a clash of ambitions.[124] Military service also paid well, 5s a day in 1512, 40s a day in 1513, but the expenses involved were large.[125] As with his marshalcies at home, the real benefit in being high marshal lay not in the office's fees but in its exercise. Not only must there have been presents to induce his favour, but many of the statutory penalties for offences against martial law involved at least partial forfeiture of goods to him, and many offenders were imprisoned until they could make fine with him.[126]

Brandon's obvious proximity to the king also brought an increasing flow of gifts from those anxious that he should represent their interests. For relatives like Edmund Wingfield, who used Charles as his first feoffee on a land purchase in July 1513, such benefits presumably came free.[127] Others paid well to court him. Edmund Bray, nephew and heir of Henry VII's minister Sir Reginald, gave him a £20 annuity in December 1511 on the understanding that Brandon would speak to the king on his behalf.[128] In 1513 the dean and chapter of Canterbury granted to Brandon and Sir Ralph Verney the presentation to a London living.[129] In April and December 1514 two monasteries presented his chaplain Christopher Lynham to London rectories.[130] As Brandon rose, so did the size of these considerations. In August 1514 Margaret, Countess of Salisbury, ordered the payment of a £100 annuity for life to the 'p[re]nobili principi' Charles, duke of Suffolk; Wolsey, she thought, was worth only 100 marks.[131]

Some tangible benefits passed to Brandon and the Guildford brothers on the deaths of Knyvet and Howard. Henry Guildford succeeded Knyvet in a bailiwick, and Howard as the king's banner-bearer.[132] Knyvet's death freed the mastership of the horse for Brandon, and the death of Knyvet's widow, Muriel, Lady Lisle, in December 1512, created for him an even more attractive opportunity. Lady Lisle's eight-year-old daughter Elizabeth was Baroness Lisle in her own right, and stood to inherit substantial estates. Even before Knyvet died, Brandon had negotiated very easy terms with the crown to buy Elizabeth's wardship, taking over seven years to pay £1,400.[133] This was a sound investment, since her lands brought in about £800 a year, and Charles could count on holding them for six years at least.[134] After December 1512, moreover, Brandon had only to contract to marry Elizabeth once she came of age, to enable the king to create him Viscount Lisle in virtue of his wife.

Until he were to marry her, though, Elizabeth's lands would not be securely his, and Brandon's resources did not readily keep pace with his rise in status. Henry did little to endow him directly, granting an annuity of 20 marks at his creation as Viscount Lisle, and £40 a year and one castle when he became duke of Suffolk.[135] The purchase of wardships provided one means for Brandon and other courtiers to convert influence with the king and his administrators, and cash in hand, into ready-made estates. Opportunities to gain control of lands which complemented both the Lisle estates and Brandon's Welsh offices arose irregularly, though, and the need to exploit them when they did come added to Brandon's financial problems. Early in 1514, for 500 marks in cash and a further 500 in instalments, he bought the wardship of Roger Corbet, son and heir of Sir Robert.[136] In the long term he probably saw Roger as a suitable son-in-law; in the short term the Corbet estates added another £150 at least to Brandon's net income, with the expectation of half as much again when Sir Robert's widow died.[137]

Investment like this necessitated various money-making expedients. Henry helped a little, ordering Brandon's annuity as duke of Suffolk to be paid in advance for three quarters in the month of his creation.[138] When the king gave him a share in the conquest of 1513 by granting him the castle of Mortain, he immediately sold it to Anthoine de Ligne, a noble from the Low Countries, for 1,000 crowns, something over £200 sterling: this was a bargain, at a third of the price Henry paid to remove De Ligne in 1521.[139] A still more controversial device was Brandon's illegal confiscation of a cargo of papal alum in spring 1514. The Florentine merchant in charge of the alum paid Charles a large sum, perhaps to secure him a royal pardon, while Brandon borrowed 1,000 marks, probably for the Corbet wardship, from Henry on the security of the confiscated goods.[140] Leo X and Margaret of Austria badgered Henry and Wolsey through letters and representatives for the alum's return, for it was valued at 12,000 ducats. By June 1515 Leo knew that Henry had ordered recompense to be made, but four years later Brandon had still not paid in full.[141]

To stay solvent Brandon resorted not only to rapacity, but to a most unchivalrous meanness. His auditors on the Lisle estates reflected this mood: the under-steward of Chaddesley Corbett had difficulties convincing them that a few pence 'hathe be alowed for p[ar]cheme[n]t by ev[er]y audetto[r] tyme out of mynde un to this tyme, as by wolde court rowlys doth appere.'[142] Another victim was Garter king-of-arms. When Brandon was created duke he gave the herald the traditional gown, as did the other peers made on the same day. Suffolk's gift was the best by far, in violet velvet with sables. Garter reckoned it worth £200, and wore it proudly all day. Unfortunately the duke's means did not live up to his motto, embroidered in gold thread all over the gown, 'Loyaulte me oblige': shortly afterwards his servant visited Garter with a cheaper gown, the money to buy a doublet, and a patent for a £4 annuity, and repossessed the magnificent garment. The herald was understandably disgruntled.[143]

Power rested in patronage as well as wealth. The right, and need, to appoint deputies in many of his offices was useful, though often limited, as in Wales and the stable.[144] In 1513 it was Brandon's military importance which above all afforded him patronage. Captaincies in his retinue paid 4*s* a day, and other posts were fairly lucrative.[145] Legal protection was available for those serving under him, and he obtained it for Mary Francis by appointing her a victualler in his retinue. She needed protection from her creditors, having failed to secure restitution of merchandise stolen from her, despite a verdict before the council nearly three years before, since her debtors were bankrupt.[146] Military success with Brandon could also pay dividends. Eight men who served directly under him were knighted on 25 September 1513, and on the day Tournai surrendered John Puleston, one of his Welsh captains, was granted the post as a serjeant-at-arms vacated by the late John Royden, a long-time friend to the Brandons.[147]

Direct influence over royal grants is hard to demonstrate. One extremely unusual piece of evidence does show Brandon's effectiveness. The signed bill by which the wardship of John Carew of Hackcomb was granted to Sir Robert Brandon was endorsed 'ad instantiam Karoli Brandon, militis'.[148] This was finally sealed on 28 January 1513, but Sir Robert and two friends had bound themselves to pay £100 for the wardship as long ago as April 1511. Obviously there had been difficulties, perhaps over a grant of the custody of some of Carew's lands to another suitor in July 1511.[149] Brandon's intervention evidently overcame these problems.

Without a large and coherent landed inheritance, though, he faced difficulties in the deployment of his own patronage. Before his grants of wardships and offices there, he had little link with the Welsh borders and south midlands. He never even became a justice of the peace in the counties where almost all his lands lay before 1515. Even securing control over the lands could be difficult: in the case of the Lisle estates the Howards, who had held the wardship of John, Viscount Lisle, Elizabeth's father, had to be removed.[150] The lands had been leased to them by the king to Knyvet's use, and before Brandon got his second grant of the wardship, that in April 1513 giving him indisputable control, they had to return this lease. Before doing so they extracted a pardon of all rent arrears (on 7 January) and a release from all demands in respect of the lease (on

12 February).[151] By mid-February Brandon had a team of three commissioners touring the estates as his surveyors, amongst other things holding manorial courts. But the team was led by Oliver Pole, a clerical servant of Knyvet and his wife much involved in the Howards' administration of the Lisle lands, and the other two had no apparent previous or subsequent connection with the new guardian.[152]

Pole became Brandon's receiver on the Lisle lands at a £20 fee, and soon rose to be his chancellor.[153] Servants of the Corbets, like George Onneslowe whom Charles made steward of all the Corbet lands in Shropshire, might have done the same.[154] But as Brandon granted out stewardships and bailiwicks on the Lisle lands in January 1513, he often had little real choice whom to appoint.[155] His officers had to have the local influence which he did not yet enjoy. Some, like Thomas Blount, were so deeply entrenched in the Lisle administration that they could not have been removed.[156] Six of his stewards were justices in the county where the manor concerned lay, one in a neighbouring county, and the remaining three sat on commissions of array or sewers.[157] Three were former sheriffs of the county, one had been named on the roll, but not chosen.[158] Of course the important men of the county made good stewards in theory, but when, like Sir Maurice Berkeley in Gloucestershire, they were reappointed every time the Lisle lands changed hands, the value of their appointments in establishing an affinity for Brandon, rather than merely reinforcing their own prestige, must be doubted.[159] The revenues were also burdened with annuities granted out by John, Lord Lisle. It would seem too that bailiffs worked less hard for Brandon than for other masters: arrears at Chaddesley Corbett were nil in 1512, over £5 by 1515, and only £6 13s. 4d. in 1521.[160] This may only show that he missed the services of Anthony Wyndesor, who acted as an efficient receiver-general on these estates both for the Howards and later for Arthur Plantagenet, but not for Brandon.

Similar problems restricted Brandon's power in Wales. As chief justice of North Wales and constable of Caernarvon Castle, he should have had, as he later put it, 'th'order and rule of the countrey there'.[161] But only local men could control the area effectively. Brandon's deputies were incapable of subduing local disputes, and he found it easiest to acquiesce in the regional dominance of Sir William Griffith, chamberlain of North Wales, a dominance effectively confirmed by the occasional interventions of the council in the marches and even the council in Star Chamber. Brandon took more personal interest at first in the marcher lordships of Bromfield, Yale, and Chirk, where his stewardships fitted well with the Lisle and Corbet estates, but there too he would lose interest once he became absorbed in the task of becoming an East Anglian magnate.

Charles Brandon's unusual situation is demonstrated by the complete lack of correlation between his land-holding and his military retinue.[162] When called upon to raise small numbers of men, he seems to have done so in Southwark. Twenty soldiers for the fleet in 1512 were paid no conduct money to London, and he mustered sixty men for the Scottish border in March 1513 at Islington.[163] None of his 1,831 men in 1513 came from his own estates, nor were any of their captains his estate officials, with the exception of Oliver Pole. During the campaign the retinue's organisation changed, but when its troops returned home, 100, raised by Brandon's relative by marriage, Lord Fitzwarin, set off for Devon and Cornwall; 100, raised by the Oxfordshire gentlemen Sir Edward Chamberlain and Sir William Essex, went to Woodstock; twenty-two went home with Sir Lewis Orwell to Wisbech; and 1,578 marched back to northern Wales.[164] The troops raised by Brandon for the cancelled invasion of 1514 were also mostly Welsh.[165]

Brandon's difficulties were reflected in his choice of captains. Eleven were Welshmen. Essex and Chamberlain may have been contacts through the Saye wardship. John Brydges, and probably Richard Cooke, had been put into the service of Brandon as a rising courtier.[166] John Shilston was Brandon's brother-in-law, Lewis Orwell linked with his uncle's cousin, Sir Thomas Lovell.[167] The remaining five, none of whom brought any troops of their own, were Brandon's East Anglian relatives, with some of whom he had remained in contact even while living at court: in October 1507 he visited James Framlingham's house at Crow's Hall, Debenham, Suffolk.[168]

Naturally Brandon exploited his good fortune to benefit his family, and when a Lisle benefice became vacant he presented his clerical cousin, John Wingfield.[169] But the abnormality of his retinue showed the failure of his local power to keep pace with his astonishingly rapid rise in status. He was knighted on 30 March 1512; within fourteen months he was a viscount, within a further nine months a duke.[170] As soon as he entered the peerage, he began to assume the trappings of great and ancient nobility. In 1513 Henry created a Lisle pursuivant for him, one of a small number of peers' private heralds: this was Christopher Barker, son-in-law of Norroy king-of-arms.[171] On 1 February, 1514, when the earl of Surrey was at last restored to his father's title of duke of Norfolk, Brandon moved a further few score places up the precedence list when created duke of Suffolk. In some ways a dukedom was merely a greater version of other peerages: more bouche of court, a herald instead of a pursuivant.[172] In others a duke, 'high and mighty prince', was set apart. The traditional link between royal blood and ducal status made a duke special, and this theory affected important issues: within a ducal household away from court, for example, the duke's steward and treasurer ranked equal with barons.[173]

The creation ceremony proclaimed Brandon's status to the assembled peerage, though they had doubtless accustomed themselves to his power as marshal in 1513, for example in presenting to him their excuses for their companies' failure to perform duties like keeping watch.[174] Such were the heights to which he was being elevated that he and Norfolk had to be created separately, since there were not enough peers of comparable status to accompany them both at once. The Marquis of Dorset did so, but Buckingham, the only duke in the country since 1504, probably absented himself, and there is evidence that he was piqued at the creations.[175]

Others were shocked. Polydore Vergil noted that 'many people considered it very surprising that Charles should be so honoured as to be made a duke.'[176] Erasmus produced a comment so insulting that it was edited out of the 1519 Basle edition of his letters. In an allusion to Persius's *Satires*, he compared the master of the horse to a drunken stable-hand whose new trappings could not hide his true nature.[177] The letters patent creating Brandon were even more eulogistic than was normal, the king explaining almost apologetically that he was bound to do something to repay the numerous meritorious services which his dearest Brandon had heaped upon him.[178]

Contemporaries also speculated about the king's reason for the creation. It must be significant that Brandon was created at the same time as Surrey and Norfolk, though of course the exact timing was determined by the session of parliament.[179] The restoration of the Howards was undoubtedly the reward for their victory at Flodden, and the creation of Brandon as Suffolk and Charles, Lord Herbert as earl of Worcester was a counterweight which stressed the equal glory of the king's own victories in France. The scale of the northern rout, when compared with the small return for Henry's huge effort in France, must have irked him: to elevate a close friend who had been central to the capture of Tournai gave a little compensation.[180] There may be armorial hints that the Brandons claimed ducal ancestry, and through his mother Charles had distant De la Pole forebears, but giving him the title of Suffolk had a far more immediate purpose.[181] This was to exclude conspicuously the possibility of restoration for the De la Poles, the last significant Yorkist claimants to the throne. Edmund, the last earl in the De la Pole line of dukes and earls of Suffolk which stretched back to 1385, fled England in 1501, but was forcibly repatriated five years later and executed by Henry VIII in 1513. That left at large on the Continent Edmund's brother Richard, who served the French as a general, called himself duke of Suffolk in succession to Edmund, and sought French support to claim the English throne. After 1515 Brandon would be called upon to supplant the De la Poles in more than name only.

In simple terms of rank Brandon had now reached as high as he could. The extent of his political power is harder to judge. He soon entered the central ceremonial role afforded by his new status, leading the glittering company which met Leonard Spinelli, as he approached London with the papal cap and sword for Henry in May 1514.[182] After the official presentation, it was Suffolk who carried the sword from St Paul's to the king's chamber. But there is little sign that he was involved in the work of government. He had been a councillor since at least May 1513, before his creation as Viscount Lisle.[183] In the spring and summer of 1514, though, he did not appear among the leading members of the council, when they witnessed grants, met ambassadors, were visited privately by envoys, or were named in letters to the council.[184]

Wolsey was certainly the rising star in council, while Suffolk's importance lay more in his very visible prominence at court. Contemporaries saw them as complementary allies, Margaret of Austria assuming that policies must belong to Norfolk, Fox, and Ruthal, or to Wolsey and Suffolk.[185] Polydore Vergil felt that they 'inter se una et mente et voce consentiebant.'[186] They had probably known each other well since at least 1511, and though Wolsey seems to have been critical of Brandon's performance as high marshal in 1513, the division of their spheres of action and influence in 1514 apparently avoided friction.[187] Later in 1514 Brandon certainly saw himself and Wolsey as working in close co-operation.

Marital Excursions

If greater involvement in government was one means for Brandon to advance yet further, another beckoned, more rapid and spectacular: an advantageous marriage. His marital history was already extremely complex, and demonstrated an asset-stripping opportunism which even contemporaries found rather shocking. At court in 1503 or so he confessed to Walter Devereux that he was 'in love and resorted muche to the companye of ... Anne Browne'.[188] She was a gentlewoman to the queen, and daughter to Sir Anthony Browne of Calais. Charles and Anne contracted to marry, before the council of his patron, the earl of Essex, and she became pregnant. Brandon then abandoned her to marry her aunt, Dame Margaret Mortimer, and shortly afterwards Anne gave birth to Brandon's first daughter, Anne, the future Lady Powis. So it was later claimed by those who argued that Lady Powis was illegitimate; Lady Powis's friends conveniently recalled that Anne Browne had miscarried with shock at her betrayal by Brandon, and that Lady Powis was born several years later. Mortimer was some twenty years older than Brandon, but her share in the Montague inheritance won the heart of the penurious young courtier, at least for a time. On 7 February 1507 he had licence of entry on Dame Margaret's lands, and in August he sold her manor of Okeford, Devon, for £260, using another of her manors as security for his side of the bargain.[189] Shortly afterwards he had this marriage invalidated on grounds of consanguinity, not only between Anne and Margaret but also between his grandmother and Margaret's first husband.[190]

Late in 1507, while Brandon was still conducting negotiations for a settlement with Mortimer's representatives, he rode off into Essex with a group of friends. They returned with Anne Browne, and Charles married her in secret in early 1508 in Stepney church. Her family and the earl of Essex, 'fearyng that the said Charles wold used her as he dyd before', ordered them to marry publicly. After Easter 1508, or possibly as late as Easter 1510, they did so, in St Michael's Cornhill, in the presence of a 'a great nombre of worshypfull people'. Anne died within a fortnight of the birth of Mary, their second, and indisputably legitimate, daughter, in the summer of 1510.

It seems clear from subsequent events that Brandon never intended to carry out his next contract of marriage, with Lady Lisle. At any rate he could wait while the eight-year-old ward grew up, and see if better opportunities presented themselves.[191] Half of Europe thought in early 1514 that such an opportunity had arisen. Possibly in October 1513, and certainly by January 1514, it was rumoured that he would marry Margaret of Austria, the regent of the Netherlands.[192] They had seen each other frequently in autumn 1513, Brandon had eagerly proffered his service even before they met, and 'whether he profered mariage or not she favored him highly.'[193] But Brandon offered his service readily to foreign princes, and other English peers like Buckingham were also expressing similar sentiments to Margaret.[194] What lay behind the rumour was the mischievous humour of Henry VIII.

He and Brandon visited her court often during the campaign. She spent lavishly on banquets, they on presents.[195] All-night dancing, gaming, and exchanges of rings flourished in these meetings, for Margaret's entourage was a famous centre of courtly love, and Henry was in expansive mood, promising a 10,000 crown dowry to a Flemish lady-in-waiting who caught his eye.[196] Despite the regent's tragic past she was vivacious, not unattractive, and little older then Brandon: their after-dinner flirtation was by no means extraordinary.[197] At Tournai, she reminded Henry, Charles 'put hymselfe opon hys knees befor me, and in spekyng and hyme playng, he drew fro my finger the rynge, and put yt upon hys, and sythe schewde yt me, and I took to lawhe.'[198] She spoke no English, and Brandon spoke – or was teasingly pretending to speak – little French. When her attempts to retrieve the ring in French, then in Flemish, broke down, Henry stepped in as interpreter. To this point dealings had been harmless, Brandon offering to be her 'rygthe humble servant', she 'to do unto hym alle honneur and plesure'. The king's maladroit sense of humour changed this: Henry, as Margaret later tactfully protested, 'by cawse off the love wyche he berethe hym, mytt have taken yt more forwarde for to enterprett mor hys desyre.' It was Henry who talked of marriage, perhaps as a misconceived political stratagem, but more likely as a witty conceit.

Brandon may later have joined the joke, but it soon began to go badly wrong.[199] Betting on a marriage opened in London, rumours soon reached the Low Countries, and by 4 March Henry had to admit that 'le co[m]mun bruyt a fort couru en divers lieux', that they would marry.[200] Those in her court who wished to see her discredited turned the story against Margaret. Her father Maximilian was shocked, and she had to reassure him that 'ce sont toutes menteries, et que aymeroie mieulx mourir mille fois ... que d'y avoir pensé.'[201]

Henry was greatly embarrassed, especially because he seemed to be the source of the rumour. Ambassadors at his court knew more than they should have done, and stirred up further speculation around Europe by their reports.[202] Henry's reaction to Margaret's complaints, threatening death for those accused of spreading the tale, was that of a guilty man. He made great efforts to ascertain the source of the rumour, protesting to Maximilian that 'ne povons bonnement penser de ou led[it] bruit peult mouvoir et proceder.'[203] To avoid difficulties he complied with Margaret's request to cancel Suffolk's mission to raise troops for the next year's war. What he refused to do was to order Brandon to marry Lady Lisle and thus solve all Margaret's problems.[204] Henry would not sacrifice his friend to Anglo-imperial amity, and, as peace with France approached, the pressure to do so decreased.

There are many parallels between this affair and the crisis one year later of Suffolk's marriage to the king's sister. Each tested the friendship with Henry which had brought Brandon almost everything he had. Each also tested the members of Suffolk's family, on whom he relied heavily early in his career. Sir Richard Wingfield, deputy of Calais, the duke's cousin, managed the delicate dealings with Margaret well, though the king seems not to have kept him properly informed of the true state of affairs.[205] Sir William Sidney, Brandon's adventurous cousin who was in the Netherlands to learn the language, involved himself in negotiations over the matter despite falling ill.[206] The final similarity lies in the effect on Suffolk's role in foreign policy. Not only was his embassy cancelled, he also had to offer partially to cut his links with Margaret's court, by recalling to England a girl he had adopted and placed there as companion to his daughter Anne, whom the regent had undertaken to bring up in her household.[207] The events of 1515 would limit more sharply his public and private contacts abroad.

By summer 1514 Brandon's power was great, but its bases were fragile. The lands he controlled were not extensive, and as he would not marry Lady Lisle they were not his own. The potential connection provided by his family could not be much rewarded with the patronage at his disposal, yet he was in no position to construct an alternative affinity using that patronage. In Wales he was strong in theory, but only in the marches did he hold effective authority.

His offices were lucrative but lent him no weight in council, and his influence in the government relied solely on his friendship with the king. As a courtier he had been supremely successful, but this in itself raised envy and enmity: he still had much to do to establish himself and his family.

2

The French Marriage and the Duchy of Suffolk: 1514–1523

In autumn 1514 Suffolk was riding high. He had identified himself closely with the French peace which had strengthened Wolsey's ascendancy, and foreigners wrote to them jointly. In November he received the first payment of a large French pension.[1] Princes like the Marquis of Mantua courted him, and continued royal favour brought gifts such as a licence to import wine. Henry had negotiated the return of at least one De la Pole estate from a previous grantee, opening the possibility that the duke would be further endowed.[2] When summoned to parliament in November Suffolk was the third layman of the realm. Distinguished relatives like Sir Robert Wingfield now no longer helped his advance, but begged him to intercede for them with the king, for the friendship between Henry and Brandon remained close: in the mummery of 31 December newer royal favourites took part, but Suffolk stayed at the centre.[3]

The First Embassy to France
In October Brandon was the obvious choice as a jousting ambassador, to attend the tournament held to celebrate the marriage of Henry's sister Mary to Louis XII, the keystone of the new alliance. With Sir Edward Nevill and Sir William Sidney he crossed to France in romantic disguise, followed by Sir Henry Guildford and a glittering detachment of yeomen of the guard.[4]

But his mission was more than a reply to the Dauphin Francis's challenge in the lists. Henry and Wolsey had entrusted him with a secret proposal for an offensive alliance against Ferdinand of Aragon.[5]

The Venetians anticipated such a suggestion, and the secrecy was less to conceal it from them or the Spanish than from Henry's other councillors. Divisions in the council were revealed when Louis XII abruptly dismissed most of his wife's English household the morning after their wedding. News of this reached the duke at Canterbury through his fellow-courtier Gerard Danett.[6] Queen Mary was distressed, Wolsey unsure how to respond. Suffolk immediately blamed the Howards, since Norfolk, who had accompanied Mary to France, had acquiesced in Louis's action. Of course Norfolk may well have acted more from obsequiousness than malice, but Brandon assumed that the Howards' 'dryeftes' were to destroy the Anglo-French amity, and with it, the dominance of Wolsey and Suffolk. In removing their appointees to her household (including old Lady Guildford) and making her unhappy, Norfolk would discredit them and their alliance. Suffolk's reaction was typical: he would abandon his heavy horses and rush to Paris, to do his business before the Howards could stop him, for 'I am suar that the fader and the son wold not for no good I schold styke wyet the Frynche kyng.'[7]

The 'bedchamber crisis' was resolved through the earl of Worcester, a veteran diplomat who had accompanied Mary throughout her journey to France, and had stayed on when the Howards left. Indeed, he remained the leading English envoy even after Suffolk's arrival.[8] Yet it was Suffolk who reported on the earl's performance to Henry and Wolsey, and as the tournament approached he and Dorset grew in importance. They hunted with Francis, arranged the jousts with him, discussed Henry's own hastiludes, and were welcomed as aids, not answerers.[9] Brandon thought that the French wore their armour awkwardly, and once combats commenced this confidence was justified. The peers themselves, wearing small red crosses all over their outfits, felt they maintained English honour well, and a Venetian observer agreed.[10] In the jousts Brandon scored brilliantly on the first day, six broken spears and an attaint in seven runs; in the tourney he nearly killed one opponent, beat another to the ground, and broke his sword on a third with such force that 'le cheval de lad[ite] Roche ne vouloit aprocher.'[11] His reaction was like that of Sir Edward Howard facing the French fleet in April 1513, who invited the king to come and share in his victory. 'Sir', Suffolk wrote to Henry, 'I see the thyem nhow that, yf et war possebbyll, I wold radar than hall that I have in the warld that you myth by wyet me anknowne, for I thynke you schold lyes non honnor.'[12]

The French reaction was less than chivalrous. They were slow with their praise, reluctant to run and be beaten, and Francis dropped out with a wound in his little finger while Brandon fought on despite injury.[13] They produced an unknown German in the foot-combats in the hope of humiliating Suffolk, but the stranger was forced to retire with a nosebleed.[14] None the less, Brandon had impressed Louis and made useful contacts among Francis's circle of friends, men like the high-scoring jouster Bonnivet whom the dauphin dispatched to Henry with a gift of horses.[15] Suffolk's ducal rank facilitated dealings with the highest peers of France, and as he carried secret verbal instructions from Henry he conducted the embassy's most important business alone with Louis. By the end of the mission, Louis was promising to conduct all his affairs with Henry through Wolsey and Suffolk, and asking Wolsey to believe the duke 'comme moy mesmes'.[16]

Most of the embassy's real achievements had been made earlier by the more practised negotiators. Suffolk's inexperience showed in his dealings with Louis's councillors, and they tried to exploit this, though Charles refused to be hustled into agreeing to the free passage to Scotland of the duke of Albany, the French candidate for the Scottish regency.[17] Brandon seems to have recognised his limitations, and was content over the Spanish scheme merely to arrange an exchange of written proposals between the kings, and begin with Francis the military planning against Ferdinand.[18] On Scottish matters too he and Dorset were not unsuccessful, and the marquis at least thought Suffolk's first embassy a triumph.[19]

With Dorset's recommendation, and Louis's verdict on him that 'no prynse gyrsynyth has sw[ch a servant] for pes and vare', Henry was pleased with Suffolk's performance.[20] But the embassy also revealed weaknesses in the duke's position. He sent gifts to Henry as tokens of their friendship, and reported French proposals directly to the king; but while away from the court he could only judge Henry's responses by asking Wolsey about them, and he was wary of taking diplomatic initiatives without explicit instructions from the archbishop.[21] While in unequivocal favour with Henry and trusting co-operation with Wolsey, all was well, but with a disgruntled monarch and a diffident minister it would be different.

The Secret Marriage

The death of Louis XII on 1 January 1515, and Henry's selection of Suffolk as the ambassador to return to France and bring home his widowed sister Mary, opened up several attractive possibilities for the duke. One of these, which he discussed with the king before he left, was his marriage to Mary.[22] They must have known each other well, through her involvement in court festivities and perhaps his contacts in her household.[23] But her later account to Henry of events in France implies that a marriage between them was far from settled when the duke left England: what Brandon promised the king was that if they did marry it would only be on their return.[24] It would in any case be foolish to judge the exact state of the matter without a letter 'revealing a most extraordinary fact in the history of Suffolk's love for the Princess Mary, of which historians have been quite at fault', sold in 1840, but now untraceable.[25]

The duke's dealings with Francis were nearly as important as those with Mary. Not only was there diplomacy to be done, but Suffolk aimed to make himself and Wolsey as close to the new king as to the old, so that 'wye bowth schall by as wyell intreated of the kyng her as hewar anne to in Yngylland'.[26] Francis was encouraging, sending Bonnivet to welcome Suffolk and his companions. But he was also manipulative, eager to extract all he could from Brandon's desire for his confidence, and need for his protection after his secret marriage to Mary.[27]

For in mid-February, in Paris, Suffolk and Mary did marry. At first they had asked Henry's permission to wed on their return, and secured Wolsey's, and even Francis's, support for this request. Henry agreed. But Mary was still afraid that either Francis or Henry would marry her off to another husband as unappetising as Louis XII, and in her desperation to escape she pressed Suffolk to marry her then and there or not at all. He gave in, later offering the unanswerable excuse that he 'newar sawe woman soo wyepe'.[28] Henry was furious when he discovered that 'the ma[n] in all the world he lovyd and trustyd best' had broken his word and compromised the king's honour.[29] His anger prompted Mary to take the blame herself, and Suffolk to submit repeatedly and humbly to Henry's mercy, which he begged Wolsey to secure. Henry could be assuaged, Wolsey replied, by a large part of Mary's dower revenues and all her goods.[30]

Both Henry's rage and the financial settlement were more complex than they might seem. Wolsey may have exaggerated royal wrath in order to magnify his own assistance to Brandon, but the marriage caused problems for him too. His control was not complete enough for him to prevent Henry writing in unfortunate terms to Francis.[31] Moreover, Henry's anger was encouraged by Suffolk's rivals, the Howards, who had opposed both Suffolk and Wolsey over the French peace. Brandon expected such opposition even to a proper marriage to Mary, and when it came it struck at Wolsey too. Norfolk dispatched a leading friar, Bonaventure Langley, to act as Mary's confessor, and he warned her not to marry Brandon, who was in league with Wolsey to control Henry by diabolical means.[32] An ambassador reported a row in parliament over the marriage on 29 March, in which only Wolsey backed Suffolk; Norfolk, Surrey, and Wolsey were certainly all in the Lords on the day in question.[33] Brandon's last appeal to Henry was cleverly couched to suggest that Henry's anger was only prompted by those around him: he assured Henry that 'I know your grace of scheth natur th[at] et cannot ly in thyr power to caus you to dysstru me for ther malles.'[34]

Mary and Suffolk had expected, before Wolsey's detailed proposals, that some financial sacrifice on their part would be needed to appease the king. Already, on 9 February, Mary had surrendered her jewels and plate to Henry: she and Suffolk knew the price and were prepared to pay it.[35] The real problem was to extract these things from the French, and here Suffolk's natural technique as a courtier rather than as a diplomat was a handicap. Since the question of Mary's precise entitlements was 'past me lerneng', he tackled it by making 'the byst frynddes th[at] I cold abowth the kyng to parsawd hem.'[36]

This in turn crippled the rest of his diplomatic mission, for he could not negotiate over sensitive issues like the possible return of Tournai to France with a French king on whose favour he was so dependent. He had to abandon the work, and the prestige, of settling with the French over such matters of state to Wolsey and others in London.[37] On his return he and Wolsey wrote together to Francis, but their letter stressed the role of 'la treshumble mediacion ... de mond[it] si[eur] d'York' in persuading Henry to accept the marriage.[38] Even before the marriage he assured Wolsey that 'hall me trost es in you.'[39] After it he confessed himself dependent on Wolsey's 'gryth assuard fryncheschyp'.[40] Other councillors had advised Suffolk how to conduct his mission before he left, and the Howards were in a strong position to oppose the marriage. But as the whole English embassy in France busied itself about buying wine for Wolsey, it was evident that his dominance was increasingly assured, and Suffolk became less an ally and more a client; even more so as Wolsey became cardinal and chancellor in September and December 1515.[41]

Henry's anger passed off very quickly. Shortly after Suffolk and Mary reached Dover on 2 May, Wolsey met them and conducted them to the king at Lord Bergavenny's house at Birling. Henry rode out with a great company to greet his sister, and despite his displeasure at the secret marriage accepted her explanation that it was her fault.[42] This, at least, was how Wolsey and Suffolk recounted the return to Francis I: an account written under such delicate circumstances cannot be unimpeachable, but it is reinforced by other evidence.

Financial settlement was reached on 11 May, on terms far more lenient than those first suggested by Wolsey.[43] Instead of paying £4,000 a year to Henry until her death, Mary was to pay £2,000 a year until £24,000 had been paid off, of which £5,000 represented debts already owed by Suffolk to the crown. Brandon had to return the wardship and marriage of Lady Lisle, and these were resold for £4,000, but he kept her lands until she should come of age and be granted livery of them.[44] Mary's earlier surrenders of plate, jewels, and half her dowry were confirmed, and on 12 May she and Suffolk bound themselves in the vast sum of £100,000 to carry out this agreement.

On 13 May they married publicly at Greenwich in the presence of Henry, Queen Catherine, and all the nobles then at court.[45] Henry's love for his sister explains no doubt the speed with which he forgave her; but his continuing friendship for Brandon was also important. It was only the timing of Suffolk's arrival in England that prevented him taking his usual place as Henry's first aid in the jousts of May Day. Suffolk himself had made careful preparations for them, and a pageant was planned involving a king, a duke, a marquis and an earl.[46] Full tournament outfits were produced for Henry, Suffolk, Dorset, and Essex, and the chronicler Hall, probably working from the accounts for these, assumed that they performed.[47] In fact the whole pageant was called off, but only after 27 April, long after Henry knew of the marriage, but once it became clear that Suffolk would not return in time. Sir Henry Guildford was Brandon's deputy as master of the horse, and he naturally replaced him in his tournament, as in his administrative, duties. It would have been incongruous for him to have jousted before the noble and experienced Dorset and Essex, so Nicholas Carew and Francis Bryan, two young men rising in Henry's favour, became substitute aids, and all three had coats made up at short notice.[48] For the moment at least, Carew and Bryan were second-choice favourites.

Endowment in East Anglia

Suffolk's absence from these jousts was not a mark of disgrace; nor was his apparent existence 'for a time in comparative retirement, as ... under a cloud'.[49] On 1 February 1515, Henry had granted him almost the entire De la Pole estate, and he had now to establish himself in it. This was far harder than it might seem, for only the few manors which the crown still held came directly to Suffolk. On the rest he held only reversionary rights, and had to buy out previous grantees, for Henry had been dispensing De la Pole manors up to the very day of his grant to the duke.[50] Margaret, Countess of Suffolk, widow of the executed Edmund de la Pole, died later in February, freeing her jointure for Brandon, though some of the manors which her feoffees had regained in a chancery case in 1513 reverted to the crown grantees deprived then.[51] While the duke was still in France his councillors began the work of buying up De la Pole estates. Oliver Pole, his chancellor, and Humphrey Wingfield, his general attorney, spent £1,000 on four manors in Suffolk, in seventeen days in February, almost all of it in cash. But this was at a time when they were also borrowing heavily to finance his stay in France, and as Suffolk's expenses for this were never refunded, he was forced to slow down his acquisition of such estates when he returned.[52]

Forming, or rather reconstituting, his estate, was merely the first phase of his establishment as a magnate to replace the De la Poles. He had to see East Anglia and be seen there, and this he did in summer 1515 while Henry hunted in the country, though late in July he visited the court and impressed ambassadors by his power.[53] That summer and the next he and Mary progressed round Norfolk and Suffolk more in triumph than disgrace. She attracted more attention than her husband, but both benefited. Cambridge sent her pike and tench in 1515, and in 1516 at Butley Priory she received a lot more reverence than her consort, as befitted her status as 'excellentissima domina Maria Francorum regina venustissima'.[54] But the huge arrays of presents produced by Norwich and Eye were directed to them both, and they were entertained together for three days when they visited Great

Yarmouth.[55] Outside East Anglia Suffolk's local power continued to expand, for example when Sir Edward Guildford passed on to him the stewardship of Sir Edward Burgh's lands in the south-east in October 1515. Within East Anglia too Suffolk's standing was not only recognised, but enhanced: in December 1515 Nicholas West made him steward and bailiff of various of the courts and estates of his diocese of Ely. [56]

It was not merely self-interest that led Brandon to strengthen his position in Suffolk and Norfolk. In the years after 1515 Henry and Wolsey wanted a strong and trustworthy replacement for the De la Poles, to counter the threat of Richard de la Pole. This was why, in June 1516, Henry sent the duke into East Anglia, 'by his commaundement ... here in thies parties feurre frome his presence'.[57] De la Pole was used regularly by the French to threaten England, and seriously too: in 1523 he nearly took ship to invade, and was paid a good deal of money.[58] More worrying still were rumours of Yorkists at home, and the boasts of Richard and the French that he could raise support among peers and people led to arrests and attempted arrests.[59] Naturally these fears centred on East Anglia, accessible by sea, and the main area where the De la Pole estates lay: in February 1516 merchants of Norfolk and Suffolk were reported to have met one of Richard's servants in Antwerp.[60] In 1522 a complex feud in East Dereham resulted in an accusation that a local notable had retained 100 men to back a landing by the rebel, a charge which the royal council took seriously enough to imprison him for nine weeks.[61] Invasion or rebellion by Richard de la Pole loomed largest in the government's correspondence, and presumably its thinking, at precisely the time when Suffolk spent long periods away from court.[62]

Suffolk made conscious efforts to replace the De la Poles, as well as more general ones to establish himself as a local magnate. He altered his seal from the classical model of 1513 to use his arms, which included the Brandon lion rampant, *queue fourchée*, surely reminding some of his older tenants of the Chaucer lion rampant, *queue fourchée* of later De la Pole seals.[63] In 1514 he had probably sponsored a play ridiculing Richard de la Pole. In

1517 he followed De la Pole precedent when the king created Lisle pursuivant, who had served Brandon loyally in France in 1515, Suffolk herald.[64] He even took into his service relatives of one of the men who had struggled to save the countess of Suffolk's estates, and perhaps one of her former servants.[65] The position of the De la Pole manors also produced some natural continuity in estate appointments: Sir Thomas Tyrrell lived close to Haughley, where Suffolk named him parker, and the same proximity had drawn Tyrrell's father into treasonable service to Edmund de la Pole; the parkership of Eye went to Edward Grimston of Rishangles, whose father and grandfather had served John and Edmund de la Pole, and whose son would become a gentleman of Brandon's household.[66]

Yet both the general and the specific tasks proved harder than they seemed. Suffolk's first problem was that he could never secure the entire De la Pole estate, and he had great difficulty in gathering even what he did. On the manors he received directly from the crown or after Countess Margaret's death, rents were paid to him from Michaelmas 1514 or March 1515, though arrears were huge and he was still trying to collect some of this first year's income in 1523.[67] The terms of his letters patent were sufficiently vague to provide plenty of business for Elizabethan lawyers.[68] He carefully secured an inspeximus of the act of parliament confirming his endowment with the holdings of Edmund de la Pole at 1499, and those of John de la Pole, Earl of Lincoln, at March 1487, but the consolidation of these estates took time and money.[69] He was still buying back De la Pole lands in 1523 and he never secured the whole estate.[70] The greatest individual holder of De la Pole manors was the earl of Surrey. Brandon produced 1,000 marks in cash in December 1515 to buy four of them, in Oxfordshire and Berkshire, but thereafter Surrey would sell no more until he needed funds to go to Ireland in 1520.[71] Determined to control Surrey's manors at any cost, Suffolk entered into an almost ruinous lease. Concluded in January 1516, this promised a cash rent of £413 6s 8d for manors which in 1522–3 produced only £401 9 s ¾d clear.[72] To secure payment of this rent in May 1516 and perhaps again in

Table 2.1 Suffolk's Acquisition of the De la Pole estates*

Manors	Percentage of total De la Pole estate, by annual value
Granted to Suffolk, 1514:	4
Granted to Suffolk, 1515:	31
Purchased by Suffolk, 1515:	6
Purchased or reverted after 1515:	9
Leased from Surrey from 1516:	14
Granted to Suffolk, 1525:	3
Dower of the countess of Lincoln, reverted in 1532:	7
Held by Catherine of Aragon and Anne Boleyn, reverted in 1536:	4
Never held by Suffolk:	22

* The values used are those for 1536–7, when available. The complete De la Pole estate is taken to consist both of the lands confirmed to Edmund de la Pole in 1493, and those then reserved to the crown. Such figures can only be approximate.

Source: S. J. Gunn, 'The Life and Career of Charles Brandon, Duke of Suffolk, *c*.1484–1545' (Oxford Univ. D.Phil. thesis, 1986), Appendix.

March 1523, and to guarantee the delivery of £1,333 13*s* 4*d* over two years for the purchase in 1520, groups of Suffolk's councillors, relatives, and feoffees had to bind themselves in ever larger sums to Surrey.[73] By 1523–4 the duke was paying the rent only three or four months late, but Surrey's longevity meant that Suffolk still owed it in 1545, after it was guaranteed on his new Lincolnshire manors in 1536.[74]

Frustratingly long life was also enjoyed by Margaret, Countess of Lincoln, widow of Earl John. Suffolk was naturally concerned to secure the central De la Pole estates first (as his councillors' spending in February 1515 shows), but she held a large dower in Norfolk and Suffolk and presumably would neither sell nor lease to the new duke. She was far from timid, confronting Brandon and fighting local notables such as the prior of Eye at law, and later entertaining Princess Mary and helping in the establishment of Wolsey's Ipswich

College.[75] She also enjoyed considerable protection from her father the earl of Arundel and her brother Lord Maltravers, who played a large role in her estate management.[76] By 1523 the duke was paying her a £40 annuity, apparently just to keep her quiet: all in all he must have been greatly relieved when she died at last in 1532, and by October his men took over her manors.[77]

Family and Affinity

Suffolk's troubles in forming an estate were accompanied by difficulties in forming a connection. There were few diehard De la Pole supporters to alienate, though one of the countess of Suffolk's estate officers was deprived of a mill by Brandon's surveyor.[78] There was also no surviving network of De la Pole retainers waiting to enter his service, for in the last two decades the East Anglian gentry had accommodated themselves to the leadership first of the De Veres, then of the Howards. Naturally, now that he did hold power near their own lands, Suffolk wanted to reward his relatives with offices. He probably trusted them more than he did others, and he was not the only peer to rely on the services of his kinsmen in posts of responsibility.[79] Most magnates utilised kinship networks among the county gentry when recruiting their supporters, and this too led Suffolk to his own relations.[80] Many of them had helped him during his troubles in France: Sir Richard Wingfield wrote to Wolsey in support of 'the sayd unhappie dewke', and Sir William Sidney was in Paris in April and perhaps March 1515, and was dispatched after Suffolk's return to ask Francis I to conceal the Parisian marriage.[81] Meanwhile Humphrey Wingfield had joined Oliver Pole in directing the duke's business in London. Yet mere loyalty to his relations cannot explain the dominance which they soon enjoyed in Suffolk's affairs.

Humphrey Wingfield is the most obvious example. By 1518 he had eclipsed Pole at the centre of the duke's finances, as the spokesman of Suffolk's council, and above all as the duke's negotiator with Wolsey: at one stage he had to ride along next to the cardinal pleading Suffolk's case.[82] Humphrey was a brilliant lawyer, and much employed in East Anglia, as steward and feoffee,

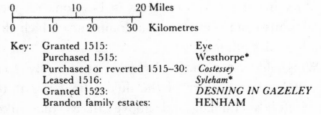

Key: Granted 1515:   Eye
        Purchased 1515:   Westhorpe*
        Purchased or reverted 1515–30:   *Costessey*
        Leased 1516:   *Syleham**
        Granted 1523:   *DESNING IN GAZELEY*
        Brandon family estates: HENHAM

Map 2.1 East Anglian Estates, 1515–1530

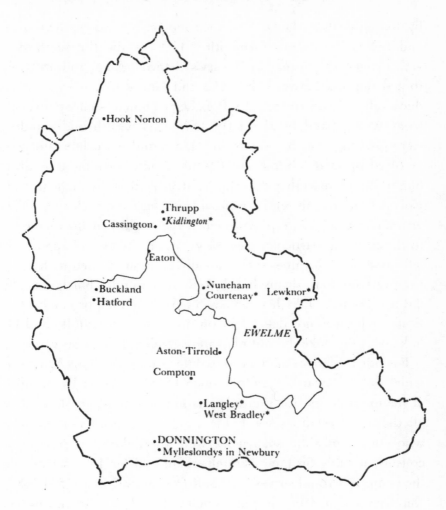

•Hook Norton

.Thrupp
Cassington. *Kidlington*

Éaton

•Buckland   .Nuneham
•Hatford   Courtenay* Lewknor*

EWELME

Aston-Tirrold•

Compton
•

•Langley*
West Bradley*

•DONNINGTON
• Mylleslondys in Newbury

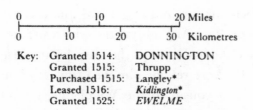

0		10		20 Miles
0	10	20	30	Kilometres

Key: Granted 1514:   DONNINGTON
      Granted 1515:   Thrupp
      Purchased 1515: Langley*
      Leased 1516:   *Kidlington*
      Granted 1525:   *EWELME*

Map 2.2 Oxfordshire and Berkshire Estates, 1514–1535

by amongst others the De Veres, the Howards, Wolsey, the crown, and towns like Great Yarmouth.[83] He was the thirteenth-most active chancery attorney of Wolsey's chancellorship, and probably forged the link between the duke and Gray's Inn, where several ducal officers were trained.[84] Suffolk helped him to secure patronage from Wolsey, and by the early 1520s his wealth and standing were growing fast, he was buying lands and wardships and was involved in local arbitrations.[85] While family ties doubtless drew him to Brandon, as they drew him and Sir Anthony Wingfield to Sir Robert Brandon, his service was evidently far from exclusive.[86] This was understandable, especially when the social benefits of service to the crown in particular were so great, and Wingfield apparently felt no clash of loyalties. Occasionally Humphrey used feoffees or sureties who were themselves linked with Suffolk, but he usually did not bother.[87] Like his nephew Sir Anthony, his prominence in East Anglia was not dependent on his service to Suffolk, and his links with the duke did not play an overriding role in his career.

For other relatives matters were different. Sir Anthony Wingfield (chief ducal steward in Suffolk since 1515) occasionally presided at manorial courts for the duke, as Humphrey (chief steward of all the ducal estates since 1515) would later do.[88] But the men who consistently did such work were the duke's less prominent cousins, notably Sir James Framlingham and Sir John Glemham, the comptroller and surveyor of Suffolk's lands.[89] In 1515–16 they were often joined by Sir John Audley, Suffolk's chief steward in Norfolk, who was only a relative by marriage, but was close to Sir Robert Brandon and the Wingfields.[90] Audley soon faded out of the duke's central and local affairs, and in general this was the fate – or choice – of all those East Anglian gentry who were not Suffolk's closer cousins. The duke had entered the area during a De Vere minority, and various De Vere retainers moved towards him briefly. Sir Richard Fitzlewis, a cousin to the Wingfields, bound himself for Suffolk's debts to Surrey in 1516, but not thereafter, and later returned to the De Veres.[91] Sir Giles Alington probably placed a son in Suffolk's household, but served the house of Oxford with dedication later, while Sir John Raynsford too flirted with

Brandon's service, but his son committed himself to the De Veres.[92] Many of those remembered in the will of the 13th Earl of Oxford did attach themselves to Brandon: but they were all Wingfields, Brews, Lovells, and Tyrrells, the duke's relations.[93]

The same trend applied among those who had not been linked with the late earl of Oxford. Thomas Jermyn and Sir Edward Echingham were sureties and feoffees for Suffolk in 1516, but there is no sign of a connection thereafter.[94] Even those who helped later showed less loyalty to Suffolk than to other lords. Sir Thomas Wyndham was bound for Suffolk's debts in 1520 and bought a wardship from him, but served Surrey as attorney-general in 1521 and named him an executor and Norfolk overseer in his will.[95] Again and again it was the duke's relatives who entered into recognizances for him and served as feoffees; when he bought the manor of East Ruston, Norfolk, in 1522 his feoffees were Sir Anthony, Humphrey, Henry and Lewis Wingfield, and Francis Hall, a brother-in-law of Sir Robert Wingfield, who brought up one of Hall's sons.[96]

In time the officers first appointed by the duke began to die: Sir James Framlingham in 1519, and Sir Humphrey Banaster in 1521. The latter had entered Brandon's service from that of Buckingham by 1511, established himself in Calais, and become mayor.[97] His absence at Calais limited his usefulness to Suffolk, though in March 1515 he spent some time in Paris, much to the distress of his subordinates, presumably helping the duke; he provided financial support, and for a spell in 1517 he helped Humphrey Wingfield run Brandon's London affairs.[98] When this generation passed on their places were filled either by other cousins, or by obscure local gentlemen. Around 1520 Suffolk's courts were often held by men with incomes of under £10.[99] That his bailiffs mostly came from this social stratum is unsurprising, though again by 1523 one in three in East Anglia was a relative or household servant.[100] Other peers who used their relations in this way – or were used by them, for the pressure on Suffolk to dispense patronage in their favour must have been constant – could comfort themselves with the thought that their cousins were in any case the leading lights of the local gentry community and thus well worth wooing. Certainly that

Table 2.2 The Brandons

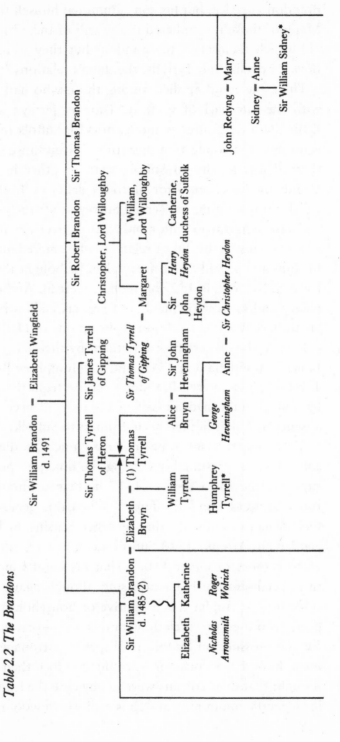

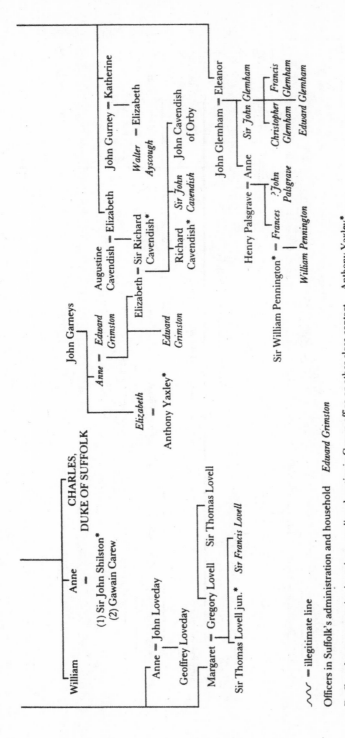

∿ = illegitimate line

Officers in Suffolk's administration and household *Edward Grimston*

Feoffees, farmers, captains in retinue, suelies, deputies in Crown office or other close contact Anthony Yaxley*

Children are not arranged in order of birth, and some are omitted.

Table 2.3 The Wingfields

Sir Robert Wingfield

Sir William Brandon = Elizabeth
d. 1491

Sir Henry Wingfield
d. 1493–4

Robert Wingfield

Elizabeth = Sir John Wingfield
d. 1481

Sir Robert Wingfield
deputy of Calais

Sir Richard Wingfield
chancellor of the duchy
of Lancaster

John Framlingham = Anne

Margaret Nevill = (1) Sir John Mortimer
= (2) CHARLES BRANDON
= (3) Robert Downes

Lewis Fitzlewis   John Fitzlewis

Sir Richard Fitzlewis*

Sir James Framlingham = Anne = (2) *Robert Browne*

*Francis Framlingham**

Sir Henry Sherbourne* = Isabel

Elizabeth = *Francis Hall*

Edmund Hall   Robert Hall*

Sir Humphrey Wingfield

Anne   Margaret = *Thomas Seckford*

*Francis   John   Anthony
Seckford Seckford Seckford*

*Lewis
Wynwood*
=

Sir John Wingfield
d. 1509

Sir Anthony Wingfield   Henry Wingfield*

Elizabeth   *Charles Wingfield*
=

William Naunton

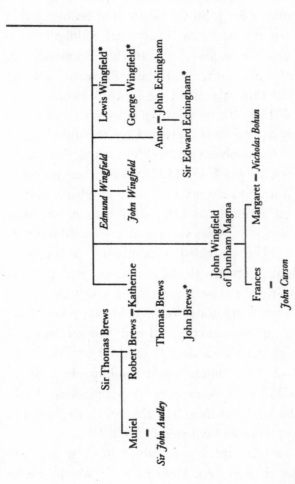

Key as in Table 2.2.

65

was the case a few years later for Henry, Earl of Worcester, the son of Suffolk's colleague on the French embassy.[101] Suffolk's cousins, on the other hand, though widespread in East Anglia, were rarely rich or powerful. Glemham's income of £60 or Sir Thomas Lovell junior's £66 13s 4d hardly placed them in the top rank.[102] Of the four active as Suffolk justices in 1514–16, Sir James Framlingham and Sir Robert Brandon were dead by 1524, leaving only Humphrey and Sir Anthony Wingfield; Sir John Glemham had been expelled from the commission of the peace by 1520 after indulging in a violent dispute with Lord Willoughby.[103] Meanwhile Framlingham, Glemham, Sir Richard Cavendish, Sir Robert Brandon, and Sir John Audley had all lost their places on the Norfolk bench in the rationalisation of 1514–15.[104] Those relatives who were successful, like Sir Robert Wingfield, had little real need for the duke's good lordship, and were less than subservient to him, as the 100 marks annuity Suffolk paid Sir Robert from 1522 onwards suggested.[105] His cousins provided a useful network of houses in which to stay, especially with William Wingfield as Prior of Westacre, and they provided plenty of brides for Suffolk's successful household servants and administrators.[106] They provided a continuity of families, though not of individuals, between Brandon and his predecessors, for the Wingfields and Brews had been prominent in late De la Pole administration.[107] But they could not provide an instant power-base for Suffolk as an East Anglian magnate, and with low income, and strong competition from the Howards and residual loyalty to the De Veres, Brandon had great difficulties in building himself an alternative one. He could hardly be expected to supplant the De la Poles properly when he held less than half the number of manors that, for example, Duke John had enjoyed in 1476.[108]

The same problems applied more generally. Suffolk was a new man with no old shoes to step into. Until he built Westhorpe he did not have a suitable residence near the bulk of his East Anglian estates. He and his wife patronised 'a mynstryll of the Fraynche Kwenys', six trumpeters, a troop of interlude players, and one or more very active bear-keepers: these proclaimed their good lordship in towns and country houses from Dover to Beverley and from Shrewsbury to Lynn.[109] Entertainers in their service appeared in Suffolk and Norfolk towns twice as often as those in Howard livery.[110] The duke could sometimes use his patronage to favour men of his choosing from outside the areas of his estates. He entrusted Donnington Castle to Roger Wolrich of Dudmaston, Shropshire, the husband of his illegitimate sister Katherine.[111] He leased Costessey with 1,000 sheep to Sir William Pennington, a Cumberland gentleman who married Frances Palsgrave, a ducal cousin and lady-in-waiting.[112] Suffolk tried to make himself a channel between East Anglia and the government, writing to Wolsey in 1517 in an unsuccessful attempt to have the deprived Abbot of St Benet's Hulme reinstated.[113] But in these early years it would seem that he made no great impact on the area. In Essex the towns, for example, looked far more to Lord Fitzwalter and the earl of Essex for favour, in Norfolk to Fitzwalter, Surrey, and the Bishop of Norwich.[114] Only from Bishop West of Ely, like him a recent entrant to the area, could the duke consistently attract patronage for himself and his followers.[115]

On the De la Pole estates outside East Anglia Suffolk spent less time and less effort, with predictable results. In Norfolk and Suffolk, at least matters close to his heart received attention. By 1538 he had 2,382 deer in his parks, with a healthily high proportion of young 'rascals' to mature stags, and prize red deer at Westhorpe; at Buckland, Berkshire, in contrast, the park was still in decay in 1535 despite orders to repair it in 1522 and 1524.[116] In Oxfordshire and Berkshire the duke was not even named to the commission of the peace, though Osney Abbey did at least make him its chief steward by 1520.[117] The scattered nature of his estates in the area and his consciousness of the role he was expected to play in East Anglia exacerbated this weakness. Only in Southwark was his local position demonstrably strong. There he could be named as a feoffee to ensure the success of a land transaction. When vagrancy searches were made in London in 1519 and 1524 he was given responsibility for the whole South Bank. In July 1523 he was commissioned to muster troops there although he held no directly relevant office.[118] Though he decorated Donnington Castle with heraldic stained glass, it was in Southwark that he put most effort into building, reconstructing the Brandon house as Suffolk Place, a large palace decorated with fashionable terracottas, including his crowned lion's head badge.[119]

Mary and the French

The year 1515 brought dramatic changes in Suffolk's life, not only through his accession to the De la Pole estates. His marriage to Mary would give their children a claim to the throne, and increased his status: he and the margrave of Brandenburg rode together at Charles V's entry into London in 1522, each the husband of a dowager queen. Similarly it brought him a leading role at the Field of Cloth of Gold, lodging with Mary in one wing of Henry's prefabricated palace there.[120] In some ways the benefits were more ambiguous, and legend has it that Brandon commented on this, in the verse

> Cloth of gold do not despise
> Though thou be match'd with cloth of frieze
> Cloth of frieze be not too bold
> Though thou be match'd with cloth of gold.[121]

In East Anglia a queen attracted more fuss than a duke: Sir Thomas Lestrange of Hunstanton sent presents and paid visits to her, but not to him.[122] At Bury St Edmunds fair he is said to have organised impressive tournaments, but she merely sat in a tent with her retinue and musicians and received a stream of admirers.[123] John Croftes placed her arms, but not Brandon's, over the gateway of his new house at West Stow.[124] Technically, she needed his authorisation to dispose of her goods, but while he and his councillors were renegotiating their joint debt to the king he was very anxious that 'sche may coum ope, to the intent th[at] sche may doo hall scheth actys, acordyng has by dyvyssed or schall by dyvyes most for your grasses surttie ... and th[at] et schall not by sayd bout et tys her dyed and fry wyell.'[125] Their joint acts were done first in her name, her seal was some twice the size of his, and at the christenings of their children the canopy over the font was decorated with her devices, Tudor roses and Yorkist suns.[126]

Such benefits as royal godparents, even for one's daughters, could not lightly be overlooked, but in other ways Mary was a burden.[127] The jointure designated for her by act of parliament included not only all Suffolk's De la Pole manors, but also eighteen on which he held only a reversion. Her frequent illness could hold him back from other important business.[128] Worst of all, her personal and financial links with France proved a political liability. Suffolk's clear landed income was around £1,500 by 1523, plus unspecified profits from office and, before 1519, perhaps £1,500 on his wards' lands.[129] In 1515 and 1516 he borrowed £12,000 from the crown with the backing of Italian bankers; he continued to stall creditors such as the earl of Shrewsbury; and between 1513 and 1523 he lent himself £3,000 out of the revenues of Bromfield, Yale and Chirk.[130] As he lost the Lisle lands in 1519 and the Corbet and Saye lands in 1522, the grant of £100 worth of Buckingham's Suffolk manors in 1523 can have made little real improvement.[131] In the light of this the £4,000 or more a year of his wife's French revenues which their arrangement with Henry left them was very attractive, and thus so was Anglo-French amity.

Moreover, the duke felt himself in Francis I's debt after 1515, and greatly admired the French king. He consistently advocated a meeting between Francis and Henry, and one in which tournaments should play a large part. When the right time came, Suffolk played a large role in organising the jousts for the Field of Cloth of Gold, working with Bonnivet, whose relationship with Francis was much like his own with Henry.[132] But when English foreign policy relied on careful fencing with the French, Suffolk became an embarrassment.

Indeed, his links with France were sufficient to generate suspicion. He enjoyed strong connections in Calais, where his councillor Sir Humphrey Banaster was mayor, and his cousin Sir Richard Wingfield was deputy from 1513 to 1519, but rumours named one of his wife's household officers as brother to a French agent, and although they seem to have had few French servants, such accusations must have been easily made.[133] About one man at least they would have been right. This was Martin Dupin, merchant of Bayonne and English denizen since 1512. Dupin secured English royal licences to import Gascon wares into England, and a French royal licence to carry grain by river from Mary's dower lands in Saintonge to Bayonne.[134] In 1515 he was in Suffolk's service in Paris, helping to buy wines for Wolsey, lending money to Bishop West, and securing Suffolk's intervention to free goods of his seized in Cornwall. In November 1518 he obtained a general pardon together with William Fellowe, Suffolk's future pursuivant, and George Hampton, Mary's treasurer. In 1517 the French government paid him 300 crowns for an unspecified secret mission.[135]

Hampton too was often in France and was arrested there in 1522, while agents of the duke were then at Bordeaux buying wine. Fellowe was involved in attempts to sell off some of the 200 or more French judicial offices at Mary's disposal, the most expensive selling at about £800.[136] Any suspicions of dangerous francophilia raised by these links were unfortunately confirmed by Suffolk's behaviour. It was no wonder that his only real, or even rumoured, diplomatic missions in these years were those in which his love for the French could do no harm.[137] Immediately after his marriage he had apparently cut his links with the Low Countries. Margaret of Austria, who had been as incredulous as her subjects when the news of the marriage broke, complied with the duke's request that she send home his daughter, though protesting that 'si vous la me eusses laissee, j'avoye inte[n]cion de la si b[ien] traicter q[ue] eusses eu cause de vous rejouir.'[138] It would be some time before Netherlanders again wrote to Suffolk for help as the Abbot of St Bertin had in January 1515. Francis, on the other hand, used Suffolk as an additional ambassador in England, and the duke either could not or would not escape from this role.[139]

When the French envoy took the news of his monarch's triumph at the battle of Marignano to each in turn, Henry, Wolsey, and Suffolk reacted very differently.[140] Henry, tragically upstaged, was close to tears; Wolsey was politely pleased, but remonstrated over Scotland; Suffolk 'answered me much more civilly than the king, and told me he was as glad of the prosperity of the king my master as any man in the kingdom of France, if not more so.' Worse, the duke assured the French that all English threats of war were a sham, advocated a meeting between the kings, and invited the envoy to visit him in Southwark. Suffolk was not excluded from the discussion, or even the execution, of anti-French policies, and when properly briefed was quite prepared to criticise the French before other ambassadors.[141] But when the French successfully manipulated him it could only bring trouble. In autumn 1515 he and Mary wrote to Albany, now established as regent in Scotland, to encourage a peaceful settlement there, but when Albany began to send all his southbound envoys to visit them, wrote to them with his version of border events, and told Wolsey to find out the truth about Scotland from Suffolk rather than the lying English borderers, it was no surprise that Brandon soon found himself excluded from the making of Scottish policy.[142]

Suffolk's longest absence from court and council in this period lasted from late May 1516 to February 1517. Some ambassadors thought that such absences betokened disgrace.[143] Yet Suffolk was active in council immediately before and after this spell, and on his summer progress Henry happily met the duke at Donnington. On 25 August he granted Suffolk the wardship of two of the sons of their dead friend Sir Thomas Knyvet, for which the duke paid a comparatively low price.[144] Relations with France were shaky, and Suffolk thus had cause to be in East Anglia, but there was also sense in keeping away from London a man who could easily have sabotaged Wolsey's careful foreign policy of restraining France by threats.

At Easter 1518 this became more clear. Wolsey was secretly negotiating a *rapprochement* with France in London, while Henry spent Easter at Abingdon, surrounded by nobles in a tense atmosphere generated by warnings of plots to overthrow him, in which Suffolk's name had probably been mentioned.[145] Though the court was surprised by the arrival of some peers that Easter, no one found Suffolk's presence unusual. Henry wanted to spend Easter with his sister as he had done in 1516, and had no objections to a long stay by her and Suffolk. For Wolsey this was ideal, for he kept the king, Sir Thomas Lovell and Sir Henry Marney informed of his negotiations, but not Suffolk.[146] Brandon was frustrated at this restraint: not unnaturally he wanted a part in any Anglo-French settlement.

He was soon accused of having taken all too great a part. Someone reported that he had told the French that they would recover Tournai (and thus sold Wolsey's chief bargaining point). He presumably denied this to Henry himself, but was eager to vindicate himself with Wolsey too, sending several trusted servants with letters to plead his case.[147] He and Mary stayed with the court, for she was too ill to be moved: he explained this carefully to the cardinal, 'wyche I thouth was meth to awartys hem of, for elles et myth fortune to abyn schowd hem th[at] et had byn doune bout for askues.'[148] In July he was still unhappy about his relations with Wolsey, which had apparently been good before the incident. Throughout the month he bombarded the cardinal with assurances of good faith, asking Pace, the king's secretary, to write on his behalf, writing directly, and sending Humphrey Wingfield.[149] He offered to confront his detractors with 'ther false & s[ur]mysed tales' face to face.[150] By late July he was relieved to 'apperceyve, as well by the teno[r] of yo[ur] said letters as by the reaporte of my said cosyn, that ye [Wolsey] be myn assured good lord and frend', and resolved that 'I therfor shall trust therunto, and laye all the trobles a parte.'[151] At the end of the month he rushed from Elmswell, the Bury St Edmunds Abbey manor where he was staying, to Enfield to meet Wolsey, and was finally convinced that the problem was over. Wolsey, with his treaty now signed, was no longer wary, and agreed to appease 'suche variance as be nowe dependyng betwen me & th'erle of Surrey & the countesse of Lincoln': this dispute, presumably over De la Pole estates, may have lain behind the accusations in the first place.[152]

Suffolk obviously found it hard to maintain his relationship with Wolsey and the king, especially when these two were physically separated. Yet he could succeed: though the policies with which he had too unequivocally identified himself were rejected, this did not imply personal rejection. In late July Henry stayed at Wanstead, where Suffolk was still keeper, and he did so again several times in the next few years, enjoying the duke's entertainment.[153] Shortly afterwards Wolsey asked Suffolk to come to London. Spoilt for choice, the duke explained that much as he would have liked to come 'spysseallie to a sen your grace', Henry wished him to stay, having 'bout fyowe to gyef atyndauns' on him.[154]

The demands of Mary's dower income, 'in which restith much of her hono[ur] and profit and myn also', always forced Suffolk to sail close to the wind. By August 1518, though working through Wolsey to arrange the matter, he had also entrusted a private mission concerning the dower to Sir Thomas Boleyn, the English ambassador in France.[155] But this raised no suspicion now. Suffolk returned to the centre of Anglo- French ceremony and festivities, appearing as a leading councillor. Mary of course played a major role too, but Suffolk was especially prominent, throwing a banquet for Bonnivet and the whole French embassy.[156] In October 1518 he was back in council.[157] Friendship with France restored him to something approaching the position of 1514–15, though Wolsey was now far more assured in his executive dominance. None the less, over the French hostages in January 1519 Wolsey acted on Henry's will as communicated by Suffolk.[158]

The material benefits of this politically uncomfortable francophilia were dubious. His French pension was paid regularly every six months until 1 June 1521, with a suspiciously early payment on 1 May 1518.[159] Mary's revenue seldom flowed freely. She was at the mercy not only of Francis, who unilaterally exchanged her rights to 10,400 *livres*' worth of salt tax for 4,000 *livres* in cash, but also of Grand Maître Boisy.[160] Francis had granted him the right to name her officers and farm her revenues, but he seems to have paid over little before his death in 1519, despite Francis's orders. His brother Bonnivet took over as farmer, but it took a mission in 1521 from Mary's chancellor and treasurer, and the intervention of English ambassadors later in the year, even to secure the payment of the rents to him.[161] This failure was despite Wolsey's apparently whole-hearted help, at least after 1518; by 1523 war had come and

Francis had sequestered her revenues of 60,250 *livres* and diverted them to pay for his own household.[162]

The French income played a larger role in Suffolk's life than its sparse payments merited. For its failure to flow freely necessitated frequent renegotiations of the couple's debt to Henry, and these were used by Wolsey as an additional brake on the duke's francophilia. As early as January 1516 Suffolk and Wolsey were again discussing 'the grete mater betwene the kyngys grace & me' and by February things were apparently settled.[163] As Easter approached something went wrong. An excellent goshawk and some jewels were dispatched to Henry, and Wolsey was assured that 'her and men ondylle trost es in your grace.'[164] Polydore Vergil suggests that Wolsey stopped Henry pardoning the debt completely, and for once there may be some truth in his interpretation. Certainly Suffolk saw Wolsey and Henry as the two men with whom he had to settle, despite the involvement of other councillors in such negotiations: in 1518 he promised Wolsey over the debt question 'suche aunswer therin, as the kinges grace and you bothe shalbe therw[ith] right well pleased and contented.'[165]

No settlement survives from Easter 1516, but the next year's dealings confirm that Wolsey, ever ready to learn from Henry VII, used Suffolk's debts as a rein on the headstrong duke, without doubt with the approval of Henry VIII. In December 1516 the terms of 1515 were softened considerably.[166] None of the total debt agreed in 1515 had yet been paid. Now the payments became smaller, they could cease while the dower rents were interrupted, and Mary's debts would be cancelled at her death. Then, in May 1517, with a delicate anti-French policy in action, Wolsey pulled in the leash. The payments stayed at 1,000 marks every six months but the duke was now to pay 500 marks a year towards his own debts even when no dower was paid.[167] The cash had to be delivered not within forty days of every payment date, but within fourteen. If Mary died, all the remainder of her jewels, hangings, and plate would come to the crown, and she had to promise not to resign her dower to Francis. Jewels worth 2,000 marks were handed over on the day the indentures were sealed, and the total debt was increased not only by the inclusion of more arrears on the Welsh lordships where the duke was receiver, but also by charging Mary and Suffolk £600 for their lodging at court, an underhand and unheard-of expedient.

All this was little more than a threat. By 1 February 1521 only a further £1,334 6s 9d of the £25,234 6s 9d debt had been paid, and the couple were still Henry's greatest debtors after Francis I.[168] Nearly £3,000 in French revenue had been sold to the crown for cash at Calais in July 1518, so the repayment must represent either one year of full payment or four years of Suffolk paying alone, but not both. Either way he and Mary were not being kept to the agreement, just as the indenture of 1517 specified that they had not been required to keep the earlier bonds 'at theyre especiall sute made unto his grace'.[169] When a little more of the dower rents came through, Suffolk sold some to the king for gambling with the French hostages.[170] The debt remained a sword hanging over his head, but was not a real burden as long as he remained in favour.

Suffolk learned his lesson well from these troubles. When England broke with France again, he set out to ingratiate himself with Charles V, and succeeded. In 1521 and 1522 he was assiduous in looking after the emperor's ambassadors. He and Devonshire led the select band of nobles and courtiers which accompanied Henry to meet Charles at Canterbury in May 1522, and on 9 June both monarchs dined at Suffolk Place and hunted in the park there.[171] Suffolk's third daughter Frances may have been named in honour of Francis I, but his fourth, Eleanor, may well have been a gesture to Charles's favourite sister.[172] The duke was also quick to tap Charles's patronage. In 1522 he secured an imperial pension to replace his French one, but that was not unusual.[173] What was remarkable was that half of Charles's English pensioners in 1522 were Suffolk's protégés. These young men, Thomas Ashby and Richard Cooke, had little to recommend them to mix with the scions of the Spanish and Netherlandish nobility except their service to Suffolk.[174] The difficulties which Henry himself and Margaret of Austria had in installing Richard Guildford, eldest son of Sir Edward, among these pensioners only highlighted Suffolk's success: he had courted Charles with his usual skill.[175]

Since his marriage the duke had not been entirely ignored by foreign powers other than France. Maximilian had communicated with him and envisaged him as commander of an army against the French in 1516, but well-informed Italian princes were wary in their overtures to Brandon despite his own fulsome enthusiasm to serve them.[176] The citizens of Tournai sent him tapestries in January 1517 to plead their cause with Henry, and Wolsey was warned to take care that 'the kynges grace shuld not tayk no prejudice for the same.'[177] In December 1517, though, Charles V and his councillors resolved to offer pensions to Wolsey, Norfolk, and Worcester, but not to Suffolk. It was thus from a genuine isolation and lack of influence in foreign affairs that the duke escaped in the early 1520s; by June 1523 he was privy to the greatest secret of the anti-French alliance, the treason of Bourbon.[178]

Household and Administration

It was not only in his finances and his diplomatic standing that Suffolk was profoundly affected by his marriage to Mary Tudor. Their household too showed great signs of her influence. Brandon had had a butler earning 40s a year and several pages by 1509, and as he made his way at court acquired a chaplain, and the adolescent son of a knight as a gentleman-in-waiting.[179] His household must have expanded greatly at his marriage, though by 1524 it was not especially large: fifty-one servants then earned 26s 8d or more each, while the earl of Oxford in 1508, for example, had employed about a hundred at this level.[180] For the Field of Cloth of Gold Suffolk was restricted to seventy followers, while Mary undoubtedly took others.[181] There were various routes to high office in the ducal household, but family relationships were again important. Lewis Wynwood and Francis Hall, who together oversaw the catering when the duke and duchess met Wolsey at Letheringham in 1517, had both married Wingfields, and Wynwood at least had been in Suffolk's service since 1514.[182] The influence of Mary was greatest over the influx of young ladies and gentlemen brought up in the household. Esquires like George Heveningham and William Tyrrell were the duke's relations, as was Frances Palsgrave the lady-in-waiting. But George Brooke, the son of Lord Cobham, Richard Manners, the son of Lord Roos, and the Ladies Elizabeth and Anne Grey had remained in Mary's household from her time in France.[183] Lord Berners himself left Mary's retinue at the 'bedchamber crisis', and his daughter did so in 1515, but his eldest bastard, Humphrey, was one of the three leading gentlemen of the household by July 1517.[184] Bastards like Humphrey Berners and Anthony St Amand may have been placed with Suffolk in the hope of a successful military and courtly career; young men with greater prospects must have been attracted mainly by the chance to serve a queen.[185] Richard Long, son of Sir Thomas who had been an executor to Anthony St Amand's father, stayed in the household in 1516–17 and then moved on into royal service; William, nephew and eventual heir to Lord Stourton, later specifically described himself as Mary's servant, although the households were entirely integrated.[186]

Mary's continental connections had little effect on the household. In 1524–5 there were only four foreigners, though two of them stayed for twenty years: one was Suffolk's physician, Master Leonard, the highest-paid officer at £20 a year, and the other was Joris Flemyscheporte, involved with the ducal stable.[187] The duke's Welsh contacts were equally unproductive. Most striking was the lack of important East Anglians. Noble households at the centre of affinities which dominated local society had always been staffed by the leading families of the area, but Brandon's two senior officers were Sir Thomas Wentworth of West Bretton and his brother-in-law Sir John Burton, both from the wapentake of Staincross in the West Riding of Yorkshire. Suffolk probably recruited them on the 1513 campaign.[188] The cost of the household is hard to calculate, but was around £1,000 a year in the early 1520s. Suffolk was thus spending about the same proportion of his landed income on the household as the earl of Northumberland or the duke of Buckingham, though this gave him a less magnificent establishment than theirs because their revenues were more than twice the size of his.[189] Household offices were used to provide fees for men who can rarely, if ever, have performed them, like Sir Humphrey Banaster as vice-chamberlain. On the other hand, esquires and gentlemen worked for their keep, George Heveningham carrying messages and Richard Manners apparently keeping the duke's privy purse.[190]

Like any great household, Suffolk's had constantly changing personnel, but remained a means to rapid advancement. This could be by long service. John Egerton was in a strong position to attract Brandon's favour, as a gentleman usher involved in the care of the duke's horses. He earned 26s 8d in 1524, but by 1533 he was bailiff of nine manors, in 1536 he secured an eighty-year lease on a manor at £60 4s 4d from the Bishop of Norwich, doubtless with Suffolk's help, and he eventually married the daughter of 'a great riche ma[n]'.[191] Advancement often came by a good marriage: Richard Freston, later favoured by the duke, probably married Alice Portington, a Lincolnshire lady-in-waiting, in 1524–5.[192] Henry Curteis, of Lincolnshire, and John Alington, of Cambridgeshire, presumably owed their Suffolk marriages to their spells in the Brandon household.[193] Controlling such a social beehive could be a responsibility as well as an advantage. In 1517 Suffolk had to deny rapidly any part in the busybodying betrothal, executed by one Mistress Jerningham, between Lady Anne Grey, a lady-in-waiting, and John Berkeley, a royal ward whom Henry had 'put ... to my rule and giding'.[194] Mistress Jerningham rather suitably took the part of 'Dalians' in a masque in the ducal household a few years later.[195] In his household, by arranging marriages and engendering loyalties, Suffolk could build a political future for himself and his sons using the status Mary brought: this was easier than forming a connection among the established gentry, but it still had its difficulties. Finally, Suffolk's household demonstrated again the importance of his links with the Lovells. Young members of the Manners family seem to have moved freely between Sir Thomas Lovell's service and that of Brandon, and this was part of a much wider pattern of connections, embracing Suffolk's relations like the Gurneys, retainers like Sir Lewis Orwell, and occasional financial backers like Sir William Paston.[196]

Influences on Suffolk's administration are harder to trace than those on the personnel of his household. Some of his councillors were very experienced. Francis Hall handled Brandon's finances with the expertise of twenty years' trading as a merchant of the staple, while John Golde, almoner by 1523, had served the duke of Buckingham, as clerk of the wardrobe by 1499 and master of the wardrobe by 1508.[197] Humphrey Banaster had been Buckingham's comptroller and treasurer, and John Peryent, an auditor by the 1520s, had been a crown auditor since 1510.[198] They had De la Pole muniments at their disposal, but did not follow De la Pole administrative structures slavishly.[199] The leading councillors often worked in London, keeping the duke informed about legal matters and questions of patronage, and negotiating with the crown and other creditors.[200] Meanwhile the surveyor, auditors, and stewards in their audits, held both in London and in regional centres such as Swyncombe and Eye, provided the link between the central council and local bailiffs.[201] Suffolk's council is elusive. When action had to be taken in London, the duke sometimes sent one individual with executive powers, rather than acting through the council; on the other hand, it sometimes acted as an executive body in Suffolk, as at Eye when 'men ... whatched by the comandement of my lord[es] cou[n]cell in the ixth yer of Henry the viiith whan P[ar]menteris wyff of Occolt was robbyd'.[202]

Survival at Court

Perhaps Suffolk's councillors bore a heavy burden in the work of making him a magnate. It seems to have been a task which he found not only practically, but also conceptually, difficult. With no noble ancestry and little experience outside the royal court, except for his brief spells in the country with Essex, it is hardly surprising that the duke was often distressed, in the early years after 1515, when away from the court which had brought him all his success. In July 1516 he begged Wolsey to tell the king that 'my hert and mynde be alwaye with hym, and daily appeteth and desireth to see his grace, and do thinke long unto suche tyme as his pleasur shalbe to licence me to acomplisshe the same.'[203] Especially when in difficulties over his debts, he feared even for his place in the king's jousts, asking the cardinal to ensure 'as me spysseall trust es in your lordysschype th[at] I may wayt on the kynges grace on hes schyed' in the tournament of May 1516.[204]

Yet Suffolk's place at the king's side was not in danger: the duke succeeded in his most pressing task in these years, that of remaining a leading courtier despite the other changes in his status and lifestyle. Henry ran at the ring on 29 January 1516; Suffolk was first aid, he and Henry wore richer clothes than the other participants, and the king gave him his outfit and all the horse trappings. When Suffolk was not at court, Henry's martial entertainments were smaller, only he dressed in superior clothes, and he took to challenging alone.[205] The duke continued to play a role in the king's more important jousts, but the nature of this role changed in 1517. Suffolk ceased to be Henry's first aid, being replaced by the men of the nascent privy chamber, Carew, Bryan, and the rest. This change, it has been argued, 'was a symbolic representation of the capture of the king's favour by the new set of intimates.'[206] But a close examination of the jousts of 1516 and 1517 suggests a different interpretation.

On 19 and 20 May 1516 Suffolk was Henry's first aid. All four challengers (Carew and Essex included) dressed alike, but only Henry's and Suffolk's servants wore yellow damask. On 19 May both king and duke jousted well, Henry scoring rather better.[207] Next day things went badly wrong. Suffolk scored excellently, ending with the highest total, and all his contests had been exciting, none of his opponents breaking less than four lances on him in their eight runs.[208] In comparison, Henry's combats were dismal: his three opponents totalled only five broken lances between them, and four of these were achieved by Lord Edmund Howard alone. Incompetent adversaries were hard to hit, and Henry shattered five fewer lances than the duke. The king was furious, and 'p[ro]mysed nev[er] to just agayn except hit be w[ith] as gud a man as hym selfe.'[209]

He kept his word. On 7 July 1517 Sir Henry Guildford, now master of the horse, took his proper place as Henry's first aid, and Suffolk led a band of experienced answerers.[210] Henry's band, many of them indeed drawn from the younger courtiers now coming to the fore, dressed in cheaper materials than the king. Brandon's aids, including leading court nobles like Dorset and Essex, dressed very much as the duke's men, with coats and bards covered with Cs and Ms for Charles and Mary. The feat performed by Carew, fitted out as 'the Blue Knight', who ran a course with an enormous lance, certainly impressed observers. It was an exact imitation of a stunt executed by Louis XII's grand écuyer in 1514 to impress Suffolk and Dorset, who perhaps set it as a challenge to their juniors.[211] None the less, what really struck all three Italian eyewitnesses was what was intended to strike them: the titanic combat between Henry and Suffolk.[212] Hector and Achilles sprang readily to mind. Unusual features of the tournament highlighted this encounter. The answerers paraded with almost equal pomp to that of the challengers, and Henry and Suffolk rode out of the lists together. Their struggle ended symbolically in renewed and undying brotherhood like that of Lancelot and Tristram. It was in this role above all that posterity would remember Suffolk: seventeenth-century surveys of the Tower of London always found complementary sets of arms and armour belonging to Henry and the duke.[213]

These jousts were intended to impress, and they did so. The new pattern remained the norm for the major tournaments of the next seven years. Henry's new aids, with the occasional exception of Devonshire, never dressed as richly as the king, and sometimes especially splendid outfits were produced for Brandon and Henry. These two always ran the first eight courses, and rarely failed to impress, as on 4 June 1522 when the king broke his spear on each run.[214] It showed Henry's true estimate of his courtiers' jousting abilities when he chose Suffolk and Dorset as his leading aids for the jousts at the Field of Cloth of Gold. Both duly won prizes, though Suffolk's scoring was not at its spectacular best.[215] One spectator was impressed by him, though, and another recorded of 19 June that 'the saying of the people was that the duke of Souffoulk had donne best that daie and many other daies before, and would have donne more, as they should have known right well yf his hand had not bine hurt by misfortune.'[216]

It would seem to have been more in disguisings and other revels that the king's newer companions predominated. But Suffolk was often involved, not only as an 'auncient persone', to counterpoint the king and his youthful companions, but also dancing with the king in groups including such mixed company as the earl of Surrey, and the newcomers Henry Norris and Arthur Pole.[217] Mary too often took part in revels, banquets, and state occasions, and in all the reorganisations within the royal household in 1519 she and her husband were always assured of a free breakfast at court.[218]

Her French connections must have involved her in some way in the arguments at court over the French affectations of Carew, Bryan, and the other 'minions'.[219] Certainly she dressed with an eye to French style, and at least by 1530 she was an important patroness of French cultural innovation at the English court. In that year she presented Henry with a French book of hours illustrated with classical architecture and playful putti, and she also received a visit from 'Maistre Ambroise', Cardinal Duprat's painter, who produced the most skilful work ever seen in England, 'passans en singularite plus que ne sauroye estimer'.[220] Brandon too kept in the forefront of fashion. He was probably painted in miniature by Lucas Hornebolte, and his seal in 1513 had borne a classically draped female figure.[221] His houses at Suffolk Place and Westhorpe were among the largest and best decorated of the reign, and Westhorpe's gardens were laid out in the French manner under Mary's influence.[222] Though Suffolk was far from educated, his servants often were: Humphrey Wingfield ran a humanist school in his houses at Brantham and Ipswich, and the duke and his wife kept in contact with John Palsgrave, her former schoolmaster and secretary.[223]

Suffolk maintained personal, as well as cultural, contacts with the French court, not only through powerful figures like Bonnivet and the nobles Brandon introduced to Henry in 1520, but also through the young French hostages, resident in England to guarantee Francis's payments for the return of Tournai. He gambled and shot with them and Henry at Buckingham's house at Penshurst and elsewhere.[224] The hostages' company was certainly not the sole prerogative of the English minions, for at dinner after the 1519 Garter festivities the young Frenchmen dined with English peers 'and none at that borde, under the estate of a lord'.[225] In any case, it would be foolish to draw great divisions between Henry's newer and older-established friends. Devonshire dined with Suffolk, and he and Arthur Pole had been in Mary's household.[226] Sir Edward Nevill, prominent in the privy chamber, had been on the fringes of Brandon's earlier circle at court. In particular Brandon seems to have been close to Sir Nicholas Carew, who became master of the horse in July 1522. Their interests were similar, and their ages not as different as has been suggested, for Carew was at least nineteen in 1515 when he first rose to prominence.[227] When the court visited Carew's home near Croydon in February 1519 Suffolk went too, and hunted in Carew's park. In March 1520 Suffolk and Mary stayed with the Carews for some time, with Mary ill and Charles visiting London on business and returning. Carew trusted Suffolk to guarantee Sir Robert Wingfield's payment of a pension to him, and was the brother-in-law of Suffolk's friend Sir Henry Guildford.[228] Both Guildfords were associated with Carew and Bryan in the affair of May 1519, while Sir William Sidney remained a feed esquire of the body from 1514 to 1520 and beyond: the advent of younger men did not sweep aside those with whom Brandon had risen.[229] And when at court Suffolk still played the courtier as much as any of the minions. He raced his black dog against Henry's for wagers, and fetched money to give to Sir William Compton for the king's private use.[230] When Sir Edward Guildford bought foreign horses for Henry in 1520, the king gave one each not only to Carew, but also to Suffolk and to Sir William Kingston, a long-standing courtier.[231]

In the Garter elections Suffolk did vote consistently for older men with military experience. Sir William Sandys was duly elected in 1518, though Sir Nicholas Vaux and Sir Maurice Berkeley, whom the duke named as frequently as Sandys, were not yet chosen. He naturally tended to back relatives and friends, like Sir Richard

Wingfield and Sir Henry Guildford, for whom he cast the only vote in 1518.[232] His disinclination to name Sir William Compton may have been a matter of personal differences, for Brandon had been accused in 1515 of giving Compton a pain in the leg by sorcery. Whatever motivated his voting, he did continue to play a large role in the order's chapters, finances, and ceremonies.[233]

In the course of 1515 the duke apparently lost three of the offices at court and in Southwark on which his position had rested. Yet he was not stripped of these honours, for the knights who succeeded him were almost certainly his nominees. Sir Henry Guildford, the new master of the horse, had been Suffolk's deputy.[234] Sir Henry Sherbourne, named to both marshalcies, had fought at sea with Sir William Sidney, perhaps commanded troops raised by Brandon, and was a relative by marriage and recent feoffee to the Wingfields.[235] At least in the king's bench, prisoners were still officially entrusted to Suffolk in 1521, and Sir Thomas Wentworth and Sir Robert Brandon continued to work as his deputies there, while in 1519 it was the duke whom a London vintner sued for releasing a man who subsequently attacked the vintner's wife.[236] Control of the prisons was obviously a more complex and informal matter than letters patent might suggest.

Patronage and Power

Suffolk employed a plethora of techniques, formal and informal, to promote and protect himself and those who called on his good lordship. Where necessary he could assist his dependents in legal procedures, calling on Robert Jenour, his own usual attorney, to defend his servant Lewis Wynwood when the latter was sued for debt over a purchase of green velvet, presumably for the ducal household. Similarly, 8d was paid out 'for making Caroo of Haccomes bill' on behalf of the relations of Sir Robert Brandon's wife.[237] Specifying that he was Suffolk's servant doubtless helped William Ellenger gain a protection as a Calais victualler in the nick of time before the case against him came into court.[238] For less straightforward problems, a letter to Wolsey was the answer. The duke's lordship had to be seen to be good, and for this reason extended surprisingly far. His maternal relative Humphrey Tyrrell was sly and hot-headed, with a fine line in threatening behaviour (promising in one dispute 'that he wyll hete some of the enh[ab] itant[es] of the seid towne as hote as his wyf heteth his oven').[239] Yet Suffolk backed him in a lawsuit with a letter to Wolsey. Anthony Savage, involved in the Pauncefote murder case, was only the brother of a servant of the French queen, but none the less both she and her husband wrote to Wolsey on his behalf. William Skelton's connection with Brandon is unclear, but he still secured the duke's intervention with the cardinal over his legal affairs.[240]

In this light it is ironic that Suffolk himself was remarkably unlitigious, though perhaps he could achieve his ends without recourse to the law. From 1509 to 1513, and from 1519 to 1523, he initiated no cases in the king's bench, and was sued only over his work as marshal. In the common pleas, where twenty-one lay peers brought three or more suits in 1513–15 alone, he was involved in only three cases between 1509 and 1523.[241] One was a fictitious action to confirm a land transaction, once he was sued over detaining land from the rightful heir, and in the third he perhaps had less his own interests than those of his tenantry at heart.[242] This was in 1515, when he sued Joan Hasilwode for trespass and damage to corn in his close at Bellington, Worcestershire, part of the Lisle estates. His heartless persecution of a widowed tenant is put into context by the court rolls of the manor of Chaddesley Corbett, of which Bellington formed a part. For Joan Hasilwode was a public nuisance. Between 1514 and 1516 she enclosed on the common field, dug an illegal ditch, assaulted someone, ploughed into headlands several times, blocked the bridge in the common field, and often failed to mend her ways under orders of the ducal stewards. Even the suit in common pleas seems not to have restrained her, though by 1518 she was simply refusing to attend manorial courts on grounds of infirmity.[243] Disciplining the duke's tenants was not always taken so seriously: the six Berkshire farmers on his manors who were supposed, under his guidance, to correct their depopulating enclosures after 1517 seem not to have done so.[244]

Despite governmental encouragement, Brandon's role in the localities was less important to him than his role at the centre. Though strained at times, his relationship with the king continued to yield patronage: the Knyvet wardship, patents confirming earlier grants of office, and in 1523 a share in Buckingham's lands and the reversion to the duke of Norfolk's post as earl marshal.[245] Intermediaries like Wolsey and Sir Thomas Lovell were directly involved in some grants, such as the arrangement of May 1517 which brought the duke the marriage of Lord Powis.[246] Suffolk's relationship with Wolsey and Henry was a complex one: they conferred closely about how to deal with him, but he could equally ask Wolsey to manipulate the king, requesting, when asking for an office, that 'if any labur by bill or otherwise be made unto the king[es] grace for the same, that it woll pleas yo[ur] grace to stoppe it till my bill may be assigned.'[247] A born courtier, he was always concerned about what those around Henry and Wolsey were saying about him, and always happier when he could explain things face to face. He found it prudent to keep both Wolsey and the king sweet with gifts of plate and furniture.[248] But his desperation in moments of crisis over finances and foreign policy must not obscure his survival as the king's friend, and his maintenance of an important, though limited, role in government.

He played the part in royal ceremonies and diplomatic meetings expected of a leading nobleman. He also participated in ritual as the king's servant, and as a leading member of Wolsey's legatine flock, assisting at the public washings of each.[249] Yet he was more than just a tame peer. He often accompanied foreign ambassadors, especially Venetians, at public functions, perhaps just because he combined status and amiability.[250] Certainly he was not a leading councillor in these years: those who wished to judge the direction of English policy visited others.[251] But exclusion from policy-making was not exclusion from power.

In 1515 he was the only non-legal witness to Warham's delivery to Wolsey of the great seal. In 1516 Henry took Norfolk and Suffolk aside for discussion between conversations with ambassadors, and in 1517 Wolsey ended a meeting between himself, Suffolk, and the

Venetian ambassador so that he could speak alone with the duke.[252] In October 1517 he was one of the only three peers named to sit in the Star Chamber twice a week to reform abuses in the courts. It seems that he tended to be present mostly at large, set-piece council meetings, and he certainly missed many.[253] But when he was at court in April 1517 he accompanied Wolsey daily to the council, and in 1520 he apologised to Wolsey that 'I of a certayn space have not gyven myn attendaunce upon yor lordship in the kinges counsaill according to my dewty.'[254] He also sat on various special commissions, though sometimes he was named with other peers to give a commission an impressive ring but then did not sit.[255] As a peer he sat at Buckingham's trial, and though he only attended in the Lords twice in the session of November–December 1515, he was named a trier of petitions in 1523.[256]

Suffolk was certainly not yet a work-horse of Henrician government like Norfolk or Surrey.[257] He was for the moment more courtier than magnate or councillor, but he was not without versatility, and many still counted him a power in the land. The Austin canons, in chapter in June 1518, looked for useful people to receive into the order, and settled on the king and queen, Wolsey, the French queen, and Suffolk. In 1519 in Lincolnshire Anthony Irby could express shock at the control exercised over Henry, by fair means or foul, by Suffolk and Wolsey. In 1515–16 the earl of Kildare, sending presents to selected influential individuals in England, included Suffolk. The countess of Salisbury obviously did not feel her pension to the duke wasted, for she increased it by £40 in 1518.[258] And when Robert Whittinton, the grammarian, assembled in 1519 a book of epigrams on important people, Suffolk was included with Henry, Wolsey, and Sir Thomas More. The name Carolus was used twice acrostically to expound Brandon's endowment with the four cardinal and three theological virtues, and the seven spiritual gifts.[259]

Whittinton's favourable comparisons between the duke and Achilles and Charles Martel must have been pleasing. Brandon had not seen action since 1513, partly because no army large enough for a duke had been set on foot. But by late 1522 England was at war, Henry was eager for his jousting companions to try their hands in the open field, and Surrey was committed to invading Scotland.[260] Suffolk was the obvious commander for the army guarding the south coast, and as Charles V applied pressure and promised assistance this became an army to invade northern France.[261] The duke faced his greatest opportunity, and his greatest test, since 1515.

3

Power in the Counties, Power at Court: 1523–1529

The Campaign of 1523 and its Aftermath

In September 1523 Suffolk led his household, family, and friends to war in France.[1] He commanded the largest army Henry ever sent to the continent under a lieutenant, and great things were expected of him. This was especially the case because his expedition was co-ordinated not only with Charles V's efforts to hold the French army in Italy and invade from Spain, but also with the revolt of Charles, Duc de Bourbon, the powerful but disaffected constable of France. At best, Bourbon's rebellion was expected to bring defections in the French peerage, disruption in the royal army, widespread collaboration with the English invaders, and Bourbon's army of German mercenaries and loyal tenants to the gates of Paris to meet Suffolk. These prospects encouraged Henry to abandon his orders to the duke to besiege Boulogne, and command instead a bold march over the Somme towards the French capital.

This plan suited Margaret of Austria very well, for it protected the southern borders of the Netherlands while she pursued her primary aim of the annexation of Friesland. But Charles V had promised that she would support Suffolk with troops and supplies, and her difficulties in meeting these commitments delayed the duke's departure from Calais, and gave disease time enough to gain a grip on his men. Only in early October, six weeks after crossing the Channel, did Suffolk join his imperial colleague, Floris,

Graaf van Buren, and march south. Expecting to meet Bourbon's supporters beyond the Somme and the duke himself near Paris, they ignored strong fortresses and seized the river crossings at Ancre and Bray. They marched on towards the capital, taking more towns and spreading panic. Suffolk commanded competently, though relying heavily on the more experienced Buren, the dashing Lord Sandys – a widely respected veteran, raised to the peerage in April 1523 – and the council of war. When necessary he took a firm line with discontented troops and even with his colleagues, insisting on a quick assault on Montdidier, and on the need to swear in the citizens of captured towns as the liberated subjects of Henry, King of France.

Unfortunately Charles V could not exert enough pressure on Francis I to prevent him from reinforcing Paris in great strength. Worse, Bourbon had failed completely: his conspiracy had crumbled, his revolt misfired and his army dissolved. Without support, and under pressure from the resurgent French, Suffolk and Buren had to retreat. On their return they were caught between Henry's determination to follow up such a dramatic incursion into France with a rested and reinforced army, and Margaret's complete inability to fund any further campaigning on her southern frontier. A freak spell of freezing weather turned Suffolk's already plague-ridden army into a mutinous rabble; Buren took the opportunity to please Margaret and disband all his troops; and Brandon was left to explain to an irate Henry why the two victorious armies which had lately promised to win him the crown of France had been replaced by a pitiful stream of sickly scarecrows drifting back into the Channel ports. As ever, the duke kept loyally to the letter of the king's instructions, telling Buren that he would rather die than return to England without royal command. But difficulties in communication forced him to take independent decisions, and he took the right ones. He allowed his troops to return home when it became obvious that Margaret would not support a further invasion, and he refused to establish English garrisons to protect her frontier when the French struck back. Henry's anger was calmed by an explanation of the circumstances, and he lost no faith in Suffolk's loyalty or generalship. On the other hand, the duke's gains were small: a few knighthoods for his followers, and the glory of the deepest English penetration into France since the days of Henry V. The hardships of war brought less reward than they had done in 1513, but left Suffolk with an undiminished martial enthusiasm and an untarnished martial reputation.

English foreign policy after the 1523 campaign was warily conducted, for Charles V and Margaret of Austria were eager for another English invasion, but unable to pay for the troops to support it, while Wolsey and Henry were determined to make an effort only if Bourbon showed signs of major success.[2] All this made for intermittent military preparations, of which Suffolk was at the heart. In April 1524 he was involved in the council's decision to advocate repetition of the 1523 invasion plan. In August it became clear that he would command any expedition that year, and this was soon known around Europe.[3] Troops were raised, and Buren gave sensible advice based on the lessons of 1523, though refusing Wolsey's suggestion that Suffolk, under Henry's instructions, should act as senior commander this time.[4] Henry's army was to be large: 9,000 English foot, 1,200 to 1,500 English horse, and 3,000 German foot, plus Buren's contingent. But English reluctance was great. No money was to be spent on Germans, for example, until Bourbon's plans were known.[5] Suffolk's preparations could only be tentative, but they were enthusiastic. He set about choosing councillors and captains, and discussed the arrangements for supplies and mercenaries with Sir Richard Jerningham. The latter, in the Low Countries to organise such matters, trusted to Suffolk's military wisdom to alter Wolsey's plans: Jerningham agreed with the duke that horse paid by Henry himself would serve him more loyally than if paid by Margaret, 'as no man[n] can tell bettre then ye, ne hath seen bettre experience therof.'[6] 1523 would seem rather to have added to, than detracted from, Suffolk's military stature.

The duke remained prominent in foreign affairs of all sorts. His role in the projected invasion of France in 1525 is not clear.[7] In November 1526 he was proposed as the king's lieutenant in Milan, under the English peace proposals for Henry to arbitrate the future of the duchy. Indeed imperial negotiators, anxious to have anyone but a Sforza, even named Brandon as a possible duke of Milan.[8] Suffolk contrived to remain acceptable to both France and Spain, a position which he had achieved in the early 1520s. His wife's French interests were great enough to make any settlement with France attractive; there were rumours that the French sought her intervention with her brother with gifts of rings. But he was an enthusiastic commander in co-operation with the Low Countries, and his imperial pension was well paid, far less in arrears than most.[9] As in the past, this European standing was not matched by consistent involvement in conciliar government, even in foreign policy. He was present at some of Wolsey's very private discussions with envoys, and larger meetings between councillors and ambassadors. More often, though, he was absent from such gatherings, or merely welcomed ambassadors and then left the subsequent discussions to Henry and Wolsey.[10]

Local Responsibilities

In the counties Suffolk's responsibilities grew fast in these years. He shared in the larger role afforded to the peerage by the expansions of the commissions of the peace after 1524. Though not named to every county, as the duke of Norfolk was, he was appointed for the first time in Middlesex, Berkshire, and Oxfordshire.[11] People appealed to him for help from areas far from his lands: someone elicited a successful letter from him to Wolsey to save Conishead Priory, Lancashire, from dissolution for the cardinal's colleges.[12] It was above all in East Anglia that the duke's standing rose, and Henry helped towards this, still within the framework of the De la Pole past. In June 1525 Brandon's second son Henry, born in 1522 after the death of the first Lord Henry Brandon, was created earl of Lincoln.[13] This marked a further stage in Brandon's assimilation of the De la Pole power, for the earldom was so closely associated with the house of Suffolk that Charles himself was sometimes called earl of Lincoln, both before his son's creation and after his son's death.[14] The spreading power of the Brandons was symbolised by Earl Henry's annuity from Lincolnshire and Buckinghamshire, while the duke's personal power too was evident in the creation ceremony. He not only witnessed the king's grants to Henry Fitzroy, the new duke of Richmond, but led this duke and the king's great friend Devonshire (now Marquis of Exeter) to Henry for their creations.[15]

In the 1520s Brandon's importance in the country grew towards the level of his importance at court. His titles in one of the Norwich episcopal registers are an interesting comment on this. When presenting to a benefice in 1517 he was just 'the duke of Suffolk', in 1524 'the man of vigour, Charles, duke of Suffolk'. In June 1527 he was 'the most powerful man, Charles duke of Suffolk, great marshal of England', and by September of that year 'the noble and most powerful prince, Charles duke of Suffolk and great marshal of England'.[16] In some ways Mary was still more honoured than Charles: the Lynn town chronicler recorded her visit but not his. When together they were jointly fêted, as at Lynn in January 1528, but more often they were apart, even when the duke was in East Anglia.[17] In summer 1527, for example, Mary stayed at Butley Priory for over a month, and in summer 1528, long enough to bring her furnishings. She made short trips to visit local friends like Sir John Glemham, and distributed largesse to the monks. The duke stayed only briefly, called on the most important local supporters like Sir Anthony Wingfield, and then rushed on with his thirty horsemen to the court at Newhall, the sessions at Thetford, or Cardinal Campeggio's reception in London. He could spare some time to hunt and picnic with Mary, but little enough to her mind, for when in East Anglia he was very much on business.[18]

The main aim of that business changed with the death of Richard de la Pole at Pavia, and the consequent disappearance of the Yorkist threat. In the later 1520s Suffolk spent time in the country primarily to counter popular unrest, and he did so in close personal co-operation with the new duke of Norfolk. This began in the spring of 1525, as they coordinated carefully the timing of their negotiations with the inhabitants of Suffolk and Norfolk respectively, over the Amicable Grant. While discussing this they also worked together in other matters, notifying Wolsey, for example, of the worrying presence of French ships off the coast.[19] When they separated, Brandon initially pursued his task successfully, commending the local gentlemen who sat with him on the commissions. As discontent in the south of the county mounted, though, Suffolk lost control, and his attempts to confiscate arms and armour to forestall opposition were counter-productive.[20] He was less successful in raising troops than was Howard, despite an appeal to his 'tenants and serving-men', and even those he did have could not be relied upon to fight the rebels.[21] Once reunited with Norfolk he bowed to greater age and experience, as in 1523. The other duke overruled Brandon's desire for a military solution, showing the same preference for negotiation as he would in 1536. Both men treated their dealings with the rebels as their joint action, but it was Norfolk who addressed the rising's leaders, and who took up the secretary's pen to write half a letter himself.[22] The dukes' shared trust in Humphrey Wingfield was demonstrated when they chose him to carry the news of the rebel submissions to Henry and Wolsey. Such co-operation between them was the best way for the government to control East Anglia, and Wolsey realised this, thanking them for their 'wyse dyscret and polityque' handling of the troubles.[23] For such control to work the dukes' own local standing was important, and Wolsey recognised this too: he suggested that to punish the rebels would be, in the dukes' words, 'convenyent for the king[es] hono[ur] and oure estimacions'.[24]

Such an arrangement seems to have suited Brandon better than Howard. While Norfolk was irritated by Wolsey's insistence that his presence in East Anglia was necessary in spring 1528, Suffolk did not complain about spending time in the country. In April and May 1528 he was even allowed not to come to the Garter chapter or serve as Henry's lieutenant at the feast, because he asked to stay in Norfolk instead: his local affairs were not yet in order, riding would be painful, and the summons for him to leave was 'somewhat hevy' for his wife.[25] When grain shortages and disruption to the cloth trade threatened popular unrest in late 1526 and early 1528, it was Howard who acted successfully to avert riots in the area of the 1525 troubles.[26] But he did not seek to exclude Brandon from the task of local control, and in April 1528 he requested a joint commission to raise the king's tenants in case of disorder. In both these periods of danger Brandon worked with Howard's followers in Norfolk to control corn supplies, vagabondage, and rioting, just as Howard co-operated in Suffolk with men like Sir Anthony Wingfield.[27]

Suffolk's work in 1528 concentrated on grain supplies. Working with Norfolk's half-brother Lord Berners, and referring their decisions to Wolsey, he organised searches for corn stores throughout Norfolk and then delegated the control over local grain movements to commissioners at hundred level.[28] When unrest did occur, he arrested those preparing unlawful assemblies at Norwich, and examined in person two malefactors at Lynn. He later appeased further trouble in Norwich and Yarmouth. In September he sat at the Thetford sessions.[29] The inhabitants responded to the duke's presence by bringing him their other concerns. In February 1528, the Marshland, south of the Wash between the Nene and the Ouse, was flooded, and its leading men secured Suffolk's support for their petition to Wolsey. Suffolk suggested that a commission of sewers be appointed, and he and Norfolk sat on it, in the following April: they were guided by Wolsey's examination of the problem in Star Chamber, Norfolk was again the dominant partner, and they seem to have referred matters back into the council.[30] The general concern about popular unrest in these years led many peers and courtiers into such increased involvement in local government, but the two dukes reacted differently to the roles they had to play.[31] Norfolk barely concealed his disagreement with the pro-French policy which cut off the cloth trade, and wrote to Wolsey of hopes for peace.[32] Suffolk merely rejoiced in Wolsey's 'favo[ur]able kinde and loving reaport[es] from tyme to tyme made unto the king[es] high[e]nes of my poer entent and mynd in executing his grac[es] pleaso[ur] and co[m]maunde-ment[es] according to my dewty'.[33]

Suffolk's role in East Anglia, then, was junior to Norfolk's and guided by Henry's and Wolsey's orders. All these relationships were natural: Norfolk's superiority in local society was neatly demonstrated by his ability to number among his guests at

Framlingham on 30 December 1526 not only his own followers like Sir Philip Tilney, but also Suffolk's officers Sir Thomas Tyrrell, Sir Anthony Wingfield, Humphrey Wingfield, and Thomas Seckford.[34] The Howard affinity was always more widespread, distinguished, and numerous than Brandon's. The imbalance in their respective incomes from Norfolk and Suffolk, though, was less marked – by 1523 Brandon, with nearly £1,100, could almost match the old duke of Norfolk's £1,300, though some £200 of Brandon's takings passed to the Howards as rent under the lease of 1516.[35] Now Suffolk was growing into the power afforded by these estates and the government's trust, not only in incidents like those of 1525 but also more generally. Local offices helped to make him a channel between centre and localities: as high steward of Yarmouth he was asked by Norfolk and Wolsey to deal with a Frenchman there who had taken a Dutchman's goods, and by the town itself to support a petition to Henry against a miscreant customs official.[36] He was also steward of Lynn for Bishop Nix, though he lost his £5 fee in the early 1520s when the king briefly controlled the town.[37] In 1527–8 Lynn gave the duke salmon and other gifts, and while Norwich in 1523 and 1524 was sending presents to Surrey and Fitzwalter, but nothing to Suffolk, in 1531–2 the city dispatched its sword bearer and chamberlain to Westhorpe with a gift almost as large as that sent to Norfolk at Kenninghall.[38] The inhabitants of East Anglia began to use Suffolk to recommend their causes to Wolsey or the king, whether they wanted a general licence to export fish or a remedy for the shortage of usually plentiful Newcastle coals.[39]

Increasing respect may account for Suffolk's continued absence from the courts. He was sued to remind him to pay a grocer's bill, and Sir John Glemham, Suffolk's surety, found himself in court over the duke's failure to complete payment in a land purchase.[40] Suffolk himself sued to encourage payment of one five-year-old debt. His only other case was in Lincolnshire, where his local power was as yet weak; it may have concerned his beloved deer parks, for the accused was claimed to have destroyed with his animals a seedling coppice in a ducal enclosure.[41]

The duke continued to be peripatetic. He visited towns like Lynn and Norwich and religious houses like Butley, Eye, Leiston, and Westacre. Of his own residences, he used Wingfield Castle, and Henham Hall, where he rebuilt the gatehouse at a cost of £2,000, and he again borrowed Rising Castle, where Sir Thomas Lovell had been farmer.[42] He had enough 'affeyres in this p[ar]ties' to stay with his 'loving ffrende' Thomas Empson, restored heir of Sir Richard, at Easton Neston in Northamptonshire in January 1527; on these grounds the duke and Mary excused to Wolsey Empson's non-appearance on the cardinal's subpoenas.[43] Brandon continued to use his Southwark house, and on his rare visits to Oxfordshire and Berkshire used Ewelme Castle, after 1525, rather than Donnington.[44]

Despite such efforts to see and be seen, the duke was still represented largely by his local officers. By the later 1520s he seems to have been able to recruit rather more substantial men from outside his family to serve as stewards and receivers. Robert Wright and Robert Dukett, who held courts at Benhall and Sternfield, had incomes of £10 or less.[45] But Robert Derhaugh, receiver at Benhall and holding courts by 1528, had £40 in goods by 1524 and was a rising man.[46] Suffolk's service also offered rapid promotion for those with ability. Robert Browne, a lawyer who had served Bishop Nix, entered Suffolk's administration as steward of two manors in 1528, became feodary of the hundred of Freebridge in 1531, and in March 1533 rose to receiver-general of all the Norfolk and Suffolk estates; these added fees of 26s 8d, £2 and £10 to the income of £80 or £100 in lands on which he was taxed in 1524.[47]

In East Anglia the duke's estates increased slowly. The death of his uncle, Sir Robert, in 1524 brought him Henham, but Sir Robert's widow and her new husband held and then sold other manors, and the manor of Cravens in Henham had been sold by Sir Robert to the duke in 1520.[48] Under the latter agreement he continued to pay 100 marks a year to his uncle's widow, but may have ended this in 1527. At least he was not involved in the tangle of debts left by Sir Robert.[49] He apparently sold out in 1527 his interest in the manor of Cleve's, sold in 1518 by Sir Robert to Thomas Wall the herald; matters are obscured by the fact that three of the five feoffees to Wall's son, also a herald called Thomas, were officers of the duke.[50] For £40 in cash, and the transfer of £140 of Tyrrell's debts, Suffolk bought in 1528 from William Tyrrell the reversion to their mother's moiety of South Ockendon, Essex. As William's son had been married ten years and had a son, Suffolk may have been doing his relations a favour; this seems likely in the light of their links with his supporters and the fact that he had helped them in the past. The reversion never fell in.[51]

Good Lordship and Arbitration

In these years Suffolk's worship grew faster than his wealth. But respect brought responsibilities, not just because Henry and Wolsey expected much from the duke's local power, but because others did so too. It was flattering to Suffolk that Anne, Dowager Countess of Oxford, appealed for his help in 1526, but it also drew him into a very difficult situation. Her feckless husband had been dominated by her family, the Howards, who had induced him in 1525 to enfeoff Norfolk and his allies Fitzwalter and Rochford (Sir Thomas Boleyn, raised to the peerage that year) in a huge additional jointure for her. Her husband died on 14 July 1526, and was succeeded as earl by his cousin, Sir John de Vere, who rightly felt himself faced with a Howard coup, and took rapid action.[52] He visited Wolsey and secured a letter of recommendation to the king, and then adopted a more spectacular course. By 11 August he had broken into Lavenham Park twice and, defying the justices' orders to keep the peace, stormed and occupied Castle Camps, part of the countess's original jointure.[53]

The new earl always intended to negotiate. He had promised to relinquish at Wolsey's command many of the manors he occupied, and was duly pardoned in July 1527 for his entry on them.[54] But his action in August 1526 understandably alarmed the countess. The Cambridgeshire justices claimed that they could not obey Wolsey's writs and remove the earl's garrison at Castle Camps, even by force; at least one of the bench, Giles Alington, may have been less than assiduous since he was a feoffee to the new earl.[55] The countess appealed not only to Henry, Wolsey, and Norfolk (in whose household she was staying by October 1526), but also to

Suffolk. As she told Brandon, since Wolsey's writs had failed, 'w[it] thowt yo[ur] grace & my lorde my brother helpe me now, I know not how to obteyne my possessyon agen.'[56] But the dukes, after consultation with Exeter and Rochford who were with them, did not try to arrogate to themselves the settlement of the affair. They wished to co-operate with Wolsey and Henry to see the countess restored to her rights, and they recognised, when writing to the cardinal, that 'we knowe not but by relation of the oon partye what is don in that behaulf.'[57]

Understandably the whole business took a long time to settle. Affairs were further complicated by the claims of the three heirs general to the late earl, who challenged the new earl's right to estates worth £2,260 annually. Wolsey intended to arbitrate, and Wriothesley produced a memorandum for Cromwell on the matter, but nothing was achieved, and attacks on Lavenham Park continued.[58] Only when Norfolk, Suffolk, Dorset, Shrewsbury, Fitzwalter, and Rochford were appointed arbitrators was the business settled. They deliberated in October and November 1529, perhaps at Wolsey's suggestion, perhaps on their own initiative after the cardinal's fall, or perhaps at the nomination of the parties to the dispute. By 19 October they had reconciled Sir Anthony Wingfield and Edmund Knyghtley – who represented the three heirs general, as husbands of the late earl's two sisters and proxies for his cousin – to the dowager countess. These parties would exchange evidences and guarantee each other's legal costs against the new earl. The second stage was to be settled by 31 November, but an award was finally produced only in the summer of 1531, and confirmed in March 1532.[59] This guaranteed Anne's jointure in reduced form, without Lavenham and other East Anglian manors; gave outlying estates and many reversions to the heirs general; and concentrated the Suffolk and Essex lands, centre of the family's power, in the hands of the earl, but only in tail male, with reversion to the heirs general. It was a predictable settlement from peers sensitive to the bases of noble power, but still an important achievement. Suffolk's part in it showed his ready cooperation with other great men, to solve the sort of dispute which had in the past caused dangerous dislocation in the body politic.

Where Brandon was more naturally drawn into a case, the parties and the government expected more from his intervention. In the early 1520s he was troubled by the complex problems of his divorced second wife, Dame Margaret Mortimer. Her only child was a bastard by an East Anglian priest.[60] This girl, Anne, married Suffolk's cousin Sir James Framlingham, and they wanted to badger Margaret into leaving her attractive inheritance to them.[61] 'Faier speche, flatyng and adulacions', removing the old lady's friends and possessions, and even turning her out of her house all failed, so she later claimed; but in August 1519 they subverted William Waller, a lawyer whom she trusted, and he told her that Sir James was very ill and would 'tacke suche a conceit and ffransy in his hert that he wold die forth[with]' if Margaret did not provide for Anne and their children. Dame Margaret bound herself in 3,000 marks to Waller and Sir Anthony Wingfield, to enfeoff trustees named by them on her estates, first to her own use, then to that of her will, and finally to that of Anne and Sir James. Nine days later Sir James died.

Waller, cousin and executor to Sir James, but feed counsel to Dame Margaret, seemed to have negotiated an acceptable settlement. He never asked Margaret to transfer her lands, though he never returned her obligation, claiming to have mislaid it among his books at Ipswich or Ramsholt. Problems only began when mother and daughter both remarried and Waller had to take sides. Margaret married Robert Downes, and began to rue signing away her inheritance. Downes had the solution: between 1522 and 1526 she alienated various properties to friends who then regranted them to him.[62] Meanwhile Anne had married Robert Browne, the lawyer who had overseen the execution of her husband's estates for Bishop Nix with an eye to the fact that he 'trustyd to mary the seyd Dame Anne, as the comen woyce went.' Browne called in Waller to save Anne's inheritance, and for over two years from Hilary term 1522 Waller and Wingfield maintained a king's bench suit on the obligation of 1519.[63] Browne also took action, allegedly threatening Downes with a dagger causing Margaret to faint, and certainly trying to stop the land transfers with a subpoena in chancery.

At about this point Suffolk tried to arbitrate, and suggested a settlement, 'the wyche ende they wold natt kepe, but brake yt'. The struggle intensified. On 6 June 1522 Margaret and Downes were arrested in London; released next day, they were caught by a bill of Middlesex and writ of *latitat* connected with the suit by Wingfield and Waller. Browne sought physically to prevent the sealing of their counter-writ, but Wolsey's agent Thomas Alvard, who would later help in their land transfers, stopped him. Downes, a Lincoln's Inn lawyer, secured royal protection as a Calais victualler, but Browne's agent laboured a London jury to invalidate the protection, and the case was referred to the Bury assizes.[64] There, on 25 July 1524, Browne, backed by Wingfield ' & other great ffryndes & alyes', used 'great labor and subornacion' to secure a verdict against Downes and Dame Margaret, leaving them liable to pay the 3,000 marks of the obligation.

In their extremity the losers turned to Wolsey, for as chancellor he could both judge by equity and regulate what they claimed were irregular issues of writs against them. They also appealed to Suffolk, with whom virtually every party was linked. Wingfield's, Framlingham's, and Mortimer's connections are obvious. By 1528 Browne had entered Suffolk's service, though his previous relationship is uncertain. Waller had stood surety for Suffolk's client John Palsgrave when the duke presented him to the rectory of Alderton in 1520.[65] The duke's interests ought to have been all on Browne's side, but he did not show this. Gainsaying important members of his connection, he accepted Downes's story of the unfair writ of *innotescimus* which had defeated his protection, and asked Wolsey on 15 October to forbid Wingfield's and Waller's proceedings.[66] Again Suffolk wanted to co-operate with the cardinal, who stayed Browne's proceedings too on 21 October, to reach a settlement where his sole arbitration had failed earlier.[67] The result was still inconclusive, since Downes went on transferring lands, and kept them at Margaret's death, despite the recognition of Anne's sons as

Margaret's heirs, leaving her son Francis Framlingham to renew the dispute in the 1530s.[68]

The duke's writ still ran more smoothly in Southwark. He retained control of the king's bench prison, with Sir Thomas Wentworth as his deputy. Fees were increased and poor prisoners not released without paying them.[69] Between 1527 and 1535 Suffolk secured the appointment of Christopher Lynham, his chaplain since 1511, to the rectory of St George's, the second-richest benefice in the borough; the patron was Bermondsey Abbey, of which the duke was steward.[70] In Oxfordshire and Berkshire Suffolk's estates expanded in 1525 with the grant of the honour of Ewelme with its wide network of courts, though in 1522 he had lost £200 or so of revenue from the lands in the area of Edward Fiennes, the heir to Lord Saye, whose wardship he had inherited from Sir Thomas Brandon. Fiennes died in 1528, and his will showed no attachment to Suffolk or anyone connected with the duke.[71]

In contrast Lord Fitzwarin, the son of Sir Thomas's last wife, kept up contact with several of Suffolk's relatives and servants. His feoffees in July 1525 included Sir Anthony Wingfield and Humphrey Wingfield, and his second marriage linked him with other Wingfields.[72] From 1522 the duke leased back to Fitzwarin for £50 a year the lands of Lady Fitzwarin's jointure in Devon, in which Suffolk had held a reversionary life interest since 1513.[73] Suffolk did not withdraw so readily from his aunt's jointure under her Sapcote marriage, and had to be prompted to do so in 1524 in the common pleas.[74] But the duke had little interest in the south-west. This period did at least see the establishment of some links between central ducal administration and the south midlands estates. John Cheyney, steward on the Berkshire manors, was a local landowner, but was uninvolved in the duke's household or personal affairs.[75] The Fetiplaces, who held most of Suffolk's other local offices, had done so before the lands were granted to the duke. Edward Fetiplace, bailiff at Buckland in 1522, and bailiff and parker at Donnington from 1524 until replaced by Anthony Fetiplace in 1526, had his own local interests to look to.[76] He used Donnington and Ewelme as bases for his involvement in leasing lands from Wolsey's colleges. But by 1528 he was Suffolk's treasurer, and his entry into local office came on a commission to deliver Oxford gaol headed by the duke in June 1530; in November he joined the Berkshire bench.[77] Suffolk's power here lagged behind its rise in East Anglia, and towns like Windsor never courted his favour, but none the less he was starting to establish himself.[78]

The greatest change in Brandon's local power in this period was the loss of all his Welsh offices in 1525.[79] As part of a string of reforms in many areas of government, Wolsey strengthened the grip of the council in the marches on Welsh administration, converting it into the council of the Princess Mary. The duke's office of chief justice of north Wales passed to his long-serving deputy, himself a member of this council, and the change probably made little difference. Suffolk's departure from his marcher stewardships was more significant. Again he was replaced by a member of the council, in the hope not only that royal revenue would flow more freely than it had done while the duke used the lordships as a source of personal credit, but also that the council might be better obeyed. Suffolk's deputy, his brother-in-law Sir John Shilston, had run the lordships in cosy co-operation with the local elite. He rode roughshod over opposition from lesser men and, more important, took no notice whatsoever of the council in the marches; it was no wonder he was replaced. Yet Suffolk's removal opened the way to William Brereton and his court-based Cheshire clique to take over in the northern marches, feuding with the local gentry and generating disorder and maladministration worse than anything in Shilston's day. The effects on the duke were less drastic, for he was carefully compensated with the castle and honour of Ewelme. He must, though, have felt the loss of military prestige in no longer being the man to lead north Wales to war. Meanwhile, the other developments of 1525–6 affected him little. In the new household ordinances he was guaranteed lodging at court, on the queen's side with his wife, or on the king's side when she was not present. He was one of the new council to hear subjects' complaints, but not one of the quorum.[80] If Sir William Compton was sorry to abandon the groomship of the stool for the under-treasurership and the council, Suffolk probably did not sympathise.[81]

Mary's French Interests

Wolsey's negotiations for peace with France in 1525–6 made a new arrangement necessary over Suffolk's debts to the crown. Before discussions began, a search was made in the exchequer for all the duke's liabilities. Various old obligations made jointly with Sir Thomas Knyvet and Sir Robert Brandon were added to unpaid Welsh revenues and unused conduct money to raise Suffolk's part of the debt to £6,519 13s 11d.[82] The procedure was comprehensive but fair: £9 15s for a wood at Wanstead purchased from the king in 1518–19 was included, but money genuinely spent on the army in 1523 but improperly accounted for, and the revenues of Lisle manors claimed by the crown, were not. The repayments were further reduced to £1,000 a year, but a clause was included to enable pressure to be applied on Suffolk to pay the 500 marks a year required towards his mounting liabilities. This specified his transfer of lands worth that sum annually to royal feoffees who would hold to the king's use should the duke default. Given the large proportion of his debt now constituted by Welsh revenue which he had in all probability received, this was only reasonable. In any case, paying was easier after 1525 because the French revenues flowed more freely. Their restoration had always been a point in English proposals for peace, and Suffolk and Mary were enabled to do more to secure them by Wolsey's greater trust in the duke. Thus in April 1525 Brandon sent a commission to treat on their behalf to the English ambassadors who were about to leave for Charles V's court, to settle with the French should Charles do so: in 1518 Suffolk would not have been aware of such secret dealings.[83] In the event the dower lands question was soon discussed in direct Anglo-French negotiations, probably in early August 1525. Suffolk and Mary remitted to Wolsey the handling of such matters as they 'boith bee greved in there, app[er]teynyng to her dote'.[84] But they were quick to remind him of their grievances, and sent George Hampton, their usual agent in France, to secure letters from Henry and the cardinal to those in France with the power to see matters put right.[85]

Louise of Savoy tried to negotiate separately with Suffolk and Mary, and allowed her agent Jean Joachim de Passano to arrange to farm the dower rents. Wolsey was firm in his support for them, though, and a treaty was settled at the same time as the others, before Passano's power to negotiate separately could have arrived.[86] The treaty was favourable to Mary: a preliminary payment of arrears on the dower was to be paid before six-monthly instalments of arrears began, and where Bonnivet had paid in theory 55,000 *livres* a year as farmer of the dower, Passano was asked for 60,000 and settled on 58,000.[87] Francis Hall, doubtless one of Suffolk's negotiators, rode out to Ewelme to explain the settlement, and the duke wrote back gratefully to Wolsey, agreeing to Passano's farm for a six-year term. Henry and Wolsey advised that Mary should send some commissioners to France 'as well for surveying of my dote and dowery, as for redressing of such enormytees as ar, or may unto theym appere to be, w[ith]in the same'.[88] She chose Francis Hall and her experienced chancellor Dr James Denton.[89]

The results of the mission are obscure. Certainly the arrears on the dower, interrupted for three years and nine months by the war, were duly paid in October and November 1525 and every six months to November 1527 and beyond.[90] At around £2,000 a year these alone would have covered the couple's obligation to Henry. Suffolk's pension of about £185 a year was also well paid, though not as punctually.[91] But Mary was unhappy with Passano's farming, and in October 1525 the English ambassadors in Paris were instructed to urge that she be given full control of her dower and allowed to appoint her own treasurers.[92] Problems continued despite Wolsey's help. The cardinal worked through Nicolas de St Martin: he had been French secretary to Mary and Suffolk from 1515 until the Field of Cloth of Gold, when Bonnivet encouraged him to enter the service of Francis I. In 1525 or 1526 Mary had Henry write to Louise of Savoy asking that he might return to work for her, being 'seant et propice a n[ot]red[ite] seur oud[it] estat de secretaire, tant pour la perfection du langaige de pardeca, que aussi

Charles Brandon

la conduyte de ses affaires en son douaire'.[93] He did so, but soon ran into difficulties. The best agent in the Calais intelligence network reported St Martin to be 'a ffalse schrew & a spey'.[94] In Paris in March 1526 he did not have the documents about the dower required by Chancellor Duprat, he could not sue to Francis because the royal court was moving around so unpredictably, and he was involved in troublesome lawsuits, one over Martin Dupin, and another against the widow of Mary's late receiver, Jean Boudet.[95]

St Martin hoped for help from the English ambassadors, but they rarely concerned themselves with the business of the dower. In June 1526 he was back in France after a visit to England, with letters from Henry to Louise asking that George Hampton be given full control over the French estates and offices. Ambassador Taylor did at least check with Jean Joachim whether he was still supposed to be in charge of the dower lands. Again, the results are unclear, but while St Martin now stayed in England as secretary to Mary and Suffolk, Hampton began to travel to and fro on the dower business.[96]

George Hampton was close to Humphrey Wingfield and a loyal servant to the duke: when imprisoned in irons for ransom in France in 1524 he had begged Wingfield to urge Suffolk to try to have him released, for 'jamais hom[m]e ne fut en plusgrant mellancoli q[ue] je suys.' The duke had certainly tried to free him, and Hampton carried out his promise that 'j'ay esperan[ce] luy faire tel s[er]vice qu'il s[er]a content avecq[ues] moy.'[97] He too was helped by Wolsey in the work of the dower, and in return served the cardinal's interests at the French court; he also frequently visited the Parisian household of Wolsey's son Thomas Wynter.[98] Hampton enjoyed useful contacts in France, and used his travels for trade, while his relationship with Wynter too was profitable, bringing ecclesiastical preferment for Hampton's scholarly son James.[99] In 1528 Hampton probably visited Paris four times, and in 1529 he was in France again.[100]

At the French court Hampton, and Mary writing directly, worked increasingly through Montmorency as his dominance there grew. Other important courtiers like Jean de la Barre also found it politic to represent Mary's interests.[101] But her lack of real influence in France made it hard for her to reward her servants there. From January to December 1528 she tried to secure a place in Francis's service for Antoine du Val, a clerk in Louis XII's household and then in hers. Her first letter to Montmorency asking for a reversion to a similar office for Du Val failed. By 18 June she had had a gracious answer from him several times, but no satisfaction, and she wrote again and persuaded Suffolk to do likewise.[102] Two days later she wrote to her old confidante Jeanne Popincourt, asking her to intercede with Montmorency; Popincourt had kept in contact, sending Mary letters by St Martin and presents for the children, a toy ship made of jet and some ornamental headgear.[103] This summer offensive also failed. Montmorency had asked another courtier to remind him about Du Val, but the prompter had then gone off to Italy, leaving Mary to write again in December. Du Val was now offering to serve without wages, but still to no avail. Mary sought the job for him 'afin que de moy eust tousjours souvenaire'; he presumably forgot her once her patronage failed, as it all too often did.[104]

The deployment of Mary's French revenue is hard to trace, but it was not simply handed over in cash at Calais as the indentures over her debts might suggest. Suffolk spent some in France, for example by giving a bill, for part payment of 3,000 crowns, to a Milanese jeweller. Some had to be diverted to buy friends in France, for instance to Admiral Brion. Montmorency used Suffolk's agents in France to transfer cash to England, while English royal envoys in France drew money from the ducal officers there which was apparently reimbursed in sterling.[105] However the money reached Brandon, it must have helped at a time when his expenses were running at a high level.

Buildings and Weddings

This was in part the cost of building a grand new brick courtyard-house at Westhorpe, decorated with terracotta figures and impressive battlements.[106] Work started in about 1527, and at a total cost of £12,000 can only have been funded by the French income. Sited among the western Suffolk estates which provided about a quarter of Brandon's East Anglian income, and within his judicial liberty based on the honour of Eye, Westhorpe was designed to be his main country residence, as the care lavished on the parks showed. Though still unfinished in 1538, it was in regular use from 1532, a symbol of Suffolk's coming of age as an East Anglian magnate.

The other reason for this increased expenditure was the marriageability of his children. Anne was married to Lord Powis by March 1525, and Suffolk or his supporters apparently paid the £1,000 price for the marriage long before.[107] The husband Suffolk found for his younger daughter by Anne Browne was half as rich again as Lord Powis, but harder to secure.[108] This was Thomas, son and heir of Edward Stanley, Lord Monteagle. From 1523 to 1527 Thomas was the object of a struggle between, on the one hand, his father's household and estate officers, and, on the other, Lord Darcy and Sir John Hussey, the successful competitors in the race at court to secure the young lord's wardship.[109] While his goods and revenues were divided in squabbles between these parties and then among the Monteagle administrators, Thomas was placed in Wolsey's household, but grew up spendthrift.[110] Plans for a marriage to Hussey's daughter or Dorset's fell through, and Monteagle negotiated for the right to marry freely, but before he succeeded Darcy and Hussey had sold the young lord's marriage to Suffolk, at an unknown price.[111] In late 1527 or early 1528, Monteagle married Mary Brandon, and by early 1529 he had not only his father's lands, but also a son to succeed him in them.[112] Suffolk had been drawn into the last stages of Thomas's troubled minority, at Easter 1528, but Monteagle's coming of age did not end the duke's liability. In September 1529 one of Monteagle's servants had to ask Cromwell or Sir Henry Guildford to speak to Suffolk about the bad influence of one of the young lord's confidants, and the marriage was only the beginning of the duke's troubles with his son-in-law.[113]

As the time approached to marry off his considerably more eligible daughters by the French queen, Suffolk ensured their legitimacy by soliciting papal clarification of his own tangled marital history. In May 1528, on the same day as a bull for Wolsey was issued, he secured a bull which solved all his problems; this was presumably handled by Sir Gregory Casale, the English agent in Rome, who

Table 3.1 The Ducal Family

Anne Browne = Charles, duke of Suffolk = Mary Tudor, dowager queen of France = Catherine Willoughby
(1)   (3)   (4)

Children of (1):

- Anne b. 1507–9 = Edward, Lord Powis
- Mary b. 1510 = Thomas, Lord Monteagle

Children of (3):

- Henry b. 1516 d. by 1522
- Frances b. 1517 = Henry, marquis of Dorset
  - Lady Jane Grey
- Eleanor b. 1518–21 = Henry, earl of Cumberland
  - Henry, earl of Lincoln b. 1522, cr. 1525, d. 1534

Children of (4):

- Henry, 2nd duke of Suffolk b. 1535, d. 1551
- Charles, 3rd duke of Suffolk b. 1537, d. 1551

illegitimate line:

Sir Charles Brandon

- Frances = (1) William Sandon (2) Andrew Bilsby; Elizabeth, widow of Sir James Strangways
- Mary = Robert Ball of Scottow, Norfolk

〰 = illegitimate line

had served with Suffolk in 1523.[114] The document was decisive in declaring ecclesiastical sanctions against any who challenged it, but suitably vague about the consanguinity which invalidated the Mortimer marriage, and about the dates of birth of Brandon's first two daughters. In August 1529 Humphrey Wingfield presented it to Bishop Nix for local authentication, and Suffolk's problems were over; this must have been a frustrating example to Henry with his apparently simpler but far more intractable difficulties.

Suffolk had other troubles, though, notably over the marriage of his son, Henry, Earl of Lincoln. An extremely suitable heiress became available with the death of Lord Willoughby de Eresby in October 1526. His total estates, mostly in Lincolnshire and East Anglia, were worth some 2,000 marks a year, and even the reduced inheritance which his daughter Catherine eventually received brought in over £900 a year.[115] Suffolk had known the now widowed baroness, a Spanish lady-in-waiting to the queen, since at least 1511 when she stood godmother to his daughter, Mary. He was a feoffee on her jointure in 1516 and to the use of her and her husband and his heirs in 1518, though not to his will in 1519.[116] His rapid bid for the wardship thus presumably found support with the dowager Lady Willoughby as well as with Wolsey, who incorporated Suffolk into his settlement of the Willoughby estates. This arrangement, 'decreyd by my lorde cardenall w[ith] the advice of my lorde of Norf[olk] and my lorde pryve seale & other of the king[es] most honorable councell', split the lands between the crown, Lady Willoughby, Lord Willoughby's executors, and Sir Christopher Willoughby, brother to the late baron.[117] Brandon was to have only a £40 pension for the maintenance of the heiress, who was not granted livery of her estates until 1539, but the real loser was Sir Christopher, who felt not only that as heir male he should have had more of the lands and the baronial title to match, but also that his brother's widow had cheated him even out of estates formally settled on him under earlier arrangements.

The price Suffolk paid was settled in November 1527; it was high, but a worthwhile investment in the future of his house. That Christmas and every Christmas for the next eight years he was to deliver 500 marks, until 4,000 marks were paid.[118] To ensure his payment (since his credit was evidently poor), estates to the value of £435 13s. were to be transferred to crown feoffees led by Wolsey. He duly enfeoffed them on his entire Oxfordshire and Berkshire holdings, and these were accepted as a guarantee of his performance although only valued at the time at £398 10s. 4½d. Suffolk had secured an important prize, and obtained a confirmatory grant of the wardship on a signed bill in February 1529.[119] The price he paid explains his determination not to let the continuing disputes between Sir Christopher and Lady Mary damage Catherine's inheritance. In 1528 the duke called in Wolsey and Paulet, joint Master of the Wards, to protect her estates when Sir Christopher occupied Eresby House, in Lincolnshire.[120] Although the lands were in the crown's hands Suffolk betrayed his profound personal interest by asking to be informed of Wolsey's decision as soon as possible. The cardinal's conciliar settlement had broken down and troubles were to continue, though Sir Christopher was at this stage careful not to confront Suffolk; he accused the duke merely of being misinformed about 'certeyn misdemeano[urs] supposed to be done by me'.[121] For his part, the duke avoided intervention in the Suffolk end of the dispute.[122]

The Court and Patronage

Even at court Suffolk's life in the 1520s suffered from new complications. On 10 March 1524 Henry tried out a 'newe harnes made of his own devise and fashion', jousting against the duke.[123] The king forgot to put his visor down, but Suffolk could not see the danger. Henry's helmet filled with splinters when Suffolk's lance shattered. Brandon 'incontinently unarmed him[self], and came to the kyng, shewyng him the closeness of his sight, & sware that he would never runne against the kyng more.' Henry was unhurt, but Suffolk must have been shaken, especially by the understandably hostile immediate reaction of the king's attendants. When they jousted again in December, they challenged together, in identical dress and disguised in silver beards.[124] This was probably the plan for 6 May 1527 too, when Henry could not joust because of a tennis injury and spectacular outfits for the king and an 'associate' were not used. This was an important event designed to impress the French ambassadors, and on less significant occasions the king himself now did not run.[125] The minions were ever more prominent in tournaments, but older courtiers like Lord Leonard Grey still played leading roles, and men of Suffolk's generation could still obtain chivalrous offices, like Sir Edward Guildford as standard-bearer.[126] Exeter, who replaced Suffolk as Henry's main opponent in the lists, was by no means the representative of a narrow privy chamber dominance, for his close social contacts included Sandys, Mountjoy, and Rutland as well as Bryan and Carew.[127] Suffolk had financial dealings with Bryan, perhaps over gambling, in December 1526, while craftsmen who worked for the duke – artists like Browne and Urmeston, and Ibgrave the embroiderer – remained important in preparing royal revels.[128] In masques he danced with the king in December 1524 and again in November 1527; on the latter occasion Henry, Exeter, Montmorency, and Suffolk wore three white ostrich feathers in their caps, the other dancers only two.[129] In the later 1520s Suffolk could reportedly be found at court playing bowls with Henry, Francis Bryan, and Thomas Wyatt, and his wife too graced the court on important occasions, though no longer dancing.[130]

The duke continued to be an assiduous attender at Garter elections, though not at the Windsor feasts.[131] In April 1526 his loyal voting for Sir Henry Guildford was finally rewarded, after Sir Henry had twice been nominated by everyone, but not chosen by Henry, whose preference seems to have been for peers. It is dangerous to construe too much from Garter voting, but it is interesting that the choices made by Suffolk and Norfolk became increasingly similar. In June 1525 their lists were identical except in order (perhaps they had discussed the elections during the Amicable Grant troubles), in April 1526 they were the only two to suggest the Marquis of Mantua, and in October 1527 their selections were again identical except in one matter of placing.

The two dukes may have been growing a little closer, but it seems unlikely that the relationship between them was ever warm.

In 1553 Norfolk deposed that he had known Brandon since the early 1490s 'and always callyd him cousyn Charles', but in 1546 he claimed that Suffolk had egged Wolsey on to persecute him.[132] There are signs that relations between their families were cool even before 1514, and Suffolk's elevation had clearly threatened the regional hegemony established by the Howards after the decline and death (in 1513) of the 13th Earl of Oxford.[133] None the less, co-operation with Norfolk was to Brandon's advantage, not only in controlling East Anglia, but also in the pursuit of patronage. For Suffolk's approach to advancing his interests and those of his dependents was eclectic, as it had to be. Wolsey was the obvious source of help in ecclesiastical matters, to overcome the Bishop of St Asaph's scruples over a presentation of a 'skoler' of the duke. As lord chancellor Wolsey could generally further Brandon's 'great causes and moost weighty affayres', as he promised to do.[134] As chief minister he could ask favours of the king and apply pressure to other subjects, as when Suffolk asked him to write to the king and to the widow of Sir Walter Strickland, in support of a marriage between her and Richard Freston, controller of the ducal household. Suffolk was grateful for Wolsey's help, but also confident of his co-operation, telling his almoner to wait with the cardinal until the required letters were produced.[135]

Perhaps Wolsey was involved in grants to the duke himself, of the chief stewardship of the duchy of Lancaster in northern England (in April 1525), of the reversion of the hundreds of Wangford and Blything, to fall in in 1531 (granted in December 1527), and of a confirmation of his office of ranger of the New Forest (in July 1529).[136] Perhaps Sir Richard Wingfield, chancellor of the duchy of Lancaster, had a hand in the grant of the stewardship with its £100 fee. Suffolk used other channels too, including the privy chamber. This was not a simple and all-sufficient patronage mechanism dominated by the minions, but for Suffolk part of a wider process, in which the grooms and gentlemen of the privy chamber provided a short-cut to the king. By 18 June 1527 Sir Edward Echingham, controller of the Ipswich customs, was 'sumwhat trobeled w[ith] sikenes and dysease' and the race began to secure his office.[137]

Henry Wingfield, younger brother of Sir Anthony, set out to do so. He was probably well informed about Echingham's condition, for Humphrey Wingfield shared with Sir Edward a 'famylyar acqueyntaunce from our childhod unto this day'. Henry also enjoyed the backing of Suffolk, who wrote to 'our ryght trusty and welbelovid Walter Walshe gentilman, oon of the gromes of the kingis grac[es] moost hono[ur]able pryvey chamber'.[138] Walsh was asked to make a 'mocion' to the king, while Suffolk wrote to, and Wingfield visited, the duke of Norfolk. Henry gave his agreement, conditional on Norfolk's 'mynde and adv[er]tisement had in the same'; Norfolk, lord treasurer and local magnate, gave Wingfield his blessing and Suffolk informed Walsh, who was to 'solicite further this mater to the good accomplishement of the same'. Norfolk arranged not only for Henry Norris, the groom of the stool and head of the privy chamber staff, to be paid off with hawks in return for backing the suit, but also 'desyred my lord of Rocheforde to speke unto the kyng[es] grace for the same'. With Wolsey abroad, Norfolk and Suffolk in the country, Rochford only just on his way to court, and Wingfield too busy to come to London, the situation may have been exceptional.[139] What is even more remarkable is that Wingfield failed. Everything but Walsh's final solicitation was completed by 15 July, when Echingham had only been dead a week or less, but William Sabin must have acted faster still, for he secured a grant sealed with the great seal on 23 August and occupied the office.[140]

Those who sought patronage from Suffolk were as wide-ranging and assiduous in their approach as he was in seeking it from Henry. John Palsgrave, once Mary's tutor, professed himself on the dedication page of his French textbook profusely grateful to Mary and Suffolk for 'their manyfolde benefytes' to him, and was closely linked with Peter Valens, schoolmaster to the earl of Lincoln, and Nicolas de St Martin.[141] In 1525, with debts to pay and a poor mother to support, he used a friend to seek ecclesiastical preferment by an appeal to Charles and Mary. But Wolsey was to be approached too, and the possible opposition of Humphrey Wingfield was to be defused not only by reporting his obstructiveness to the first three, but also by instructions to 'handyll Syr Robart, Master Wyngfeld[es] prest, accordi[ingly].' Part of Palsgrave's plan succeeded, part failed: he managed to resign one living to a priest who had paid him for it, but the benefice of Cawston went to Christopher Lynham.[142]

Palsgrave had stressed his affection for Mary and Suffolk, and 'howe myche it hathe bene agaynst my wyll that ever I went from theym.' The duke could with more justice claim the same for his friendship with the king. Henry could be hard to please, but Suffolk knew well how to handle him, and their relationship remained the basis of the duke's position. In summer 1526 Henry was enraged when Suffolk warned him not to pass through Woodstock since a ducal servant had died of the plague there; he thought Brandon should have informed him sooner.[143] The duke replied by sending a trusty servant to apologise 'in as humble and soryfull man[er] as could be'. Henry promptly 'p[ar]donned and forgave his mysfaicte in the p[re]misses, and telled his said s[er]v[a]nt a right good tale to be shewed unto hym', which presumably cheered Suffolk up.

Foreign Affairs and Domestic Politics

The standing of Suffolk and Mary remained as constant as their relationship with the king, as their place among the recipients of New Year's gifts from the royal family showed.[144] The duke's position in government is more questionable. The (very thin) evidence shows few attendances in council, and it has been argued that his lack of major office made him entirely dispensable.[145] Certainly he was not eligible to attend when sheriffs were chosen, under the ruling of 1516, but it must be doubted how far this damaged him: in the fourteen years between 1515 and Wolsey's fall, eight saw a relative or associate of the duke, or a man with a son in ducal service, as sheriff of Norfolk and Suffolk. These were not Brandon's closest followers, and he certainly could not match the grip on the shrievalty exercised by locally dominant peers in previous or later generations.[146] None the less, such appointments hardly represented a damaging exclusion of the duke from local influence, especially since he was still very much Howard's junior as an East Anglian magnate. In 1525–6 Suffolk retained a prominent ceremonial role, and after 1526 the strengthening of the French alliance brought his return to a leading executive role in foreign affairs. In November or December 1525 the French ambassadors travelled to Reading to thank Mary for her part in bringing about the *rapprochement*, and Suffolk answered on her behalf that she would do her best to maintain it.[147] The Anglo-French alliance gave Suffolk's admiration for Francis I full rein. On 9 May 1526 he and Mary wrote to congratulate Francis on his release from captivity in Spain after the disastrous battle of Pavia.[148] Mary assured him that the ladies of England had been praying for his liberation, both 'icelles qui vous ont veu, et aultres qui ont ouy parler des v[er]tuz et graces que Dieu vous a faictez'. Suffolk's pledge to Francis was far warmer than anything he ever wrote even to Margaret of Austria, 'vous offrant ce que ung gentilhom[m]e peult offrir: c'est de mourir a voz piedz pour v[ot]re s[er]vice.'

The duke was at the forefront of the ensuing discussions about war with the Low Countries, in which Henry too took great interest. When the council met the French ambassadors in March 1527 he was as much a leading figure as he was in the accompanying social events.[149] Others conducted detailed negotiations while the duke prepared for war, buying armour and discussing strategy with Henry.[150] Suffolk had been appointed – he was the French king's choice – to attack the Netherlands with 10,000 English troops in 1528, should Charles V refuse to return the French princes held hostage for their father's compliance with the humiliating treaty of 1526. Norfolk co-operated with this policy, visiting the leading French ambassador with Suffolk on 5 April, but he was soon disgruntled with the French alliance.[151] For Suffolk, in contrast, all was going well, with plans afoot for another meeting between Henry and Francis. The second-in-command of the tiny English contingent accompanying Lautrec's Italian invasion that summer was the duke's step-cousin and client John Carew of Hackcomb, recently appointed a feed esquire for the body. Carew succeeded to command the company when his superior died of plague, but he too then succumbed, and

Brandon's sense of family loyalties did not extend to buying up the wardship of his ten-year-old son.[152]

As Suffolk's campaign approached, his importance increased. Despite Buren's pleadings and continued dissension in the council, he and Wolsey prepared for war.[153] Troops were mustered in London, Sandys sent in April 1528 to prepare Guînes, and Suffolk and the cardinal devised with Francis three possible strategies, discussing which they should present to Henry. They promised Francis that, whichever plan he chose, 'ilz mectront peyne de le faire trouver bon au roy leur m[aitre]'; Wolsey and Brandon were working together more closely than at any time since 1514.[154] Disruption to the cloth trade and the fishing industry forced a truce with the Netherlands in June 1528, and Suffolk's captains disbanded their troops, but the duke had no reason to break with the cardinal.[155]

In summer 1527 he probably rejected the chance to do so. Norfolk, seen by contemporaries as the cardinal's leading opponent, at least over foreign policy, filled the court in late July with the Boleyns and 'atros sus aliados'.[156] Norfolk and Rochford dined frequently in Henry's privy chamber with Exeter and Suffolk. With Wolsey away on embassy in France, and progress on Henry's divorce unsatisfactory, the Howards and Boleyns criticised the work of Wolsey's agents in the foundation of his colleges, and the king listened. But Suffolk was apparently not among the conspirators.[157] Unlike Anne Boleyn and her father Rochford, he had no personal reason to demonstrate to Wolsey his influence over the king, and in the matter of the colleges he had far less to lose than Norfolk. Both dukes witnessed the charter of the Oxford college, both would supply bucks for dinners at the Ipswich college, and both had to sign away their inherited founders' rights over dissolved monasteries.[158] But Humphrey Wingfield was much involved in the Ipswich project, and Suffolk and Mary surrendered their rights to only two manors and one religious house: of these Sayes Court (or West Greenwich) in Deptford had been sold or given to Wolsey in 1517, Bickling was still held by the countess of Lincoln, and Snape Priory was officially counted a royal foundation despite the involvement of the countess of Suffolk in the presentation of the prior in early 1515.[159] Wolsey's reaction to these criticisms also reflected Norfolk's involvement. Howard was constituted a joint founder of the Ipswich college, while the cardinal tried to alter the terms about the consent of all interested parties, in the bull enabling his suppressions, avowedly to prevent malicious opposition.[160]

Religion and the Opposition to Wolsey

Suffolk's apparent attitude in 1527 was the one he pursued throughout 1528 and 1529. He stayed close to Henry, obeyed with enthusiasm the king's every command, especially during the public order problems of 1528, and avoided explicit commitment for or against Wolsey. It has been suggested that John Palsgrave was pandering to Suffolk when he composed a vehement critique of the cardinal, over which the council apparently disciplined him in April 1528, but his charges did not specifically reflect the duke's interests, and he was more likely driven by his own ire at his dismissal as schoolmaster to the duke of Richmond.[161] It has been argued that the duke 'led' 'a hostile aristocracy' against Wolsey, consistently advocating an attack on the power and wealth of the church, and that this was motivated by religious views of an anticlerical and perhaps reformist nature, but this seems to be an inaccurate picture.[162] Suffolk's convictions are hard to establish. His only demonstrable ecclesiastical enthusiasm was for church music, and in his correspondence even his more explicit comments were purely conventional; he signed his small psalter with its French commentary among the psalms for times of tribulation, but this was also the only spare space apart from the endpapers.[163] In 1522 a fraternity in Dunstable was praying for Mary and the duke, in 1525 he ordered religious processions to celebrate the battle of Pavia, and while no religious books were dedicated to him around the time of Wolsey's fall, those dedicated to her were translations of foreign works of orthodox piety or Erasmian morality.[164]

The most that can be said is that Brandon seems to have been tolerant of unorthodoxy, as perhaps anyone aspiring to wide connections in East Anglia had to be. In January 1526 Anthony Yaxley recanted various Lollard, or perhaps Protestant, heresies. Yaxley was the husband of one of Mary's ladies-in-waiting, may have been a relative of Brandon, and was probably the nephew of Robert Yaxley the physician and his wife Margaret who were close to Brandon in London in 1508–10. In June 1527 Anthony Yaxley stood surety for a chaplain of the duke when Suffolk presented him to the rectory of Melles.[165] Suffolk had good reason to employ his only other reformist contact of this period. This was Peter Valens, a Norman educated at Gonville Hall in Cambridge, who had criticised indulgences as early as 1517. By 1530 he was schoolmaster to the earl of Lincoln, presumably chosen less for his doctrine than for the pedagogical talent he was later to employ on Thomas Cromwell's son Gregory.[166]

None of the priests presented to livings by Suffolk before 1535 later became a notable Protestant; two were deprived for marriage in 1554, but one put away his wife and was reckoned chaste.[167] Of four who left wills between 1526 and 1546, three were orthodox conservatives, and the last seemed less concerned about his soul than that 'ev[er]y man woman or childe being at my buryall shall have a penye, a pere, a pastie and a halpenye Ioffe, and good duble bere, the best thei canne bye'.[168] Suffolk's ecclesiastical patronage reserves were very poor, and he had to seek benefices from other patrons for well-qualified clerics whom he wished to reward. The great majority of his livings were worth less than £9, and between 1516 and 1531 he made only two more presentations than the countess of Lincoln, who retained many De la Pole advowsons.[169] He often granted out advowsons to supporters like Sir Anthony Wingfield or Sir Thomas Wentworth, to provide for their own priests, or to tenants and household servants like Nicholas Arrowsmith, Henry Curteis, or Ralph Hughson.[170]

The richest of Suffolk's livings usually went to his chaplains. Christopher Lynham made good use of his dispensation for pluralism, receiving Cawston in 1526 and Huntingfield in 1531 until in 1535 his income from English benefices totalled £47 14s 2d.[71] John Johnson, a chaplain active as an attorney and feoffee, was presented to Melles in 1527.[172] When not appointing chaplains, the duke sometimes chose the sons of his tenants, like John Pratyman at Wyverstone in 1524, sometimes apparently contacts from his past, like William Steres at Geldeston in 1534.[173] Other advowsons were used to reinforce his relationship with local religious houses like Langley, while Butley returned a similar favour to one of his supporters.[174] Suffolk took an interest in the De la Pole college at Wingfield, presenting one of its priests to a living in 1524 and installing one of his chaplains as its master in 1531.[175] He looked after the families of his local officers: in 1526 and 1533 he gave benefices to Brian Carter, an associate and presumably a relative of his south Midlands receiver-general, Thomas Carter.[176] Lastly, the duke cared for his own family through the church: in October 1528, having secured a legatine dispensation from Wolsey, he settled the rectory of Stemfield on sixteen-year-old Francis Glemham, third son of Sir John, who kept it for ten years, and then resigned it for an illegally large pension.[177]

Suffolk, then, showed little sign of theological commitment, nor of interest in learning (presenting only two graduates in these years, though admittedly his livings were rarely rich enough to attract them). He demonstrated no opposition to pluralism, dislike for the religious orders, or even distaste for legatine authority, when it could be useful. If there were Lutheran books at the English court in 1529 – and it is quite possible that the story of their circulation was a fiction devised to coerce the papacy – then Anne Boleyn was a far more likely source than Suffolk.[178] Indeed, the threat to the church came less from Suffolk than from Henry's own imperial inclinations, his frustration over the divorce, and the insistent arguments of the common lawyers.[179]

The issue on which Henry was unequivocally committed was the divorce, and in that Suffolk followed his sovereign. When apparently good news came through in early 1528, he rejoiced, 'thinking verily the good succession therof hath been specially by the dyvine p[ro]vidence of almighty God.'[180] He played a large role in welcoming Cardinal Campeggio, and he and Mary were very prominent in the court's activities at Christmas 1528.[181]

From November or December that year Norfolk, Rochford, and Anne Boleyn joined in clear opposition to Wolsey, encroaching further on his position with the king. Earlier in 1528 Rochford had discussed policy over the divorce with Henry; by March 1529 the king was sharing all his latest European correspondence with Rochford, Norfolk, and Suffolk.[182] In February Suffolk was for the first time named among Wolsey's enemies, significantly after Henry had begun openly to criticise the cardinal.[183] In January both the imperial and the French ambassadors had defined the opposition as Anne Boleyn plus 'le duc de Nortfoch et sa bande'; now Suffolk was moving, not so much against Wolsey, as with the king.[184]

Suffolk's caution was hardly surprising. He had no reason to risk anything for the Boleyns' ambitions or Norfolk's Burgundian loyalties.[185] Indeed, the price of his support may have been the softening of Norfolk's anti-French stance around Wolsey's fall. Nor was Brandon obviously impelled by a desire to attack the church. Perhaps simple greed led him to advocate disendowment, though if so the problem remains of why the 'Parliament Matters' memorandum of 1 July 1529 should be in Lord Darcy's hand. This blueprint for erastianism contained many matters of personal interest to Darcy, none so to Suffolk, and there is no evidence that it 'did justice to Suffolk's views at the moment of Wolsey's destruction'.[186] If Brandon took any interest in historical precedents, he could as well have seen himself in the situation of 1371, when Edward III replaced his clerical ministers with laymen after parliamentary complaints of their corruption and unaccountability, as that of 1410, when the Lollards pressed for ecclesiastical disendowment. Even Chapuys, sensitive to any hint of anti-clericalism, could report on 4 September that parliament was summoned to 'ouyr et entendre les querelles contre les administrateurs de la justice et deniers du royaulme, là ou l'on dit y a eu grande faulte pour le passé.'[187]

Embassy to France
Suffolk's reluctance to throw in his lot entirely with Wolsey's critics did nothing to lessen his political importance. Du Bellay, the French

ambassador, spent money on both dukes to 'entretenir leur amytié'.[188] Suffolk's role in government too remained central, writing letters at Henry's command to Francis I and Albany about Scotland.[189] In May the alarming prospect of a Franco-imperial peace demanded that a weighty English embassy be sent to Francis, and Suffolk and Sir William Fitzwilliam were chosen.[190] After a careful briefing from Henry and a large payment for their expenses, they set off on 17 May. Within six days Henry knew that Franco-imperial talks would definitely take place at Cambrai: the embassy was doomed.[191] Suffolk was to promise English troops and money for war against Charles, and Francis was still considering an invasion of Italy. But Louise of Savoy and Montmorency were eager for peace, and Francis would not reject an attractive settlement should they produce one.[192]

Suffolk began his mission enthusiastically, and was honoured by allies and enemies from 1523 alike. Every Frenchman he met spoke only of peace, though, and while he hurried, as Henry had ordered, the French delayed him. Money was spent on entertaining him, and once at court he had plenty of access to Francis and Montmorency, but it was hard to secure anything but vague assurances that Francis would 'cleve as nere on to the kyng [Henry] as the naylys doth to hys flesh.'[193] Eventually Fitzwilliam was dispatched with satisfactory answers to Henry's military proposals; but meanwhile the peace conference approached, Wolsey would not be able to attend, and Montmorency's policy worked well, detaining but negating the duke, 'lequel le roy amusera cependant a chasser'.[194]

As Cambrai drew nearer, rumours spread that Suffolk would attend the conference. The French peace party was keen to avoid this, and was helped by Henry's conviction that if only Wolsey could be there he could use the meeting to further the divorce.[195] By mid-June Francis was admitting that he favoured the conference, though he hoped it would serve Henry's ends. Meanwhile he was drawing huge gambling expenses to keep the helpless Suffolk quiet, while Du Bellay delayed Fitzwilliam's return from England.[196] Francis persisted in military preparations and promised support at Rome, but Margaret of Austria and Louise of Savoy, architects of the forthcoming 'Ladies' Peace of Cambrai', travelled inexorably towards one another. Wolsey fell into despair, warning Du Bellay that Suffolk's servants might open his dispatches, and sharing the ambassador's fear that the duke would take over English policy and head for Cambrai, 'comme s'il se y debvoyt trouver, dont je vous asseure que le cardinal d'York ne seroyt content'.[197] Suffolk intended nothing of the sort: he returned rapidly once Henry ordered him to do so, for it had become clear that Wolsey would not have finished with the legatine divorce court in time for the conference, and in that contingency Henry had long planned to send Bishop Tunstal to Cambrai.[198]

The embassy had hardly been successful. But Suffolk cannot be blamed for accepting the French line that it was Charles who was pressing for peace, when Wolsey too believed it.[199] Francis did continue to discuss an Italian campaign even after Suffolk's return; whatever his private fears, Henry gladly received French assurances of undiminished support; and Wolsey realised that peace was inevitable.[200] Yet the significance of the embassy went far beyond its failure to keep Charles and Francis apart. For Henry had entrusted to Suffolk alone an additional very secret charge: this was to pursue an earlier hint by Francis that not all Henry's agents were loyal, and ask if he thought that Wolsey was obstructing the divorce.[201] Francis's answer was equivocal. He blamed Campeggio as 'entiere imperialle', and suggested that Wolsey did desire the divorce because 'he loved not the quene'; but he added that Wolsey was rather close to the pope, and advised that Henry should trust no one too far, but 'loke substauncyally upon his matiers hym self.' Suffolk admitted that he could not fathom the French king's true mind, but thought that he was not deceiving Henry.

The duke promised to try to elicit further information from Francis; unlike Du Bellay and Montmorency, Francis did not believe that the French hold over England could only be maintained by preserving the cardinal, and there is thus no reason to think that Suffolk was fabricating the French king's replies.[202] Henry's impatience over the divorce was enough to prompt questions about Wolsey, and Norfolk and Suffolk apparently encouraged this impatience, but it would have been rash indeed for Suffolk to have probed Francis without Henry's instructions, or falsified the response. Even before he left for France, the duke had interrogated Du Bellay about the French knowledge of Charles's attitude to the divorce.[203] He reported back directly to Henry, just as he sent all the news from his embassy directly to the king, rather than have it filtered by Wolsey as had been the norm. Others were beginning to act as intermediaries between the king and his servants: the only extant version of Suffolk's first letter from the French court is a copy in the hand of Viscount Rochford.[204] Henry felt that he could trust Suffolk when he was no longer sure if he could trust Wolsey.

On the other hand the duke did nothing to alienate the cardinal. He was polite about the 'towardnes of witte and vertue' of Thomas Wynter, whom he visited in Paris.[205] He brought back general assurances of Francis's trust in Wolsey. But it was Fitzwilliam, long trusted by Wolsey, who carried a credence to the cardinal from Louise of Savoy, spurring Wolsey's enemies later to suggest that these two had had treasonable contact in the past.[206] Wolsey's and Du Bellay's suspicions of Suffolk were soon confirmed, as news reached them of his conversations with Francis, and Wolsey complained about this to Henry. But with Suffolk 'du tout planté auprès de son maistre' they grumbled in vain, and by 1 September even Du Bellay had to recommend that Francis thank Suffolk, Norfolk, and Rochford for their 'bon office' towards French interests.[207]

The Fall of Wolsey and the New Regime

Du Bellay saw the duke's embassy as part of a greater struggle between Wolsey and the Boleyns. When Suffolk returned in late June the outcome of this struggle rested on the success of the Blackfriars legatine court.[208] Some of Wolsey's enemies were already planning his downfall in secret, like Thomas, Lord Darcy, whose charges against the cardinal, 'shewed by me Thomas Darcy' were as personal as his plans for parliament; he was especially proud of his own devices to secure Wolsey's wealth for the king.[209] It is impossible to say how far he colluded with Norfolk and others. Certainly tension in London must have been high and discussion animated as most of the political nation, including Darcy and the returned Suffolk, gathered to testify before Wolsey and Campeggio. Yet the peers continued to work with Wolsey as long as Henry's trust remained in him, and even the suspension of the court did not make a final break.[210] It is unclear exactly when and how the court closed, but it seems that it was Suffolk who announced the termination, on the king's orders, not in terms of passionate personal outrage, but of a considered royal statement against papal intransigence.[211]

None the less, Suffolk's ringing declaration at the court's last session that 'the olde saied sawe is true, that there was never legate nor cardinall, that did good in Englande' boded very ill for one cardinal legate in particular. From the moment the court failed, the queen thought that Wolsey was doomed, and in the next two months Norfolk, Suffolk, and Rochford grew from critics of the cardinal to a clear group of rivals.[212] They were far from united, though. In May and June the imperialists thought Norfolk was influencing policy in their favour. In August the French rewarded Suffolk with about £500 worth of silver plate, and sent smaller gifts to others through Nicolas de St Martin who was in France.[213] The peers were often physically apart, too. Through August and September Rochford was usually at court, acting as spokesman for the king and commenting on Wolsey's advice.[214] Norfolk did the same when he was at court, but was away in early and later September.[215] Suffolk was ill in early August, and in late August he left court with Norfolk after hunting at Woodstock with the king.[216] Wolsey's most vociferous opponent was still Anne, perhaps because her position was safest. But by early September both French and imperial ambassadors recognised the triumvirate of peers who 'pevent beaucoup envers leur maistre', being 'les plus continues aupres de la personne du roy, et ceux que maintenant a la court (puysque mons[ieur] le cardinal en a esté absent) despeschent tous les affaires.'[217]

In September, as Wolsey failed to perform the miracle in foreign policy needed to secure the divorce, the king's trust in him finally crumbled – and that, rather than an attack by his enemies, was how the cardinal himself described the situation.[218] In the vital weeks, Suffolk was again at court. He may have organised the snub of 19 September, when Wolsey arrived at Grafton with Campeggio to see the king, only to find no lodgings available, but outwardly he remained courteous.[219] They apparently co-operated in council as late as 6 October, for until Henry committed himself 'tous les grans d'Angleterre' had to work together, making it hard for Chapuys to guess 'que seroit de ce nouveau gouvernement.'[220] Wolsey's following was dissolving, Brian Tuke, Stephen Gardiner, and others abandoning him, but the peers' coalition too now showed signs of strain.[221]

Even before the first *praemunire* charges against Wolsey on 9 October signalled that the cardinal's fall was complete, Rochford was trying his strength against his allies. He was so disgruntled that the French had not honoured him as they had the dukes, that he blocked in council French proposals to which they were agreed. On 12 October, with Rochford and his daughter imitating Wolsey's behaviour towards Henry, praising the king's own ideas and pointing out how well they were managing his affairs, Du Bellay attended another council meeting.[222] There Rochford was 'si glorieulx fol pour m'avoir voulu monstrer son credit et ce qu'il sçait faire', that he let all the others agree to accept Du Bellay's proposition and then 'vint proposer tout le contraire.' His daughter's known hold over the king was such that he could 'renverser a ma veue leurs opinions'. With his son George on the way to France as ambassador, Rochford was taking significant control over English policy: it was no accident that a premature report in Paris of Wolsey's dismissal as chancellor named Rochford as the replacement.[223]

In the next month the dukes redressed the balance. For Du Bellay they were 'les ducz' on 12 October, 'noz ducz' by 2 November. He regarded them as the leaders of the new regime, they had spoken with him often, and the perhaps chastened Rochford was 'comme tout ung avec eulx'.[224] It is possible that in this period Norfolk also reproved an ambition on Suffolk's part to succeed as chancellor, though this rests only on gossip over a fortnight old, and seems unlikely considering Brandon's realistic estimate of his own abilities and questionable dedication to work.[225] It is more probable that Norfolk was tiring of the Boleyns' pretensions. It may not have been merely politeness to Charles V that prompted him to tell Chapuys of the divorce that 'il voudroit luy heu cousté une de ses propres mains et qu'il n'eust jamais ceste question de ce d[it] affere.'[226]

Norfolk and Suffolk seem to have worked well together. They did so on official business, like depriving Wolsey of the great seal, and also more informally, as in their visits to Du Bellay.[227] Howard was the senior partner, as both Chapuys and Du Bellay recognised. He announced in council on 19 October the plans for meetings in Star Chamber three days a week.[228] But Suffolk was to deputise as leader of the council in his absence, and Chapuys felt him to be the only other councillor worthy of a letter of ingratiation from Charles V. His ducal status alone gave him a prominent role in official business, in a regime where power had returned to those whose nobility fitted them for it.[229]

Brandon took a share in the spoils of Wolsey's fall. The cardinal's prize mules were added to the duke's stable; the clerk of Wolsey's kitchen entered his service; the manor of Sayes Court in Deptford returned to him.[230] The office of president of the council was revived for him: in Henry VII's reign it had involved real, though flexible, responsibilities in the council's work, though for Brandon it soon became merely honorific.[231] Norfolk may also have made concessions to Suffolk's interests, as well as to necessity, in foreign policy. Howard continued his fulsome professions of dedication to Charles V, but he also joined Suffolk in promising that they would keep Henry close to Francis, and in redressing any impression given by Wolsey that they had stirred the king against France in the past.[232] Governing was no easy task, especially since Henry was not 'si aisé a manyer que l'on pense', and they had to apologise to Du Bellay because 'leur maniere de negocier envers leur maistre n'est encores bien dressee.'[233] But the rewards of power were welcome.

There was some debate about what form those rewards should take. Some lords planned to expropriate the church, reported

Du Bellay on 17 October, 'qu'il ne seroyt ja besoing que je misse en chiffre car ilz le cryent en plaine table.'[234] Chapuys feared the same, but neither named Suffolk as the author of these plans, and the evidence points rather to Darcy and, more important, the Boleyns.[235] By 1529 European precedents made disendowment a political option which a radical clique did not need to invent, merely to encourage. That it was for the moment rejected suggests that Norfolk and the new chancellor More, and perhaps Suffolk too, agreed that it was not for the best, and Henry was persuaded.[236]

When parliament gathered on 3 November it apparently proclaimed the maturity of Suffolk's power.[237] Many of those elected had links with the duke: the knights for Suffolk were Sir Anthony Wingfield and Sir Thomas Wentworth of Nettlestead, the latter knighted by the duke in 1523. But since Wentworth had succeeded his father in 1528, each was presumably of sufficient local standing to be elected without the duke's help. Humphrey Wingfield sat for Great Yarmouth, a borough for which he provided legal counsel. Suffolk's connections with others lay at varying distances in the past: Sir William Essex, Sir Thomas Cornewall, Sir Richard Cornewall, Sir John Brydges, Sir Edward Chamberlain, and Roger Corbet are examples.[238] Only Sir John Shilston in Southwark could certainly be named as a client elected through Suffolk's influence, and he died shortly afterwards, his will witnessed by ducal servants.[239] His fellow member Robert Acton would have known the duke, as king's saddler, and may have had other links with him. Such connections demonstrate the wide range of Brandon's contacts in many areas of the country, and in the case of Southwark the effectiveness of his influence on local society. What they do not demonstrate is the existence of a docile ducal affinity in parliament. Essex was part of the staunchly conservative Queen's Head Tavern circle, and Brydges too opposed royal religious policy.[240]

This was symptomatic of Suffolk's condition in 1529. He was gathering his share of the spoils of a political victory in which he had not been a leading combatant, a victory over a minister whose rule in recent years had harmed him little. His prominence was now seemingly more assured than under Wolsey, but in council, in foreign affairs, in patronage and in personal influence with the king there were others more important than he. His power was everywhere evident, but so were its limitations.

4

Years of Eclipse: 1529–1536

From the fall of Wolsey to that of Anne Boleyn, Suffolk displayed neither the ambition nor the ability to play a dominant role in government: as the Venetian ambassador reported in 1531, he sat in council only to discuss important matters, 'passing his time more pleasantly in other amusements'.[1] The same envoy stressed the role of the French queen in her husband's career, and this was perceptive. At a time of turmoil in the royal family and consequent dislocation in European politics, her proximity to the throne and attachment to Catherine of Aragon affected the duke profoundly, and her death in 1533 forced him to reassess his position both in England and beyond.

Role in Government

In late 1529 Brandon was at the heart of the regime. He ranked third in council as lord president, and was named to every commission of the peace from December.[2] He was prominent in the prosecution of Wolsey, Rochford's elevation to the earldom of Wiltshire, and the conciliar settlement over John Roper's will.[3] In October he was pensioned by the astute Bishop Longland, and in December he was privately courted by the French ambassador. With other leading councillors he entertained both the French and imperial envoys.[4] To the latter he avowed his impartiality, insisting 'qu'il estoit vray que le principal de son bien estoyt en France, mays qu'il aymeroit mieux estre mort, quant yl en auroit dix foys autant d'avantage, que pour ceux-la conseyllier au roy chose que fust a son desavantage.'[5] But by January 1530 Suffolk was not one of the active inner circle of the council.[6] It was probably his work-shyness rather than his views that excluded him. More significant was Wolsey's neglect of the duke in his machinations to regain favour. Though Suffolk and Norfolk had dealt together with the cardinal at his fall, it was consistently to Norfolk and to his other dire foes the Boleyns that Wolsey looked for help in 1530. Even other courtiers like Norris, Sandys, Fitzwilliam, and Sir Henry Guildford took priority over Brandon in Wolsey's plans.[7]

Suffolk had not become a nonentity. His absence from court in May 1530 was noticed, and that autumn he harangued ambassadors with Norfolk and Wiltshire.[8] Between 1531 and 1535 the Abbot of Furness granted him a £10 pension, and in 1533 the pewterers' company lobbied for his support in parliament with a gurnard, a pike and an eel.[9] But when the duke of Milan relied on Suffolk's influence in September 1530, he was ignoring the advice of his well-informed ambassador.[10] The politics of 1530 and 1531 were complex and frustrating, and the duke may have been happy to stand aside: unlike Wiltshire, for example, he had no personal or ideological axe to grind.[11] His religion remained pragmatic and conservative, and rumour had it that in council he argued against dangerously radical démarches. He would abuse the pope to please the king, but sued for a papal dispensation in January 1532. He was thought to favour the persecution of heresy.[12] In 1535 he presented to Ewelme a graduate cleric who mixed with court reformists and later left a Protestant will, but who was also a protégé of the conservative Bishop Longland.[13] In the same year the chapel at Suffolk Place contained six gilt statues of saints.[14] When he spoke to ambassadors he loyally furthered the king's policy, but they were more likely to meet him at dinner with Henry, or at the door of the privy chamber, than in council or in private rendezvous.[15] His conciliar attendance was erratic, as was his presence in parliament in 1534, and even his title as president of the council fell into disuse.[16] In the momentous events of these seven years he was neither an indispensable executive nor an influential adviser.

At court and in the country he played the part expected of him. He helped to present to the House of Commons the collected verdicts of the European universities on the king's divorce, and the plans for new border fortifications.[17] He put on his collar of the Order of Saint-Michel and showed a French ambassador around Westminster Palace.[18] He was commissioned to report on the defences of Calais, to examine the Protestant John Frith, and to swear the members of parliament to the succession.[19] He examined and tried More and Fisher.[20] In March 1530 he was sent to Oxford to coerce recalcitrant dons and rioting townswomen into support for the divorce, and he was ready to repeat the trip.[21] He was involved, too, in the king's and Cromwell's arbitration of disputes between the town and university authorities.[22] In February 1535 he went to Suffolk, as many other courtiers went into the localities, to oversee the dangerous levy of a peacetime subsidy.[23] All these activities demonstrated and reinforced his authority: by 1535, for example, Oxford corporation made him steward of the town. He was even offered the command of an army against the Irish revolt.[24] But in March 1534 the Venetian ambassador did not think him worth bribing, and in March 1535 Suffolk was not even among 'thow personages' Henry 'most trusts' to negotiate a marriage alliance with France.[25]

Catherine of Aragon, Anne Boleyn, and Thomas Cromwell

Superficially the duke's friendship with the king held firm. They continued to exchange gifts, Suffolk's offerings ranging from greyhounds to a gold-bound book containing a clock.[26] Henry visited Ewelme in 1531, 1532, and 1535, and he and Brandon gambled together, played tennis, and listened to the French queen's sackbut players.[27] The king now jousted rarely, and spent far more time with the gentlemen of the privy chamber than with the duke. Yet their personal friendship was still important: Henry would snap at other councillors who advised him to conciliate Charles V, but not at Suffolk.[28] The royal divorces strained this relationship, and threatened the duke, in several ways. The disinheritance of Mary, and later of Elizabeth, gave Suffolk's children a strong claim to the throne. This opened the way to an attractive diplomatic marriage for his daughters, but the fact that observers from Edinburgh to Rome saw the earl of Lincoln as a strong contender for the kingdom placed an enormous premium on Suffolk's loyalty, and must have made him wary.[29]

The duke's links with Catherine of Aragon were also a problem. Chapuys claimed that he and his wife opposed the divorce in secret and merely lacked the courage to do so more openly, and a case can be made that Suffolk consistently disapproved of the divorce.[30] It is more significant, though, that Brandon failed to press his sentiments to any great lengths, presumably out of personal loyalty to the king and a sense of self-preservation. In her last illness the French queen protested her love for Henry, but she was popularly believed to sympathise with her sister-in-law and niece, and one contemporary thought that she died of grief over Catherine's troubles.[31] Lady Mary Willoughby, the earl of Lincoln's prospective mother-in-law, stayed close to Catherine, and rushed to see her on her deathbed; Catherine Willoughby was second mourner at the ex-queen's funeral in February 1536, when the first mourner was Suffolk's daughter Eleanor.[32] The duke found the repeated missions to humiliate Catherine on which the king dispatched him distasteful. In May 1531 he was impressed by her dignity, and reportedly resolved to try to dissuade Henry from his folly. In April 1533 he had to tell her that she was no longer queen, and in December was ordered to disband some of her servants and move her to an unhealthy home at Somersham.[33] He was prepared to deal with a riot in her favour, but was defeated when she locked herself in her room. Lady Mary Willoughby told Chapuys that the duke had confessed and communicated before setting out, wishing some accident on himself to relieve him of this hateful duty. In these years it was easier to live by the French queen's motto, 'La voullente de Dieu me suffet', than by Suffolk's 'Loyaulte me oblige'.[34]

The duke's relations with the Boleyns were another handicap. He may have gambled with Wiltshire, and leased crown lands with him, but they were not close.[35] Suffolk did not vote for Anne's brother George, Lord Rochford, in Garter elections, and Rochford's friends at court were no friends to the duke.[36] But Anne herself was the most hostile. No informed commentator ever linked her and Suffolk as allies in power. To Norfolk, Wiltshire, and others she was sharp-tongued enough, but against Suffolk, who was admittedly never an enthusiastic supporter of her cause, she prosecuted a feud.[37] In May 1530 there was trouble over Suffolk's report of a previous affair between Anne and Sir Thomas Wyatt, a matter apparently raised by the duke less out of malice than 'upon zeal that in his conceit it was true.'[38] In July 1531 she blended personal with political venom in the charge that Brandon 'se mesloit et copuloit avec sa propre fille', and in April 1532 the French queen insulted Anne, against whom she may have borne an old grudge.[39] Such difficult relations with a queen so politically active help explain Suffolk's quiescence in these years; to his credit he was not prominent in Anne's arrest and prosecution, and at her trial followed his usual principles, 'wholly applyinge himself to the king's humor'.[40]

Suffolk's dealings with Cromwell were easier than those with Anne, but from an early stage the duke was more petitioner than colleague. By December 1531 Brandon needed Cromwell's 'good mynde, favo[ur]s and helpe' and by autumn 1532 was grateful for the 'faithfull[e] and contynuell kindnes which I dayly fynde and considere in you toward[es] me and all myn'.[41] The duke's agent with the rising minister was Edward Fetiplace, Suffolk's treasurer, for whom Cromwell procured 'good avauncement ... in the counties of Oxford and Berkshir[e]'.[42] This was as wise a choice as that of Humphrey Wingfield as negotiator with Wolsey, for Fetiplace had known Cromwell since at least 1527, and counted him his 'right trusty friend' by 1529.[43]

The duke often asked Cromwell to favour his suits and those of his servants, and his servants sought Cromwell's help on the grounds that it would please Suffolk.[44] When their interests clashed, Suffolk was firm, but profusely apologetic. He once found himself explaining that he could not surrender his lease of Water Eaton, Oxfordshire, to a friend of Cromwell, because he had already granted it out to Lord Powis and Lady Anne, 'the wyche I am sorre for, for and et war threas as moche land as [that] es, I cold fiend in me hart to gyfet you, accordyngle as I am beholden to doo, most hartylle prayyng you to thenke non ankendnes in me, for in me fayth et es nat in me to doo.'[45] Brandon hunted with Cromwell in August 1535, and granted him a stag from one of his parks.[46] But he was never as close to the new minister as he had been, at times, to Wolsey. In 1532 he reacted bitterly when Cromwell passed on to the king hostile rumours about him; in 1533 he sent the French government some mysterious 'propoz de Monsr de Suffoz touchant Cramouel'.[47]

Suffolk's success as a patron was limited, whether asking Cromwell to favour his brother-in-law Gawain Carew to be sheriff of Devon, or attempting in one year to place a kinsman, a servant and an old soldier in the Calais retinue by letters to Lord Lisle.[48] With Lisle the French queen had more success, while Suffolk did obtain a benefice from Cromwell for the Abbot of Tilty.[49] Those far from court still asked the duke to use his influence with the king on their behalf, as did the earl of Cumberland and Lord Audley; but Audley usually sent his requests to Cromwell, and Suffolk had to pass on Cumberland's letter to the minister.[50] Suffolk's military reputation drew some suitors, like Stefan von Haschenperg, the military engineer.[51] More often he was petitioned either by those whose information was outdated – like Cardinal Campeggio in 1536 – or by those who appealed to him and Norfolk together as the senior adult peers.[52] In these lean years for royal favour, Suffolk's ducal rank and his eminent offices preserved for him some of the power and standing he had won in his earlier career. He appeared as a pillar of the regime at many state occasions, and was lieutenant at the Garter feast twice (though he missed three chapters).[53] But he proved unable to retain the office which had guaranteed him a proud and prominent place in royal ceremonial and the chivalrous life of the court and nation.

The Earl Marshalcy

By April 1533 the coronation of Norfolk's niece, Anne Boleyn, was imminent. With this in mind, the senior duke requested that Suffolk relinquish the office of earl marshal to him, 'whose

auncesto[ur]s of longe tyme hadde the same untill nowe of late'.[54]
As compensation Norfolk asked the king to appoint Suffolk as
warden and chief justice of the royal forests south of Trent, but
Henry realised that he was asking Brandon to make an important
sacrifice. The king declared himself pleased that Suffolk showed
'moche more estimacion and zele to norisshe kyndenes and love
bytwene my saide lorde of Norff[olk] and you, then ye have to
thatt or any office', but Brandon surrendered with ill grace, and
Norfolk was warned in June that 'my lord of Suff[olk] is looth to
let falle a noble on lesse he toke up a ryall for it.'[55] As high steward
and constable for a day Suffolk presented a splendid and powerful
figure at Anne's coronation, presiding at the court of claims and
seeing his unknighted sons-in-law made knights of the bath. But
at every stage of the ceremonies he was accompanied by Norfolk's
deputy, and at the end of the day Howard and his heirs were earls
marshal in tail male.[56]

The importance to Suffolk of the earl marshalcy can only
be inferred. Once he was lord president it conferred no extra
precedence, and its fee was only £20.[57] But Brandon was always
enthusiastic about the trappings of chivalry, and it must have
flattered him to be the nation's arbiter in such matters. After his
herald, Christopher Barker, entered royal service in July 1522, he
created William Fellowe his pursuivant 'in his place in Sudwarke
... w[ith] hys owne hande'.[58] He named Fellowe 'Merlyon de
Aye', after a badge he used widely enough for it to be the object
of court humour, and maintained contact with him long after he,
too, became a royal herald.[59] Barker and Fellowe played many
roles in the ducal household, organizing revels, preparing epitaphs,
rehearsing Suffolk's Latin style in different grammatical cases,
copying military treatises, and providing for 'Master Palgrave' 'iiii
pec[es] of green say for the anging of ys chambre'.[60] Their interest
in jousts equalled that of their master, and they bear testimony to
the enthusiasm and expertise which he surely brought to the earl
marshalcy.[61]

The scope of his activity is hard to judge. There was little
business in the court of chivalry, and for many matters the heralds

formed a self-regulating corporation.[62] Orders to the heralds and licences for visitations passed directly from the king to Garter king of arms, and heralds were appointed under the great seal and created by Henry in person.[63] Pursuivants could be created by peers, like the chamberlain of the household, who could even create heralds when commissioned with Garter.[64] The earl marshal had no control over the heralds' fees, and so varied were their roles in royal service, often verging on diplomacy and spying, that they could not look to him alone for political support.[65] Even Suffolk's title was vague, ranging from earl marshal to the more impressive steward marshal or even great marshal.[66] His influence in the selection of heralds was variable: every earl marshal had to secure the decision of the office of arms that candidates were 'hable and sufficient to have theyr said romes', but the need for Cromwell to favour the appointees was new in the 1530s.[67] Fellowe, Lancaster herald in 1527, and Thomas Wall junior, Windsor herald in 1524, probably did benefit from the duke's patronage.[68]

Suffolk's duty, as 'head & superiour judge over all the officers of arms', was to 'see a due order in [that] same office as to honour doth appertain.'[69] The heralds petitioned him with their corporate grievances, but many of these were insoluble in the short term and some, like their claim to legal immunity in any court but the court of chivalry, were preposterous.[70] In disputes within the college of arms he was slightly more successful. By an order decreeing a fixed scale of fees for the granting of arms, and placing constraints on such grants by Clarenceux, he partly settled a jurisdictional dispute between Clarenceux and Garter, which broke out in 1530.[71] But he could not solve the long-term problem of Garter's anomalous position, which persisted into the next century, or the short-term personal rivalries between the heralds which Cromwell and Norfolk took until 1539 to appease.[72]

East Anglian Rivalries

Despite the problems of the earl marshalcy, Suffolk could with justice resent his enforced resignation. It formed part of a series of difficulties between him and Norfolk, which explain Henry's 'contentacion' in 1533 'to see and p[er]ceve twoo so greate and hono[ur]hable p[er]sonages his subjectfes] so lovynglie and ffrendlie th'oon to love th'other.'[73] The cause was less personal animosity between the two peers than friction between their East Anglian followers. The greater local respect for Brandon evident from the later 1520s was matched in the 1530s by an expansion in his estates which doubled his East Anglian income between 1531 and 1538.[74] At the same time Howard wealth and influence in the area continued to expand, and Norfolk's greater resources – at the start of the decade a nationwide income almost twice the size of Brandon's – enabled him, for example, to buy Snape Priory in 1532 despite Suffolk's claim as heir to the founder.[75] Brandon tried to respond, increasing the scale of his hospitality, but at a period when the potential influence of both peers in local society was expanding, Suffolk's good lordship proved itself to be insufficient protection for his friends against those attaching themselves to Norfolk.[76]

On 20 April 1532 Suffolk's tenant and relation by marriage, Sir William Pennington, was murdered in the Westminster sanctuary by Norfolk's followers Richard, Robert, and Anthony Southwell and five or more accomplices.[77] The court was stunned, and Henry had to send Fitzwilliam to intercept Suffolk, who was reported to be on his way to remove the Southwells from the sanctuary. The king secured a promise from Suffolk to control his own retainers, but in July court rumour told of an oath by Brandon's servants to be revenged on the Southwells 'although it were in the king[es] chamber or at the high aulter.'[78] Though Suffolk denied this and Norfolk discounted it, such frustration was understandable, for the murderers escaped justice almost entirely. Howard's support, and Cromwell's friendship for Richard Southwell, secured them a pardon on 15 June after a perfunctory investigation.[79] The pardon halted their prosecution in king's bench, in September they gave two manors in Essex to the king to meet the £1,000 price of forgiveness, and in 1533 an Act of Parliament confirmed their immunity.[80] In 1534 Richard Southwell was named sheriff of Norfolk and Suffolk.[81]

Bacton

WALCOTT

West Somerton **

Drayton
Tolthorp in Drayton

Hellesdon

WHEATACRE •

•MENDHAM*

•SOUTH
ELMHAM

HOXNE   •*Fressingfield*

Sorrells and Dagworth
in Old Newton

•*Eye*

Stoke Ash •   •*Occold*   •*Laxfield*

Hurtes in Saxmundham   •*Darsham*

*Bedfield Benhall** •*Theberton*
•*Leiston*

BACTON•   *Debenham*•*Great Glemham*   *Knodishall*
Stratford St Andrew•   •*Aldringham*

Harleston•.   *Pettaugh*•   *Glevering*   Bickling•   *Thorpe*•
Finborough••   *Bilford in Little Glemham*   in Snape

BATTISFORD►   *Wantisden*•

Kettlebaston •   *Butley*• •*Chillesford*•
Culpho   *Tangham*•
•*Gedgrave*•
WIX BISHOP IN IPSWICH•   •*Boyton*
•*Howes in Alderton*
•*Bawdsey*•

Stratford St Mary*•

Langham*•
•Dedham*•

0   10   20 Miles
├─────────┼──────────┤
0   10   20   30   Kilometres

Map 4.1 East Anglian Acquisitions, 1530–1540

Pennington and the Southwells may well have quarrelled over local matters, as Sir William did with at least one other aggressive Howard farmer.[82] But Pennington was also a neighbour of the Howards near Kenninghall, and had recently joined the Norfolk bench very much as Suffolk's protégé: he leased land and livestock from Brandon, and the intended feoffees for his wife's jointure included Suffolk, Sir Anthony Wingfield, Sir John Glemham, Humphrey Wingfield, and John Johnson.[83] After his death his widow stayed in Suffolk's household, where her son became a henchman, Humphrey Wingfield did her legal business, and the ducal council negotiated for her son's wardship.[84] However private the argument between Pennington and Southwell, it looked alarmingly like a Brandon–Howard feud, one which the Venetian ambassador linked ominously with the French queen's hostility to Anne Boleyn.[85]

Other local disputes ran along similar fault-lines, rather as Suffolk disorder in the 1430s was channelled by the antipathy between the Mowbray and De la Pole affinities.[86] Norfolk seems to have taken Sir Christopher's side in the Willoughby dispute. Dame Frances Pennington could get no justice in the liberty of St Edmund, where Norfolk was the active steward.[87] Richard Cavendish of Trimley was a cousin of Suffolk with a brother in the ducal household, and was regularly involved in business dealings with the duke. He was an enterprising military engineer and diplomat, but found himself blocked at every turn in his local ventures.[88] Suffolk and other royal councillors restrained him when he challenged the town of Ipswich in 1533, but he met more consistent opposition from Norfolk's local representatives. Duke Thomas himself was a model of rectitude, returning Cavendish's kidnapped shepherd and appointing Sir Anthony Wingfield to arbitrate between Cavendish and the Howard tenants.[89] But Cavendish received little support from friends of Suffolk. Such defeats occurred even at the highest level of county society. Sir Arthur Hopton, one of Suffolk's richest allies with lands taxed at £400 in 1524, acted as a feoffee for the duke and placed his son as a henchman in the ducal household.[90] In April 1536 the abbot of Sibton contracted to sell his lands to

Hopton by Michaelmas, but when the time came Sir Arthur found himself gazumped by Norfolk. Howard claimed a vague verbal licence from the king, and, more importantly, showered benefices on the former abbot; Hopton was left with no redress at law because the abbey no longer existed.[91]

Perhaps Suffolk's power in East Anglia had for the moment reached its natural limits. Cromwell's network of correspondents slightly devalued Brandon's role as a link between centre and localities.[92] Both the duke himself and his local officers increasingly sought solutions to their problems in the central courts, and Suffolk even had to sue one of his own bailiffs.[93] He appointed ever more household servants to estate offices, though whether this was a cause or a symptom of his limitations as a local magnate is hard to say. It certainly resembled the policy of ineffective local lords, like Edward IV's brother Clarence, rather than effective ones like Brandon's contemporaries Darcy and Worcester.[94] His influence in county affairs rested on an alarmingly narrow base: no one closely connected with him sat regularly as a justice in Norfolk or in western Suffolk.[95] Sir Arthur Hopton was active at Ipswich and Blythburgh, Sir Anthony Wingfield and Sir Thomas Tyrrell less so, while Humphrey Wingfield – Suffolk's only contact among the quorum, the trusted inner ring of the commission – was assiduous at Ipswich and Woodbridge.[96] Both Sir Anthony and Humphrey continued to hold ducal courts, and Humphrey's local and central career flourished, bringing the speakership of the Commons and a knighthood.[97] But three cousins and a friend did not make an affinity.

The Ducal Affinity

The extent to which East Anglian society was polarised by the competition between Brandon and Howard interests is hard to judge. Neither duke abused his influence so grossly as to alienate large sections of the gentry community, as fifteenth-century magnates in the area had done.[98] Towns such as Norwich and monasteries such as Butley cultivated both peers, and of Leiston Abbey's three leading officers two were servants of Brandon, one of Howard. This was no sign of harmony, though, for the past reaction of towns to magnate feuding had generally been to seek friendship with both sides.[99] Many monastic administrations were dominated by the Howard clientage, and there was no overlap between the bailiffs and administrators of the two magnates, except the 40s legal retainer paid by Norfolk to Humphrey Wingfield.[100] Talented lawyers like Wingfield or Lionel Talmage could maintain links with both peers, but for most members the exclusivity of the Suffolk retinue seems to have been increasing.[101] Robert Jenour and Humphrey Wingfield did legal business for each other, and for Sir Anthony Wingfield and Robert Wright.[102] William Naunton and Walter Wadlond perhaps entered Suffolk's service through their links with Lord Monteagle and Sir Arthur Hopton.[103] Estates passed between ducal followers: in 1536 Naunton sold to William Ellenger, Lord Powis to Robert Wingfield.[104] Such links were closest in the household. When Syrres Gwynello, a French servant of the duke in 1524, died in Southwark in 1534, the witnesses to his will included Thomas Holmes and John Shotter, both Suffolk's servants; Gwynello had left his brooch with gentleman of the household Thomas Huntley and some money with the ducal embroiderer William Ibgrave.[105] The duke apparently tried to encourage such identity of interest by rather indiscriminate distribution of his 13s 4d livery coats.[106]

This drawing together was not necessarily the product of conflict. As Brandon's power matured his affinity was probably bound to become more cohesive – the retinue of a new magnate, like that of Lord Hastings two generations earlier, was often amorphous and internally troubled until it stabilised under the lord's leadership, though such problems may have been eased for Suffolk by the recruitment of so many of his relations.[107] Yet the duke could not or would not promote such homogeneity by consistently settling differences among his followers. He apparently did nothing about the renewed dispute between Francis Framlingham, son of Sir James, and his increasingly active administrator Robert Browne, who was backed by other ducal officers.[108] Even when cohesion was evident, it was by no means always the product of ducal discipline or encouragement. The geographical distribution of those Brandon recruited inevitably produced other links between them which might explain their co-operation: Robert Derhaugh acted as feoffee to Humphrey Wingfield, but both were involved with the town of Ipswich.[109] Some bonds, however, like that between Francis Hall and Thomas Holmes, were surely forged in Suffolk's service, and it was these in particular that made the ducal connection an identifiable body for those within and without.[110]

Complete exclusivity was never attained, especially among the knights and esquires of the affinity. At the funeral of the French queen on 21 July 1533, Brandon's cousin Sir Francis Lovell carried the coffin, and in February 1534 he became chief steward of the ducal estates in Norfolk, but his feoffees in 1532 were led by the earl of Sussex and included no close associates of the duke.[111] Such total exclusivity had not marked many affinities of the previous century and a half, nor was it always desirable: Walter Wadlond's auditorships for the earl of Northumberland and three religious houses increased his income and standing without threatening his loyalty to Suffolk.[112] Any affinity consisted of a core of household servants and administrators, and concentric circles of followers of decreasingly strict loyalty, ending in the vaguest of well-wishers. Indeed, in counties like Norfolk and Suffolk, where the gentry were comparatively numerous, rich, and apparently either active or inactive at will in local and central government, goodwill might often be all a peer could expect.[113] None the less, the ducal affinity arrayed at the French queen's funeral gave cause for concern, for mutual trust and co-operation could avail little if the lord and his men were not strong enough to defend one another's interests, especially at a time when Suffolk's difficulties at court made it harder for him to deploy influence there to counter that of rivals in the country.

At the heart of the funeral ceremonies was the household. Suffolk's servants were loyal: of the four gentlemen ushers who sat on the carriage with the coffin, Nicholas Slyfield and John Egerton served him for over twenty years, Denis Lowe for more than ten.[114] But the leading household officers were often ducal relatives by blood or marriage – Lord Powis was chamberlain,

John Wingfield master of the horse – and the same was true of the young gentlemen of the household who carried the coffin at Westhorpe – Christopher and Edward Glemham, Edward Grimston and William Naunton.[115] The leading mourners, after the duke's children and the ladies Willoughby, were the wives and widows of the duke's most prominent followers, again often relatives after nearly twenty years as an East Anglian magnate. Knights from the affinity took prominent parts in the ceremonial: Sir Anthony Wingfield, Sir Christopher Heydon, Sir Thomas Tyrrell, Sir Arthur Hopton, and Sir Humphrey Wingfield.[116] So did former members of the household: Sir Thomas Wentworth of West Bretton and Lord Edward Grey.[117] But so too did many local notables more closely aligned with other peers, or whose interests clashed violently with those of the duke. Excluding the ducal sons-in-law there were twenty-two knights and a peer present, but few were more than the loosest of well-wishers. At her funeral East Anglia paid its last respects to the French queen, respects rarely extended to her husband; and even so the turn-out was paltry compared with the 900 lords, knights, and gentry who had followed the old duke of Norfolk to the grave in 1524.[118]

The prestige of the ducal household was bound to decline at Mary's death, for Suffolk would not be served again by henchmen like the son of the Marquis of Exeter.[119] Yet Brandon managed to keep up a good establishment: in 1535, for example, he still had six choirboys to sing spiritual and profane music.[120] The affections of the monks at Butley concentrated on the dead queen rather than on the living duke, yet he still managed to secure free bed and board for his choir at the priory from November 1534 to July 1535.[121] The death of Mary was a political as well as a personal bereavement, but all was not lost.

The Ducal Family

Unfortunately Suffolk derived only minimal consolation from the marriages of his daughters. He bound himself closer to his existing sons-in-law, voting for Lord Powis in Garter elections, serving as his feoffee, and seeing Powis and Monteagle enfeoffed in the jointure of his daughter Eleanor in 1535. But Powis may already have been at loggerheads with his wife, and Monteagle's fecklessness forced the duke to intervene in his financial affairs by 1533, if not as early as 1531.[122] In March 1533 Monteagle gave over £250 worth of his estates to Suffolk and four ducal servants, to be used to pay off the young lord's debts. These totalled £1,452 17s 9d, almost half owed to the duke and the rest to thirty-one creditors, from the king, through the king's shoemaker, two drapers, an embroiderer, and a goldsmith, to 'the goodman of the Bor[es] Hede at Westm[inster]'. Fifteen days after this agreement Monteagle still could not cope; he borrowed £300 from Suffolk, who took charge of his entire income and provided an allowance to support Monteagle and Lady Mary, but in July he needed to offer another bond to the duke for his compliance.[123]

In September 1534 Suffolk attempted a long-term settlement, returning Monteagle's income on three conditions. His debts were to be paid in regular instalments, and if he defaulted the duke would take back the £250 of lands to his own use. Financial sobriety was imposed on Monteagle: he and Suffolk signed a book prescribing his household expenditure, and he promised not to leave this budget without the assent of the duke and the baron's own councillors. Marital propriety was also dictated. Monteagle promised that he would 'from henceforth fro tyme to tyme hono[ur]ably handle & entrete the seyd Lady Mary, as a noble man ought to do his weyff, onles there be a gret default in the seid Lady Mari'.[124] Monteagle was bound in £2,000 to keep these arrangements. Nine days later, Suffolk's paternal affection overcame his strictness. He gave to Monteagle, Mary, and Monteagle's heirs, 'of hys mere goodnesse' jewels worth £523 19s 9d, rings, necklaces, partlets, and an 'egg' studded with ninety large pearls and fourteen diamonds.[125]

Monteagle's financial demands perhaps restricted Suffolk's attempts to find husbands for his more eligible daughters by the French queen, Frances and Eleanor. In 1530 Norfolk turned down Frances as a match for Henry, Earl of Surrey, because her dowry was too small.[126] Fortunately an alternative soon presented itself. Thomas, Marquis of Dorset, died in October 1530, leaving both Suffolk and the earl of Arundel as feoffees to his wife.[127] It was Arundel who had succeeded in arranging a double marriage alliance with Dorset's son and daughter, and obtaining the son's wardship to enable this. But young Dorset refused Arundel's daughter, and the earl withdrew his bid for the wardship. Suffolk stepped in, secured the approval of the dowager marchioness and the king, produced the first instalment of the 4,000 marks price, and was duly granted the wardship.[128] Then the French queen's death constricted ducal finances, and in late 1533 Brandon reneged on his agreement to support the young marquis at court until his majority. After a barrage of appeals to Cromwell and some sly sniping by her lawyers, the dowager forced surrender on Suffolk: he was left to support Marquis Henry and Frances for another four and a half years.[129]

Only the duke's youngest daughter was married without major complications. By 1530 the earl of Cumberland had strained his finances to arrange an impressive match for his heir with Eleanor Brandon, the king's niece.[130] Royal approval was given before Easter 1535, final indentures sealed in May, the marriage celebrated in the king's presence in June, and the conditions confirmed in parliament in February 1536.[131] The marriage contract provided for a reduction in the dowry payable to the Cliffords should Eleanor inherit part of Brandon's estates at his death; in 1535 this was all too real a possibility, for in March 1534 the duke had lost his only son, Henry, Earl of Lincoln.

The Willoughby Marriage

Lincoln was ten at his mother's death in June 1533, while Catherine Willoughby, his intended bride, was fourteen.[132] The young earl was probably sickly, for his elder brother had died young and he himself would be dead within nine months of his mother.[133] Suffolk took no chances, and married Catherine himself in September 1533. This intensified his interest in the defeat of her uncle Sir Christopher in the dispute over her father's lands. Sir Christopher tried to avoid confronting Suffolk, with whom he had long-standing links. He took part in the French queen's funeral, and concentrated his legal attacks on Lady Mary Willoughby and her vulnerable mistress, Catherine of Aragon.[134] But Suffolk could not be avoided. As a councillor he sat on the case in Star Chamber, and as a feoffee on Lady Mary's jointure he sued Sir Christopher and his brother George on her behalf.[135] As Sir Christopher pointed out, Lady Catherine was too young to initiate legal action, and petitions in her name were inspired by her guardian.[136] When the Master of the Wards went to law in her defence, his attorney was Humphrey Wingfield, who also acted both for Lady Catherine and for the feoffees to Lord William's will.[137] Lady Mary herself demonstrated her collusion with Suffolk when insisting that it was the royal council, not she alone, that prevented, with a writ of *supersedeas*, Sir Christopher's efforts to have inquisitions held on Lord William's estates. She asserted triumphantly that 'she wilbe reported by my lorde of Suff[olk] whither the said sup[er]sedeas were obteyned by the king[es] counsaill or not.'[138]

Sir Thomas More's three chancery decrees on the case all recognised the need to abandon Lord William's impossible will, and balance Lady Mary's large jointure of 1516 against Lord William's promise that 300 marks of his inheritance would pass in the male line to Sir Christopher.[139] Though these settlements were replaced by another, concluded between Suffolk and Sir Christopher in spring 1536 'by medyac[i]on of the kyng[es] highnes', after unseemly bickering between them in the royal presence, More's principles remained.[140] Sir Christopher never won the further 400 marks of income he claimed, but he himself admitted that he had a right to this only if Lord William had no heir of either sex.[141] Sir Christopher's son had to wait for Lady Mary's death for some manors, but 1536 concentrated the junior line's Lincolnshire holdings by the exchange of Fulstow Beck and Fulstow Arseck for Cockerington, Ingoldmells, and Fulletby.[142] Suffolk had fought hard to protect his new estates, but by no means unfairly. Sir Christopher's grandson, born in 1536 or 1537, was named Charles, perhaps in token of the Willoughbys' reconciliation to the Duke.[143]

Oxfordshire, Berkshire, and Southwark

Meanwhile Brandon's local power was healthier in Oxfordshire and Berkshire than in East Anglia. At Oxford he headed commissions of gaol delivery, while at Norwich and Ipswich he was named after Norfolk. In the diocese of Norwich he held scarcely any ecclesiastical estate offices, but in Oxfordshire he was named in 1529 constable and steward of the castle and town of Banbury and other manors in that hundred, in survivorship with the earl of Lincoln.[144] Abingdon Abbey, leading knights like Sir Adrian Fortescue, and the struggling Cardinal's College, Oxford, all paid court to the duke and his servants, doing so more easily because he spent increasing amounts of time at Ewelme.[145] In the early 1530s Suffolk was invited to settle disputes among the gentry of western Buckinghamshire, and between the Oxfordshire gentry and the abbot of Bruern.[146] In November 1530 he bought from Sir Nicholas Carew for £400 in cash the constableship of Wallingford Castle and the stewardship of Wallingford. This carried a £50 fee and the chance to secure a link with another local knight by appointing him deputy: Suffolk chose Sir Walter Stonor.[147] Ducal servants in the area were also rising to prominence. In 1531 Thomas Carter joined the Oxfordshire commission of the peace. He had been Suffolk's receiver and surveyor in the area since at least 1522, as well as clerk of the ducal kitchen.[148] In 1534 and 1535 the duke leased two local manors to him, including the repaired manor house at Swyncombe where he settled.[149] In 1533 and 1534 he appeared on the sheriff roll, in 1535 served on the commission for spiritual tenths, and in 1535–6 was sheriff of Oxfordshire and Berkshire.[150]

Suffolk's dominance in Southwark was still remarkable. In 1530 even Wolsey's bailiff there was a ducal servant, and in 1534 or so Cromwell's parliamentary lists gave Suffolk the patronage of the borough.[151] The ducal household servant John Shotter married a local girl and settled in Southwark, farming the rectory of St George's for Brandon's chaplain Christopher Lynham; in 1542 Shotter was working closely with Thomas Holmes, the duke's secretary, who was by then in charge of the king's bench prison as Suffolk's deputy.[152] In London itself the duke had less influence, as a chaplain of the French queen discovered, when he could not be released from prison because he 'was a stranger & cold fynd no fre men of the seyd cyte to be suarte for him.'[153] But a baker of St Martin's, Ironmongers Lane, 's[er]vyd the said same Charles [Suffolk] w[ith] bread and was a reteyn[er] to hym', and John Watson, elected into the livery of the mercers' company in 1528, described Suffolk as his master in 1535, presumably saving entered Brandon's orbit through his links with Francis Hall.[154]

In neither Southwark nor the south Midlands was Suffolk's domination long to continue. The French queen's death in June 1533 necessitated a financial settlement between the duke and the crown, and Henry enforced an exchange of lands, probably having taken a liking to Ewelme on his visits there. Cromwell researched Brandon's previous financial arrangements and set Brian Tuke to work to analyse the ducal debt. By summer 1535 it was agreed to cancel Mary's liabilities, leaving £6,722 3s 7d for Suffolk to pay, including £2,666 13s 4d for the Willoughby and Dorset wardships.[155] The duke handed over a large number of jewels, hoping they would be reckoned sufficient to cancel this sum, but they were valued at only £4,361, so the exchange had to proceed.

In the ensuing negotiations Henry, working through Cromwell and Richard Rich, struck a very hard bargain.[156] The basic exchange was harsh enough. Suffolk surrendered all his Oxfordshire and Berkshire estates, the Wallingford stewardship, and the reversion of Suffolk Place after his death, for various ex-Percy manors at the southern end of the Lincolnshire wolds. He lost lands valued at £487 16s 4d a year in exchange for £175 8s 2d in income, £2,333 6s 8d in cash, and a pardon for his debts. But the royal agents demanded more: Sayes Court in Kent and, worse still, the reversion to the new palace at Westhorpe and the nearby manor of Wyverstone. Suffolk gave way, accepting in return a Percy manor in Essex, a handful of reversions on De la Pole estates, a further £849 3s 4d in cash and the promise of new letters patent, granting to the duke's heirs by any marriage the Stafford manors given to Suffolk and the French queen in 1523. He extracted one concession, the confirmation of various leases to his local followers on the estates he was to lose, including one made on 28 May to Thomas Carter for a term of forty years to begin in 1543.[157] On these terms indentures were sealed on 19 July, but when Henry heard of the arrangement he 'mervelyd gretely' and sent Rich back to demand that Suffolk cancel the leases, return the De la Pole reversions and justify his claim to have spent large amounts on building repairs.[158]

The duke fought hard to defend the settlement, to keep the entry fines on the leases, and to demonstrate that he had spent £1,000 on Ewelme Castle and £1,500 on a hunting lodge at Hook Norton. He promised that eighty red deer would be left at Hook Norton and offered to give up the De la Pole reversions in exchange for Sir Thomas More's house in Chelsea. Henry was undeterred: he thought the last-minute leasing a sign of 'som ingratitude and unkyndenes', he had seen Ewelme and Hook Norton and knew their condition, and had heard that Edward Fetiplace had wasted the woods and game at Donnington. Suffolk had used the ploy which repeatedly rescued him from Henry's anger, protesting that he would submit entirely to the king's gracious pleasure, since 'youre highnez only under God have brought hym to his estate.' Henry did not reply with his usual bluff magnanimity; instead he exploited Suffolk's submission, arguing that the duke should therefore 'frankly and frely' return the De la Pole reversions, 'w[ith]out looking for other recompence then shall please the king[es] highnes of his mere lyberalite to extende toward[es] him.' He even warned Suffolk, who had received such 'manyfold benefit[es]', not to cause his master 'to conceyve any jalousie or mistrust in him.' Cromwell, Rich, and even Thomas Carter pressed Suffolk for a generous surrender, so that the king 'may thereby p[er]ceyve the said duk[es] gentill herte and naturall zele toward[es] his majeste'.[159]

It was to a strangely hostile king that Suffolk capitulated in late November. Suffolk Place, Sayes Court, Westhorpe, and Wyverstone were transferred to royal feoffees, and the De la Pole reversions and even the Percy manor of Quendon in Essex handed back.[160] Only then did Suffolk secure the Lincolnshire lands, the regrant of Buckingham's manors, and a pardon to himself and his sureties for his own debts and those of the French queen.[161] The final indignity was that Henry demanded Suffolk Place immediately, and by mid-December the duke's servants were moving his goods to the London palace recently surrendered by the Bishop of Norwich.[162]

The settlement negated years of patient construction, both of houses and of local influence. Several candidates immediately asked the duke to give up the stewardship of Banbury, and in October it was regranted to Suffolk and Henry Norris in survivorship, passing to Cromwell at Norris's fall.[163] More worrying still was Brandon's failure to deter Henry, a clear demonstration that he had temporarily lost the unique position in the king's friendship which had enabled him to survive such crises in the past. From the early 1530s onwards several of Henry's noble subjects were pushed into damaging exchanges of lands with the king, but it must have been intensely depressing to the duke to be treated just like any other peer.[164] The events of 1535 made clear not only the reduced wealth and status enjoyed by Suffolk after the French queen's death, but also the difficulty of his position in an England dominated by Anne Boleyn, Thomas Cromwell, and an increasingly irascible and dictatorial king.

Finances

It was time to take stock, and Suffolk did so. Early in 1535 he carefully examined the state of his finances, working from a book compiled by 'hold Fransses Hall and me' to make up in his own hand lists of creditors and debtors. He owed £2,415 13*s* 4*d* to a wide range of creditors, including six months' rent to Norfolk under the 1516 lease, £370 to a draper called Holt, and £100 towards the drainage of the Plumstead marshes (as lord of Sayes Court).[165] Others owed him £2,210: £1,200 from Lord Monteagle would be paid eventually, because 'I hef land bond to af yerlle cc markys, to the holl sum be payed.' Lancelot Lowther, a deputy to the duke in the Welsh Marches, still owed Suffolk £200, but again land had been recovered to pay £20 a year of this.[166] The other debts were all of about £100, from courtiers – Sir Francis Bryan, Lord Berners – or ducal followers – Sir Anthony Wingfield, Sir Humphrey Wingfield, Sir Arthur Hopton, Richard Cavendish, and

Edward Fetiplace. At the same time the duke reviewed his income, concluding: 'the holl som [that] I Charlles ducke of Suffolke may dyspeynd de clarrow by exstemasseun m^{1}m^{1}v^c li. with me pynsseun howth of France'.[167]

For the 1534 subsidy he was assessed on a clear income of £2,000, and paid promptly.[168] Some of his other debts were less readily discharged, notably the interest on a £2,000 loan from a German merchant at Antwerp due for repayment in 1531; though the capital was apparently returned, the duke and Francis Hall, who had acted as his agent, were still being pursued for the interest in October 1532.[169] But the duke could find sufficient cash to expand his estates by occasional purchases. Late in 1529 he bought a house in Lynn and the hundred of Freebridge, Norfolk, from the Marquis of Dorset.[170] In April 1534 he spent £220 on expanding his estate at Henham, and later in the same year he gained his first taste of monastic spoils when the Prior of Mendham, of which the De la Poles had been patrons, transferred his house's estates to ducal feoffees.[171] He would sell outlying manors when others wished to consolidate their estates, taking £800 from Sir Nicholas Carew in May 1530 for the De la Pole manor of Ravensbury in Surrey.[172] Quite how efficiently Suffolk exploited his estates is hard to judge, but he seems to have been a successful landlord. The fifteen years from 1523 to 1538 saw an average rise of 12 per cent in his income from East Anglian manors, similar to the increase in the revenues of the vigorous Bishop Nix, rather than to the level takings of the lax Percies in the same period.[173] Crown surveyors managed to raise the income from some of the lands transferred in 1535, but they also seem to have provoked opposition.[174] The duke certainly sought to profit from his feudal rights. In 1531 he raised an aid from the honour of Eye for the marriage of his eldest daughter. This brought in only £1 11s 6d, but manumissions were more lucrative, at £20 each; Suffolk freed one bondman in 1522–3 and two bond families in 1536.[175] He also enforced his rights over those who were still villeins, inserting his own farmers, even into copyhold lands held of other lords, at the death of his bond tenants.[176]

Like his income, Suffolk's movable wealth was reduced after

1533. In 1534–5 he gave away jewels worth nearly £5,000. In 1533 he had used jewels to secure a loan of £700.[177] Yet even after 1535 his goods were of great value: when Suffolk Place was cleared in December the plate alone was worth £1,475.[178] Both his capital and his income remained substantial, but the change in the sources of that income affected his career in two ways. Lincolnshire, rather than the south Midlands, became for the next few years his secondary area of landed power; and the loss of his wife's rents transformed his relationship with France.

France, the Emperor, and Christendom

Before Mary's death, her income was still used to finance English agents in France, and refunded in sterling. Her officers were active at the French court, George Hampton selling 'trois grandes pieces de diamans' to Francis I for some £6,800.[179] An increase in the rate of payment of the wartime arrears was promised, after prolonged badgering of successive French ambassadors and Montmorency himself, but never took effect.[180] Though Suffolk counted Montmorency 'le plus grant amy que aye de pardela', and Jean de la Barre still interested himself in Mary's affairs, the duke's petitions for Antoine du Val fell on deaf ears.[181] On the other hand, French envoys in 1531 and 1533 spent much time dealing with Suffolk and Mary, and Hampton was regularly in France, where he kept in contact with Thomas Wynter, and made himself of assistance to Cromwell.[182]

The French queen's death on 25 June 1533 destroyed this network of useful, if limited, contacts. On 7 July Francis sequestrated her revenues, and his auditors began to calculate the sums outstanding to Suffolk.[183] It was said at court that Henry diverted to the duke the revenues of the vacant see of Ely to pay for Mary's funeral and, perhaps, to compensate temporarily for the loss of the French income.[184] Brandon was determined to extract his due from the French. He cultivated Montmorency, and secured first the recommencement of the arrears payments, and then in December the release of Mary's last half-year's revenue.[185] As the mine of French income neared exhaustion, extraction became harder: by September

1535 the arrears payments were four months overdue, and the death of Hampton late in 1534 forced Suffolk to use his French secretary Nicolas de St Martin as an envoy. The duke became increasingly reliant on English ambassadors, first Sir John Wallop, then Bishop Stephen Gardiner, to secure him 'a fenneall yend' in France.[186]

In particular he wanted 'noo fardar bessenes in the lawe'. He inherited from George Hampton a suit over Hampton's imprisonment in 1522, and despite verdicts in several courts and petitions to Francis and the chancellor, could not have judgement executed.[187] By 1537 the outstanding arrears on the dower lands totalled only 8,000 or 9,000 *livres tournois*, and Suffolk was hopeful that these would soon be paid.[188] But Hampton's lawsuit dragged on, as did another at Bordeaux against the executors of Martin Dupin. Suffolk went to considerable lengths to settle these cases. To authenticate an obligation of 1513–14 in the Dupin suit, Suffolk had to send William Fellowe to Boulogne in October 1535 with a certificate from five heralds proving that in 1513—14 he had been Viscount Lisle, and ask the current Viscount Lisle to send gentlemen over from Calais to testify to this effect.[189] All this effort was in vain, as both suits continued, and at least one was still running in June 1547.[190]

Such frustrations urged Suffolk to reassess his commitment to the French, as of course did the removal of his financial incentives to Anglo-French amity. The role of the Boulogne conference of October 1532, to exalt Anne Boleyn and ease her route to the throne, made the occasion distasteful to the duke's wife, who pointedly did not attend. Suffolk was said to have opposed the meeting in council, incurring royal obloquy, and when he took ship in Suffolk, avoiding the shipping shortage, Chapuys thought he was avoiding the conference.[191] Though he played his part in the meeting dutifully, he had not been involved in planning it. Afterwards Francis rewarded him with plate worth less than two-thirds of that given to Norfolk, and Norfolk's pension was raised to 3,000 crowns, Suffolk's to only 1,500 (nearly £320 sterling).[192] For a time Suffolk played second string to Norfolk in promoting the French interest, but Anne Boleyn's links with France discouraged Brandon's efforts, and by 1536 Chapuys detected a clear move on the duke's part towards Charles V.[193]

This was an easier stance to take after the death of Catherine of Aragon in January of that year, and Cromwell and others, even Anne Boleyn, were ready to stress the importance of Anglo-imperial friendship.[194] But Suffolk had special motives. One was an eagerness to invade France again, if necessary commanding English auxiliaries for Charles V, as he offered to do several times.[195] The other was an apparently genuine indignation at the French betrayal of Christendom through alliance with the Turk. Other councillors vaguely promised English help for Charles's crusading ventures, but Suffolk was more vehement and more consistent.[196] In July 1536 he quoted the Emperor Maximilian to the effect that there was no greater Turk than the king of France; in June his animosity towards France stemmed explicitly from the Franco-Turkish understanding. These remarks were part of Suffolk's enthusiastic response to Charles's search for support in England.[197] But as early as September 1533, when Henry was courting Francis and even the German Protestants, Suffolk spoke out over dinner with Chapuys and Norfolk, Audley, and other councillors. During a discussion of Barbarossa's Mediterranean raids, the duke praised Charles for doing his duty, and more, to defend Christendom against the infidel, and detected divine judgement on France and England for their inactivity.[198] A zeal for the crusade could easily have coincided with Brandon's other chivalrous preoccupations; its rhetoric, at least, was an important element in his move from France to the emperor.

That move was part of a general recovery in Suffolk's career in the summer of 1536. On 18 September 1535 one of his anxieties had been relieved by the birth of a son, again named Henry, to whom the king and Cromwell graciously acted as godfathers.[199] In spring 1536 he was quick to sue for a share in the lesser monasteries, and was apparently well received.[200] Above all, the fall of Anne Boleyn in May brought Suffolk both tangible and intangible benefits. Three De la Pole manors in her jointure reverted to him, adding over £100 to his income.[201] At a time of insecurity great enough for Norfolk to hear a rumour that he was himself in the Tower, the king relied more heavily on his old friends. In June and July 1536 Suffolk sat regularly in council, and was prominent in the opening of parliament and the multiple aristocratic marriage ceremony of 3 July. His parliamentary attendance was more regular than in 1534, and his bill to secure the duchess's jointure passed with ease.[202]

Other changes augured well for the future. In June William Rugge became Bishop of Norwich: he had preached at the French queen's burial, his brother was married to the daughter of a Brandon officer, and he was soon granting generous leases to Suffolk's servants.[203] Potentially even more important were Suffolk's links with the Seymours. He had knighted Edward in 1523, had some financial dealings with him in the early 1530s, and granted him a £10 annuity in March 1533. In December 1536 and April 1537 Suffolk and Edward Seymour gambled together, and in March 1537 they dined at Beauchamp Place.[204] Brandon could certainly expect better treatment from the Seymours than he had received from the Boleyns. By autumn 1536 he was emerging from yet another of the crises which afflicted his career, less spectacular and less alarming than those of 1515, 1518, or 1523, but longer and more frustrating. Yet his role in government was far from assured, his power in East Anglia was questionable, and he had not even begun to establish himself in his new wife's inheritance in Lincolnshire.

5

The Move to Lincolnshire: 1536–1540

The revolt of October 1536 transformed the duke of Suffolk's relationship with Lincolnshire. Before it his interest in the county was minimal; soon after it he was a frequently resident magnate with more power than he had ever enjoyed in East Anglia. Since 1516 he had leased two former De la Pole manors in Lincolnshire, and at some time between 1523 and 1533 he secured a third.[1] In 1535 he added the former Percy estates in the county from his exchange with the crown, but the De la Pole and Percy lands were widely separated, and they produced together only £200 or so, less than the Oxfordshire income the duke had lost.[2] Over his wife's inheritance Suffolk exercised no control. Lady Mary Willoughby kept firmly in hand not only her jointure, but also the lands held to the use of Lord William's will, and her officers ran both sets of estates and sometimes confused them.[3] Performing the will and paying £100 a year to the crown can have allowed Lady Mary to contribute little to Catherine's support, but at least she tried to manage the lands well. The disruption caused by the dispute with Sir Christopher made this hard, but the dowager realised that her revenues 'stonde muche by fermes', and was enterprising enough to be among the first lessees of dissolved Lincolnshire monasteries.[4] Indeed, she was probably too efficient a landlady for her own good, as she and her officials discovered during the rising.[5]

The Lincolnshire Rising

So it was not as an established Lincolnshire magnate, but as a 'great inherito[ur] in those p[ar]ties' that Brandon was sent to deal with the revolt.[6] Like other peers who were called on to raise troops against the 1536 risings, he must have been delighted at the scope of the commission given him as the king's lieutenant: it provided for him alone to lead all East Anglia to war, forced Norfolk to beg to serve under him, and gave him full authority to stamp his power on the area which would become his home. None the less, he acted carefully, meeting Norfolk and the Earl of Oxford in northern Essex to discuss the mobilisation of their men, while Sir Anthony Wingfield, Sir Arthur Hopton, Sir Francis Lovell, and Sir Thomas Tyrrell assembled the ducal tenantry.[7] Then, on 8 October, four days after the king first heard of the outbreak, increasingly alarming news of its progress brought a new urgency. Suffolk set off without his troops, reaching Huntingdon next morning with his riding household of two dozen servants.[8]

Brandon travelled fast, and followed the king's instructions assiduously. When the gentry among the rebels requested a pardon, Henry demanded dispersal and total surrender, and threatened destruction; the duke reinforced this with a letter stressing 'the greate slaughter that ys like by stroke of sworde whiche ys p[re]payrede shortly to ensue among[es] you.'[9] In these first contacts with the rebels Suffolk already had an eye to cultivating friends among the gentlemen, warning that he would have to attack them if they advanced, 'whiche I wold not gladly do, if the occasyon thereof shuld not ryse & procede of yo[ur] self[es]'.[10] These carrot-and-stick tactics betrayed too that Brandon was anxious to buy time. The loyal John Harrington was finding as much difficulty as the dithering Lord Hussey in raising troops in southern Holland, and even around Peterborough; only 150 men from Holland ever joined the duke. Even the common people around Huntingdon were 'evyll willing to come out' for a commander without arms, armour, or money save his own.[11] Worst of all, at Huntingdon Suffolk heard that his own retinue had been ordered by the king to stay in East Anglia: 500 ducal tenants led by Tyrrell and Sir John

Glemham, and half that number raised by Hopton, Lovell, and Wingfield from their own estates. He begged for, and obtained, the reversal of this decision. If he had to fight, he would need not only supplies but also 'some of myn own frynd[es] and s[er]v[au]nt[es] to s[er]ve yo[ur] grace at this tyme'.[12]

Fortunately the rebels did not force the issue. By next evening Suffolk had joined Sir John Russell and Sir William Parr at Stamford, the king's vulnerable forward base, and they had been reinforced by Sir Francis Bryan, Richard Cromwell, and Sir William Fitzwilliam with the first contingents from the grand royal musters at Ampthill.[13] In the next few days morale, numbers, and resources rose, and with them Suffolk's aggression, just as in 1525. But by the time he had 3,000 fighting men (including his own retinue), nearly £5,000 in cash, and sixteen cannon, there was no enemy left to fight.[14] The earl of Shrewsbury, himself at Nottingham and with troops at Newark, was well placed to exploit divisions among the rebels exposed by the intransigence of Henry and the duke; on his own initiative he sent a herald to Lincoln to order their dispersal. The disheartened Commons scattered and the relieved gentlemen agreed to ride to Stamford and submit.[15]

Suffolk did not begrudge Shrewsbury's role, and sent on to him almost half the money arriving from London.[16] But Henry was not so gracious. Astonished that his army should wait for five days, some 40 miles from the rebels, when a mere proclamation sufficed to disband them, he upbraided his commanders at Stamford for fearing their own shadows.[17] Perhaps Henry read the rising as a 'regional demonstration' which presented no real military threat,[18] but his earlier panic does not suggest so. Nor could Brandon afford to take such a view. In Suffolk there were rumours of his defeat, and his troops expected to have to fight. In London the rebels were expected to march south, and several groups of insurgents indeed planned to move to Ancaster on 8 or 9 October.[19] The gentlemen had claimed on 10 October to be doing as much as they dared to hinder the revolt, by persuading the Commons to halt at Lincoln. Whether he believed them or not, Suffolk could not deny their claim that 'if we had not stayed them there by good policy ... they had bin this present day at Huntingdon.'[20] On 10 October the duke would have been quite unable to repel them.

The gentlemen, anxious to excuse their implication in the rebellion, painted for Suffolk a picture of the common rebels as an irresistibly mutinous mob, and this made him cautious as he planned his advance. He contemplated sacking Louth and Horncastle, and the gentry offered their help in such reprisals, but instead he resolved to join Shrewsbury and occupy Lincoln.[21] Shrewsbury's shortage of cash, and concern about the burgeoning Yorkshire revolt, prevented this junction, but the hostile reaction to Suffolk's advance guard when it did enter Lincoln, late on 16 October, vindicated the duke's precautions.[22] Next morning he set about fulfilling the king's very specific instructions for dealing with the county. Louth, Horncastle, and Caistor, the first centres of revolt, were not to be pillaged, but fresh outbreaks were to be punished brutally. By careful interrogation of gentlemen and others, the origins of the rebellion were to be investigated and the guilty parties detained. A garrison was to be established in the cathedral close, perhaps permanently, but military assistance should be made available to the commanders further north. Suffolk was to co-operate with Shrewsbury, and consult with Fitzwilliam, Russell, Bryan, and Parr; Richard Cromwell was circumspectly co-opted onto this council.[23]

The duke's task was complicated by the inconsistencies of these instructions. A few circumstances favoured him: popular rumour depicted a very abject surrender by the rebels, and gentlemen under suspicion like Edward Dymoke the sheriff were understandably eager to please, handing over leading agitators even before the occupation of Lincoln.[24] But there was little spoil to distribute, and financial provision for November, when the initial large deliveries of cash would run out, was a worry. Suffolk had persuaded Henry to pay 8*d* rather than 6*d* a day, but with 4,000 men by early November daily charges of nearly £150 were hard to justify.[25] Shrewsbury needed whatever cavalry Suffolk could spare for his march north from Newark, and Norfolk grumbled when horsemen were sent to Lincoln, hinting that 'men wold have them more for

1. Double portrait of Mary and Charles Brandon, by an unknown artist. Brandon's marriage to the king's sister, dowager queen of France, crowned his rise to power but shocked contemporaries. It gave their children a claim to the throne but compromised his position in Anglo-French relations.

Left: 2. Henry VII, from *Pictures and Royal Portraits illustrative of English and Scottish History*, 1878. Brandon's uncle's service to Henry VII at court and in war built the foundations for his own career. *Right:* 3. Richard III, portrait from 1641. Brandon's grandfather, father and uncles gambled their lives and careers to join the revolts of 1483–5 against Richard III's usurpation.

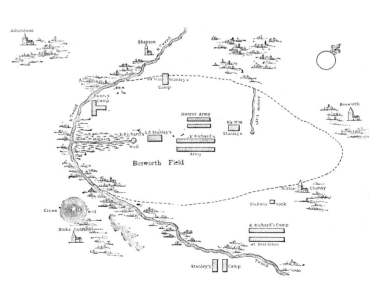

4. Conjectural plan of the battle of Bosworth, from *British Battles on Land and Sea*, 1882–87. Brandon's father William, standard-bearer to Henry Tudor, was killed by Richard III in his final desperate charge.

Above: 5. Bosworth Field today.

Below: 6. The Bosworth Field memorial.

7. Charles Brandon late in life by an unknown artist, perhaps after Holbein, *c.* 1540–45. His heavily furred gown and richly embroidered jacket were signs of wealth, but his collar of the Order of the Garter was the ultimate badge of honour at Henry VIII's court.

Left: 8. Henry VIII by an unknown artist, *c.* 1520. In his prime the king was handsome and physically powerful but at times, as this portrait perhaps hints, insecure.

Right: 9. Jousting in replica armour. The reinforcing armour plate across the shoulder and chest is a reminder of the massive force with which a well-aimed lance strikes the jouster's body.

10. Henry VIII jousting at the tournament to celebrate the birth of a prince, February 1511. It was at this tournament that Henry and Brandon fought one of their most dashing combats.

Above left: 11. Thomas Howard, duke of Norfolk, print after the portrait by Hans Holbein, 1624–30. Norfolk's relations with Brandon at court and in East Anglia were never easy, though Norfolk claimed he always called him 'cousin Charles'. *Above right:* 12. Bishop Stephen Gardiner, portrait print by Pieter van Gunst. Gardiner was one of the pricklier politicians at Henry's court, but Brandon managed to work with him and Gardiner shared in taking the duke's funeral service. *Below:* 13. An imaginative depiction of Cardinal Wolsey learning of his dismissal as lord chancellor and the king's chief minister.

Above left: 14. St Michael Cornhill. This was the church where Brandon publicly married Anne Browne in an effort to tidy up his messy early marital history. *Above right*: 15. Tattershall Castle. Tattershall, built by Henry VI's lord treasurer Ralph, Lord Cromwell, was granted to Brandon by Henry in 1537 to form a base for his power in Lincolnshire in the wake of the rebellion there. *Below*: 16. Grimsthorpe Castle. Grimsthorpe was part of the inheritance of Brandon's last wife, Catherine Willoughby, but they greatly extended it to host the king and his court on his progress to Lincolnshire in 1541.

17. Suffolk Place, Southwark, from Anthonis van den Wyngaerde's Panorama of London. With its domed turrets, Suffolk Place dominated the High Street in Southwark and showed Brandon's power in the borough.

18. Henham Hall, Suffolk. Brandon rebuilt the gatehouse to give himself a substantial house in eastern Suffolk as an alternative to Westhorpe in the centre of the county.

19. Terracottas from Suffolk Place, Southwark. Terracotta was a fashionable material associated with the Italian and French Renaissance. Brandon used it both for classical imagery and for heraldic badges, in this case his lion's head with a ducal coronet.

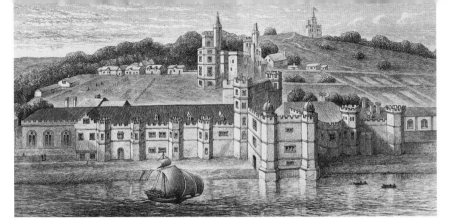

Top: 20. Greenwich Palace from *The Palace and the Hospital; or chronicles of Greenwich*, 1886. It was at Greenwich that Brandon and Mary married before the king and queen in 1515 and from there that he set out to invade France in 1544. *Middle left:* 21. Charles V, king of Spain and Holy Roman Emperor, etched by Jacques Reich, from an engraving by Iovita Guravaglia after the portrait by Niccola Bettoni. Brandon met Charles on the 1513 campaign and again in 1522, when Henry and Charles hunted in his park at Suffolk Place. *Middle right:* 22. Calais, from *The Chronicles of E. De Monstrelet*, translated by T. Johnes, 1840. Brandon passed through Calais on each of his French campaigns and wrote from there begging Henry's mercy after the botched retreat from Boulogne in 1544. *Bottom:* 23. The battle of the spurs, from *The Popular History of England*, 1856. Henry made much of his victories in 1513, commissioning paintings including the one on which this print is based, and promoting Brandon to celebrate his role in them.

Left: 24. Henry VIII by Hans Holbein. In his forties, as he stopped jousting, Henry began to fill out but also became increasingly convinced of his supreme power. *Right:* 25. Map of Westminster showing Whitehall Palace and the sites of the institutions of Henry VIII's government.

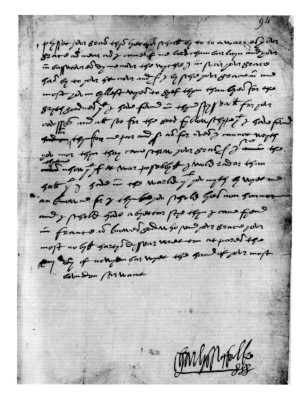

26. Charles Brandon – Henry VIII, Paris, 14 November 1514. Brandon's handwriting was not untypical of noblemen of his generation, but his spelling was always idiosyncratic. Here he wishes the king could be with him incognito ('anknowne') to take part in the French court jousts.

Above left: 27. Perhaps Anne Boleyn, a sketch by Hans Holbein the Younger. Brandon's relations with Anne were bad and while she was queen he found Henry alarmingly distant. *Above right:* 28. Thomas Cromwell, portrait print from 1737–39. Brandon worked well with Cromwell, whose reforms of the royal household gave him the powerful position of great master. *Below:* 29. The coronation procession of Anne Boleyn in front of Westminster Abbey, 1 June 1533. Brandon's enforced surrender of the office of earl marshal before Anne's coronation was a sign of his waning power.

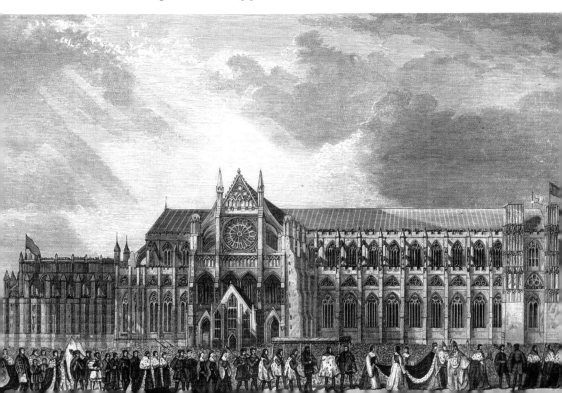

30. Leiston Abbey, Suffolk. One of the dissolved monasteries granted to Brandon and then passed back to the crown in exchange for Lincolnshire lands.

31. Donnington Castle, Berkshire. The fourteenth-century castle was the first of the De la Pole estates granted to Brandon to mark his creation as duke of Suffolk.

D KATH DUCISSA S'UFFOL
VIDUA ÆT: 25 A° D 1554
DEINCEPS UXOR D RICA
BERTIE.

32. Catherine, Lady Willoughby, duchess of Suffolk, 1548, by an unknown artist.
By the time of this portrait, Brandon's widow was trying to bring up his sons amid
the turbulent politics of Edward VI's reign.

Left: 33. Anne of Cleves, portrait by Hans Holbein the Younger, 1539. Brandon and his wife led the party that met Anne on her arrival at Dover.

Below: 34. Windsor Castle. Henry had Brandon buried in St George's Chapel, Windsor, where he himself would be laid to rest.

Above: 35. Sixteenth-century painting by an unknown artist, known as *An Allegory of the Tudor Succession: The Family of Henry VIII.* Brandon's sons would be close to Henry's son Edward VI, while his widow would go into exile for her faith under Philip and Mary and return to be a staunch patron of Protestantism under Elizabeth.

Right: 36. Lady Jane Grey, nineteenth-century portrait in stained glass in the chapel of Sudeley Castle. Lady Jane, briefly recognised as queen in 1553 before a successful challenge by Mary, traced her royal blood to the marriage of her grandparents Charles Brandon and Mary Tudor.

37. Henry
Brandon, later
2nd Duke of
Suffolk, 1541,
miniature by
Hans Holbein
the Younger.
Brandon's son
and heir, named
for the king,
was groomed
to be a great
man in Edward
VI's England,
but survived his
father by less
than six years.

38. Charles
Brandon, later
3rd Duke
of Suffolk,
1541, by
Hans Holbein
the Younger.
Charles died
of the sweating
sickness later
on the same
day as his
elder brother,
a tragic end to
Brandon's hopes
for his sons, all
four of whom
died before
they reached
adulthood.

there glory, thenne for nede.'[26] Henry was generous in reinforcing Suffolk, realizing that troops in Lincolnshire could join in a royal offensive against Yorkshire, or hold the Trent, should Shrewsbury be defeated.[27] But maintaining a large army of occupation was hard to reconcile with avoiding provocation to further revolt. Suffolk's suggestion of a tax on Lincolnshire to pay for its garrison was wisely vetoed.[28] In victualling he was more tactful, forbidding his troops to take food without payment, forestall it on its way to Lincoln, or even buy in the ordinary markets. Instead, farmers from Gainsborough to Louth were to sell at Lincoln to the army, on the promise of 'reasonabylle prises' and redress for injuries on appeal to the duke.[29]

The developing Yorkshire revolt conditioned Suffolk's handling of Lincolnshire. Excessive cruelty could turn sympathy for Yorkshire into a disastrous new rising, but rebellion also had to be deterred by the 'terrible example' of selective executions. The overriding danger of spreading revolt, and Suffolk's awareness of his future interest in the county, combined to make him avoid quick executions and rely on the gentry to deliver rebels and maintain order.[30] Again the king was impatient, urging more hangings and a more suspicious attitude to the local gentlemen, but when the difficulties were explained he stressed his satisfaction with Suffolk's service. He shared his lieutenant's worries that the Lincolnshire rebels were 'attempting as moche as they dare to renovell' their revolt.[31]

This made the pacification and occupation of the north of the county a priority. On 15 October Suffolk had secured the release of the rebels' prisoners at Louth, but their keeper had to promise to return them to the Commons on request. On the 17th it was reported at Lincoln that beacons were burning at Louth. Ten days later, when Fitzwilliam, Russell, and Richard Cromwell entered the town and disarmed the inhabitants, the men of Louth were still 'veray hollowe', though the churchwardens did welcome the king's captains with a fire in the market place.[32] Simultaneously Bryan disarmed Horncastle and Sir Anthony Browne Market Rasen, fulfilling a central point in Henry's instructions.[33] In so doing, Suffolk had been careful not to repeat his mistake of 1525, when over-hasty confiscations of arms precipitated revolt in Suffolk. Now he first received the submissions of individuals and communities, imprisoning or bailing whatever leading rebels they presented: on the 21st Horncastle had sent in Brian Stones, the killer of the bishop's chancellor, Dr Raynes. Next he swore the inhabitants, wapentake by wapentake – 'otherwise called hundred[es]', as the local novice Suffolk pointed out – to an oath of loyalty specially composed by the king.[34] Only then did he order the leaderless and oath-bound rebels to surrender all their weapons. Where no detachment of troops was sent to collect them, each community gathered its arms and armour and sent them to Lincoln: at Hagworthingham their transport cost the churchwardens 4s.[35]

At every point Suffolk requested very specific instructions from Henry, was duly sent them, and kept to them zealously.[36] But in dealing with the Lincolnshire gentry he could not please the king. In part this was because Henry did not know his own mind. He suspected strongly that the gentlemen 'did wynke at this rebellyon', yet he eagerly showed mercy to Sir John Thimbleby, who had joined the revolt, with men raised for the king's service, only two days before its end.[37] Under pressure from the sudden rush of gentry loyalty, Suffolk had sworn ninety-six gentlemen to serve the king even before royal instructions about the oath arrived, while those under the greatest suspicion, like Dymoke the sheriff, were necessary to organise the swearing and disarmament of the county as a whole, especially as Suffolk and his colleagues knew Lincolnshire so little.[38] The duke did oversee the investigation personally, filling Lincoln Castle and four temporary gaols with some 120 prisoners, and sending others out on surety to inquire further.[39] By 21 October detainees were being examined, and with one exception the officials involved were irreproachably strict.[40] But when Henry and Cromwell scrutinised the evidence, only Thomas Moigne could be selected as a gentle victim, and further questioning produced no more.[41] As the investigations spread beyond Lincoln, Suffolk tried to maintain impartiality. He committed the task to his own captains – Sir Anthony Wingfield, Sir Arthur Hopton – gentlemen from other counties – Sir John St

John, William Sharington – or at least local men who avoided the rising, like Edward Sapcote. All too soon, though, leading figures in the rising like Sir William Skipwith and Edward Forsett were taking depositions, and surely enough the process of investigation became a series of accusations by Lincolnshire gentlemen against the Commons, the opposite of what the king wanted.[42]

There were some signs of inefficiency in Suffolk's administration of Lincolnshire, and by November victuals were running short, though that was hardly surprising.[43] Such problems were small compared with the continuing difficulty of combining the settlement of Lincolnshire with opposition to the Yorkshire rebels. Suffolk blocked the routes to Yorkshire on his own initiative by 22 October, but once Norfolk's and Shrewsbury's armies had withdrawn under the Doncaster truce of 27 October, Lincolnshire had to be properly defended.[44] After a period of confusion, it was evident by 16 November that the Yorkshire revolt was not over, and Bryan and Russell examined the Trent fords around Newark where Suffolk had posted them.[45] Meanwhile, plans were made to remove victuals from the rebels' path, and the lower Trent and Humber coast were garrisoned from Gainsborough to Grimsby.[46] By late November, Suffolk's force of 3,600 was arranged in an impressive system of defence. Seven hundred men held Newark, where a new blockhouse and drawbridge were under construction; Suffolk occupied Lincoln, with all the county's weaponry and large stores of corn; every boat on the Trent could be sunk at an hour's warning; and most of the army, including the ducal retinue, was spread in a string of garrisons from Grimsby to Winteringham.[47]

All this may have deterred the northern rebels from invading Lincolnshire. It also had other profound effects on the main events of the Pilgrimage. The Doncaster agreement did not bind Suffolk to disperse his army, but the rebel leaders were quick to accuse him of infringing the truce, and the Yorkshire Commons feared he would invade.[48] Suffolk broke the spirit of the agreement in many ways. He maintained a productive spy network in Yorkshire, using his own and his captains' servants.[49] He encouraged Yorkshire loyalists like Sir Brian Hastings.[50] He supported with supplies or encouragement royalist enclaves like Hull (until its fall), Scarborough, and the Cliffords' castle at Skipton; by late November he was also the king's link with Berwick, Newcastle, Sir William Musgrave, and the earl of Northumberland.[51] He even sought to detach whole areas from the rebel obedience. Marshland, Howdenshire, and Axholme had been in arms under Robert Aske since 10 October, but in mid-November two gentlemen from the area asked Sir Francis Lovell and John Cavendish to secure Suffolk's mediation for a royal pardon for their locality. Henry was delighted, an unofficial truce was established, by late November the rebels could find little support in the area, and early in December Suffolk obtained a separate pardon and oath of loyalty to be proclaimed there.[52] Similarly the duke exploited the provision of the Doncaster agreement that he should suspend his blockade of Hull. He made contact with the town's richer citizens and tried to subvert them into surrendering to the king, but the common rebels discovered this and cut off trade before the plot could succeed.[53]

Such developments reinforced Suffolk's view that time was on the king's side, and that if negotiations were postponed and more royal troops raised, then neither concessions nor conflict might be necessary.[54] But he did not chafe at Henry's plans for a multiple assault on the rebels, in which he was to attack Hull. This involved the rearming of Lincolnshire. The Yorkshire rebels were watching the treatment of Lincolnshire closely, and the government must have intended at least the gentlemen of the north to note the evidence of the king's disposition to mercy in the release of confiscated arms and armour to the gentry, which accompanied the Lincolnshire pardon of 16 November.[55] An army of 5,000 was to be raised for the attack on Hull, while 'sure and certain steyes' remained to hold the county in the duke's absence.[56] Suffolk was quick to capitalise on local loyalty. On 8 November Lincoln common council had ordered every able citizen to hold a horse ready for the king's service. By the 26th Suffolk had promised Wingfield, Hopton and Cavendish that their watch on the Humber would imminently be relieved by local gentlemen. On the 27th Henry suggested that Suffolk deal separately with each gentleman to raise men at his own expense to serve against Yorkshire for a month. In early December the duke, his captains and the local gentry mustered the whole shire and prepared its forces to march at an hour's warning.[57]

The conclusion of a second agreement with the Yorkshire rebels denied Suffolk the chance to lead his new county to war, but he was able to win its heart in other ways. He assured the king of the innocence in the revolt of the Dean of Lincoln, a member of the influential Heneage family. He told Henry that the gentry were sufficiently trustworthy to be armed.[58] In late November Cromwell issued orders, without informing Suffolk, that pensions and debts on the late monasteries in Lincolnshire should go largely unpaid; the duke overrode him, to command their payment in part or in full. Brandon thought it foolish to affront a community lately in revolt against irresponsible commissioners, but he also stressed that 'for asmoche as it is the king[es] pleaso[ur] I shulde be here at this tyme to stey and order this countrey, me semythe it were requysite I shulde be made p[ri]vey to suche thing[es] as shulde be doon in theise p[ar]ties.'[59]

The benefits of Suffolk's role for his relationship with Lincolnshire were matched by benefits in his relationship with the king. Early in December they exchanged their most fulsome letters in years. Suffolk's good service gave Henry 'as moche cause to rejoyse of o[ur] favo[ur] and goodnes hertofor extended unto you as of any like thing that we have doon sithens o[ur] reign'.[60] Brandon felt he could never 'recompence and deserve the hundreth thousande p[ar]te' of these sentiments, and vowed not only to pray for Henry's preservation 'but also to employe my poore bodie and harte in this worlde to the maynten[au]nce of the same'.[61] Suffolk even invited Cromwell to share this warm glow, 'considering moche of the king[es] goodnes therin is shewed unto me by yo[ur] good meanes and furtheraunce.'[62] Henry also granted Suffolk's request to come to court at Christmas, should the pardon of December disperse the Yorkshire rebels.[63]

The pardon had the desired effect, and as the rebels disbanded, so did Suffolk's troops. Though money had always arrived in time to pay them, it was short by early December, and by the 12th Suffolk had sent all his men home bar 500 or 1,000 to guard the prisoners and the ordnance at Lincoln. By 24 December a deputy had taken charge there, and by 18 January at least the duke was back at court.[64] Everyone expected him to return soon to occupy Hull, attack Bigod's rebels or just 'set order in the country', and his future role in Lincolnshire was indeed under discussion: one plan suggested that he hold the new county militia ready to enter Yorkshire in support of Norfolk and the council of the north, while reducing the county to obedience through godly preachers.[65] Such detailed arrangements were never established, but when Suffolk left court in April 1537, Henry did instruct him to move his main residence to Lincolnshire.[66] He was to become a magnate there at royal command, as he had done in East Anglia.

Lincolnshire after the Revolt

While in the south, Suffolk missed the trials of rebels at Lincoln and the indictment of Lord Hussey. The local barons who had escaped the revolt, Lords Burgh and Clinton, and knights from adjoining counties, presided at these, though Lincolnshire knights sat on 1 August 1537 when many rebels pleaded their pardons.[67] In Suffolk's absence overall supervision of the county rested in Sir William Parr, who kept in close touch with Cromwell. Parr oversaw the sequestration of the lands and goods of Hussey and of the implicated monasteries, and distributed the benefits to himself, local gentlemen, and the other midlands knights involved in the trials.[68] This weakened Suffolk's position. Of course, Thomas Cromwell and even Richard Cromwell had been the targets of suitors for many of the spoils of the rebellion, and Suffolk's request for lands for two royal servants and his cousin John Wingfield was stymied by the pardon of the rebels who owned the estates.[69] But Suffolk's effective replacement by Parr during spring 1537 deprived him of his last chance to exercise largesse with the rebels' property, and later grants from it showed no certain sign of his influence.[70]

The duke was back at Lincoln for Hussey's execution in early July.[71] This by no means put an end to disquiet in Lincolnshire, or governmental concern about order in the county: there was certainly a job for Suffolk to do. In March 1537 Parr reported the shire to be quiet, but in February there had been a plot for a new revolt and in June there were riots in Lincoln.[72] On 1 August four local men were tried for treason, only one of them for participation in the revolt.[73] The others' offences, allegedly committed in March and May 1537, between them raised almost every issue of the late rising. One, it was claimed, said simply 'the devylle gyff the kyng sorowe of Brodham Abbey.' Another supposedly announced that 'all men beyng worthe in good[es] ix *d*. shuld paye to the kyng[es] grace ii *d*. ob & so ratiable above the sayd value, and that ther was a comyssyon comen downe to Lincoln for the same & was in the house of one John Gawley of the sayd cytye.' More idiosyncratic, but equally worrying, was the Scottish labourer who explained 'that our kyng shuld sende unto hys kyng vii moylles lodyn wyth gold & sylv[er] & plate', and 'that as longe as your kyng shuld sende unto hys kyng to by your peace ye shall nev[er] have a good world.'

All four were acquitted, which may suggest that these were malicious accusations to exploit governmental fears. But in August 1538 a Winterton man was found guilty of declaring, on the day after the twenty-ninth anniversary of Henry's accession, that 'the kynge hathe lyved ov[er] long by thre yeres, & that I wyll avowe for I care not for my lyff.'[74] In early 1540 the rumour spread from Louth to Boston that the king would take the tenth penny of every man's goods, and from January 1541 to August 1543 three priests of parishes between Bourne and Sleaford plotted a new revolt against the royal supremacy, for which they were tried in February 1544 and executed.[75] Seditious words and conspiracies were widespread after 1536, but in a county so recently in revolt they demanded special attention.[76]

Unlike Norfolk in the north or, later, Russell in the west, Suffolk had no regional council; nor, after the revolt, did he enjoy any special powers as lieutenant. It was left to him to build up his position in the county by normal means. Of course he headed crown commissions there, like that to defend the coast in 1539. He had some control over the disposition of local crown wardships, though only those of his tenants and servants.[77] He enjoyed no prerogative over crown patronage in Lincolnshire, suing to the king in competition with others, though local interests could support him: the Stamford authorities valued his visits and backed his bid for the Greyfriars there.[78] Naturally his power attracted local patronage. The repentant Louth churchwardens regaled him with venison when he first visited the town in the wake of the revolt, sent him pears in the following year, and were generous thereafter to his servants, whether his secretary or his 'fabule actoribus'.[79] On 1 March 1537 Revesby Abbey named him and his heirs chief stewards of all its lands for ever.[80] In November 1536 Lincoln invited him to name a new recorder for the city, and he chose Anthony Missenden, a very active steward on the Willoughby estates from at least 1526 to 1540.[81] The choice was significant, for Suffolk's first and best foothold in the county was provided by the Willoughby connection.

The Willoughby Affinity

At Christmas 1536 nine gentlemen and seven others were 'sworn unto my lord's grace and my ladye' at Tattershall. Nine were bailiffs or parkers of Willoughby manors, and four were appointed to minor offices in the duke's new Lincolnshire household. Their homes were concentrated in the Willoughby heartland around Spilsby and Alford, slightly to the south of Suffolk's Percy manors; such a pattern was probably normal for the affinities of the lesser nobility.[82] They were not great men, but in a poor county they were substantial: five were taxed on between £20 and £50 in lands, four on between £20 and £50 in goods.[83] Some had supported Lady Mary passionately during the Willoughby dispute, and in the revolt they and all her officers had been tested again in their loyalty to her.[84] Most had done their best for their lady and the king, and this must have made Suffolk confident of their good service. They shared their devotion readily between the duke and the dowager lady. The will made by Francis Stoner, Lady Mary's surveyor, in August 1537 left plate and money to his executrix the dowager lady, and to Duchess Catherine, but his best animals 'towarde my lorde of Suff[olk's] greate honorable household'.[85] The Willoughby officers were particularly useful to the duke in two ways. Thomas Gildon, the receiver, and Anthony Missenden were experienced county administrators. Gildon had been feodary of the duchy of Lancaster, escheator, a justice in all three parts of the county (sitting at Boston and Horncastle) and feed by Stixwold Nunnery and Revesby Abbey.[86] Missenden, taxed on £40 in lands and fees, became a serjeant-at-law by 1540, and combined a London chancery practice with local estate offices for the crown and five religious houses.[87] Like Gildon, he was one of the quorum of the commission of the peace in both Lindsey and Kesteven, and in the later 1530s he was active on the bench at Caistor, Horncastle, and Spital-in-the-Street, and in holding manorial courts for Suffolk.[88] As recorder of Lincoln he attended some common council meetings, and was deputed in May 1539 to 'speke w[ith] the duykez grace conc[er]nying [the] harneys that lythe in the hale and what order shalbe taken ther in.'[89] Judicial activity elsewhere, and work on the council of Suffolk's friend the Earl of Rutland, detracted little from his usefulness to the duke.[90]

Gildon, Missenden, and the intermarried network of lesser gentlemen sworn to Brandon's service, also had useful contacts with the greater gentry of south Lindsey.[91] This made it more natural for the local knights to co-operate with Suffolk. Sir John Copledike kept an eye on the Willoughby dispute for the duke, and the close friends Sir William Sandon and Sir Andrew Bilsby led the commissioners for Revesby Abbey's surrender to Suffolk in 1538.[92] Other relations of the Willoughby retainers were recruited into the ducal administration. George St Poll entered Suffolk's service as a lawyer in 1537, Hugh Grantham as an auditor by 1541. Each had experience in local crown commissions and monastic administration, and St Poll was an active Lindsey justice.[93] But only at Horncastle were he, Gildon, and Missenden joined on the bench by Copledike, Bilsby, and Sandon, and this was symptomatic of Suffolk's position: the Willoughby legacy made him strong, but only in a small area.[94] The only known trespass on his Lincolnshire lands in this period took place outside that area; conversely, the

Map 5.1 Lincolnshire, Nottinghamshire, and Yorkshire Estates, 1515–1537

only Lincolnshire monastery to surrender directly to Suffolk was Revesby, only 6 miles from Spilsby.[95]

Suffolk's preferred residence was imposing Tattershall Castle, slightly to the south-west of the Willoughby and Percy estates, a gift from the king in April 1537.[96] But even before Lady Mary's death he used her houses at Eresby and Grimsthorpe, and by summer 1538 he was taking over her affairs, for example approving her presentations to benefices.[97] She kept control of her estates to the last, signing a copy of court roll on or after 7 May 1539, but by the 20th she was dead and Suffolk was negotiating for livery of her lands. With the formal grant of July 1540 over £900 of Willoughby income, all but £85 or so from Lincolnshire, was finally in the duke's hands.[98]

Good Lordship, Local Government, and the Church

Even before he took charge of the Willoughby estates, the duke was able to introduce some of his East Anglian followers to Lincolnshire. Some, like Robert Wingfield and Richard Freston, already held offices or leased lands there before 1536.[99] Others entered in 1537–8, taking joint leases with local ducal officials or buying land from them.[100] John Cavendish made the greatest impact, marrying the widow of Sir Robert Sheffield of Butterwick and racing to build up an estate on the Isle of Axholme before his stepson came of age. In 1538 he joined the Lindsey bench, in 1541 he was knighted and by 1543 he had turned Axholme Priory into 'a goodly manor place'.[101] By 1544 his taxable income was £80, and meanwhile his younger brother John was establishing himself at Orby.[102] In June 1539 the ducal treasurer William Naunton joined Cavendish as a justice of the peace.[103]

Of course such men could help the duke in his general oversight of the shire: Cavendish and his chaplain dealt with the traitorous vicar of Newark.[104] But Suffolk himself resided at least every summer and sometimes more often, and frequently left his wife there while he was at court.[105] No one expected him to exercise close control over the whole county. In areas far from his estates others were more suited to the task, like Sir John Markham in the area east of Newark. Nor could he make much impact on the long-running feud in north Lindsey between Sir William Ayscough and Sir Robert Tyrwhit, in which Cromwell and the council intervened directly.[106] When Lord Chancellor Audley wanted to

Table 5.1 The Willoughby and Suffolk Affinities

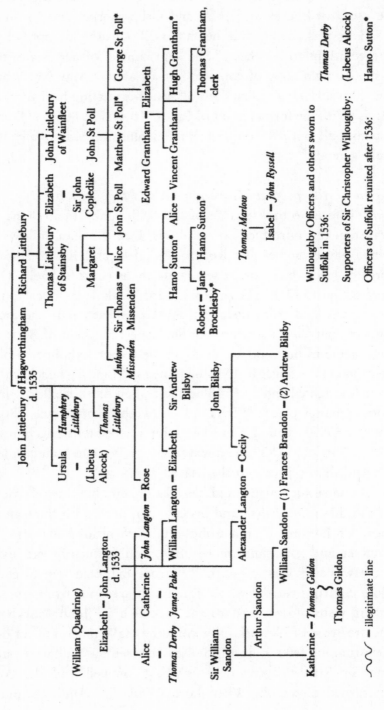

help a chancery plaintiff restrain abuses by Sir William Tyrwhit, he asked Sir William's courtier brother Robert to write to Sir William.[107] Only within his affinity did Suffolk arrogate all such matters to himself, but there he did so tenaciously. After Thomas Gildon's death in 1538, his widow Katherine disputed the lease of a house in East Kirkby with Richard Skepper, her son-in-law. Suffolk appointed Anthony Missenden and George St Poll to arbitrate on his behalf, but both parties initiated legal action, one at the Lincoln assizes and the other in chancery. The duke's response was a sharp letter to Gildon, requesting the withdrawal of her suit and promising a hearing 'be for us & ou[r] counsell apon Wedenssday in Ester wek at ou[r] castell of Tatteshall'.[108]

Yet Suffolk was expected to investigate the general condition of the county, and in particular threats of popular unrest. He took it upon himself to report to Henry that the people were 'as sorye for there offences ... as any men can be'.[109] He supervised the execution of the 1538 proclamation against vagabonds, and was active as a commissioner of sewers.[110] He was busy in the defensive arrangements of spring 1539, claiming that the men of Lincolnshire were 'as wyllynge men ... as ever I sawe' to offer themselves and their equipment to regain their honour in the king's service; he had to be excused from the Garter chapter because 'oon my faythe as yet I have don nothing yn a maner of myn owne, but oonlye the kyng[es] busynes.'[111] Lastly he was expected to further government religious policy, though what that involved is unclear. Local Protestants equated support for them with opposing the heirs of the rebels: in 1539 the Horncastle reformists sighed, 'Wold God my lord of Suffolk's g[ra]ce did know the trewth of ev[er]y thyng with hus, and how the most p[ar]te of hus favor[es) the word of God, and what a great no[m]ber favour[es] the pope's doctryne, and especyally owre prest[es].'[112] They described their opponents as 'success[ors] to the trat[or] Leche in word[es] & condicyons', but as their chief enemy was the bishop's chancellor, it was far from clear which side the duke should be on.

Bishop John Longland certainly did his best to counter the spread of Protestantism in Lincolnshire.[113] But did the leading layman of his diocese do much to further it? He told Cromwell what Cromwell wanted to hear, that by August 1539 the people were beginning 'to seware the worde of God somewhate better then they dydd, and I trust in Gode wylle doo daylye more and more, for I here many of the gentilmen speke very welle.'[114] His actions, though, were more ambiguous. It has been suggested that he introduced the popular preacher, Hugh Latimer, to Lincolnshire, for example, but on Latimer's own evidence this was not the case; and in the years from the fall of Anne Boleyn to the fall of Cromwell, his religious patronage was dominated not by missionary zeal but by the need to relieve himself from paying monastic pensions.[115] Revesby's surrender, arranged with royal consent, was purchased by Suffolk's payment of the house's debts, £66 13s 4d to the abbot, and life pensions ranging from £50 to £6 13s 4d to him and his nineteen brethren. By 1543 the duke had presented at least five of them to livings.[116] Two-thirds of all the clergy presented to benefices by Suffolk from February 1537 to June 1540 were ex-religious, usually from Revesby, Leiston, or Butley.[117] Some may have leant to the new learning, but the vast majority did not.[118] The same was apparently true of the ducal chaplains, and others presented.[119] Suffolk looked after his chaplains well, but not because they were model Protestant clergy. He tried to help the multi-beneficed dean of his chapel, Christopher Lynham, hold onto an Irish prebend.[120] He sued to Cromwell on behalf of Dr Arthur Bulkeley, a ducal chaplain and canon lawyer of 'lernyng, gravite and discretion' who was 'in all matters sp[irit]uall of his grace's [Suffolk's] counsaill'.[121] Bulkeley's suspected papalism did not invalidate the usefulness of his legal skills, and in 1542 the duke reaped further reward, when Bulkeley became Bishop of Bangor and made Suffolk and his son chief stewards of all the see's lands in survivorship.[122]

The duke continued to grant advowsons to his servants and administrators, and present their relatives himself.[123] Even in his rhetoric he was a far less committed promoter of the new faith in Lincolnshire than, for example, Thomas Lord Burgh, and most of his actions matched his words.[124] Yet Suffolk supported some of the most prominent reformist clergy of the 1530s, and continued to do so after the establishment of the conservative Act of Six Articles, when he could not have been innocently or ingratiatingly following the government line. The foremost example was Alexander Seton, a leading Scottish Dominican and royal confessor, who began to preach justification by faith and fled to England. Brandon may have secured his denisation, and certainly presented him to the rectory of Fulbeck in July 1539.[125] Seton set off for London, for a career of inflammatory preaching, Protestant writing, and clashes with ecclesiastical authority.[126] Though the eulogies of the Protestant exiles may exaggerate his confrontation with the conservative hierarchy, he certainly set the self-conscious 'we' of the gospellers against the official teaching of the Paul's Cross sermons, and had to recant publicly in December 1541.[127] Yet the duke gave him a second Lincolnshire rectory in September 1542, only months before his death in Suffolk's London house.[128]

Suffolk apparently exercised little control over Seton, and in his recantation Seton suggested he lost his own self-control in the excitement of preaching. But the duke cannot have been unaware of the friar's background, views, and connections, and it was well known that Seton was Suffolk's chaplain.[129] Most other evidence suggests that Brandon held no strong religious views, and after 1540 he had no strong political motive to support reformers. It is possible that his wife already influenced him in favour of Protestants, for she did show by 1539 an unusual interest in matters ecclesiastical. But her choice in clerics, her absence as yet from court Protestant circles, and perhaps her use of the Assumption of the Virgin in dating a letter, make this less likely.[130]

It is more probable that Suffolk's patronage was influenced by Protestants in his household and affinity. The duke may have chosen the reformist Thomas Lawney as a chaplain merely because of his legendary wit.[131] But Lawney was a friend of Thomas Marbury, a Protestant London haberdasher who had occupied a financial post in the ducal household in the 1520s, at which time Marbury's sister Elizabeth was a lady-in-waiting to the French queen.[132] By the later 1530s Thomas's trusted cousin John Marbury was comptroller of Suffolk's household, and was the 'syngler frynd' of at least

one cleric presented by the duke.[133] By 1540 Thomas Marbury
worshipped at St Pancras, Soper Lane; the incumbent there was
Richard Marsh, like Lawney a protégé of Cranmer, and by 1544 a
chaplain to Suffolk.[134] At least by his death in 1553 John Marbury
too was of Protestant views, and he may well have provided the
link between London radical circles and the duke's patronage.[135]

In East Anglia too, pressures in the affinity encouraged ducal
ambiguity. Unlike Norfolk or Lord Wentworth, Suffolk did not
have a clear local reputation as a conservative or a reformist.[136]
This, however, helped to preserve his good lordship in the face of
appeals for help from followers who took very different views of
the Protestant onslaught. The new faith gained ground in the 1530s
in the Stour valley and north-central Suffolk, both areas where
the duke held land, but this was due to local conditions rather
than to Brandon's influence. Though he was lord of the reformist
stronghold of Stratford St Mary from 1536, innovation there had
gone a long way before the manor came to him.[137] Similarly at
Thorndon, the duke was more troubled than cheered by the advent
of Protestantism. In October 1536 the ex-friar John Bale was
preaching there, but he met opposition from the wives of some of
Suffolk's leading tenants, including the wife of William Kirk. Kirk
had been a ducal servant since 1520, and bailiff of Thorndon and
Wattisfield since 1522.[138] He had gone off to Lincolnshire in the
duke's army, but had told his wife that he would not 'fyght ageynst
hys cosyns and kyndred', because '[the] good cristen men of Yngland
were in [the] North, and [there] were than rysyn for [the] common
welth.'[139] When Kirk returned, he set about persecuting Bale and
using his power as bailiff to coerce the villagers into denouncing
the preacher. Kirk found an ally in Thomas Bek, under-steward
of the ducal courts in Suffolk. In January 1537 they convinced Sir
Humphrey Wingfield that Bale should be 'wyseley suppressed',
and he recommended this to Suffolk.[140] But Bale was not without
friends. Thomas Culham of Thorndon ignored Kirk's threats to
the tenantry of 'dysplesor' from 'my lorde of Sothfolke', and stood
surety for Bale. Bale assured Cromwell that not only his friend
Lord Wentworth – not, it must be remembered, a close associate

of the duke – but also Edward Grimston, a coffin-bearer to the French queen, would testify against Kirk.[141] Suffolk's response was less than decisive, though whether this reflects tactical cunning or ineffectual lethargy is hard to say. He passed on Wingfield's letter to Cromwell, who called Bale before the royal council, but he took no obvious steps against either party, and Kirk was still bailiff in 1539.[142]

Some of Suffolk's correspondents merely wanted to discover the government's real view of local excesses. The rector of Stratford St Mary, presented by the duke in March 1537, contacted him to ask whether Cromwell really intended his congregation to rip every image out of the church, as they were doing on pretext of the 1538 royal injunctions.[143] Others expected action from the duke. In 1537 Sir Thomas Tyrrell was shocked by the open marriage of the vicar of Mendlesham, and asked Suffolk's 'plesure whatte is beste to be done for the reformacion off hys opyn cryme, whyche is abomynable in the jugement off the laye peopell; and hys ensample wnponnyched shall be occacion for other carnall evyll dysposed prestes to do in lyke maner, whyche God defend.'[144] Again, Suffolk referred the matter to Cromwell. This might be seen as a commitment to Cromwell's version of reform, but then again most of the duke's correspondents expected conservative rather than reformist action from him.

If Brandon preserved an ambiguity which not even his clergy and officers – and quite possibly not even he himself – could penetrate, it may well have been to the advantage of his good lordship. Richard Freston, comptroller of the ducal household to April 1537, then receiver and surveyor of the Norfolk and Suffolk estates, led a group of religious conservatives at the heart of Suffolk's service.[145] Walter Wadlond, Robert Brampton, Thomas Seckford and probably Sir Thomas Tyrrell shared his views, and Wadlond worked with Freston to channel ducal patronage to their clerical allies, men like John Righton and Robert Budde.[146] Both Budde and Righton, as master of Wingfield College and Prior of Blythburgh respectively, repaid Freston with substantial leases of land.[147] Any magnate who could combine the services of men like these with those of the Marburys and Seton must have cared more about good lordship than good doctrine, but that probably did his position in local politics no harm at all.

Departure from East Anglia

In East Anglia that position was threatened by more than religious strife. In the early 1530s Sir Humphrey Wingfield had still conducted some routine business for Suffolk,[148] but as his own local and national importance grew, his role at the centre of ducal administration had to be filled by someone else. The task fell largely to Thomas Holmes; he was the duke's secretary, a post of increasing responsibility in most contemporary households, including of course that of the king.[149] In 1517 Holmes had acted as Suffolk's attorney in a land transaction, in 1523 he paid money into the household accounts, and in 1524 he collected the subsidy on the ducal household.[150] By 1537–8 he was still collecting cash from bailiffs, and acting as an attorney, but he was also regularly dealing with Cromwell for Suffolk.[151] In 1539 and 1542 he acted as the duke's London agent, but in July 1540 he was with Suffolk and witnessed the duke's deposition about his negotiations with Anne of Cleves.[152] Until 1542 he was active, as 'clarke to the said duk[es] grace', in the administration of wood sales in royal forests; and from at least 1542 he held courts twice a year as surveyor on Suffolk's Devon manors.[153] He must have been reliable and he was certainly industrious, but he did not have the prestige and connections of a Humphrey Wingfield either locally or nationally. Autumn 1537 removed another ducal stalwart. Sir John Glemham held his last court for Suffolk on 18 September, made his will on the 22nd and died soon afterwards. His sons Christopher and Edward followed him into Brandon's service, but Christopher was named to the Suffolk bench only after the duke's interest in the county had largely ended.[154]

Trouble continued between Brandon and Howard followers. Richard Cavendish and others exploited Norfolk's absences in 1536–7 to discredit the duke and indict his tenants. Norfolk's response was to ask Cromwell to urge Suffolk to restrain his retinue.

Howard professed surprise at his recent discovery that Brandon bore a grudge against him, and promised that neither he, nor his men 'w[ith] my gode will', would give Suffolk cause for enmity, since 'the better we agre, the better the kyng shalbe s[er]ved.'[155] But Suffolk either would not or could not restrain Cavendish, and disputes continued beyond October 1538, with Cavendish forced to seek help wherever he could find it.[156] Animosities emerged in the joint effort against the rebels of 1536, Sir Arthur Hopton taking four horses from Norfolk's land to carry Suffolk's soldiers to Lincolnshire, and returning two 'so sore travayled that they myght labour no further' and the other two only when sued at law for them.[157] Meanwhile, Norfolk used his supervision of East Anglia in 1536–7 to arrogate wide control to his personal council: it was before that body that Bale was first called to account for his preaching. The dissolution too still gave cause for friction, as when Richard Freston was beaten to a monastic lease in Wangford by Norfolk's treasurer.[158]

For Brandon there were some encouraging signs. Sir Anthony Wingfield and Sir Arthur Hopton gave each other financial support in these years, and Edward Grimston acted as a feoffee to Sir Humphrey Wingfield.[159] More important, several ducal officers had joined the Suffolk bench in February 1535 and sat regularly in the later 1530s.[160] Two of them, Suffolk's feodary Walter Wadlond and his receiver- general Robert Browne, were typical of the ambitious, but unestablished, men the duke had recruited from the later 1520s: only now were they able to enter the county elite.[161] Nicholas Bohun and Richard Freston were in a similar position, becoming justices by 1539 and 1543 respectively.[162] The third new justice of 1535 was Thomas Seckford, a ducal cousin and bailiff of Wingfield.[163] Seckford, Wadlond, and Browne all held manorial courts for Brandon, and Wadlond, Browne, and Freston collected most of his rents in this period.[164] The rapid expansion of the ducal estates in Suffolk in the 1530s probably reinforced the claim of Brandon's active estate officials to a place in county government, conveniently at a time when the commissions of the peace were expanding to include talented gentlemen from outside the established county families. Now at last Suffolk had followers with a voice in local affairs who owed no loyalties to other peers, and served the duke, not out of familial duty, but because they valued his patronage and good lordship: his affinity was taking a more satisfying shape. Another active justice was John Harman, who was linked to Suffolk through the Willoughby marriage: this also strengthened the duke's relationship with Sir Thomas Tyrrell, for he was the duchess's uncle by marriage, and with Sir John Jenny, who had helped to defend Orford against Sir Christopher Willoughby.[165] Meanwhile in Norfolk the commission of sewers of July 1538 introduced two of Suffolk's men to county administration: John Curson, who had held courts and collected reliefs for the duke, and Robert Brampton, his bailiff of Sedgeford hundred.[166]

In 1536–7 Suffolk himself was still very much a force in East Anglia. Butley Abbey still offered him favours, and he remained steward of King's Lynn, though Cromwell had to arrange how town courts would be held under the new charter, to avoid arguments between the duke and the corporation.[167] When Brandon was in East Anglia in May and June 1537, his mind was partly on Lincolnshire, seeking to have the right candidate elected Abbot of Revesby, doubtless with an eye to the abbey's future surrender. But he also co-operated with Norfolk justices and Howard councillors to deal with popular sedition, interrogating suspects, stopping some popular gatherings, investigating a play in which a character had deviated from the text in an inflammatory manner, and requesting royal orders for all justices to take 'good respect & spyalle among[es] the light p[er]sons'.[168] That summer Cromwell even asked him whether his presence in Lincolnshire or Suffolk would be more conducive to public order, but the duke was happy to leave Suffolk in the hands of the worshipful gentlemen of the shire. Before he left, the Norwich city chamberlain presented him with a porpoise.[169]

It was his last gift from Norwich corporation. Henry's order to move the ducal household to Lincolnshire led within a year to the start of negotiations for another exchange of lands. The duke had not contemplated a wholesale departure for Lincolnshire before the revolt. His wife's jointure, assured by act of parliament in 1536, included East Anglian De la Pole lands.[170] In May 1536 he had secured a forty-year crown lease of the manor and hundred of Hoxne and four other manors, scattered in the same areas of Suffolk as his own estates, which had belonged to the see of Norwich.[171] He was already negotiating for the lands of Suffolk monasteries: in December 1536 his councillors badgered the Prior of Butley to surrender, but he as yet held firm. In the ensuing spate of monastic grants to the peerage, when other leading nobles secured lands worth £100 or 100 marks net, Suffolk and Norfolk were each endowed with estates worth £200, clear of the reserved rent to the crown: to Brandon came, in April 1537, the sites and lands of Leiston Abbey and Eye Priory, both in Suffolk.[172] Just as the duke's enthusiastic empire-building came near to fruition, however, it was terminated by the king's insistence that he establish himself in Lincolnshire, primarily to secure the good order of that county, but also to eliminate the threat posed by conflict with the Howards to the good order of Norfolk and Suffolk. Perhaps this was the sort of by-product that appealed to the tidy mind of Thomas Cromwell.[173]

By late summer 1537 the duke was preparing for an exchange. A list was produced of all monastic houses over which he had any claim by patronage, surrender or royal grant. New rentals of some of his manors were drawn up, presumably to raise their value.[174] He began to make noticeably longer leases, some probably for large fines, others to favoured candidates, like his brother-in-law Nicholas Arrowsmith who secured Newhall in Huntingfield for ninety-nine years. After 10 August 1537 he made no lease shorter than eighty years.[175] William Naunton, Edward Glemham, Francis Framlingham, and Richard Cavendish all gained ducal manors by long lease, purchase, or exchange.[176] Soon those outside the duke's circle sought the opportunity to buy from him before he concluded terms with the king. On 24 May 1538 Suffolk sold Burgh-next-Aylsham to a London mercer for £220 in cash.[177] On the same day he obtained a licence to alienate five of Buckingham's former manors to Lord Chancellor Audley. They concluded a complex bargain on 11 June at a price of £3,000, made up of cash in hand, future payments, £500 worth of monastic lead, and cancellation by Audley of the £900 dowry of his wife Elizabeth, sister of Suffolk's son-in-law Dorset.[178]

Thomas Manning, Prior of Butley and suffragan Bishop of Ipswich, recognised this as the right moment to throw in his hand, encouraged no doubt by Suffolk's grant to him of an eighty-year lease on the manor of Nedging in September 1537. His monastery surrendered on 1 March 1538, its lands passing to the duke.[179] On 20 March Suffolk agreed to give him 50 marks in cash and lands for life worth 200 marks, provided the bishop leased them to ducal nominees. When these lands passed to the king, Suffolk obtained for Manning instead a life interest in Monk's Kirby, Warwickshire, with reversion to the duke. Finally, in November 1539, Suffolk secured Monk's Kirby in return for presenting Manning to the mastership of Mettingham College, with the proviso that the manor would be given back if the college were dissolved.[180]

Meanwhile negotiations continued for the main exchange. In late March and early April 1538 Sir Richard Rich, chancellor of the court of augmentations, led an impressive team on a thorough survey of the ducal estates. They reported to Cromwell on the tenants' military capacity and soundness in religion, and the construction and situation of Suffolk's houses and parks. Their survey was more comprehensive still, numbering deer and bondmen and describing Westhorpe and Henham minutely.[181] Court profits were assessed so that the exchange would not rest merely on rental income, though they reckoned without Suffolk's last-minute attempts in summer 1538 to find gold on his estates through the prospecting of Richard Cavendish and two foreign goldsmiths.[182] A separate team viewed and valued all the ducal woods, finding £250 worth of timber of between two and eighty years' growth, presumably a sign of good management. Soon after their return Rich led an augmentations delegation to Suffolk's London house to begin detailed negotiations.[183]

The duke had fired the first shot, presenting over-ambitious proposals directly to Henry. The king received him graciously, but wrangled hard once his surveyors had given him accurate figures.[184] The struggle was both shorter and less one-sided than in 1535. Suffolk did not want to give up both Henham and Westhorpe, but he had to do so. Henry was reluctant to grant the lead from the monasteries of Barlings and Kirkstead, which he valued at £4,000, but by 10 July Suffolk had won this point, reckoning the lead at £1,600 (one-fifth lower than the rate he allowed Audley).[185] The duke had to relinquish the lands of Butley and Leiston, which he had hoped to keep.[186] But he prevented the inclusion of undesirable Lincolnshire lands in the exchange, replacing them with more attractive estates in other counties. Throughout Suffolk maintained the principle that 'I somyth me self hallwayes to hes henes' goodnes', but it was a mark of his recovery of the king's favour that this tactic brought far better dividends than in 1535.[187]

A preliminary agreement was sealed on 6 July. This gave Henham to the crown, with another manor and park nearby, and the reserved rent of £50 on the duke's earlier grant in fee of Mendham Priory to Richard Freston.[188] The sale was for cash, £3,000 at twenty years' purchase, the same rate as the private sales. At the same time Suffolk prepared to convert other estates into cash indirectly. Particulars of lands outside Lincolnshire were prepared by the augmentations staff and included in the crown's side of the exchange, while the duke found potential purchasers for them. On 13 July Suffolk, Sir Arthur Hopton, and Richard Freston bound themselves in £500 for the sale of Trentham Priory, Staffordshire, to William Whorwood, who paid in advance £450 of the £1,800 price.[189]

'The Last Agrement', as the relieved augmentations auditor Thomas Mildmay entitled it, was completed on 30 September. Suffolk's estates were finally valued at about 10 per cent more than in the spring 1538 survey, a fairer reflection of their revenues over the last four years, and of the income the crown could expect from them.[190] He handed over his entire East Anglian holdings, including Butley, Eye, and Leiston, though he had already leased the last two to his clients, Nicholas Cutler and Robert Browne.[191]

The only exceptions were the Willoughby manors, several distant reversions, Gapton Hall and the manor of Tasburgh, Norfolk. The last he claimed to keep for sentimental reasons, holding it 'by discent of inheritaunce from his auncettours', but he overcame his scruples and sold it in 1542.[192] His career as an East Anglian magnate was effectively ended. From Michaelmas 1538 his £2,231 12s 8d of revenue there was paid to the king; from summer 1539 courts were first held in the king's name; and it was left to men like Browne, Freston, and Wadlond to make their own way in the county using the offices and monastic leases left to them by the duke.[193]

The Lincolnshire Endowment

The grant of lands to Suffolk was made in two instalments, in December 1538 and March 1539.[194] Nearly all the estates were formerly monastic and so were subject to a reserved rent to the crown of one-tenth of their annual value. Most had already been leased out for terms of twenty-one years by the court of augmentations. Small imbalances in value between these and Suffolk's estates were corrected by the grant of numerous advowsons, scattered from Cornwall to Cumberland, but many were unused before the duke's death. The Lincolnshire estates in the grant were one-and-a-half times more valuable than the combined De la Pole, Percy, and Willoughby lands in the county: by 1543–4 they were bringing in more than £1,650.[195] Of the others he kept only five manors in Devon and Somerset – used to pay Norfolk's rent under the 1516 lease – one other Devon manor and three in Warwickshire. By the same date these produced less than £100, clear of the payments to Norfolk. The remainder of the new estates was converted as rapidly as possible into cash. Between December 1538 and May 1539 Suffolk received £3,327 on five sales alone, and made at least four other bargains whose details are unknown. The purchasers ranged from augmentations men involved in the exchanges – one at least reaping his reward for helping the duke – through courtiers and crown officials, to Londoners and local gentlemen.[196] In July 1540 Suffolk also disposed of Maxstoke Priory in Warwickshire, to a London goldsmith, for £1,500 in cash and the promise of a further £603.[197]

Some of this money was reinvested to concentrate the duke's estates. From March 1539 he leased three hundreds in Somerset, in the same area as his manors there, but also formerly part of Lady Margaret Beaufort's lands as were the duchy of Richmond estates granted to him in 1539. (Suffolk was proud of the honour of Richmond, commissioning Holbein to design a special seal for his use within it).[198] In the same month he bought the little park and coney-warren next to Tattershall Castle from Lord Clinton, and in July he obtained from James Standyshe of Coningsby the promise of first refusal, should Standyshe sell his manors at Billinghay, Walcot, and Spanby. In February 1540 he bought out for 250 marks Sir William Skipwith's lease on Markby Priory, on which he had been granted the crown's reserved rent and the reversion.[199] What could not be spent in this way or on building was invested in continental jewels. The sum of £800 bought one diamond ring from a Florentine operating in London, Bartolommeo Compagna, in July 1538 and August 1540 the duke did unspecified business with the Antwerper Lieven Terle and his colleagues, and in March 1540 Terle was bound 'for the delyverey of certein dyamondes to be made to the said duke'.[200]

Such jewels could be converted into land at a later date, and in this case were. Meanwhile Suffolk made good use of the lands he had just acquired. The Revesby estates, worth nearly £350, lay among the central Willoughby manors, but none of the lands from the exchange was so conveniently placed. Something over £400 worth of these were scattered among the Percy and Willoughby lands between Louth and Alford, and the existing office-holders on these estates included useful contacts like Sir Andrew Bilsby, and future enthusiastic ducal officers like Brian Newcomen.[201] The rest of the new acquisitions were spread across the centre of the shire, with outliers at Thornholme, Elsham, and Newsham in the north, and Vaudey, Edenham, and Scottlethorpe in the south around Grimsthorpe. Suffolk did alienate some of these new lands, but with clear aims. He concentrated his holdings, exchanging Owersby and Thornton, near Francis Ayscough's home at South Kelsey, for Ayscough's manor at Sausthorpe, close to Spilsby.[202] When he sold outright, it was to his officers or their relatives. George St Poll borrowed money from his father to buy Westlaby Grange in Wickenby from the duke.[203] St Catherine's Priory, Lincoln, was sold to Vincent Grantham, elder brother of Hugh and a leading figure in the city.[204] Leases were kept short, and Suffolk's auditors managed to prove to the augmentations that the lands produced some £24 less than their guaranteed value under the exchange agreement. A further selection of monastic farms and rectories, with the friaries of Boston and Stamford, was assembled to compensate for this, and the lands were duly granted to Suffolk.[205] The duke's final requirement was for a country house just outside London. He bought the manor of Dunsford, in Wandsworth, from the augmentations, only to resell it to Cromwell, from whom he purchased a house at Kew in July 1538.[206]

These exchanges made Suffolk the greatest landowner in Lincolnshire, but they did not make him the only channel between county and court. The Heneages, based at Hainton, also profited greatly from the dissolution; from his position as a leading gentleman of the privy chamber, Sir Thomas easily gathered numerous lands and leases, mostly in the area between Market Rasen, Wragby, Louth and Horncastle.[207] Where this sphere of influence met Suffolk's, Heneage could still be successful, for example in obtaining the wardship of John Gedney's son in July 1537. Local suitors to Cromwell could look to the Heneages for help, and other families had their own routes to court: Robert Tyrwhit was close to the earl of Hertford in the later 1530s.[208] Suffolk may not have needed or even wanted to be sole mediator between county and king, but he must have worried that the influence of Heneage and the Tyrwhits would devalue his good lordship to the gentry of Lindsey.

Family and Friends

Ruling Lincolnshire was still easier than ruling the ducal family. In these years his daughters Anne and Mary both suffered marital

Newsham

•Elsham
•Keadby•   •Thornholme

• Thornton•
•Owersby•   •SWINHOPE
WILLOUGHTON•   • BINBROOK
•Glentham
Caenby
•Linwood   Gayton-   • Louth Park
•Legsby•   le-Wold   •Carlton
Westlaby Grange• Benniworth •Maltby• •Gayton-le-Marsh
Sturton   Snelland WITHCALL   •Strubby
Scampton Lings Grange• Swinesthorp BURWELL•   •MALTBY
North Carlton Scothern in Snelland   •CLAYTHORPE
Riseholme Stainton• Bullington BELCHFORD Greenfield •Markby
St Catherine's Lincoln• •Barlings   BRINKHILL •DRIBY
Canwick• •CHERRY WILLINGHAM   Ashby   Mumby
Boultham •Washingborough •Waddingworth Puerorum •Claxby
Sheepwash Grange Hameringham •SAUSTHORPE
LANGTON• •Mareham HUNDLEBY •SCREMBY
Nocton Roughton WOOD East Hundleby
WADDINGTON• •Dunston Kirksteade Woodhall •ENDERBY Hagnaby Keal Toynton•BRATOFT
Harmston• Metheringham •Kirkby on Bain •Revesby Abbey WINTHORPE•
COLEBY MARTIN• Tattershalle •TUMBY Grange
Thorpe• TATTERSHALL •TATTERSHALL PARK
•Flawford• TATTERSHALL •CONINGSBY •Stickney
Billinghay Rectory STICKNEY
Leadenham •Temple Bruer• BILLINGHAY Sibsey•
•Fulbeck Wildmore Fen •
Armtree Fen

Boston
Wilsford• Burton Pedwardine Skirbeck• •Blackfriars
•Allington   •Skirbeck•
Frampton•
•Welby HELPRINGHAM/ Kirton
•Donnington
Ingoldsby• •Hanby Grange

•HOLBEACH
Vaudey•
Scottlethorpe• •Edenham
CAREBY •LOUND TRETON HALL IN TYDD ST MARY
•TOFT

KILTHORPE •Stamford Greyfriars
IN KETTON• •EASTON   0   10   20 Miles
MANTON TIXOVER   0   10   20   30
Kilometres

Key: Granted 1538–9:   Welby
      Granted 1540:   *Hundleby*
      Purchased from the crown, 1542: *Maltby**
      Alienated by the duke: Legsby*
      Purchased or gained by exchange: *SAUSTHORPE*
      Granted 1545:   TOFT

Map 5.2 Acquisitions in Lincolnshire and Rutland, 1538–1545

crises, largely of their own making if one retailer of contemporary gossip is to be believed. Though 'handsome women', they reportedly 'took to evil courses, and became common women, the father, however, taking no notice of it.'[209] This is unfair on Suffolk. He asked Cromwell to mediate between Lord and Lady Powis, and to favour the latter only if she live in 'such an honest sort as shalbe to yo[ur] hono[ur] and myn'.[210] Following the violent removal of Lady Powis's lover from her lodgings in a night attack by Lord Powis, Cromwell negotiated a maintenance agreement, preparatory to a legal separation. Lady Powis continued to enjoy court society thereafter, borrowing the necessary cash from both Cromwell and her father.[211]

The Monteagles' troubles were less sensational, but still serious. Suffolk rightly thought his son-in-law incompetent, and had to ask Cromwell to interfere in Monteagle's estate administration. In February 1538 Lord Thomas still owed the duke £1,063, and to cancel this Suffolk arranged to take the custody and marriage of Monteagle's son and heir William, with £100 in land to pay for William's upkeep.[212] By July 1540 further problems had arisen, and Monteagle was bound to keep an agreement between him and Suffolk arbitrated by a crown surveyor and two leading civil lawyers.[213] Trouble between Monteagle and his wife probably exacerbated these difficulties. As he lamented to Cromwell in asking for help to reform Lady Mary's 'abuses',

> sum greatt men arre myndyd to hold more of hur p[ar]tie then of myn, natw[ith]standing the ungoodlye conv[er]sacion she ys of, the whiche in tymes paste I have nat p[er]fitly knawne, but have been bly[n]ded w[ith] collusions; and as farre as I can considre, my sufferaunce haithe been cause sufficient to move the king his g[ra]ce & your lordship not oonly to thinke lesse witt and honestye to be in me then I thanke God ys in deed, but alswell in me to be a weyke spirite and lakke of audacyte.[214]

At least the Clifford marriage alliance worked well. Suffolk secured Cromwell's help and advice for Lord Clifford. He mediated between Cumberland and Lord Richard Grey, the uncle of the Marquis of Dorset, over the dower for Lord Richard's wife. He looked after Cumberland's London business, and tried to satisfy him over a debt owed him by Sir Thomas Wentworth, once Suffolk's servant.[215] Suffolk did complain that Cumberland's financial provision for Clifford's stay at court was inadequate, and that Clifford and Lady Eleanor were living in an unhealthy country house. But he felt free to ask for any tame red deer Cumberland might have to spare, and in 1540 he completed some complex manoeuvres at the court to gain the Cliffords an important lease.[216]

The move to Lincolnshire fostered Suffolk's contacts with the northern peerage, but perhaps weakened those with the nobles of the south and court. Lady Lisle was happy to send presents to Duchess Catherine, but most reluctant to place her daughter in the Suffolk household.[217] On the other hand the earl of Shrewsbury happily entertained the duchess at Sheffield, and one of the brokers who tried to commit Lady Lisle's daughter to the 'vertuous, wise and discreet' duchess of Suffolk was the countess of Rutland.[218] When the latter bore a daughter in summer 1539, she named her Catherine, explicitly after the duchess. Proximity rekindled the Brandon-Manners connection which dated from Sir Thomas Lovell's days, and in August 1539 Suffolk paid a visit to Belvoir. The stables there were repaired, extra wood and coals were brought in to keep the duke warm, 10s reward was paid to the ducal cooks, and at Rutland's command 3s 4d was spent on 'Doctor Lee's shawmes and shagboshes that playt before my lorde of Suffolk'.[219]

Politics and Patronage

In about 1538, an anonymous commentator described Suffolk as 'a good man and captain' but 'sickly and half lame'.[220] Yet his developing local commitments were matched by continuing activity at the centre of government. He was a member of the reformed privy council and, when available, attended regularly though by no means always. His attendances covered the range of conciliar business from routine administrative and judicial work, through negotiations with ambassadors, to the examinations of suspected traitors and heretics.[221] As lord president, he should have been active in various committees, though how far he took part in their deliberations cannot be gauged.[222] He played many other roles expected of a councillor. He echoed the king's views and boasted of the royal revenues to the French ambassador. He watched the king's review of his artillery in February 1537, the burning of a Welsh image and a romanist friar in May 1538, and the London musters in May 1539. He was a leading judge for the treason trials of 1538–9.[223]

Suffolk's attendance in the parliament of 1539–40 showed the same tendency to reasonable, but not devoted, assiduity. He missed twenty-one of the 100 days, not to be compared with Norfolk who missed only seven, but rather better than average for the temporal peers.[224] Sometimes when he was absent it was on official business, and he was careful to attend when important legislation was under discussion. In November 1539 he was one of the councillors who prorogued parliament; on 13 April 1540 he introduced a bill confirming his jurisdiction as great master of the household; and on 2 July, in the absence of both Audley and Norfolk, he took the chancellor's place as director of government business in the Lords.[225]

His participation in royal ceremony and his proximity to the royal family remained important. He was prominent in the opening of parliament, the christening of Prince Edward, the burial of Queen Jane, and the obsequies for the empress.[226] His daughter Frances led the ladies of honour at Queen Jane's funeral, his cousin Sir William Sidney became chamberlain to Prince Edward, and the duke himself supplied New Year gifts to the prince as to the king.[227] But Suffolk did not develop a special relationship with the Seymours. He stood godfather to Edward Seymour's son, but so did Norfolk. By 1538–9 he dined or supped at Beauchamp Place only when most of the council did so: this brought him half as many meals as Gardiner, one-third as many as Norfolk, and far fewer than Seymour's real intimates.[228] It is harder to judge how far

Suffolk had regained a special relationship with the king. When at court, the duke and his attractive duchess were feted by Henry. But Suffolk was often away, continuing to miss Garter chapters until April 1540, for example.[229] The king's letters stressed his goodwill, but when away from him Suffolk needed Cromwell's help almost as much as he had needed Wolsey's.

Their relationship was friendly, but its effectiveness sometimes questionable. Suffolk provided Cromwell with comparatively large gifts at New Year; Cromwell provided Suffolk with medicinal potions distilled by a servant of the minister.[230] Petitioners could appeal to them jointly, and the duke naturally supported his servants' suits to Cromwell, or their causes under his consideration as arbitrator or vicegerent in spirituals.[231] At least in the sale of augmentations lands, though, Suffolk's appeals were often unsuccessful. Edmund Hall, son of the late ducal treasurer Francis, farmed Greatford in Lincolnshire, and with Suffolk's and Cromwell's help managed to buy up the manor. But Brandon's suits to Cromwell availed nothing for William Naunton at Butley or Tangham, and the duke himself wanted the sale of the demesnes of Fountains halted until he could 'schow your lordschepe therin schyth thynges as you schall thynke et worth the stayinge', only to see them sold to Sir Richard Gresham.[232]

Some of Suffolk's servants and relations did obtain crown patronage – Richard Freston, John Cavendish, Gawain Carew, and the auditors John Peryent and Robert Wingfield – but there is no proof of the duke's involvement in these grants.[233] John Verney married the French queen's servant Dorothy whose jointure was paid for by the duke, and in 1540 named Suffolk overseer of his will, but he sought Cromwell's help directly, while Suffolk's half-nephew Humphrey Tyrrell became Cromwell's servant.[234] Sir Anthony Wingfield became vice-chamberlain and captain of the guard in March 1539, but he was by no means the duke's creature. Many of these successes may have been the result less of good lordship than of self-help, like that employed by Sir Thomas Lovell junior or Richard Cavendish in their land disputes.[235]

Yet Suffolk still disposed of large reserves of patronage and influence. His advice was useful to towns such as Great Yarmouth (organizing its fortifications) and Oxford (sending to Henry and Suffolk 'for the townys besynes').[236] Royal offices too continued to reinforce his power. As chief justice of the forests south of Trent he controlled between £170 and over £570 of annual income from timber sales, until 1542 when these were brought under the court of general surveyors.[237] Discretionary rewards to subordinates could be made on Suffolk's command, and fees to patentees like Sir Francis Bryan were paid on terms negotiated by the duke. Posts like that of salesman for particular woods could be given to clients such as Robert Wingfield, and the office was a useful source of credit: by Michaelmas 1542 the duke owed the crown £478 16s 1 ½d on eight years' account. Suffolk issued letters patent to confirm liberties claimed within the royal forests, and warrants for the delivery of bucks.[238] Of course local matters were taken to local magnates, ducal deputies in the New Forest taking their troubles to the earl of Arundel. But power, and probably profit, accrued to the duke from the revival of his judicial responsibilities. In November 1539 Cromwell discussed this possibility with Suffolk, in July 1540 legislation empowered the duke to appoint subordinates to execute forest justice, and by August Suffolk and Lord Chief Justice Mountague were hearing indictments for waste.[239]

In 1539 Suffolk acceded to a far more important office, one that demonstrated that he enjoyed not only the favour of the king, but also the confidence of the chief minister. This was the lord stewardship of the royal household, renamed the great mastership, and upgraded to take precedence over the lord chamberlain. His appointment, apparently without letters patent, overrode the earl of Sussex's reversionary rights on the death of Lord Steward Shrewsbury, and formed part of Cromwell's complex and repeated attempts to reform the household. Sussex, perhaps edged out by Cromwell because of his close relationship to Norfolk, was compensated by the transfer to him in December 1539 of Suffolk's chief stewardship of the duchy of Lancaster in the north.[240] Brandon's new title was established by late June 1539, Cromwell's new household ordinances came into effect on Christmas Eve, and when parliament restarted Suffolk put through his bill confirming that the lord steward's jurisdiction rested in him as 'greate maistre' or even 'grande maistre d'hostel du roy'.[241] Fundamental to Cromwell's new order was the reorganisation of the board of greencloth as the administrative centre of the household, with Suffolk as its chairman, like the peers or bishops leading regional councils. The board's records suggest that the duke earned his £100 fee, sitting repeatedly when major decisions were taken.[242] Unfortunately at least some of these attendances were fictional, for the duke was certainly elsewhere on the dates in question. He may well have sent written instructions to the board, though, and he does seem to have exercised his judicial duties in person on occasion: on 17 March 1540 he tried a theft within the verge of the household together with the steward of the marshalsea court, a serjeant-at-law, and four other commissioners.[243]

The rewards of this promotion in terms of patronage were immediately apparent. An important feature of the revised household was the new band of fifty gentlemen pensioners, and candidates linked with Suffolk were highly successful in the competition for places. Only one entrant was listed as 'my lord of Suffolk's man': Thomas Bolles, a younger son of the family of Gosberton, where there was a Willoughby manor.[244] But John Cavendish, Richard Freston, and Edward Grimston were all included. So were John Wingfield, eldest son of Sir Anthony, and another John Wingfield, probably the steward of Suffolk's household.[245] John Banaster had had no recorded contact with Suffolk since the death of his father Sir Humphrey, and Francis Sidney probably relied on the influence of his brother Sir William rather than his cousin Suffolk, but Francis Framlingham had maintained his family's links with the duke.[246] Gawain Carew remarried after the death of Suffolk's sister, by July 1540, and Sir Osborn Echingham probably had patrons apart from Suffolk, who had recommended him during the Lincolnshire revolt, but Edward

Ferrers was probably a gentleman of the ducal household, and so was Lord Edward Grey who joined the gentlemen pensioners by 1544.[247] Magnates were anxious to recommend candidates for these posts, and with good reason – they gave Wingfield, Carew, and Cavendish the entrée into the court jousts of 1540, for example – and Suffolk's support seems to have been especially effective in securing places.[248]

In part this sprang from his influence as great master, but it probably reflected too an increasingly strong relationship with Cromwell. Whatever his religious views, the duke did not abhor Cromwell's policy as Norfolk or Gardiner did. His inclination was to follow the king, and his involvement in the Cleves marriage displayed this obedience, but also demonstrated an acceptability in Cromwell's eyes which did not make the duke part of a simple aristocratic anti-Cromwellian faction. Brandon played an enthusiastic role in the negotiation of the Cleves alliance.[249] He and the duchess led the party which met Anne at Dover. When her household was established, the duchess was one of her six 'great ladies', the countess of Rutland a lady of her privy chamber, the earl of Rutland her chamberlain, and Richard Manners, who once kept Suffolk's privy purse, her cupbearer.[250]

The duke was both able and willing to benefit from Cromwell's other successes in 1540. When Bishop Sampson was imprisoned in late May, the horse-loving duke was granted the use of the bishop's mule and the expectation of it as a gift should Sampson's goods be forfeited. But unlike the earl of Southampton or Archbishop Cranmer he did not stand conspicuously with Cromwell up to, or even beyond, his fall. He did not obviously take sides at all until the king's mind was very clear, and only one account suggests that he was even involved in the minister's interrogation thereafter.[251] In the aftermath of Cromwell's arrest Henry's greatest aim was to rid himself of Anne, and Suffolk set loyally to his part in that task. He had been involved in Cromwell's attempts to extricate the king, and he was an important witness to the details of the negotiations for the marriage treaty. He was no longer among the king's daily intimates, who could testify to the non-consummation of the marriage or Henry's complaints about his wife.[252] But he was still the king's trusted servant. He became Henry's leading negotiator with Anne, assuring her of the king's brotherly affection, securing her consent to the divorce, and persuading her to explain the situation to her brother, the duke of Cleves. He reorganised her household, explained the whole affair in the House of Lords, and gave evidence for the divorce in convocation.[253] Anne was more pliable than Catherine of Aragon, but Suffolk performed the task with a fine mixture of persuasion and coercion: he spent eight days wheedling her into writing to her brother, but he took care to set up an effective spy system in her household.[254]

The latter days of Cromwell's ministry, like those of Wolsey's, had been kind to Suffolk. Certainly they were a great improvement on the years before 1536. Lord Bray gave up paying his £20 annuity to the duke in 1533, presumably because Brandon's influence was no longer worth buying. In 1536–7 Suffolk sued for the arrears, though the verdict is unknown. Then in May 1538 Lord Bray granted the duke a new annuity of £30.[255] The fall of Cromwell, like that of Wolsey, affected Suffolk less than it did more overtly political figures. In April 1540 letters from Calais to the leaders of the Privy Council were addressed to Cromwell, Norfolk, and Suffolk; in August 1540 letters from Ireland to the leaders of the Privy Council were addressed to Norfolk and Suffolk.[256] But in 1540 as in 1529 it was Norfolk who led the new regime. Suffolk could never dominate the government sufficiently to bend it to his private ends, for example over his French lawsuits and the outstanding £850 or so of dower income. He badgered ambassadors to pursue these matters, but they only really paid attention when Cromwell insisted, either because Suffolk's complaints were temporarily a useful counter to French demands, or because the minister had special reason to be grateful to the duke.[257] Without the administrative control of a Cromwell, or the queen-making ambitions of a Norfolk, Suffolk had always to pursue his ends by his personal means. In France these were unsuccessful, the more so because of the death of his agent,

Nicolas de St Martin, in 1538.[258] But in Lincolnshire, in the royal household, and as the king's trusted servant, the private power at the duke's disposal had been greatly increased by the events of the last four years.

6

The King's Lieutenant:
1540–1545

Wars and rumours of wars had always furthered Suffolk's career, and Henry's return to battle in the 1540s, first against the Scots, then against the French, gave the duke a central place in national government and the king's affections. Brandon's military responsibilities grew steadily: rumours of a trip to check the Calais fortifications in November 1540 and an expedition to defend the Calais Pale in August 1542 came to nothing, but in October and November 1542 he guarded the border while Norfolk and others invaded Scotland.[1] From January 1543 to March 1544 he served as Henry's lieutenant in the north; from July to November 1544 he commanded the king's own ward of the vast army sent to France. In June and July 1545 he reviewed coastal defences and organised the defence of southern England, and in August he had begun to fortify Portsmouth and was about to lead an army to the relief of Boulogne when he died.[2] When not on campaign, he was needed in council for his military experience. From October 1540 to March 1541 he attended only 60 per cent of council meetings.[3] As war approached and parliament sat, he was present at 97 per cent of meetings from November 1541 to April 1542.[4] From March to June and in November and December 1544 he sat in the vast majority of known sessions; from January 1545 to his death he attended assiduously, for an overall rate of 62 per cent concealed several prolonged absences from court on military business and at least one illness.[5]

For all this activity was maintained through years of declining health. In November 1540 the French ambassador Marillac thought Suffolk neither 'en aaige ny disposition de voiager'.[6] In January 1542 the duke was allowed to sit during the opening of parliament, and in October of that year a bad leg immobilised him for over a week.[7] On 17 March 1545 his treasurer William Naunton turned away a desperate suitor because Suffolk 'had byn very seke all the night before, and was then newly fallen aslepe.'[8] By the 20th he had recovered, but by 21 August he was too ill to sit in council, and he died next afternoon at 4 p.m.[9] Concern for his health was reflected in a proliferating retinue of foreign medical advisers: to 'Doctor Leonarde', employed since 1525, were added John Vandernot, surgeon, by April 1543, Dr Marten Kyrnbeck by November 1543, and 'Frances Grevyn, physician' by 1545.[10]

The Northern Border

Command in the north was a new challenge for Suffolk. As royal lieutenant his authority was not just military: he had to 'give accompte to the kinge for the hole countre'.[11] He found himself settling feuds in the York oligarchy, obtaining licences to excuse northerners from fish days, raising northern horse to serve in France, and wondering whether to restrain all the northern peers and MPs from going to parliament in case of war.[12] He had to defend the north from Scottish piracy and from popular insurrection.[13] Border conditions generated endless accusations of treason or disloyalty, and the duke had to investigate these, oversee trials, and administer punishments, though in all these matters he could receive strong directions from the king and council.[14]

Suffolk's control extended to less sensational aspects of border life, licensing Scotsmen to pasture their animals unmolested, or ensuring that the proper sums were spent on repairs to Berwick bridge.[15] He was the king's local agent in minor matters, the arrest of an errant servant, or the restoration of confiscated Norwegian goods.[16] But his powers could be sweeping. When cash did not arrive in time to pay his garrisons he could demand payment of the king's rents in the north directly to his treasurer. Though his financial position was easier than that of his successors in the lieutenancy, he did divert the rents in late summer 1543, and in November extracted a large loan from the mayor and aldermen of Newcastle.[17] He was not a northern magnate in his own right and this perhaps complicated his task. But he was a great man about the king, and could play on the fact. In urging the city of York to let his son-in-law, now the earl of Cumberland, command its contingent of troops, he pointed out that 'the nowe erle haif freynds redy to be medyatours unto the king's majestie in all his laufull affayers.'[18]

Soon the north clamoured for Suffolk's patronage. In late 1542 local suitors appealed to Bishop Tunstal of Durham, Norfolk, and Suffolk; by July 1543 entire communities, like the inhabitants of the Yorkshire coast, sued to Suffolk alone.[19] Even after he left the north, his long presence there and his role in central government brought him a string of requests for help, and he was often successful in responding. In 1545 he secured one man's release by the Scots, gained the council's intervention to save another from the oppression of the Archbishop of York, and helped a third obtain an important lease: in the last case the king's decision even echoed Suffolk's phrase that his friend's opponent was 'somwhat to strayt laced'.[20] During his lieutenancy the duke had been given a considerable role in northern appointments. Minor posts were his to grant: as post-rider at Wetherby he probably appointed a relation of one of his followers.[21] More important positions were filled by the king, and Suffolk was merely notified. But he named temporary substitutes when border offices fell vacant, advised on suitable replacements, and in one instance drew up a short-list of candidates with Tunstal and Lord Parr.[22] Suffolk claimed to co-ordinate patronage in the king's service. Ignoring the suits of numerous friends, he advised delay in granting out the offices of the late Sir Reginald Carnaby, so that these might be deployed to support a new keeper of Tynedale.[23] He also influenced patronage to his own ends. Sir Thomas Wharton requested Suffolk's good lordship to help secure the stewardship of Sheriff Hutton for Wharton's son; two months later it was granted to the duke's own bastard son Charles, who went on to make a career for himself in Yorkshire and on the borders.[24]

Suffolk's influence as commander-in-chief was more direct. He regularly ordered gentlemen of his choice throughout the north and midlands to prepare troops to serve under him.[25] He adjudicated disputes over the division of ransoms after the battle of Solway Moss, pronouncing that one party's claims were 'against all reason, and all the lawe of armes that ever have bene; nor never the like demaunde hathe bene redde of in any cronnycle, nor harde tell of in any contre.'[26] He protected the captains of his retinue and other clients. In November 1542 he asked Hertford, then warden-general of the Marches, to let Philip Tyrwhit of Barton-on-Humber return home to see his ailing father.[27] Suffolk's intrusive cousin Sir John Cavendish faced numerous lawsuits in his attempt to establish himself in the Isle of Axholme, but the duke spared him one appearance before the court of augmentations in September 1543 by insisting that military necessity prevented Cavendish leaving the north.[28] In the Yorkshire musters of March 1544 one gentleman was 'spared and discharged' at Suffolk's request, and in January 1545 Suffolk asked Shrewsbury not to summon a ducal deputy in a Yorkshire office for renewed border service.[29]

Despite all these powers, Suffolk's lieutenancy was a difficult and unsatisfying job. His inexperience on the borders was demonstrated in October 1542 before he even left Yorkshire, when he suddenly realised that half the 6,000 troops with which he was supposed to counter any Scottish invasion were border tenants, who were bound only to defend their own locality and not to march against the Scots. That year he ventured to Alnwick only with reluctance, and hurried home to Lincolnshire as soon as he could.[30] When he returned he braved Newcastle for a few weeks, but then settled down at Darlington with Tunstal.[31] From there it would have been hard to exercise tight control over the borders, though Darlington was well sited for communications with Carlisle. The retreat to Darlington also marked the end of Suffolk's serious involvement in Scottish affairs. From January to March 1543 he dealt directly with those Scottish nobles who favoured Henry's plans for a marriage between the infant Mary, Queen of Scots and Prince Edward, notably Sir George Douglas and the earl of Angus; with Arran the vacillating governor; and with the anti-English dowager Queen Mary of Guise.[32] Even then he was not Henry's only link with any of the Scots, but from mid-March, when the king sent Sir Ralph Sadler to Edinburgh to expedite a favourable settlement between the nations, Suffolk's role in Henry's Scottish policy was minimal.[33] Until the autumn he merely collected news and sent it south, and received Henry's letters and sent them north.

The failure of Sadler's mission drove Henry back into reliance on Douglas and Angus, and Suffolk again supervised English relations with them. He did not find this an easy task. By December 1543 he would not venture to explain their actions to king and council, since the general untruthfulness of the Scots made this, in his judgement, impossible. By February 1544 he concluded that the Scots were 'straunge men to medle with, and lytill to trust to'.[34] Perhaps Suffolk was hoodwinked by the Douglases who could never sacrifice their own political survival to their English loyalties. He seemed consistently impressed by their protestations of faithfulness to Henry's interests, and tried to mitigate the council's harshness in rebuking their inactivity.[35] Yet he did warn them of the dangers of Henry's wrath, he was far less generous with cash than with encouragement, and he dealt firmly with their attempts to protect their uncommitted friends from English attack.[36] They were confident enough of their indispensability to flaunt offers from the Francophile Cardinal Beaton to betray the English cause, and so badly did Henry need Scottish friends that large pensions were on offer for any nobles who made the slightest overtures to the English.[37] In such circumstances Suffolk had no option but to trust the Douglases, and he did his best not to let them have everything their own way.

A major issue in his wrangling with them was the fate of their friends' border estates. Suffolk bore responsibility for the state of the borders, but exercised little direct control over raiding. In June 1543 he turned this to advantage, advising the warden-general Lord Parr to instruct those suffering Scottish raids to revenge themselves on an unofficial basis, thus satisfying the aggrieved English borderers, but appearing to uphold the truce.[38] This was the natural reaction of all borderers anyway, and once the truce broke down in September, at Arran's defection to Beaton's party, large raids co-ordinated by Parr and Suffolk were interspersed with local efforts.[39] Such incursions needed little encouragement: even the gentlemen Suffolk brought from Lincolnshire, and Parr's captains from Warwickshire, soon caught the local enthusiasm for nocturnal devastation.[40] In any case, raids and the ensuing local negotiations were better directed by a warden-general at Alnwick or Warkworth than by a lieutenant at Darlington. From January to April 1543 John Dudley, Viscount Lisle had executed the warden-generalship with proper deference to Suffolk and with considerable skill, but also with a degree of confident independence which must have made the duke feel rather redundant.[41] Dudley's replacement, William Lord Parr, expected and received rather more guidance from Suffolk, but still had to take important decisions by himself.[42] Parr corresponded directly with Henry and the council, and was most irritated when Suffolk declined to forward one of his letters, despite Tunstal's assurances that this was for Parr's good.[43] Otherwise the two peers co-operated well, and there were signs of a friendship: in May 1543 they arranged to meet at Greatham, first to course with greyhounds, then 'whan the horse run[n]yng shalbe'.[44] At Suffolk's funeral Parr, by then earl of Essex, was a leading mourner.[45]

In theory Parr directed the deputy-wardens, but in the case of Sir Thomas Wharton, based at Carlisle, he was fortunate even to be notified of his deputy's activities. Wharton, very much the rising star on the borders, only called in Suffolk when he needed help to discipline his raiders.[46] Often Sir Thomas dealt directly with Henry and the council, and with Scotland's western borderers, merely informing the lieutenant of these negotiations and the intervening raids. But however far Wharton's independence and geographical isolation deprived the duke of control over him, they could not deprive the lieutenancy of its honour: even Wharton found himself thanking Suffolk humbly for 'your honorable goodnis shewid unto me at my lait being at Darnton'.[47]

Suffolk's supremacy would have become more practical had he

commanded an invasion of Scotland. He was eager to do so, and resoundingly dismissed suspicions that he was physically unfit. 'I thanke God of his grace', he told the king, 'I dowt not to sustaigne not oonly that jornaye, but I trust many worse then that, as well as they that arr more yonger then I.'[48] Henry was keen for Suffolk to lead an invasion, assuring him that 'we wold be loth but that youe shuld have th'onour therof in recompence of your former travail.'[49] An invasion would have been the natural culmination of many of his efforts in the north. In 1542 he had been attentive to problems of supply, entrusting them to his household servants, and saving many of the returning army by his prompt provision of victuals.[50] In 1543 he kept a tight rein on food supplies – as all northern lieutenants had to do – ready to victual an army at any point.[51] Meanwhile he sought to reduce the costs of border warfare, saving the king's money for a decisive campaign.[52] Strategic planning also suited Suffolk's talents better than trying to manipulate Scottish politics. On the latter he developed his own views only in the autumn of 1543, but from the first attempt to arrange an invasion, in February 1543, he played an independent role in military preparations.[53] Suffolk appreciated the impossibility of victualling a large army in Scotland by conventional means, and each time he was called upon to plan an invasion – in February, April, July, August, and September 1543, and in February and March 1544 – he contrived a different solution. His suggestion of September 1543, to avoid problems of insufficient carts and poor roads by carrying small beer barrels on the soldiers' mounts, was met with derision by the privy council.[54] The duke turned with enthusiasm to a possibility repeatedly raised by the king throughout 1543, the use of ships.[55] Previous frustrations with ships had discouraged him from this option, but his view changed when the Douglases finally deserted the English cause in January 1544. This made the projected invasion less an intervention in Scottish politics than an offensive against a hostile nation.[56] Suffolk's consequent planning, and gathering of ships, horses and victuals from the entire north, laid the foundations for Hertford's successful attack on Edinburgh in May.[57]

In all these preparations Suffolk co-operated with other councillors, notably Gardiner in 1544.[58] He also worked closely with local experts. He was still a comparative novice on the borders, reminding the king in February 1544 that he could not advise which local gentlemen should accompany an invasion because 'I nevour sawe noone experyence of noon of them.'[59] Tunstal was a great help, but Suffolk called on the borderers for real expertise. Twice their indisputable judgement on local conditions saved the duke from attempting dangerous expeditions conceived by the king.[60] Their advocacy of the maintenance of strong defensive garrisons and of thorough devastation of the Scottish borders sprang from self-interest, but they did give Suffolk an appreciation of the role in border warfare of careful victualling and of destruction of the enemy's crops which helped his planning in 1544.[61] Such consultation also gave the borderers increasing confidence in the duke, leading them to present their schemes for the north and its defence to him rather than directly to the king.[62]

Suffolk left the north in March 1544 without any notable achievement. His policy had always been cautious: he took numerous bonds and hostages from the assured Scots, was sceptical of the fickle promises of the border clans, dismissed an agent in Scotland whose loyalty was questioned, and managed to avoid Henry's more reckless military schemes.[63] The king could be a hard taskmaster, whether asking the duke shamelessly to break a truce 'without the manifest offence of his majestie's honour', or responding to the bewildering fluctuations of Scottish politics, by constantly changing his mind about invasions.[64] Yet Suffolk executed his lieutenancy to the satisfaction of the usually ungrateful monarch. In November 1543 Henry assured him that he appreciated his hard work, and only wished him to remain in the north to reap the reward of honour for which he had laboured. In January 1544 he promised Suffolk a double reward: the leadership of the Scottish invasion, should it be mounted before the royal expedition to France, and the choicest command at Henry's side in the French campaign.[65] The first of these prizes had to be left for Hertford, but the second and greater was eagerly claimed by Suffolk.

The Expedition to Boulogne and the Defence of Southern England

Henry's aim in 1544, perhaps confided only in Brandon, was to ensure tangible gain by refusing to advance on Paris until Boulogne was taken.[66] This left Norfolk and Russell to besiege Montreuil with insufficient forces and poor lines of supply, as a sop to Charles V and a cover for the king's siege. Norfolk was particularly embittered by this situation, and so were his and Russell's troops.[67] Suffolk bore the difficult responsibility for setting up the siege of Boulogne, in such a way that the king could safely come and supervise it and be assured of a great victory. But at least he had all the resources he needed, and his successful execution of the task guaranteed the affection of his grateful master. By October, in Henry's words, the fact that Suffolk was 'o[ur] chief minister in the wynnyng of Bulleyn' reinforced the 'sp[ec]iall love, confidence and good affection w[hich] we beare to you before others'.[68] The contrast was evident to Norfolk as early as 5 August. He was desperately worried about criticism of his conduct at Montreuil, and reflected significantly that 'it is oftentymes sene, that som[m]e men[n]ys doyng[es] be taken moche better, than som[m]e oth[er] mennys be.' He thanked Suffolk for speaking up to the king on his behalf, and begged his help in procuring the dispatch of a sympathetic observer to Montreuil, appealing to 'all th'oulde love and acquay[n]taince that of longe co[n]tynua[n]ce hathe bene bytwene us.'[69] At no other point in the reign could Norfolk have written Suffolk such a letter. Howard continued to hope for his junior's help in the council at Boulogne, for their respective roles in the French campaign marked a large change in their relationships with each other, with the king and with the rest of the council, a change which left Norfolk increasingly isolated.[70]

As the invasion was planned, Suffolk had been relaxed enough to crack jokes in privy council meetings, and as the armies landed on the continent, his combination of firmness and courtesy in co-operation with the regent Mary of Hungary contrasted sharply with Norfolk's complaints.[71] While Norfolk and Russell bickered, Suffolk led a harmonious council of war composed largely of his friends. Sir Anthony Browne had worked with the duke in September

1543, was at his side in 1544 all the way from Greenwich to Boulogne, and signed his most secret letters; Lord St John acted as Suffolk's trusted logistical expert. Both were executors of Brandon's will, made in June.[72] The Earl of Arundel, marshal of Suffolk's ward, was second mourner at the duke's funeral, when the leading mourner was Suffolk's son-in-law Dorset, who led the foot in the advance to Boulogne and was to have captained the rearguard in the duke's expedition of 1545.[73] The other prominent member of Brandon's council was Sir John Gage, a respected captain whom Suffolk had twice requested from Henry as a lieutenant for Scottish invasions.[74]

It is unsurprising that Suffolk's leadership was consultative, as it had been in previous campaigns.[75] Even after Henry's arrival important decisions were made in the council of war, 'remytting nevertheles the alteration therof to the king[es] moost excellent wisedome'.[76] Suffolk also played a distinctive personal role. He reconnoitred and skirmished ahead of his army, and braved the garrison's fire as his pioneers dug trenches towards the town.[77] His retinue was not large – 400 foot and 100 or 150 horse, recruited from Lincolnshire tenants and household servants – but was prominent in the fighting. His servant Edmund Hall organised transport; a gentleman of his household, Leonard Veale, was killed in a skirmish with French foragers; and of his captains Sir John Cavendish was paid a special reward of £6 13s 4d, and Francis Ayscough and the bastard Charles Brandon were knighted.[78]

Every observer commended the duke's conduct of the siege in the week before Henry's arrival. He established batteries on a commanding mound and within eighty paces of the walls, rewarding the gunners for the dangers this entailed; he took the outlying defences, began mining, and dug trenches to impede sorties.[79] Thereafter Henry built on this foundation unimaginatively, pursuing his original intention to bludgeon the town into surrender by an artillery battery of astonishing scale.[80] After Henry took charge, Suffolk concentrated on one quarter of the siege, though continuing to exercise a general command under the king.[81] He dealt with ambassadors and messengers, often working with the king's secretary, William Paget, or with Sir Anthony Browne, but referred their detailed requests to the whole council. Others conducted formal negotiations, including those for the surrender of the town, and this was wise, for Suffolk was not always master of the subtleties of diplomacy. But when Boulogne capitulated, the treaty was made in the duke's name, and he rode in on 14 September to occupy the town, as he had done at Tournai thirty-one years earlier.[82]

When Henry himself resolved to rest on his laurels and return home, Suffolk was appointed to press on to the aid of Norfolk and Russell at Montreuil. Before he could do so, the French advance, enabled by Charles V's decision to abandon the unco-operative English and make peace, enforced a general retreat to Boulogne.[83] Henry then gave Brandon 'specyall favour and credyte for execucion of his com[m]andem[en]t': to defend Boulogne with the reunited army, and refortify it in accordance with plans made by the king himself.[84] Unfortunately Henry's designs were impractical, supplies were short, the weather was bitter, and the French attacked on 1 October.[85] They then marched on to threaten Guînes, and the disgruntled mercenaries mutinied and abandoned the English. On 2 October Mary of Hungary issued the inevitable order to her troops to withdraw, but by the time they left on the 4th the English too had 'soudainem[en]t dep[ar]ti.'[86] For on Friday 3 October, with the agreement of John Dudley, Viscount Lisle, who was left to hold Boulogne, the dukes and Russell beat a ragged retreat to Calais.[87]

Henry was furious, especially since they had abandoned many of the town's supplies in the unfortified lower town where the French could take them.[88] The councillors at Calais replied jointly to the king's irate letters, to justify the withdrawal, point out their zealous defence of Guînes and the Pale, and explain that the French advance prevented the return to Boulogne which Henry had ordered.[89] Suffolk characteristically went further. He wrote alone to the king of his distress at the enforced withdrawal, distress caused in part by the grief the retreat would cause Henry. Echoing numerous submissions in the past, he begged the king 'whatsoever it shall please your ma[jestie] to doo with me', not to be too hard on his colleagues lest they be discouraged. He hoped Henry would pardon them all, since he knew well that the king 'ever aftre the trouth knowen useth to take thing[es] in suche sorte as they have been doon.' Finally, as humble subject but as true friend, he waited 'in greate care of mynde till I here of your majesties good pleas[ou]r.'[90] Henry did relent, and in late October when Norfolk and Russell went home, he asked Suffolk to stay on at Calais to relieve Boulogne if necessary. Brandon was to have a free choice of subordinates and, added Henry affectionately, 'to have a good respect to your own he[a]lth'.[91] The French withdrew, reducing Suffolk's duties to arranging the Pale garrisons and playing second string to Paget in fruitless peace negotiations.[92] By mid-November even these were petering out, and the duke occupied himself in apparently unsuccessful attempts to procure an obscure French humanist as teacher for his sons. By 22 November he was back in the privy council.[93]

The 1544 campaign brought Suffolk honour, patronage and even more tangible benefits. Before the invasion he was influential in appointments in the army, during it in appointments in Boulogne, and after it in appointments for those who had served under him.[94] His personal reward was Tattershall College. When he bought monastic lands in February 1541, the price was exactly twenty years' purchase, with additions for woods. Over 80 per cent of the price was paid in jewels at the time of the sale, the remainder was paid within two years, and the only possible concession was that Suffolk's surrender of his reversion on lands sold to the king by Sir William Sidney was generously valued at £500.[95] After three years of faithful military service, in February 1545, the duke negotiated terms for the grant of the lands of Tattershall College as what was rightly called by the augmentations officials a purchase and gift. At £2,666 13s 4d the total price was less than eight times the clear annual value, though Suffolk was bound to pay pensions and certain charitable provisions; the college's goods, debts, bells, and lead were included at no extra cost, and only half the purchase price was paid in cash.[96]

Had he lived through it, the fighting of 1545 might have

brought Suffolk further landed wealth; it certainly did bring him unaccustomed powers and useful patronage. He was licensed to retain 100 liveried gentlemen as a cavalry company.[97] As Henry's lieutenant in the southeast and south, directing preparations against a French invasion which in the event reached to the Isle of Wight but no further, he found the captains of local fortifications and the gentlemen raising local troops looking to him for instruction and help.[98] As designated commander of any English counter-attack across the Channel, he found foreign mercenary captains suing to him for assistance and employment.[99] Again he was working among friends. The commissioners of array for the southern counties were his three executors (St John, Browne, and Lord Chancellor Wriothesley) and the Earl of Arundel. Sir John Gage supervised the defence of Sussex, while the Sussex and Hampshire levies were led by Dorset and Sir Anthony Wingfield (another prominent mourner at Suffolk's funeral). When the confrontation with the French fleet in the Solent ended late in July and Henry left Portsmouth, Suffolk stayed on in charge there with St John.[100]

Because his command lay in the south, Suffolk was able to attend the council far more often than Russell or Norfolk, whose lieutenancies on the west and east coasts took them far from the king. Even when not in council he communicated advice to the king through Paget, who carefully sent him government correspondence to read. In August he was recalled to court as soon as he had prepared Lisle's fleet for sea and made Portsmouth partly defensible.[101] At least in wartime he was evidently a leading member of the council. This increased role in government extended well beyond military matters, though fellow councillors like Russell and Hertford respected him primarily for his martial abilities.[102] In particular, his recent experience in the north also gained him a special voice in Scottish policy.[103]

Politics and Government

In council he was no mere warmonger. In May 1545 he and Wriothesley urged Chapuys to help forge an Anglo-French peace, but not to mention their request to Henry who was unenthusiastic about a settlement. Such co-operation with Thomas Wriothesley, who joined the council on succeeding his master Cromwell as royal secretary in 1540, and then replaced Audley as Lord Chancellor in May 1544, was significant. In March 1545 Paget bracketed the chancellor and the duke together, apparently sincerely, as two loyal, intelligent, painstaking, just and honest royal servants; and often in 1544–5, when Suffolk was at the heart of government, he was working with Wriothesley.[104] They talked to ambassadors together, and reported to Henry on the council's discussions. In June 1544 they oversaw with Browne the king's borrowing at Antwerp, they settled with Paget a treaty with the earl of Lennox, and Suffolk named Wriothesley his executor.[105] In December 1544 they headed the audit commission for accounts from the French war, and in January 1545 they sat together at Baynard's Castle to assess London's citizens for the benevolence.[106] Both Hertford and Paget tended to mention them in letters as a pair, and they sometimes worked together in matters of patronage.[107] In 1542–3 Wriothesley had kept Suffolk in touch with the court and council; in April 1545 the duke stood godfather to the chancellor's son.[108]

Another godfather on that occasion was Arundel, who joined Wriothesley in advocating policies of moderate conservatism during the next reign. In 1547 Wriothesley alone opposed resolutely Hertford's assumption of the protectorate, failing because the support he might have expected from Browne, St John, and Gage was not forthcoming.[109] All these men were close to Suffolk, and had he survived they could perhaps have formed a less radical and more stable Edwardian regime than that which ensued. Indeed, only after Suffolk's death could the Howards contemplate, or reasonably be charged with, the pretensions to a protectorate 'both for services done and for estate' for which they were destroyed in Henry's dying months.[110] Had Suffolk lived, the events of 1546–7 might have taken a different turn. Unlike Hertford, or perhaps Norfolk, he was not statesman enough to aspire to the protectorate. Out of loyalty to Henry he would presumably have aimed at a stable conciliar regency, playing Bedford or Hastings rather than Humphrey or Richard of Gloucester.

His experience since 1540 fitted him for a leading part in such a regime. His attendance rate in the 1542 session of parliament was 84 per cent, well above the average, and he was active in at least one debate.[111] In 1541–2 he had more official and unofficial contact with ambassadors than ever before, and in 1544 he spoke to them authoritatively on Scottish affairs.[112] He took a more prominent part in the imprisonment and interrogation of Queen Catherine Howard than in any such affair since the fall of Wolsey, and played a role in the other investigations and trials of 1541 and 1542.[113] Even before the war, Henry's resolution to rule by council, rather than by one minister, elevated Suffolk and his colleagues. In this atmosphere the duke throve, taking on increasingly varied work. In 1544–5 he was even named to several financial commissions, and though experts must have done the detailed auditing he did, for example, sign indentures with purchasers of crown lands.[114]

Despite his prominence in government, Suffolk was apparently inactive in the political conflicts of the period. He missed their most acute moments by his absence in 1543 and his death before 1546, and indeed he was away in the north when he supposedly led an attempt to arrest Gardiner.[113] Suffolk worked well with all his colleagues, and there is no sign that any of them bore him the sort of animosity that Russell felt for Browne and Norfolk, or Paget, Hertford, and Lisle felt for Gardiner.[116] Suffolk's executors Browne and Wriothesley were close collaborators with Gardiner in conservative plotting; yet Hertford looked to Suffolk for help, readily took Suffolk's candidates into his service, and found the duke amenable to the requests of his brother Sir Thomas Seymour in military appointments.[117] Perhaps all the leading politicians thought Suffolk either too friendly or too feckless to be a threat. Norfolk does seem to have taken advantage of him in November 1542, promising to see Suffolk's retinue relieved of duty in the border garrisons and then advising Henry to order the very opposite.[118] But Brandon's attempts to evade his commitments throughout the campaign justified such treatment, and otherwise his fellows treated him as nobody's enemy but nobody's fool.

Politics and Religion

The strength of Suffolk's political position was reinforced by his wife's increasing involvement with reforming groups at court. Her early links with Queen Catherine Parr signified little, for she was expected to draw near to any important female members of the royal family. She spent time with Anne of Cleves and Catherine Howard, and played cards and frequently exchanged gifts with Princess Mary.[119] Before she attended Catherine Parr's wedding in July 1543, she did not move in the Seymours' rather reformist social circle. By spring 1544 she could be found visiting the countess of Hertford and sending a horse to the earl, but that summer the queen still paid far more attention to the countess and her friend Lady Herbert than to the duchess.[120] At some point before August 1545 Duchess Catherine supposedly insulted Gardiner over dinner, but only once widowed did she plainly take sides.[121] Perhaps she was freed by Suffolk's death to reveal her true views; perhaps her weakness forced her to choose one end or the other of the rapidly polarizing political and religious spectrum; most likely Suffolk's death was coincidental to the gradual development of her friendships and beliefs.

In November 1545 the queen spoke to the king on the duchess's behalf, and in the same month the duchess stood godmother to Lady Lisle's daughter.[122] In February 1546 those who bound themselves for the payment for her son's wardship included most of the leading evangelical courtiers: John Gates, Sir Philip Hoby, Sir William Herbert, Sir Anthony Denny, Sir Ralph Sadler, Sir William Paget, and Dr George Owen, lately the queen's doctor.[123] In June of that year she was accused of helping the imprisoned Protestant Anne Ayscough, and in early 1547 Chapuys named her for the first time among the queen's dangerous reformist friends, in the company of Lady Lisle and the countess of Hertford. Whatever the truth of later suggestions that the duke's daughters Frances and Eleanor were also involved, it was clear by 1547 that Duchess Catherine had found her lifelong home in the Protestant camp.[124] In the last years of Suffolk's life, her views were probably less clear cut, but none the less must have eased her husband's relations with the rising generation at court and in the council.

The duke's own beliefs remained on the conservative side of ambiguity. Though English exiles in Germany mourned him as a thorough favourer of the gospel, those around him knew better.[125] At his death Christopher Lynham was still dean of his chapel: then aged sixty-seven and in ducal service for thirty-five years, he conformed to both the Edwardian and Marian settlements.[126] Suffolk was allowed by statute six resident household chaplains. Of the six at his funeral, two were probably undistinguished former Oxford fellows.[127] Another left a Protestant will in 1556, though he had been happy to be appointed a chantry priest in 1540, only two years before Suffolk first took him up.[128] Thomas Launcelyn's will was doctrinally neutral in 1551, as perhaps befitted his role as the duke's receiver-general.[129] Alfonso de Salinas, presumably a maternal relation of the duchess, went on to be made a prebendary of Westminster by Queen Mary.[130] Suffolk's other chaplains and presentees in his last years were an equally mixed selection. One chaplain was deprived for marriage under Mary, restored under Elizabeth, and left a reformist will; another became a royal chaplain under Mary.[131] Two ex-monks of Revesby and the former Abbot of Hagnaby, a client of Lady Mary Willoughby and a long-standing Willoughby administrator, received benefices.[132] Under Mary one of the Revesby monks conformed, to die a conservative in 1559; the Abbot of Hagnaby was deprived for marriage and restored only in 1559; and William Newton, presented to Scarborough in March 1545, was consistently troubled, but for misconduct rather than for heresy.[133] Of all the clergy linked with the duke only one seems to have gone into exile under Mary, as the duchess did.

This was John Parkhurst, the future Bishop of Norwich. Ordained by the radical Bishop Shaxton, known as a breaker of the Lenten fast, and already mounting verse attacks on the conservative bishops, he was clearly of convinced reforming views in 1542 when he entered the Suffolk household.[134] At that time, though, he made no mention of the duchess's good doctrine, and he soon passed on into Catherine Parr's service.[135] His presence at Grimsthorpe and Kew largely coincided with Suffolk's absence in the north, and he was far more the duchess's man than the duke's. When he died twenty years later he left an impressive cup to Peregrine Bertie, her son by her second marriage, 'for a token onelie of my love to hym and all his stock'.[136] And it was by no means only – probably not primarily – his theology that made Parkhurst a good chaplain. He embellished the ducal entourage with his learned Latin verses, imploring God to heal Duchess Catherine's illnesses, rejoicing at the duke's return from the north, and flattering his master with lines such as

> Mauors cum Carlum vidisset in arma ruentem
> Obstupuit, dicens: Carolus alter ego est.[137]

Parkhurst's learning reportedly impressed the king, and it would be no surprise if it attracted Suffolk, who had by 1542 to think of 'th'onest brynging upp of my sonnes in lernyng[es] and other vertuous education'.[138]

Parkhurst was only seven years older than the duchess; both were a generation apart from Suffolk and Lynham, and the duke was never likely to take up the new faith with the enthusiasm of his juniors. His will does suggest familiarity with the reformers' phraseology, leaving his soul to God 'who hath redemed the same by the merytt[es] of his passion' and requesting burial 'w[ith]owt any pompe or owtward pride of the world'.[139] But, like Henry, he still valued prayer for the dead, requesting dirges from his chaplains and the priests of Tattershall College, and leaving £100 to his poorest tenants 'to th'entent to pray for my soule'. At his death Suffolk was still firmly attached to what he called 'the aunciaunt and laudable custome of the church of England'.

Continental Contacts

Suffolk was, however, prepared to employ people of more radical religious views than his own, and not just as chaplains. John Dymmock was an English merchant who had picked up Protestantism in Antwerp, where he spent most of his life, and married a local woman.[140] He did business for the English government for three decades, but always felt the need of a patron alongside the king.[141] Between Cromwell and Paget he served Suffolk, who needed his skills badly.[142] The duke had been trying to sell lead from his dissolved monasteries on the continent, since by 1539 the domestic price had collapsed.[143] In May 1539 the Cologne merchant Derich Born bound himself to Suffolk in £1,000 to buy £600 worth of the duke's lead, but then defaulted, and by August 1540 Suffolk persuaded Lord Chancellor Audley to threaten all the Cologne merchants in the London Steelyard with distraint.[144] In January 1541 the duke went ahead and confiscated a ship full of cloth. He pursued his grievance at Cologne, through Bishop Gardiner (in Germany for the Diet of Regensburg), and a personal representative, and at Westminster, with a successful lawsuit against Born, until he had the Steelyard itself on his side. By February 1543 a settlement was under arbitration – it emerged that most of the problems were due to a split between Derich and his brother Johann – and by September Derich was at work with Dymmock in the exchange market. By July 1545 Suffolk again counted Born as his 'fey[th]ful serviteur', but in 1540 Dymmock seemed a safer choice of salesman.[145] In October 1540 Dymmock was licensed to export bell metal, bought from Suffolk, from the port of Boston. A mutually satisfactory relationship soon developed: by July 1545 Dymmock was selling large volumes of Suffolk's lead, on a difficult Antwerp market, at a price over 25 per cent higher than that notionally paid by the duke to the crown.[146] The real benefit to Suffolk was greater still, for he had never paid for the lead and bells of Leiston and Eye, and eventually he (or his executors) agreed to repay the crown with the same amount of Lincolnshire monastic lead, thus exploiting the deflated market price.[147]

An associate of Dymmock in these sales was Dr Marten Kyrnbeck. He too moved between Antwerp and England: in September 1545 he was at Suffolk's funeral, in October he took the executors' instructions to Dymmock.[148] Kyrnbeck was the duke's physician, but he played many other parts. He was intimate with councillors and ambassadors in the Low Countries, and provided useful intelligence for Suffolk and the English government.[149] Suffolk's patronage of men like Kyrnbeck and Dymmock, overseas servants of the crown, increased his own importance in the regime. It also brought him contacts among the German and Dutch intellectuals and artists fashionable in England. As Martinus Corenbeckius, Kyrnbeck was a correspondent of the humanist physician Hadrianus Junius, while Kyrnbeck's host in Antwerp on at least one occasion was Derich Born.[150] Born and Derich Berck, his colleague in the purchase of Suffolk's lead, were both early patrons of Hans Holbein.[151] Holbein's executor was Jan van Antwerpen, who mined Suffolk's estates for gold in 1538; Jan's partner then was Hans Fromont, with whom the duke did business again in 1543 and 1545.[152] It seems no coincidence that it was in the early 1540s, when his contacts with these merchants were most frequent, that Suffolk commissioned a spate of drawings and paintings by Holbein, including two delightful miniatures of his sons.[153]

Brandon also had a servant among the Italian merchants of London. This was Baptista Borone, a Milanese who held a financial office in the ducal service. When he was robbed of rings by another Italian, Suffolk and the duchess intervened with Chapuys to secure the return of his goods, which had been recaptured in the Low Counties. In July 1544 Suffolk, Wriothesley, and Browne arranged for Borone to transfer his wool-export licence to Bartolommeo Compagna, who had also done business with the duke.[154] In 1545–6 Borone increasingly served the crown, and was rewarded with denisation. But like Dymmock, Born and Kyrnbeck he maintained his links with Suffolk, attending the duke's funeral and in 1552 still leasing London houses from the duchess.[155]

Connections and Influence

This network of continental contacts had no connection with the duke's earlier activities in France. By the 1540s, the lawsuits of Suffolk, Hampton, and Dupin merely provided a fossilised phrase in the litany of English complaints about French injustice.[156] But many other elements of Brandon's earlier career did produce legacies enduring into the 1540s. He retained friends from his first days in the court. Sir Griffith Don attended Brandon's marriage to Anne Browne; when Don made his will in 1542 much of his clothing lay 'in my chamb[e]r at my lorde of Suff[olk's] place besides Westminster'.[157] The young men raised in the ducal household had sometimes reached positions of influence. By 1545 Sir Richard Long was a gentleman of the privy chamber, well placed to mention Suffolk's suits to the king, and ready to do so. Lord Cobham was by then deputy of Calais, able to appoint the duke's nominees to posts in the garrison, and eager to provide hospitality for the duke and duchess when they toured the defences of his native Kent.[158]

Nor were Suffolk's links with Wales and the borders at a complete end. In 1541 or 1542 he sent one Welsh servant to north Wales in search of merlins, and in 1545 he secured the wardship of the heir of another ducal servant, resident in Conway, for a third ducal dependent.[159] In the same year he sponsored the appointment of a constable of Holt Castle.[160] He retained contact with both branches of the Cornewall family. George, son of Sir Richard, had had to be expelled from Suffolk's service after violent affrays in the ducal household in 1532.[161] But Lady Jane, Sir Richard's widow, presented a ducal chaplain to a living in 1544, while Richard, son of Sir Thomas, mustered his troops among Suffolk's retinue that year.[162] In Oxfordshire too Brandon kept a foothold, retaining his lease at Water Eaton and keeping his place on the bench for the county town. He led the town's arbitrators in negotiations with the university in 1541, was named by the king to settle such disputes in 1542, and took Oxford's troops with him to France in 1544.[163]

With East Anglia he naturally retained still greater links. His relations were still deeply entrenched there: three of the four justices sitting at Woodbridge on 2 October 1544 were Sir Humphrey Wingfield, Christopher Glemham, and Thomas Seckford.[164] He apparently married off a bastard daughter, Mary, to a Norfolk gentleman, and his brother-in-law, Nicholas Arrowsmith, though settled at Huntingfield, remained in the ducal service.[165] His alienations of land to his followers involved him in lawsuits in defence of their titles, and the business of the Willoughby estates kept his council in contact with local towns and gentlemen, but it was personal bonds that tied Brandon most tightly.[166] John Drury of Rougham, a Suffolk commissioner of sewers, attended his funeral.[167]

So did William Naunton, still the duke's treasurer though settled at Alderton in Suffolk, and Thomas Huntley, a gentleman of the household who still held the East Anglian bailiwicks granted to him by the duke.[168] The Seckford family in particular linked the duke with his Suffolk past. Thomas was chamberlain of his household and still held the offices at Wingfield given him by Brandon. His sons Francis and John served under Suffolk in the north in 1542, and at the duke's funeral Francis carried the banner of the ducal arms and John, and a third brother Anthony, were coffin-bearers. Both John and his brother Thomas made Lincolnshire marriages, one to the daughter of Suffolk's follower George Metham.[169]

Other members of Brandon's family were of continuing importance to him. In 1545 John Wingfield was still steward of his household and Charles Wingfield, Sir Anthony's son, was his master of the horse.[170] Robert Wingfield was still a ducal auditor, and Edmund Hall was named chief feodary of Suffolk's Lincolnshire and Nottinghamshire estates in 1541.[171] Edmund Hall and Charles Wingfield commanded garrisons under the duke in 1542, as did George Wingfield, one of the sons of Lewis Wingfield whom Sir Robert Wingfield had raised.[172] More distant cousins still proved useful, Geoffrey Loveday of the Calais retinue pursuing Suffolk's affairs in Paris; and Suffolk kept an eye on his relations far away, inquiring into the argumentative Richard Cavendish's disputes with his fellow officers in Boulogne in July 1545.[173]

Outside East Anglia the duke had scarcely any relatives, and outside Lincolnshire he had scarcely any land. Yet his power spread by other means, especially through military command. By his death he was becoming a magnate across the northern midlands and the north, not on the scale of the Earls of Shrewsbury or Rutland but in the same mould. He remained close to the Earls of Rutland: Lord Roos, Duchess Catherine, and the servants of both families travelled between Grimsthorpe and Belvoir, and a room at Belvoir was kept for the duke, painted in June 1541 with fashionable 'anticke warkes'.[174] When the young earl's brother-in-law, Henry Lord Nevill, found he was being blackmailed by a magician – who offered first gambling success and musical skill, and then the deaths of unloved relations – he naturally turned to Suffolk for help.[175] The duke was less close to the Talbots, but could still ask Shrewsbury for a stag to feed the king at Grimsthorpe in 1541.[176] Lesser northern families courted Suffolk by placing sons in his household. Sir Arthur Darcy, a rising power in Yorkshire, was one of the duke's chosen subordinates for the Scottish invasion of September 1543; his second son Thomas commanded under Suffolk in 1542 and carried his coffin in 1545.[177] George Metham was standard-bearer at Brandon's funeral, and also led a garrison in 1542; he was the third son of Sir Thomas Metham of Metham in Yorkshire.[178] Henry Nevill of Chevet, son of the executed Sir John, bought land in 1544 from the father or brother of Suffolk's officers George and Matthew St Poll, and attended the duke's funeral in the following year.[179] Oswald Sysson was then a corpse-bearer; he was the ambitious and successful farmer of the former monastic estates at Selby, just rising into county society.[180] All these men were second-rate: younger sons, those recovering from family disaster, or arrivistes. But for a peer with Yorkshire estates worth less than £110 a year they were an impressive selection.[181]

Even further north the duke was beginning to make useful friends, like Cuthbert Horsley, the Northumberland justice of the peace and augmentations receiver.[182] In the midlands too Suffolk was growing in influence. In Northamptonshire he was asked in 1541 or before to arbitrate an alimony settlement.[183] From the same county came Francis Barnard of Abington, who bore a banner at the duke's funeral and continued in the duchess's service.[184] He was the son-in-law of John Haselwood of Maidwell, a recurrent candidate for the shrievalty of Northamptonshire who also leased and purchased lands in Lincolnshire.[185] Haselwood protected Katherine Gildon after the death of her husband Thomas, the Willoughby administrator: this link combined with his lease of Hanby Grange in Lenton to bring Haselwood and Barnard into Suffolk's orbit.[186] Though he retained some monastic estates there, Suffolk apparently had less contact with Warwickshire, presumably because of its greater distance from Lincolnshire. Nevertheless, Edward Ferrers of Baddesley Clinton commanded one of his garrisons in 1542.[187]

Office-holding contributed to Brandon's wealth and influence as it had done in his earliest days. In May 1544 he was appointed chief steward of all the lands controlled by the court of augmentations north of the Trent. The position carried a fee of £100 and no discernible duties besides the nomination of a deputy, whose fee was £20: Suffolk chose George St Poll.[188] The forest justiceship involved a little more work. Wood sales could be authorised by a general warrant to the master of the woods, in the court of general surveyors, but the supervision of the local judicial officers of the forests did necessitate the regular dispatch of letters requiring the proper keeping of courts 'as you tendre the contynuance of yo[ur] office.'[189] In this the duke had the help of regional deputies – in Hampshire, Wiltshire and Somerset, for example, his friend William, Lord St John.

The great mastership of the household was more onerous, but again Suffolk could work with friends. St John was lord chamberlain from May 1543, Gage comptroller, Browne master of the horse, and Sir Anthony Wingfield vice-chamberlain.[190] In his long northern absence Suffolk can have played little part in the running of the household, and the marshalsea court, for instance, was conducted by a large staff of well-qualified deputies, but on the French campaign he was very active in supervising the household and its provisions.[191] If he tried to keep household expenditure down to Cromwell's target he was, not surprisingly, unsuccessful, but the cost of the household did not rise dramatically until after his death, and at least he and his subordinates could exercise some control over the spending of the establishment's offshoots.[192] In any case, efficiency mattered less to Suffolk and his contemporaries than honour. He sometimes referred to himself as 'magnus magister Anglie', an assimilation of his post to the great offices of the kingdom rather than merely those of the royal household; and Lord Lisle for one thought that the prestige of the great mastership itself had been increased by the tenure of the noble duke.[193]

Ducal Finance

These three offices carried substantial fees and various other profits. Suffolk had done well from the dissolution too, but at his death John Dymmock at least thought his finances were in a dire state. Dymmock warned Brandon's executors in October 1545 that 'hyt ys not unknowen to those that do belonge unto me lord's grace but that me lord's grace dosse owe a good deall of mon[e]ys.'[194] In fact the problem was not as bad as it seemed. Just as he had used his Welsh offices and control of wood sales in the past, Suffolk had used his debt to the court of augmentations as a credit account. The complexities of crown finance enabled him, for example, to lend the king £2,000 in 1544 and earn £100 interest, at the same time as the augmentations claimed he owed the crown £3,256 16s 5d.[195] Between April and July that year his auditor Hugh Grantham negotiated away £1,212 12s 6d of the debt, by proving that the lands sold or leased to the duke had been undervalued or burdened with crown annuities.[196]

Two years earlier – when the crown reckoned Suffolk a good payer of debts – a similar process had ended in a lump payment of £1,986 11s. 4d. by the duke, and the latest debts would have been paid had he not died.[197] In due course his executors did pay them off one by one, and meanwhile Suffolk had enjoyed extended credit: the total in 1544 included the rent on Hoxne and other Norwich episcopal estates for 1537–8.[198] By 1553 Brandon's total debt to the crown was only £3,059 13s 6½d.[199] In his will he had assigned fifteen years' revenue from lands worth some £620 a year to pay his debts, provide for his younger son and fund other bequests, and in March 1546 his executors gave his widow control over these, professing the 'specyall truste and confydense that they beare towardys the seyd Ladye Katheryn.'[200] Even before she leased back many of his estates from the court of wards, her jointure and the Willoughby lands brought her a taxable income of £1,333 6s 8d, among the top ten peers.[201] She could manage comfortably, especially since her son's household as a minor would cost less than his father's, and the debt to the crown could be readily paid, just as the executors of Thomas, Earl of Rutland, whose income was little larger than Brandon's, paid off £10,000 within four years of his death in 1543. The wrangles over Suffolk's debts which permeated the next three reigns were the product not of his irresponsibility, but of the division of his estates and liabilities amongst numerous squabbling co-heirs.[202]

By 1545 Suffolk's estates produced over £2,500 a year, from which Norfolk's pension subtracted £413 6s. 8d., but to which the Willoughby lands added over £900, providing a net income of some £3,000.[203] The annual value of Tattershall College was bound to rise by over £120 as the late master and fellows died off or were beneficed – the duke's grants of pensions to them specified that they would be void if the holders were presented to a living of equal value, and at least one priest of the college was reimbursed with a chaplaincy in the household before long.[204] How far the duke sought to raise his landed income by other means is hard to tell. He did take some part in estate management, signing receipts in place of his auditors, and most of his leading servants, like John Wingfield, were involved too.[205] Whoever designed Suffolk's policy, it was a sound one. Woods were carefully husbanded, and leases kept to twenty-one years, however favoured the recipient. Improvements were encouraged, Suffolk providing the timber and stone for a local carpenter to construct three new mills at Tattershall and repair two old ones, all five of which he then leased from the duke.[206]

Suffolk's estate policy was coherent on the larger scale too. He consistently alienated lands outside Lincolnshire to concentrate his estates within the county. Some of his sales may have been short-term expedients, like that of Tasburgh in February 1542 for £400 cash in hand.[207] But when the duke secured grants of monastic lands in other counties, their destination could be plotted long in advance. The details of the 1542 grant had been worked out by 24 February 1541; on 26 September Henry, Earl of Cumberland, paid Suffolk £365 13s 5d for three manors in Craven, and the duke bound himself to deliver them; only in February 1542 did Suffolk secure his letters patent, and on 1 March he recognised in chancery his commitment to Cumberland.[208] Similar dealings must have lain behind the duke's other rapid alienations, often to local men. [209] Complex bargaining could continue long after the royal grant, as it did in the sale of Nottinghamshire and Northamptonshire lands to Richard Andrews, a dealer in monastic lands.[210] Other sales cannot have been planned at the time of the grants. Of the acquisitions made in 1538 Suffolk disposed of Stockingford, Warwickshire only in December 1542, and the Lancashire rectory of Leigh in February 1545.[211] He made little, if any, profit on these transactions, since the prices were always close to the twenty years' purchase he paid to the crown. But they provided him with the cash – including Tasburgh perhaps £3,650 in 1541–2 alone – which he needed to persuade the court of augmentations to sell him further blocks of land, always including Lincolnshire estates which he retained for himself.

Inside Lincolnshire Suffolk's dealings still aimed to raise cash, but also sought to concentrate his estates and reward his supporters. The July 1540 exchange with Francis Ayscough did all three, for Ayscough was described as the duke's servant, and paid £264 15s 4d in cash as part of the bargain.[212] One of Suffolk's attorneys in that transaction was Matthew St Poll; to him, and to his brother George, the duke alienated two outlying monastic properties in February 1541 and June 1544.[213] On the other hand, Suffolk snapped up the smallest scraps of land when they complemented the central Willoughby estates around Spilsby.[214] Even on the fringe of that area he alienated land only under special circumstances. When he sold the manor of Ashby Puerorum in 1545 it was to Thomas and Humphrey Littlebury of Stainsby, the nephews of the patriarch of the Willoughby retinue, John Littlebury of Hagworthingham. It was also for nearly twenty-two times the annual value.[215]

The Lincolnshire Affinity

Brandon's concentration on Lincolnshire was illustrated by his only purchase of non-monastic land outside the county after 1540. This was of a stable and meadows in Ware, Hertfordshire, conveniently on the road from London to Stamford and thence to Lincoln.[216] Such intensity of effort was rewarded in just nine years with a position of dominance in the county far more impressive than anything he achieved in East Anglia. The captains of the Lincolnshire levies he marched up to the border in 1542 explicitly counted Suffolk their master, and were referred to by Hertford as Suffolk's gentlemen.[217] They included sons of Sir William

Ayscough, Sir Robert Tyrwhit, Sir John Thimbleby, and Nicholas Girlington, each already taxed on, or at least the heir to, an income of £20 or more.[218] John Booth of Killingholme and Edward Bushey of Haydor served in person, and the latter was soon a Kesteven justice of the peace.[219] Other magistrates attached themselves to Suffolk in other ways. Hamo Sutton of Washingborough, a justice in Kesteven by 1540, accepted the duke's fee of four marks as steward of his lands there.[220] Sutton's son-in-law Robert Brocklesby of Glentworth took Suffolk's fee in 1542; he had been a Lindsey justice since the 1530s, and was the county feodary for the duchy of Lancaster.[221]

Gentry with such formal links with the duke were never in a majority, even in Lindsey, but they were numerous enough to give him remarkable influence. He could not match the followings of those peers before or after him who enjoyed overwhelming supremacy in their shires – the forty-one out of sixty Lancashire Members of Parliament elected between 1369 and 1397 who were retainers of John of Gaunt, the seven out of ten Devon sheriffs in the 1380s who were close associates of Edward, Earl of Devon, or the eleven out of eighteen Norfolk justices in 1564 who were closely linked with Thomas, Duke of Norfolk.[222] But such magnates were the exception rather than the rule, and by normal standards Suffolk had a useful grip on the county. In the 1540s ducal servants continued to join the justices' bench, John Wingfield and Matthew St Poll for Lindsey in 1540, John Dyon for all three parts in 1543.[223] Dyon, Brocklesby, Sutton, and both St Polls sat in various parts of the county, and Dyon was particularly active as a link between the national and local judicial systems; Sir John Cavendish, Sir Francis Ayscough, William Naunton, John Dyon, and the two St Polls constituted almost half the Lindsey quorum in 1543–4.[224] Anthony Missenden sat with the assize justices before his death in 1542, and John Wingfield sat at Stamford in June 1545 with only four others under a special oyer and terminer commission. In August 1544 John Wingfield and George St Poll sat on a commission of sewers at Boston.[225] Sir Francis Ayscough was sheriff in 1544–5, Hugh Grantham under-sheriff in about 1541.

Anthony Missenden, Geoge St Poll, Edmund Hall, and William Naunton all represented Lincolnshire boroughs in Parliament between 1542 and 1547.[226]

Suffolk reinforced his followers' part in county affairs using the patronage generated by his estates. John Wingfield, for example, could not have been taxed at £30 in lands and fees without his £20 annuity as steward of the household and his £10 annuity as constable of Tattershall Castle.[227] Many others took advantage of leases on ducal manors: among them John Marbury, comptroller of the household, Charles Wingfield, master of the horse, and John Hastings, a Suffolk retainer of William Lord Willoughby.[228] George Metham ended his life in 1589 still living at Willoughby-in-the-Marsh, and by then a loyal follower of Peregrine Bertie, declared Lord Willoughby in 1580 in right of his mother.[229] Even estates leased from the crown could be sublet to ducal clients, such as Robert Hall.[230]

Bailiffships too could be used to reward the ducal entourage, as they were at Eresby and Spilsby.[231] But even at this level offices could be used to draw men of more local importance into the ducal affinity. John Porter was already bailiff of the town of Tattershall for the college when Suffolk arrived in the castle. In 1544 he bought a house and lands there from John Dyon, at some point he leased land at Haltham from the duke, and in 1545 he acted as a ducal attorney and carried Suffolk's coffin.[232] Similar lesser gentlemen or substantial yeomen were often chosen bailiffs of manors near their homes: Brian Newcomen of Saltfleetby All Saints in Gayton Soke, Nicholas Vero of Skidbrooke at Saltfleet Haven, Rise Wymbish of Blankney on the estates around Sleaford.[233] Other officers from the same social stratum – taxed on between £20 and £35 in goods, or even £20 in income – were drawn from the central area of the ducal estates. John Bowes of Raithby was clerk of the ducal courts, Thomas Dale of Alford bailiff on three Warwickshire manors.[234] Dale bought lands in 1542 in Farlesthorpe; Farlesthorpe was the home of John Spenluffe, godfather to the son of Richard Caterton; Richard Caterton served Suffolk and the dowager duchess; at his death in 1588 John Spenluffe left his best gelding to Peregrine, Lord Willoughby.[235] The land-holding dominance of Suffolk and his heirs in this area created a natural affinity for them.

The twin foundations of the duke's affinity, in his concentrated estates and the pre-existent Willoughby retinue, should have made it a cohesive body, and there are signs that this was the case. George St Poll and John Dyon did legal business for various ducal officers and tenants.[236] Dyon was named supervisor or trustee in the wills of Robert Brocklesby and Sir John Copledike, while Copledike's feoffees in 1541 were John Langton of Langton and John Littlebury of Wainfleet.[237] Sir Francis Ayscough was executor to Sir John Cavendish and supervisor to Hugh Grantham, employed a Marbury and sold land to Humphrey Littlebury of Hagworthingham.[238] Robert Brocklesby was close to Nicholas Girlington and Philip Tyrwhit, and dealt in land with Richard Thimbleby, Robert Hall, John Dyon, and George St Poll.[239] Hugh Grantham obtained the wardship of Francis Cracroft, son of the Willoughby bailiff John Cracroft, to provide a husband for his daughter; in the ensuing lawsuit over Cracroft's lands Grantham was supported by Roger Grey, a gentleman of the ducal household.[240] Such cohesion outlasted individuals: Sir Andrew Bilsby died in 1539, Sir William Sandon in 1545, but first Sandon's grandson William, then Bilsby's grandson Andrew married the same ducal bastard, Frances.[241] It could operate independently of the duke: Thomas Gildon, the bastard son of the Willoughby administrator, joined his cousin William Sandon and the rather wild Richard Cracroft of Hogsthorpe and Legbourne in a series of robberies.[242] But by encouraging lawful cooperation between his followers, by granting offices or leases to successive generations of local families, as the Staffords and Percies did, and by introducing new men to the county, Suffolk could construct a durable basis for the power of his house.[243]

The affinity as a whole was never as exclusive as some had been in the past: 70 per cent of land transactions entered into by the retainers of Edward, Earl of Devon, in Richard II's reign, were with fellow retainers, for example.[244] In their own relatives and friends, in their professional lives (as lawyers or auditors) and in the affairs of their own estates, most of Suffolk's men had some close contacts who were unconnected with the duke. In the ducal household loyalties were narrower. In 1546 John Wingfield, the steward of the household, and Robert Ingoldson, keeper of the house and park at Eresby, both died. Each bequeathed his best animals to the duchess and her sons. Wingfield left rings to his cousin Charles Wingfield, master of the horse, and to Roger Grey; Ingoldson left rings to Grey and to George Metham. Wingfield's supervisor was the duchess, his executors a former priest of Tattershall College and his cousin Robert Wingfield, the ducal auditor; Ingoldson's sole executor was Barnard Archimbold, who succeeded him as keeper of Eresby.[245] Wingfield also made bequests to Edmund and Robert Hall; Ingoldson to three ladies and four gentlemen of the household. The wider ducal connection might have grown more enclosed in this way in several sets of circumstances. Had it been the only effective political network in the county, it might have subsumed the entire gentry community, as Lord Hastings' affinity had done in the honour of Tutbury, but its identity as Suffolk's personal following might then have been at best ambiguous.[246] Conversely, it might have become more inward-looking in the face of competition for recruitment, or conflict with another affinity, but in either case would have been smaller and more embattled, like Suffolk's East Anglian connection in the 1510s and 1530s. In practice neither of these situations arose.

Suffolk's followers showed no distinctive religious identity. In the 1530s they left bequests for altar lights, church repairs and trentals.[247] Two produced neutral wills between 1540 and 1548, but five requested the prayers of Mary and the saints.[248] Under the godly imp and the enthusiastic duchess, six produced more or less Protestant wills.[249] But Mary's reign showed only one possible reformist and three conservatives, and the years from 1558 to 1569 provided three uncommitted testators and the strangely ambiguous George St Poll.[250] In the era of a supposedly decisive shift in the religious beliefs of the Lincolnshire gentry, revealed in their wills, the ducal connection was not self-consciously in the vanguard.[251] Nor was the affinity faced by major conflict on secular grounds.

Yet there was very clearly an alternative axis in the society of Lindsey, whose separation from the ducal affinity had four main causes. It enjoyed a clear route to the king without Suffolk's mediation, through the influence of Sir Thomas Heneage as chief gentleman of the privy chamber. It linked several of the senior knightly families of the area, who doubtless enjoyed managing their own affairs without recourse to the duke. Through Sir Robert Tyrwhit senior it stood in opposition to the Ayscoughs, who now identified closely with Suffolk. And through Heneage's continuing close contact with his daughter Elizabeth Willoughby, it backed the Parham rather than the Eresby interest in the Willoughby dispute, which the 1536 agreement had not properly terminated.[252] The Heneages and the Skipwiths, the Skipwiths and the Tyrwhits were intermarried, and worked together in local matters; at court Sir Thomas Heneage co-operated with Robert Tyrwhit.[253] Heneage installed his son-in-law Sir William Willoughby at Tupholme Abbey, where Willoughby forged links with the Dymokes of nearby Scrivelsby, relations by marriage of the Skipwiths.[254]

This connection was not defined by its faith or by alignments at court. Heneage was no radical in religion, and was elbowed aside by reformists in 1546. His closest ally at court seems to have been William Fitzwilliam, Earl of Southampton, who died in 1542, while Sir Robert Tyrwhit junior and his wife were leading servants and close friends of Queen Catherine Parr.[255] But Heneage and Tyrwhit found common ground in their efforts to tap royal patronage for the benefit of their families and friends, and their efforts were successful. Tyrwhit secured various local wardships, and Heneage gained that of Andrew Bilsby and married him to the daughter of Robert Heneage.[256] The Heneages continued to amass grants and leases of monastic land.[257] There is no sign that Suffolk was in direct competition for any of these grants, but both he and his followers were notably unsuccessful in the quest for wardships. It was symptomatic that the only wardship allocated to the duke in the 1540s was one over which the crown had no claim, since all the knight-service lands of the deceased were held of Suffolk.[258] As a landholder, or as a great man in long-term dealings with the king, Brandon had no local rival, but in the rapid bustle at court to secure signed bills for single grants of lands or wardships, men like Heneage and Tyrwhit had the edge.

Such competition did not split local society into two separate camps. The Tyrwhits, for example, were related to the Girlingtons, Thimblebys, and St Polls; Philip Tyrwhit served under the duke, and in 1542 Suffolk sold Sir William Skipwith a house in Walmsgate.[259] In 1545 Edmund Hall stood surety for Sir William Willoughby, not surprisingly, as they were brothers-in-law.[260] None the less, five of the seven richest knightly families of Lindsey had remarkably little contact with the duke and his friends.[261] Such men had less need of the duke than the rising gentlemen from among whom he recruited his officers, and even the less prosperous knights sometimes paid him little attention.[262] But there were signs of considerable friction between Suffolk's men and the Heneage group.

The duke's officers were properly zealous to extend his power. His clerks slipped an improper 'dei gratia' into his title.[263] George St Poll found more practical ways to exalt his master. From his appointment as chief steward of the honour of Richmond estates in September 1541, he systematically spread the vague jurisdiction of the duke's soke courts, especially that of Gayton Soke around Louth. By 1543 he was taking bonds from local husbandmen to guarantee that they would sue in the duke's court and abide by its judgement.[264] The soke courts of Kirton and Mumby attracted many pleas from a distance of up to 6 miles, but at Gayton St Poll tried too hard. In Welton-le-Wold he enforced the court's jurisdiction by distraint, protecting the rent-collector who had withheld the rents from the lord, and making the farm of the demesnes so unattractive that no one would take it on; he refused to let the king's writ challenge his actions.[265] In part this was policy. Matthew St Poll in the same area, and other ducal officers far away near Sleaford, were busy enforcing and extending Suffolk's jurisdictions at the same time. In part it looked like persecution. 'W[ith]out knowledge of the said lorde of Suffolk, as your said orateur is well assured', St Poll had tried to foment legal trouble between the duke and the lord of Welton, and had harrassed the latter's son over a bondman. The struggle was unequal because St Poll's authority 'under my lord[es] grace in all his causes' enabled him to concentrate the whole of the duke's local influence on his victim.[266] That victim was John Monson, a close ally of the Tyrwhits.[267]

Other disputes ran along similar lines. Lady Tailbois was the sister-in-law of Sir Robert Tyrwhit of Kettleby, and the mother-in-law of Sir Christopher Willoughby and of Edward Dymoke. Both St Poll and Hugh Grantham fought her at law, and in one of these cases she was supported by Sir William Skipwith.[268] Members of the Curtis family were in dispute with Sir William Ayscough, Richard Thimbleby, and the veteran Willoughby retainer, Anthony Gunby; Anthony Curtis was the servant of Sir Thomas Heneage, who obtained for him the wardship of Brian, son of Leonard Curtis.[269] These confrontations did not constitute a full-scale feud. Monson was careful to avoid implicating Suffolk, and it was probably inevitable that the intrusive duke and his ambitious followers would upset the established interests of the intermarried knightly elite, just as John of Gaunt and his officers had done in Sussex a century and half earlier.[270] What must have worried Brandon more was trouble between those to whom he extended his good lordship. He faced a dilemma, in that in employing some of the cleverest and most unscrupulous men in the county, he risked that they would prey on his friends and perhaps even on himself.

John Dyon was a good example. From 1532 to 1534 he cut his teeth in manorial administration for the Ayscough family, and from 1534 to 1536 he served an energetic apprenticeship as Lincoln's common clerk. From Michaelmas term 1536 he practised as an attorney in common pleas for Lincolnshire clients, and this probably cost him the common clerkship.[271] He displayed his considerable legal skills, acquired at the Inner Temple, at the Lincoln assizes too. From 1538 he began buying lands with his profits, though in 1545 he was taxed on £30 in goods.[272] He did not achieve success without making enemies, men who said he 'trobled them that ys better than hym selffe.'[273] Robert Mason opposed him in a land dispute; he hit Mason's wife and she later died.[274] Dyon survived by exploiting, his enemies said perverting, the local and central legal systems. He was 'a sotell & trobelous p[er]son having great mayntenaunce & berynge of the questmongers and barrectours in Lincolnshire'.[275] From 1543 to 1546 he was also the most active steward in Suffolk's manorial courts, and even there he made enemies, two tenants at Raithby accusing him of malpractice.[276] Dyon was a hard man to control, as his defiance of his fellow justices in 1550 would testify.[277] But Suffolk found him a useful servant, and sought to reward him by securing his appointment in 1545 to the bench for the city of Lincoln. The duke insisted that Dyon was 'a man of good learnyng, judgement and right mete for the same', but the members of the common council were aghast, and sent two of their number to explain their rejection of the former common clerk. Dyon was successfully excluded.[278]

Sooner or later Dyon's ambitions would lead him into conflict with another ducal servant. In the event this only happened at the end of Suffolk's life, but George St Poll made himself important enemies earlier, at greater cost to himself.[279] He worked closely with his brothers Matthew and John to build up estates for themselves and for his son Thomas. By 1545 George and Matthew, both younger sons trained at Lincoln's Inn, had reached taxable incomes of £20.[280] But by 1544 they had made an enemy of the ducal auditor Hugh Grantham. A dispute between their respective clients led Grantham to expound in Star Chamber the 'malice, ylwyll & displeaso[ur]' which the three St Polls 'beare spe[ci]ally unto the said Hugh.'[281] Such feelings cannot have made for a healthy atmosphere in the ducal council, but worse was to come. In May 1545 it came to Suffolk's attention, doubtless with the help of Grantham or another enemy to the St Polls, that George stood accused of taking bribes. A Suffolk gentleman who had taken possession of Brandon's lands at Halesworth had been called to London to speak with the duke. On 3 May he reportedly announced that he was confident of the outcome, declaring, 'I dought nott but I shall do well inough in my matter betwyxt the duke of Suff[olk] & me, for I have gyven to one George Sayntpole … one of the seyd duk[es] counsell iii angell[es] & he hath p[ro]-mysyd me to helpe to ryd me in the sayd matter.'[282] When Suffolk heard of this, he was enraged. St Poll was dismissed from his council and banished from his presence, with no recourse but to sue the detractor for damages. The duke died before St Poll could clear his name. He attended Suffolk's funeral, and held a court at Fulstow in September 1545, but he was not among the leading councillors of the duchess in 1546–7.[283]

The Maturity of Power

The duke, then, was not fully in control of Lincolnshire, nor even of his own affinity. Yet the position he left to his wife and sons was very strong. In part his local power depended on his role as a royal confidant – hosting Henry at Grimsthorpe in 1541 during the royal progress – and as a leading councillor, overseeing the collection of the subsidies voted in 1540 and the loan of 1542 throughout the county, or the subsidy anticipation of 1545 in the city of Lincoln.[284] His position in the state also partly determined his ability to command patronage from local sources. Lincoln readily accepted his nomination of George St Poll to replace Anthony Missenden as recorder, not just because he was a great local landowner (with whose council the city had to negotiate, for example, over the enclosure of nearby lands), but because his 'petycion & suyte had unto his majestye' could reinforce the city's pleas for royal help. Thus within three months of Suffolk's death they sought help, not from the duchess, but from Norfolk, 'a man able at al tymes to doo for you and for the wealthe of yo[ur] citie'.[285]

Similarly, Suffolk helped Boston obtain a charter of incorporation, and in reward the town may have offered him its high stewardship.[286] Such relationships could not be preserved for his children. But some local patronage, like that granted by Tattershall College before its dissolution, sprang from landed domination of a small area.[287] Concentrated estates and an affinity based on them were a transmissible inheritance. So were houses fit for a ducal dynasty, and Suffolk left not only Tattershall, but also a much enlarged Grimsthorpe, and at least plans for expansion at Eresby. By 1539 he was planning a building project, for when he leased out Bullington Priory he reserved the right to remove construction materials from the site. He faced competition from Heneage, who had by 1543 'doone much cost' at Hainton, erecting a new building of brick and abbey stone.[288] In the end a new courtyard at Grimsthorpe was put up rather 'on a sudden' to accommodate the king in 1541; the hall was supposedly designed around a 'fair suit of hanging, which the duke had by his wife Mary the French Queen'.[289] Certainly the level of wealth displayed within the duke's residences was impressive. After his death, bedding for nearly 100 individuals was removed from Tattershall Castle to Grimsthorpe and Eresby, with thirteen Turkish carpets and numerous and varied tapestries.[290]

The material and landed wealth Suffolk left to his sons was matched by a strong set of alliances within the English aristocracy. He had arranged no match for his heir, but bequeathed to his younger son Charles the wardship of an heiress whom he had purchased from Sir Anthony Wingfield.[291] He kept in contact with the husbands of his wayward older daughters, casting the only vote for Lord Powis in the January 1541 Garter chapter, and leasing monastic estates with Lord Monteagle. For Monteagle's son William he arranged a good marriage with Anne, daughter of Lord William Howard, and made provision in his will for young William to have the lands taken by the duke to pay for his upkeep.[292] Suffolk bequeathed £200 worth of plate bearing the ducal arms to each of his daughters by the French queen, and he had more contact with their husbands than with Powis or Monteagle. He bought lands for Cumberland and worked with him in the north, and guided Dorset through his military apprenticeship in France. Frances, marchioness of Dorset, and her daughters were drawn by Holbein with Suffolk's two sons, and Lord Edward Grey, Dorset's brother, commanded a garrison under the duke in 1542.[293]

In time, leadership of the family network passed to Dorset – himself created duke of Suffolk in 1551 – with sad results. The short-term distribution of power in Lincolnshire was less clear. The duchess was said in December 1546 to rule the county, but Sir William Willoughby – created Lord Willoughby of Parham in 1547 – rose fast, and in 1546, for example, a ducal servant who had occupied attainted lands without royal warrant was readily exposed.[294] Suffolk's high offices mostly passed to his friend St John, and as executors St John and Wriothesley did their best to tidy up the duke's unfinished business.[295] The duchess enjoyed sufficient favour at court to buy monastic lands, and to obtain patronage for others.[296] Most important, the Brandons had secured a stake in the next reign. Suffolk left Prince Edward a gold cup worth 100 marks, and both he and the duchess ensured that there was plenty of contact between Edward and Henry Brandon, some two years his senior.[297] Suffolk did his best to provide his heir with the greatest advantage he himself had ever enjoyed, a friendship with the king.

When contemporaries passed a verdict on the duke, they were surprisingly unanimous. It was his military qualities that struck them first. Thomas Wilson, tutor in the next reign to Brandon's sons, implied that they inherited learning from their mother, horsemanship and martial vigour from their father. Charles Wriothesley lamented the death of Suffolk who 'had been so valiant a captaine in the kinges warres ... to the great dammage and losse of the kinges enemies'.[298] Even Elis Gruffydd, usually grudging in his praise, admitted that Henry grieved for the duke 'with reason, because of his courtesy and ability, for he was the flower of all the captains of the realm and had the necessary patience to control soldiers.'[299] The second dominant trait in the duke's character helped to explain his military success and political survival. This was that he was 'almoste of all estates and degrees of menne hygh and lowe, rych and poore, hartely beloved'.[300] Henry himself allegedly told the privy council that throughout his career Suffolk had never sought by word or deed to injure anyone. In politics, as in religion, Suffolk had usually tried to accommodate both parties in any argument. His funeral neatly reflected this, with services performed jointly by Stephen Gardiner and by Henry Holbeach, the radical Bishop of Rochester who would sit at Gardiner's trial.[301]

The network of relationships on which Suffolk had built his power was fittingly incarnated in the prize stable of horses he left to his wife.[302] His military role was reflected by gifts or purchases from mercenary captains like the 'cursare Granadoe' and 'baye moselde horse Lyghtmaker'. There were animals from both sides of the widening political divide: the 'baye Flanders mare Aroundell' and 'baye geldinge Pare'. Brandon's family provided the duchess after his death with 'graye Sakford' and the geldings of John Wingfield. The duke's growing influence across the north midlands and the north brought the 'mare Newna[me]' and the 'dunde geldinge Coneas'. A distant client had sent the 'graye gelding Horsle'. But the majority were Lincolnshire bred, starting with a 'whight geldinge Willowbe'. Just before his death Suffolk had bought 'certaine great stude mares' in Skidbrooke, and indeed the Willoughby estates and the retinue based on them provided a significant part of the duke's stable, such as the 'baye horse Palmer' and the 'yownge mare Curwine'.[303] Many others came from new relationships forged by Suffolk himself: the 'old mare Bostone', the 'sorell Flanders mare Barnarde', and the two 'coltes bowght of Master Askewe'. Lastly there were several products 'of the kinges stood'. All that Suffolk achieved rested on his friendship with and service to the king, as Henry showed at the last by insisting that Brandon should be buried at Windsor, just as Edward IV had promised a tomb at Windsor to his most loyal friend and servant Lord Hastings. As the duke put it in his will, by Henry's 'moost bountefull liberalitie and p[re]f[erment] I have ben and remayn advaunced to that estate I p[re]sently am of.'[304] Such preferment was one reward for Suffolk's dogged obedience to his motto, 'Loyaulte me oblige'. For the duke and his contemporaries, loyalty's other reward was just as significant: Brandon would surely have been pleased that, seven years after his death, his late servants still met to reminisce about 'the said lord of Suffolk's hono[ur] in his lyff tyme'.[305]

7

Conclusion

Charles Brandon's career was made possible by a family background sufficiently distinguished to place him at the heart of the court; but any advance beyond the heights attained by his uncle Thomas rested on Charles's close friendship with Henry VIII. The bonds between king and courtier, reinforced and displayed in the hunt, the masque, the tournament, and the tennis court, held firm to the end of Brandon's life. The relationship was never one of slavish obedience, and this made it stressful, especially during the reign of Anne Boleyn, when a summons to court or a royal visit could involve implicit coercion to accept the new order, as well as a reassurance of royal favour.[1] Suffolk obeyed Henry to the letter when he could, but the very responsibility of the jobs the king gave him – especially in military command – forced him to take risky decisions and rely on their mutual trust for the outcome. Henry's temper was unnerving, but from 1515 Brandon received an effective education in the politics of personal monarchy, learning both how to handle Henry and how to subordinate his personal interest to the demands of national policy. One contemporary even noted in the margin of his copy of Lydgate's *Fall of Princes*, 'Kardinall Wolsey yoused this theame to the duke of Suff[olk] when he was in th[e] kinges displeasu[re]', next to a passage recommending that kings delay action 'til that ther ire aswage'.[2]

The same section warns of slander, for 'to folk absent it is myschevable.' The risks of courtly calumny worried Suffolk at several periods when he found it hard to combine the roles of courtier and local magnate. Sent into the shires as the king's trusted lieutenant, whether in East Anglia or Lincolnshire, he was more reliant on Wolsey or Cromwell than he might have wished. But at the same time he knew the truth of the medieval commonplace:

> Bewar, squier, yeman and page,
> For servise is non heritage.[3]

The house of Brandon could be solidly founded on large and concentrated estates, a loyal and powerful gentry affinity, and the concomitant local power, in a way that it could not on the simple amity of Henry and Charles, nor even on the central and local offices through which Brandon exercised so much of his influence. He had to avoid the fate of several contemporaries, Henry, Earl of Worcester and Sir Ralph Egerton among them, who were so reliant on office-holding for their income and local dominance that their families faced devastating setbacks when these offices could not be passed on to the next generation.[4]

Before 1515, Suffolk's estates were in the Welsh borders and southwest, his natural followers in East Anglia, and his personal influence in Southwark. After 1515 he could combine his family and the De la Pole estates as the basis for an East Anglian affinity, but the weakness of this foundation, his reliance on his wife for status and income, and competition from other peers, hampered his efforts. As his earlier initiatives began to show some reward in the 1530s, his good lordship clashed repeatedly and unsuccessfully with that of Norfolk; less through the machinations of the peers than through the ambitions of their followers, and the absence of the mechanisms of arbitration between affinities which Suffolk sought to operate within his affinity, but still with dangerous effects on the relationship between the two magnates. Finally, in Lincolnshire, everything went right. With the Willoughby estates came a close network of local gentry supporters, loyal to the duke's new wife whose own status (unlike that of the French queen) posed no threat to Brandon. Suffolk could work outwards from this core, along the lines of natural connection in local society, to construct a large affinity, while the availability of monastic land enabled him to assemble valuable and concentrated estates, as the Stanleys, Howards, and others did at the same period.[5] Though he operated on credit for his entire career, he never overreached himself, and left his finances in a comparatively healthy state. His debts look paltry compared with those of the Duke of Buckingham, and more so – even allowing for inflation – compared with those of Elizabethan courtiers like Leicester or Hatton, and this was partly thanks to competent landlordship, admittedly exercised under easier circumstances than those confronting the Elizabethans.[6] He was never among the richest peers in terms of landed income, for not only Buckingham and Norfolk, but also the Marquis of Exeter and the Earls of Northumberland and Derby enjoyed considerably more profitable estates.[7] On the other hand wardships and offices added substantially to his revenue, substantially enough to enable him to rebuild Suffolk Place in Southwark at a time before the regular French rents paid for Westhorpe. Though he did not profit in cash terms – legally or illegally – to the same extent as Edwardian or Elizabethan officials like John Beaumont or Robert Cecil, his office holding gave him some income, and considerable honour, patronage and credit. At the same time he escaped the crippling indebtedness to the crown and other creditors which often afflicted Elizabethan and Jacobean peers, faced with the rising cost of service at court, on embassy or in regional office, and unable to obtain the restricted number of very profitable posts, like Huntingdon, Elizabeth's lord president of the council in the north.[8]

This placed Suffolk inside the smallish circle of noblemen who served Henry in senior positions and reaped significant rewards.[9] Yet among them he was unusual only in the length of his career in the front rank and in the heights to which he rose. Several of Henry's other courtiers and personal friends – William Fitzwilliam, John Russell and William Sandys for example – faced the same problems of reconciling the demands of service at court and in council with the need to establish themselves in the localities, of commanding difficult armies for a distant king, and of negotiating the white water stretches of political life. Russell, for instance, miscalculated the proper balance between court and country, and had to put more effort into cultivating the loyalty of the south-west after he had failed to prevent the rising of 1549.[10] Such mistakes were easily made, for Suffolk and his contemporaries stood at a point of transition in that balance. The tendency of late-medieval government, accelerating under the Tudors, to centralise the distribution of royal patronage at the expanding court and to increase direct contact between crown and gentry, made aspiring magnates of necessity court patrons. Brandon's readiness to beg favours for his followers from Wolsey, Cromwell, Henry Norris, or whoever else might help, showed his realisation of that. No peer could now resent and resist the penetration of direct royal patronage into the region under his command, as John of Gaunt in the 1390s, Clarence in the 1470s, or even the Percies before the 1520s had done.[11]

Yet the court was not everything. It was not only the daily and intimate courtiers who obtained the king's favour. William Compton in the first five years of the reign, like Thomas Heneage in the last ten, outgunned Brandon in securing innumerable signed bills for lands and offices, yet each ended his career rather less wealthy and considerably less honoured than Suffolk. And to be a court magnate alone, without power in the country, was not enough, as those who tried to prevent Mary's accession in 1553 found.[12] In Elizabeth's reign the process went further. Rather more than half Leicester's income in 1575 came from offices, licences and fees, rather less than half from lands, while Essex faced financial ruin when he lost his patent to import sweet wines. Essex succeeded for a while in building a nationwide following held together by little more than his command of royal patronage, but when that command failed he was forced to discover that he was no Thomas of Lancaster, Henry Bolingbroke, Warwick the Kingmaker, or Richard of York, able to fall back on his own resources to coerce the monarch.[13]

In the long run, though certainly not before the last years of

Elizabeth, the same process also created a court-based and fully factional system of politics with some ideological overtones, a system in which to be Essex's man marked one out as an anti-Cecilian in the country as much as at court. By the early Stuart period one can even speak of the local affinities of some politically active peers – the Rich interest in Essex for instance – as identifiable by a coherent 'political philosophy'.[14] Such ends were still far distant in Suffolk's day. Though Kent local politics from the 1530s may have been characterised by a struggle between reformist and conservative parties taking their cue from leaders at court,[15] such was not the case in East Anglia or Lincolnshire. Even at court political alignments were far more complex than historians sometimes suggest. Though the fluidity of court faction is often stressed, there is still a tendency to write about early Tudor politics as a series of bipartisan conflicts – Wolsey against the courtiers, Cromwell against the nobles, reformists against conservatives. Brandon clearly avoided the taking of sides on such a crass level whenever he could, and Russell for one did the same, maintaining links with all parties in religious and political debate and winning a reputation as everyone's friend, except Anne Boleyn's.[16] They did both enjoy unusually close friendships with the king, and in their political conduct they may have been exceptional. Brandon claimed in 1515, expecting Henry to believe him, that in court politics 'I ne[ver went] abowth to hert non mane', that 'ther was newar non of thym' (his detractors in the council) 'in trobbyl bout I was glad to helpe thym to me pour and [that] your grace knowes byst.'[17] Even the one man who felt that Suffolk consistently showed 'olde undeservyd evyll will' towards him, Sir Thomas Wyatt, who was imprisoned in 1536 at the duke's suggestion, trusted Brandon enough to appeal to his testimony, when imprisoned again in 1541, that the charge against him on that occasion was false.[18]

Certainly Brandon appears one of the more affable, probably even one of the less ambitious characters of the Henrician court. Yet he, like Russell, survived and prospered, without taking spectacular political gambles. He combined with other councillors to advocate policies which promised to serve their own or the national interest

– with Wolsey to preserve the French peace in 1514, with Norfolk and the Boleyns to provide an alternative to the rule of the faltering cardinal, with Wriothesley to advocate an end to the war in 1545. He co-operated with other courtiers in the pursuit of patronage – with Knyvet and Howard in his early career, with Norfolk, Norris and Walsh in 1527, with Wriothesley and Long in 1544–5. He doubtless shared with others at court his personal dislike for individual politicians, notably Anne Boleyn. But he did not work consistently with others in a 'faction', whether in securing patronage for himself and his followers or advocating policies to the king. Of course more coherent groups did exist – those who prospered and fell with Anne Boleyn and the privy chamber reformist clique of the 1540s are the best-documented examples – but they were probably far from the norm.

The approach towards Henry as patron and policy-maker by Suffolk and his contemporaries looks very like the approach of Suffolk's servants to the duke himself. The members of his household readily secured minor estate offices from him, presumably by the same well-timed importunity that brought the king's attendants myriad piecemeal grants. But the great positions and the great rewards went to men of talent and apparent trustworthiness, making Suffolk's wrath all the fiercer when it seemed that his trust had been betrayed by George St Poll, just as Henry exploded at the apparent betrayals of Wolsey, Anne Boleyn, Cromwell, or the Howards. In the search for ducal patronage, a search coloured for some by religious ideology from the 1530s, Brandon's followers combined into loose groupings, most obviously that of Freston and the conservatives. Their influence with the duke won them a place in the distribution of others' patronage: Freston's leases from Righton and Budde were the equivalent of Suffolk's pension from the countess of Salisbury or stewardships from Bishop Longland. The duke's courtiers had to keep a wary eye on those who bore them grudges, like Humphrey Wingfield's animosity for John Palsgrave. Just as Grantham and the St Polls fell out over the activities of their respective clients, so Brandon's problems with the Howard affinity complicated his relationship with Norfolk at court. Yet neither at

Westhorpe nor at Westminster could these relationships be simple ones of co-operation or enmity. Too many other factors intervened: bonds of blood and marriage, the memory of past favours or old slights, shared friendships or hostilities towards others, preferences in religious doctrine or foreign policy, and the ultimate imperative of good service, whether by counsellors to the king or by the affinity to the duke.

For Brandon lived by the fundamental loyalties of his age. His relatives – immediate and distant, legitimate and illegitimate – expected both to help him and to receive his help, and were not disappointed. His household generated a stricter loyalty between his servants and between servant and master, and he in turn rewarded old servants with generosity.[19] He was loyal to Henry, who rewarded him well. But these simple loyalties were exercised in a complex society, and Suffolk had also to live by the wits of his experts. There is no reason to doubt that he appreciated the music of his choir, the skill of his terracotta-makers, and the startling realism of Holbein's miniatures, but they all proclaimed too that the duke was a great man. Able merchants like Francis Hall, Thomas Marbury, and George Hampton handled his money. Expert heralds like Christopher Barker handled his status. Efficient auditors like John Peryent handled his accounts. And a string of brilliant lawyers handled his affairs both in and out of the courts. The loyalty of a Humphrey Wingfield or an Anthony Missenden could never be to Suffolk alone, even less so that of John Spelman, Robert Jenour, Christopher Jenny, or Francis Monford.[20] But Wingfield, George St Poll and John Dyon served the duke first and foremost, and that the others could be called upon both demonstrates and helps to explain Suffolk's success.

That success ran into the sand with the deaths from sweating sickness of both Brandon's sons in 1551. The duchess found consolation in her zeal for religion, but that was not part of Suffolk's legacy to her. From Oliver Pole and Arthur Bulkeley to Thomas Launcelyn and even John Parkhurst, his chaplains were more administrators, lawyers, teachers, and poets than preachers. In religion as in politics, he held the middle ground out of an incalculable blend of mediocrity and cunning, at times, no doubt, even of confusion. Above all he avoided commitment out of loyalty to the king. The values of chivalry motivated Suffolk more than the dogmas of Christianity: duty combined neatly with self-interest to keep him to his motto, 'Loyaulte me oblige'.

Abbreviations

AAJB	*Ambassades en Angleterre de Jean du Bellay*, ed. V. -L.Bourrilly, P. de Vaissière
ADN	Archives Départementales du Nord, Lille
AN	Archives Nationales, Paris
BL	British Library
BN	Bibliothèque Nationale, Paris
Bodl.	Bodleian Library, Oxford
CAD	**Descriptive Catalogue of Ancient Deeds in the Public Record Office*
CAF	**Catalogue des Actes de François Ier*
Cam. Soc.	Camden Society
CCJB	*Correspondance du cardinal Jean du Bellay*, ed. R. Scheurer
CCR	*Calendar of the Close Rolls*
CCRO	Coventry City Record Office
CIPM	*Calendar of Inquisitions Post Mortem*
CPR	*Calendar of the Patent Rolls*
CSPM	**Calendar of State Papers, Milan (1385–1618)*, ed. A. B. Hinds
CSPS	**Calendar of State Papers, Spanish*, ed. G. A. Bergenroth, P. de Gayangos, M. A. S. Hume, G. Mattingly
CSPV	**Calendar of State Papers, Venetian*, ed. R. Brown, C. Bentinck, H. Brown
DNB	*The Dictionary of National Biography*, ed. L. Stephen, S. Lee, 2nd edn (22 vols. London, 1908–9)

EETS	Early English Text Society
EHR	*English Historical Review*
ERO	Essex Record Office
FOR	*Faculty Office Registers, 1534–1549*, ed. D. S. Chambers
GEC	*The Complete Peerage*, by G. E. C., ed. V. Gibbs et al. (13 vols, London, 1910–40)
Hall	E. Hall, *Hall's Chronicle*
Harl. Soc.	Harleian Society
HMC	Reports of the Royal Commission on Historical Manuscripts
KLBRO	King's Lynn Borough Record Office
LAO	Lincolnshire Archives Office
LJ	*Journals of the House of Lords*
LL	**The Lisle Letters*, ed. M. St C. Byrne
LP	**Letters and Papers, Foreign and Domestic, of the Reign of Henry VIII*, ed. J. S. Brewer et al.
NRO	Norfolk Record Office
PRO	Public Record Office, Chancery Lane
SBT	Shakespeare's Birthplace Trust Record Office, Stratford-upon-Avon
SR	*Statutes of the Realm*, ed. A. Luders et al.
SRO	Suffolk Record Office, Ipswich branch
StP	*State Papers, King Henry the Eighth*
TRP	*Tudor Royal Proclamations*, ed. P. L. Hughes, J. F. Larkin
ULC	University Library, Cambridge
VCH	*The Victoria History of the Counties of England*

* In these works references are to document numbers unless otherwise specified. For further details of books and archive collections, see the Bibliography.

Notes

Preface

1. *The Sword and the Rose*: L. Maltin, *The Disney Films* (London and New York, 1973), pp. 110–12.

1 The Rise of Charles Brandon: c. 1484–1514

1. *LP* I. i. 20.
2. R. Boyle, *English Adventures* (London, 1676).
3. *GEC* xii, pt. i, p. 454. The following is based on the fuller treatment of Charles Brandon's grandfather, father, and uncles in S. J. Gunn, 'The Life and Career of Charles Brandon, duke of Suffolk, *c.* 1484–1545' (Oxford University D.Phil. Thesis, 1986), pp. 1–8.
4. *CIPM 1485–95*, pp. 377–9; PRO C1/258/52; E198/4/21, 26.
5. *Materials for a History of the Reign of Henry VII*, ed. W. Campbell (2 vols, Rolls Series 60, 1873–7), ii. 495; *The Great Chronicle of London*, ed. A. A. Thomas, I. D. Thornley (London, 1938), p. 311; *Letters and Papers Illustrative of the Reigns of Richard III and Henry VII*, ed. J. Gairdner (2 vols, Rolls Series 24, 1861–3), i. 397–400; PRO E101/414/ 6, fos. 13ʳ, 24ʳ, 70ʳ; 414/16, fos. 33ʳ, 43ʳ, 44ʳ, 59, 62ʳ; 415/3, fo. 49ᵛ. For Sir Thomas Brandon, Sir Thomas Lovell, and others of their circle see my book, *Henry VII's New Men and the Making of Tudor England* (Oxford, 2016).
6. *GEC* iv. 381, v. 510, xi. 483; *CPR 1485–94*, pp. 345, 439; *LP* I. i. 218(30); J. Smyth, *The Lives of the Berkeleys*, ed. J. Maclean (2 vols, Gloucester, 1883), ii. 144–5, 157–8; *CAD* iii. D819; PRO C1/333/30.
7. PRO E405/479, fo. 2ʳ; *LP* I. i. 94 (12), 158 (90), 190 (35, 41), 218 (30, 52), 289 (35).
8. N. H. Nicolas, *Testamenta Vetusta* (2 vols, London, 1826), ii. 496; *LP* I. i. 157, 353.
9. Bodl. MS Ashmole 1109, fo. 111ʳ (*LP* I. i. 353); PRO E36/214, fo. 194ʳ; *LP* I. i. 447(23); PRO C24/28, Randal Haworth and Lady Powis v. Henry, duke of Suffolk, deposition of William Thorpe.
10. PRO C24/29, Haworth and Powis v. Suffolk, deposition of Sir William Sidney.
11. *Test. Vet.* ii. 497; *LP* I. ii. 2055 (104); III. i. 1070; G. Cavendish, *The Life and Death of Cardinal Wolsey*, ed. R. S. Sylvester (EETS 243, 1959), pp. 7, 9–10.
12. *Test. Vet.* ii. 497; *CPR 1494–1509*, p. 503; PRO E150/677/2; CP40/1037, rot. 793; *Wreyland Documents*, ed. C. Torr (Cambridge, 1910), pp. 118–19; W. A. Copinger, *The Manors of Suffolk* (7 vols, London and Manchester, 1905–11), iii. 102.
13. PRO PROB11/17/28; *SR* 27 Henry VIII, c. 39, s. 3; *LP* III. ii. 2486, XIII. ii. 219; PRO C24/28, Haworth and Powis v. Suffolk, depositions of William Thorpe and David Johns.
14. F. M. Heal, *Of Prelates and Princes: a Study of the Economic and Social Position of the Tudor Episcopate* (Cambridge, 1980), pp. 35–6; *CPR 1452–61*, p. 395; *LP* I. i. 381 (17).
15. D. J. Johnson, *Southwark and the City* (Oxford, 1969), p. 100.
16. *SR* 19 Henry VII, c. 10; *Great Chronicle*, p. 206; PRO C1/114/21; E101/414/16, fo. 24ʳ.
17. R. B. Pugh, *Imprisonment in Medieval England* (Cambridge, 1968), p. 161; *CPR 1452–61*, p. 395, 1467–77, p. 85; M. Blatcher, *The Court of King's Bench, 1450–1550* (London, 1978), p. 75.
18. Pugh, *Imprisonment*, pp. 179, 242; BL Add. Ch. 5835.
19. Johnson, *Southwark*, p. 70; *LP* I. i. 731 (28); ii, p. 1544; PRO C260/161/13, C260/ 202/4.
20. *LJ* i. xxxviii.
21. E. Herbert, *The History of England under Henry VIII* (London, 1870 edn), p. 380; *LP* IV. iii. 5774.
22. PRO E101/415/3, *passim*; LC2/1, fo. 73r; C1/671/18; C24/28, Haworth and Powis v. Suffolk, *passim*; BL Add. Ch. 29269.
23. *CPR 1494–1509*, p. 332; PRO C24/29, Haworth and Powis v. Suffolk, deposition of Walter, Viscount Hereford.

24. PRO C24/28, Haworth and Powis v. Suffolk, deposition of Rose Cornwall; C24/29, same case, deposition of Sir Anthony Wingfield.
25. Hall, p. 512; *LP* II. ii, p. 1445.
26. PRO E36/214, fo. 10ᵛ; BL MS Add. 21480, fo. 22ʳ; *Excerpta Historica*, ed. S. Bentley (London, 1831), p. 132; *LP* I. i. 244.
27. PRO E36/214, fo. 20ʳ; *LP* I. i, *passim*; IV. iii. 5774 (3, 13).
28. Hall, p. 512; *LP* I. i. 635.
29. *LP* I. i. 1123 (65), 1221 (9); D. R. Starkey, 'The King's Privy Chamber, 1485–1547' (Cambridge Univ. Ph.D. thesis, 1973), p. 23; *CCR 1500–09*, p. 316.
30. S. T. Bindoff, *The History of Parliament: The House of Commons, 1509–1558* (3 vols, London, 1982), ii. 262–5; PRO C24/28, Haworth and Powis v. Suffolk, deposition of William Thorpe; C24/29, same case, deposition of Christopher Lynham.
31. *Report of the Deputy Keeper of the Public Records*, 36 (London, 1875), 146; *LP* I. i. 604 (12), 682 (5); PRO E36/214, fo. 261ʳ.
32. *LP* I. i. 888, 1144; BL Add. Ch. 7925; MS Egerton 3025, fo. 26ᵛ.
33. PRO LC2/1, fo. 73r; E36/214, fos 31ᵛ, 123ᵛ, 132ʳ, 153ᵛ; LP III. i. 1160.
34. W. C. Hazlitt, *Remains of the Early Popular Poetry of England* (4 vols, London, 1864–6), ii. 128.
35. *LP* I, II, Hall, *Great Chronicle, CSPM, passim.*
36. *LP* I. ii. 2359; *Great Chronicle*, p. 370; *The Antiquarian Repertory*, ed. F. Grose, T. Astle, 2nd edn (4 vols, London, 1807–9), ii. 309; PRO E36/214, fo. 24ʳ.
37. Hall, pp. 516, 520.
38. M. J. Tucker, *The Life of Thomas Howard, Earl of Surrey and Second Duke of Norfolk* (The Hague, 1964), pp. 93–4, 98; S. J. Gunn, 'The French Wars of Henry VIII', in *The Origins of War in Early Modern Europe*, ed. J. Black (Edinburgh, 1987), p. 43. The research of Mrs S. Vokes on the Howards in the earlier part of Henry VIII's reign will clarify some of these issues.
39. *LP* l. i. 880, 1201.
40. *LP* I. i. 1414,1661 (4); ii. 3608; Hall, pp. 534–5; *CSPV* ii. 200; *The Anglica Historia of Polydore Vergil A. D. 1485–1537*, ed. D. Hay (Cam. Soc., 3rd series, 74, 1950), p. 187.
41. *The Works of Sir Thomas Malory*, ed. E. Vinaver (3 vols, Oxford, 1947), i. 210; *Letters of Richard Fox 1486–1527*, ed. P. S. and H. M. Allen (Oxford, 1929), p. 58.
42. *LP* I. i. 1771; *CSPM 635*; Hall, pp. 533, 537.
43. *LP* I. ii. 1480, 1748, ii. 2055 (96); *Test. Vet.* ii. 534.
44. *LP* I. ii. 1844.
45. Hall, p. 515.
46. Sources as n. 35 above.
47. *LP* II. ii, pp. 1490, 1496, 1497–8, 1500.
48. J. Anstis, *The Register of the Most Noble Order of the Garter* (2 vols, London, 1724), i. 275. Unfortunately, no details of the election survive.
49. *LP* I. i. 1480, 1748, 1804 (2, 26, 55–7); ii. 1948 (68, 93).
50. S. Anglo, *The Great Tournament Roll of Westminster* (2 vols, Oxford, 1968), i. 37, 38, n. 4.
51. *LP* I. i. 698; ii, App. 9; Hall, pp. 510–12, 516, 518; *Great Chronicle*, pp. 341–3, 372.
52. Hall, pp. 533, 566, 568. R. Macquereau, *Traicté et recueil de la Maison de Bourgoigne*, ed. J. A. C. Buchon (Chroniques et Mémoires sur l'Histoire de France, 16, 1838), p. 55, is controverted by *LP* I. ii. 2562.
53. Macquereau, *Traicté et recueil*, p. 55, apparently admitted by Hall (p. 566), but not by Paulo de Laude (*CSPM* 669).
54. Anglo, *Great Tournament Roll*, i. 113–15.
55. PRO E101/418/1, fo. 20 (*LP* I. ii. 2506).
56. Hall, pp. 516, 520.
57. *LP* I. ii. 2562; Hall, p. 566; *CSPM* 669.
58. *LP* I. i. 975, ii. 2575 (ii), 3436; Add. i. 367; *Report on the Manuscripts of His Grace the Duke of Rutland* (HMC 12.4, 1888), p. 21.
59. *LP* I. i. 969 (62); ii. 2964 (37); Hall, p. 534; *CPR 1494–1509*, p. 566.
60. Johnson, *Southwark*, map at end; Bodl. MS Ashmole 865, fo. 242ᵛ; PRO C1/435/ 18, 439/19.
61. Pugh, *Imprisonment*, p. 121; PRO C1/383/43.
62. *CPR 1485–94*, p. 129, *1494–1509*, pp. 34, 115, 566, 637, 664; Bodl. MS Ashmole 852, pp. 302–3.
63. *CPR 1467–77*, p. 367, *1476–85*, p. 233.
64. Johnson, *Southwark*, p. 69; *Rotuli Parliamentorum* (7 vols, London, 1832), vi. 537.
65. A. R. Myers, *The Household of Edward IV* (Manchester, 1959), p. 161; PRO KB9/ 547/1; KB27/1100 Rex, m. 11.
66. Hall, p. 526, *Great Chronicle*, p. 379; PRO SC6/Henry VIII/344, m. 9.
67. *LP* I. i. 1221 (9); *CPR 1553*, p. 248.
68. PRO C47/7/4/22/2–9; J. Manwood, *A Treatise and Discourse of the Lawes of the Forrest* (London, 1598), fo. 166.
69. *LP* I. i. 1123 (65); Starkey, 'King's Privy Chamber', pp. 27, 32; *VCH Essex* vi (1973), pp. 324, 328.
70. *CSPS* I. 481; *LP* I. i. 168, 190 (34); ii. 3101, 3226 (10); VI. 578 (41); PRO SC6/ Henry VIII/745.
71. *Rutland Papers*, ed. W. Jerdan (Cam. Soc. 21,1842), p. 79; *LP* I. i. 381 (76), 2053 (2); II. ii, p. 1459; PRO SP2/Fol. A, fos 69–70 (*LP* II. ii, App. 58); E101/107/15. For Brandon's appointment, see E405/89 m. 68r.
72. PRO E101/107/17 (*LP* IV. ii. 3734).
73. *LP* I. i, p. 19, III. i. 1114; PRO SP1/19, fo. 268ʳ (*LP* III. i. 704 (3)); E101/107/15, fo. 5, 17, fo. 2; *A Collection of Ordinances and Regulations for the Government of the Royal Household* (London, Society of Antiquaries, 1790), p. 206; College of Arms MS Mbis, fo. 23ʳ.
74. *Household Ordinances*, p. 144; Myers, *Household*, p. 65; *LP* I. i, pp. 19, 40; 370, 428, 453, 651 (5), 1177, 1255.

75. *LP* I. i. 1785; ii. 2679; II. ii, pp. 1459–61, 1464.
76. *CSPV* ii. 237, 385, 434, 438, 446.
77. *CSPV* ii. 438.
78. Hall, p. 544; Macquereau, *Traicté et recueil*, p. 53.
79. O. de la Marche, *Memoires*, iv, ed. H. Beaune, J. d'Arbaumont (Société de l'Histoire de France, 1888), p. 58.
80. *LP* I. ii. 2141.
81. Hall, p. 537; *StP* i. 23; CCRO A79/26; *LP* I. ii. 1869.
82. *Richard Fox*, p. 64.
83. *LP* I. ii. 1859; *Richard Fox*, p. 61.
84. PRO SP1/229, fo. 158 (*LP* I. ii. 1869).
85. *LP* I. ii. 1852, 1883.
86. *Richard Fox*, p. 64.
87. *LP* I. ii. 2062; BL MS Cotton Faustina EVII 4 (*LP* I. ii. 2575); MS Add. 6113, fo. 6 (*LP* I. ii. 1880).
88. *Richard Fox*, p. 69; *LP* I. ii. 1874, 1882, 1944, 2544 (ii); CCRO A79/26.
89. *LP* I. ii. 1898, 1899, 1912.
90. Ibid. 1907.
91. Ibid. 2544 (ii).
92. *Richard Fox*, p. 72; *LP* I. ii. 1969.
93. *LP* I. ii. 1965, 1971, 1976,1978, 1992.
94. CCRO A79/26; *LP* I. ii. 1948 (68); H. Miller, *Henry VIII and the English Nobility* (Oxford, 1986), p. 14.
95. *LP* I. ii. 2575.
96. *LP* I. i. 1176, 1484; ii. 1869 (iii, v).
97. *LP* I. ii. 1948 (93).
98. *The Chronicle of Calais*, ed. J. G. Nichols (Cam. Soc. 35, 1846), p. 71.
99. *LP* I. ii. 2556, 3046.
100. Ibid. 2053 (3–6); Hall, pp. 540, 542; *Polydore Vergil … 1485–1537*, p. 209.
101. BL MS Lansdowne 818, fo. 11ʳ.
102. *LP* I. ii. 2078; *TRP* I. 73.
103. BL MS Lansdowne 818, fos 11ʳ–12ʳ.
104. C. G. Cruickshank, *Army Royal: Henry VIII's Invasion of France 1513* (Oxford, 1969), pp. 36, 49; *TRP* i. 73; Hall, p. 540.
105. *TRP* i. 73–4.
106. *TRP* i. 74; *CSPM* 657; *LP* I. ii. 2391.
107. Hall, pp. 549–50; *LP* I. ii. 2391; Macquereau, *Traicté et recueil*, p. 39.
108. *LP* I. ii 2391; Macquereau, *Traicté et recueil*, p. 33; Hall, p. 549.
109. Hall, p. 551; *Négociations diplomatiques entre la France et l'Autriche*, ed. E. A. J. Le Glay (2 vols, Documents Inédits sur l'Histoire de France, 1845), i. 535; *LP* I. ii. 2172 (2); *TRP* i. 73; Macquereau, *Traicté et recueil*, p. 35.
110. *LP* I. ii. 2171.
111. A. Hocquet, 'Tournai et l'Occupation Anglaise (1513–19)', *Annales de la Société Historique et Archeologique de Tournai*, NS 5 (1900), 379; Hall, p. 565.
112. *CSPM* 660; Hocquet, 'Tournai', pp. 381, 384.
113. Macquereau, *Traicté et recueil*, p. 44.
114. C. G. Cruickshank, *The English Occupation of Tournai, 1513–1519* (Oxford, 1971), pp. 7–8; Hall, p. 565; BL MS Lansdowne 818, fo. 8ᵛ; Macquereau, *Traicté et recueil*, p. 48.
115. *LP* I. ii. 2391; *CSPV* ii. 350.

116. PRO E36/214, fo. 16ᵛ; *LP* III. ii, p. 1529.
117. *LP* II. ii, pp. 1482, 1499.
118. *LP* I. ii. 244, II. ii, p. 1445; S. J. Gunn, 'The Regime of Charles, duke of Suffolk, in North Wales and the Reform of Welsh Government, 1509–25', *Welsh History Review*, 12 (1985), 466–7, 491.
119. *LP* II. ii, p. 1465; PRO E405/89, m. 68ʳ.
120. *LP* II. i. 1804 (2, 26).
121. *LP* I. i. 1804 (2); PRO SC6/Henry VIII/7056, 7057. The other grant took effect (SC6/Henry VIII/3686, m. 9ᵛ).
122. *LP* I. ii. 2055 (26); PRO E36/214, fo. 227ᵛ; E101/676/2, *passim*.
123. *LP* II. i. 630; PRO E101/676/2, mm 1, 3; S. J. Gunn, 'The Act of Resumption of 1515', in *Early Tudor England: Proceedings of the 1987 Harlaxton Symposium*, ed. D. T. Williams (Woodbridge, 1989), 87–106.
124. *Report on the Manuscripts of Lord Middleton* (HMC 69, 1911), p. 515; *LP* II. ii. 3285; *Trevelyan Papers*, iii, ed. W. C. Trevelyan, C. E. Trevelyan (Cam. Soc. 105, 1872), p. 10; G. W. Bernard, 'The Rise of Sir William Compton, Early Tudor Courtier', *EHR* 96 (1981), 758–62, 777.
125. *LP* I. i. 1414, ii. 2575.
126. *TRP* i. 73.
127. PRO CP25 (2)/51/360/9.
128. LAO lAnc 11/C/la; PRO CP40/1095, rot. 531.
129. *HMC Ninth Report* i (1883), p. 120; Lambeth Palace Library, Register Warham II, fo. 358ʳ.
130. G. Hennessey, *Novum Repertorium Ecclesiasticum Parochiale Londinense* (London, 1898), pp. 109, 248.
131. BL Harleian Ch. 43F8; *CAD* v. A13349.
132. *LP* I. i. 1524 (3), ii. 1948(96).
133. PRO E36/215, fo. 335ʳ.
134. *LP* I. ii. 2537.
135. *LP* I. ii. 1948(68), 2684(5).
136. Gunn, 'North Wales', p. 462; *LP* I. ii. 2617 (44); PRO WARD9/147, fo. 13ʳ.
137. PRO C54/390, m. 8; C142/28/5, 39, 70, 87, 120, 133, 134, 144, 148–51, 157–9; El50/678/5.
138. *LP* II. ii, p. 1463.
139. *Négociations diplomatiques*, ii. 182; *LP* III. ii, p. 1544.
140. *LP* I. ii. 2916, 3107 (11), 3205; II. ii, p. 1464.
141. *LP* I. ii. 2867, 2916, 3205, 3241, 3490, II. i. 571, ii. 4561.
142. SBT DR5/2915, 2918.
143. BL MS Egerton 985, fos 60ᵛ–61ᵛ; College of Arms MS M4, fo. 45ʳ.
144. Gunn, 'North Wales', p. 466.
145. *LP* I. ii. 2575.
146. *LP* I. i. 1805 (I. ix), ii. 2772, (21, 33); PRO STAC2/15/300.
147. *LP* I. ii. 2484 (3), App. 26; Gunn, 'North Wales', p. 463.
148. *LP* I. i. 1602 (35).
149. PRO E36/215, p. 662; *LP* I. i. 833 (20).
150. SBT DR5/2892.
151. *LP* I. i. 1602 (12), 1662 (26), 1804 (57).
152. SBT DR5/2913–14; *CPR 1494–1509*,

p.486; *Registrum Ricardi Mayew Episcopi Herefordensis*, ed. A. T. Bannister (Canterbury and York Society 27, 1921), p. 279; PRO PROB11/17/20; *LP* I. i. 1524 (5); ii. 2575 (ii); II. ii, p. 1482.

153. SBT DR5/2913, 2916; PRO SP1/4, fo. 19 (*LP* I. ii. 2537); BL MS Egerton 985, fo. 61.
154. *LP* I. ii. 2628; PRO E150/8/2, E150/678/5.
155. BL Add. Ch. 73511 (*LP* I. i. 1556); I. H. Jeayes, *Descriptive Catalogue of the Charters and Muniments at Berkeley Castle* (Bristol, 1892), no. 675.
156. *LP* I. i. 1803 (2, m. 2); SBT DR5/2892, 2913.
157. *LP* I. i. 804 (52), 833 (58, iv), ii. 2537, pp. 1537, 1539, 1543, 1545–6.
158. *LP* I. i. 257 (49), 438 (2, m. 5), 833 (19), 969 (23).
159. Smyth, *Lives of the Berkeleys*, ii. 202; S. M. Wright, *The Derbyshire Gentry in the Fifteenth Century* (Derbyshire Record Society 8, 1983), pp. 62–3.
160. SBT DR5/2913, 2916, 2923.
161. Gunn, 'North Wales', pp. 461–79.
162. For the retinues of other peers, see Miller, *English Nobility*, pp. 138–41.
163. PRO E36/2; *LP* I. ii. 2305 (329).
164. BL MS Cotton Faustina EVII 4 (*LP* I. ii. 2575 (ii)); PRO E101/56/25, *passim* (*LP* I. ii. 165. This can be calculated from their conduct money: *LP* IV. i. 1854 (4).
166. PRO C24/28, Haworth and Powis v. Suffolk, deposition of Sir John Brydges; *LP* III, i. 926.
167. Bindoff, *Commons* iii. 31A; *HMC Rutland* iv (HMC 24, 1905), p. 563; *Test. Vet.* ii. 642.
168. Sir Robert Brandon, John Glemham, James Framlingham, Thomas Lovell, and Richard Cavendish; PRO C24/28, Haworth and Powis v. Suffolk, deposition of William Thorpe.
169. Lambeth Palace Library, Reg. Warham II, fo. 273ᵛ.
170. *LP* I. ii, App. 26.
171. *GEC* xi, App. C, p. 75; Bodl. MS Ashmole 1115, fo. 256ʳ.
172. *LP* I. ii. 2590, 2684 (5); Myers, *Household*, p. 94; *Household Ordinances*, p. 162; *GEC* xi, App. C, p. 87.
173. *Manners and Meals in Olden Time*, ed. F. J. Furnivall (EETS 32, 1868), pp. 188, 315, 381; Myers, *Household*, p. 95.
174. BL MS Add. 29549, fo. 1 (*LP* I. ii. 2620); *TRP* i. 73.
175. BL MS Egerton 985, fos 60–61ᵛ; Bodl. MS Ashmole 862, p. 304; *LP* III. i. 1284 (ii).
176. *Polydore Vergil ... 1485–1537*, p. 223.
177. *Opus Epistolarum Desiderii Erasmi Roterodami*, ed. P. S. Allen (12 vols, Oxford, 1906–58), i. 550–1; *LP* I. ii. 2610; Persius, *The Satires*, ed. J. R. Jenkinson (Warminster, 1980), v. 76–81.
178. T. Rymer, *Foedera, Conventiones, Literae et cujuscunque generis Acta Publico*, 3rd edn (10 vols, The Hague, 1739–45), vi. 55.
179. Miller, *English Nobility*, p. 14.
180. *LP* I. ii. 2284, 2268.
181. BL MS Cotton Claudius CIII, fos 5ʳ, 17ʳ,

34ʳ, 73ᵛ; *Excerpta Historica*, p. 333; *GEC* ii. 356–8.
182. *LP* I. ii. 2929 (ii).
183. PRO SP1/229, fo. 151 (*LP* I. ii. 1869).
184. *LP* I. ii. 2718, 2782, 2913, 2959, 3018, 3049 (11).
185. *LP* I. ii. 3210.
186. *Polydore Vergil...1485–1537*, p. 198.
187. PRO E36/215 p. 664; *LP* I. ii. 2576.
188. For what follows see PRO C24/28, 29, Haworth and Powis v. Suffolk, *passim*. As this case concerned the legitimacy of one of his daughters, dates and details in different depositions conflict, making it impossible to be certain about the true sequence of events.
189. *CIPM 1485–95*, p. 75; *CPR 1494–1509*, p. 553; *CCR 1500–09*, p. 316.
190. *LP* IV. iii. 5859.
191. *LP* I. ii. 2654, 2941.
192. Hall, p. 566; *CSPV* ii. 371.
193. *LP* I. ii. 2171; Hall, p. 566.
194. *CSPV* ii. 438; *Analectes historiques*, ed. A. J. G. Le Glay (Paris, 1838), p. 202.
195. *LP* I. ii. 2255, 2262, 2281, 2355, 2375, 2380, 2391; ADN B3345/3, fo. 10ʳ; BL MS Stowe 146, fos 96, 104, 105.
196. *CSPM* 654, 656, 657; J. Strelka, *Der burgundische Renaissancehof Margarethes von Österreich und seine literarhistorische Bedeutung* (Vienna, 1957), pp. 48, 56–7; E. W. Ives, *Anne Boleyn* (Oxford, 1986), pp. 25–6.
197. *HMC Ninth Report*, ii (1884), p. 412; M. Bruchet, *Marguerite d'Autriche duchesse de Savoie* (Lille, 1927), p. 30.
198. For what follows, see *Chronicle of Calais*, pp. 71–4.
199. Hall, p. 568.
200. *Chronicle of Calais*, p. 75; *LP* I. ii. 2654; ADN B18864/31263 (*LP* I. ii. 2700).
201. *Chronicle of Calais*, p. 74; *The Renaissance, 1493–1520*, ed. G. R. Potter (New Cambridge Modern History 1, 1957), p. 252; *Négociations diplomatiques*, ii. 572 (*LP* I. i. 2670).
202. *LP* I. ii. 2736, 2940, 3104; *Chronicle of Calais*, pp. 73–4.
203. *LP* I. ii. 2654; ADN B18864/31262 (*LP* I. ii. 2701), B18864/31263.
204. *LP* I. ii. 2654, 2684 (34, 88); *Chronicle of Calais*, p. 76.
205. Ibid., pp. 68–76; *LP* I. ii. 2940.
206. *LP* I. ii. 2488, 2924, 2940.
207. W. C. Richardson, *Mary Tudor, the White Queen* (London, 1970), p. 162.

2 The French Marriage and the Duchy of Suffolk: 1514–1523

1. BL MS Cotton Caligula EII, fo. 292; *CSPS* II. 191.
2. *LP* I. ii. 3281; II. i. 19, p. xiii; PRO CP25 (2)/51/360/16.
3. *LP* I. ii. 3253, 3464, II. ii, pp. 1500–1; Hall, p. 580.
4. *Chronicle of Calais*, p. 16; *LP* I. ii. 3426, 3578.
5. Hall, p. 571; *LP* I. ii. 3580.
6. *CSPV* ii. 469; *LP* I. ii. 3355, 3356, 3376, 3378, 3379, 3381.

7. Ibid. 3376.
8. Richardson, *Mary Tudor*, pp. 110–11; *LP* II. i. 3416, 3440, 3441, 3449.
9. Ibid. 3387, 3430, 3438.
10. Ibid. 3430, 3461; Hall, p. 572; *CSPV* ii. 518.
11. BL MS Add. 30543, fos 83^r–85^r, 99^r–100^r; Hall, p. 572. An attaint was a hit that did not break the lance.
12. *CSPM* 635; PRO SP 1/230 f. 303 (*LP* I. ii. 3437), reproduced in Plate 5.
13. Hall, p. 572; *LP* I. ii. 3461; BL MS Add. 30543, fos 101^v–105^v; *Journal de Louise de Savoie*, ed. C. B. Petitot (Collection Complète des Mémoires Relatifs à l'Histoire de France 16, 1826), p. 396.
14. Hall, p. 572; *LP* I. ii. 3461.
15. *LP* I. ii. 3461; BL MS Add. 30543, fo. 114^r.
16. T. Godefroy, *Le Cérémonial françois*, 2nd edn (2 vols, Paris, 1649), i. 745–6; *LP* I. ii. 3411; Rymer, *Foedera* vi, pt. i, p. 81.
17. *LP* I. ii. 3424, 3449, 3472.
18. Ibid. 3476–7.
19. *LP* I. ii. 3430, 3472, 3485, II. i. 1.
20. *LP* I. ii. 3472: 'gyrsynyth' meaning 'christened', or 'Christian'.
21. Ibid. 3387, 3411, 3424, 3449.
22. *LP* II. i. 224.
23. Hazlitt, *Early Popular Poetry*, ii. 109–130; *LP* II. ii, pp. 1492–3, 1497; PRO C24/28, Haworth and Powis v. Suffolk, deposition of Dorothy Vemey; C24/29, same case, deposition of Sir William Sidney.
24. PRO SP1/10, fo. 79^r (*LP* II. i. 227).
25. T. Thorpe, *A Catalogue of the most Splendid, Interesting and Truly Important Collection of Autograph Letters ever offered for Sale* (London, 1840), p. 4.
26. BL MS Cotton Caligula DVI, fo. 177^r (*LP* II. i. 106); *LP* II. i. 145.
27. ULC MS Add. 4875, fo. 50. This interpretation generally follows that of Richardson, *Mary Tudor*, pp. 128–85, which provides a detailed narrative of the events from January to May.
28. BL MS Cotton Caligula DVI, fo. 186^r (*LP* II. i. 80).
29. *LP* II. i. 203; PRO SP1/10, fo. 77^r (*LP* II. i. 224).
30. *LP* II. i. 224–6, 256, 367.
31. Richardson, *Mary Tudor*, pp. 179–80; *LP* II. i. 203.
32. Ibid. 106, 113, 138. Langley's only diplomatic employment had been under the Howard-led regency of Queen Catherine (*LP* I. ii. 2394, 2423).
33. *CSPV* iii. 1486; *LJ* i. 38.
34. BL MS Cotton Vespasian FXIII, fo. 80.
35. *LP* II. i. 80, 223, 237. There seems to be no good reason to assume, as the editors do, that the last is misdated.
36. PRO SP1/10, fo. 88^r (*LP* II. ii, App. 7).
37. *LP* II. i. 224, 300–2; Richardson, *Mary Tudor*, pp. 181–5.
38. BN MS Dupuy 462, fo. 4^v.
39. BL MS Cotton Caligula DVI, fo. 167^v (*LP* II. i. 134).
40. Ibid., fo. 175^r (*LP* II. i.192).
41. *LP* II. i. 80, 136, 159.
42. *CSPV* ii. 618; *Chronicle of Calais*, p. 17; BN MS Dupuy 462, fo. 3^v: 'Barking' (Richardson, *Mary Tudor*, p. 187) is surely a misreading: Henry was at Birling on 6 May (PRO E36/215, fo. 188^v).
43. *LP* II. i. 224; PRO C54/383, m. 17 (*LP* II. i. 436).
44. PRO SP1/11, fo. 11 (*LP* II. i. 660); PRO C66/624, m. 29 (*LP* II. i. 696); *LP* II. ii, p. 1487; SBT DR5/2921.
45. *LP* II. i. 468.
46. *LP* II. i. 82; ii, pp. 1503–4.
47. *LP* II. ii, p. 1504; Hall, p. 582; D. R. Starkey, 'The Age of the Household', in *The Later Middle Ages*, ed. S. E. Medcalf (London, 1981), p. 275.
48. *LP* II. ii, pp. 1466, 1503–4; Hall, p. 581.
49. *DNB* ii. 1127.
50. *LP* II. i. 94; Miller, *English Nobility*, pp. 213–14.
51. *LP* I. ii. 2055 (50), 2055 (95), 2617 (33), 2772 (25); II. i. 113; XXI. ii. 773 (i, 36); PRO SC12/18/58, fos 2, 3, 5; C43/2/42–7; C142/28/1; SRO HA18/DE1/7.
52. BL Harl. Ch. 54I27, 56G52; LAO lAnc 2A/19/11; ERO D/DRg 1/92; *LP* II. i. 134.
53. *CSPV* ii. 638.
54. *HMC Third Report* (1872), p. 321; *The Register or Chronicle of Butley Priory Suffolk 1510–1535*, ed. A. G. Dickens (Winchester, 1951), pp. 33–4.
55. NRO Norwich 7g, 1515–16, m. 19; SRO EE2/L2/2/24; H. Swinden, *The History and Antiquities of the Ancient Burgh of Great Yarmouth in the County of Norfolk* (Norwich, 1772), p. 936.
56. BL Harl. Ch. 51A13; ULC MS Mm 1.41, p. 107.
57. PRO SP1/13, fo. 249 (*LP* II. i. 2170).
58. *LP* III. ii. 2856, 2869, 2870, 2919, 2922; *CAF* i. 1858.
59. *LP* II. ii, App. 39; III. i. 1221, 1266; ii. 2446, 2769, 3365, 3368; IV i. 68; *CSPS* Further Supplement, p. 219; HL MS El. 2652, fo. 13^r.
60. *LP* II. i. 1510 (ii).
61. *LP* III. ii. 2737; PRO STAC2/14/1,18/20; Cl/634/448; 'Norfolk Subsidy Roll, 15 Hen. VIII', ed. W. Rye, *Norfolk Antiquarian Miscellany*, 2 (1883), 402.
62. The index to *LP* III (1519–23) mentions Richard thirty-six times, that to *LP* II (1515–18) eighty-three times.
63. BL Add. Ch. 73511; University College of North Wales Library, Bangor, MS Penrhyn 48; W. de G. Birch, *Catalogue of Seals in the Department of Manuscripts in the British Museum* (6 vols, London, 1887–1900), iii. 398.
64. *Two Tudor Interludes: The Interlude of Youth, Hick Scorner*, ed. I. Lancashire (The Revels Plays, 1980), pp. 32–4, 59–63; Bodl. MS Wood F33, fos 19^v, 23^r; *LP* II. i. 437.
65. *LP* I. ii. 2055 (95); NRO Bulwer NRS 2567, m. 14^v, 2568, m. 5^v; PRO PROB11/18/ 16; LR12/21/636. I owe the last reference to Dr R. W. Hoyle.
66. *The Visitation of Suffolk 1561*, ed. J. Corder(Harl. Soc. NS 2–3, 1981–4), i. 107;

BL Add. Ch. 16573; *CAD* v. A10951; SRO T4374/Box 9, no. 5.

67. PRO SC6/Henry VIII/345, mm. 12–13; LR12/21/636.
68. Clwyd RO, Hawarden, D/PT/1020.
69. LAO 2Anc 3/B/l.
70. See table 2.1.
71. PRO C54/383, m. 15; *LP* XIII. ii. 1215 (1).
72. *SR* 27 Henry VIII, c. 38, s. 13; PRO LR 12/21/636.
73. PRO C54/384, m. 2; 388, m. 26; 390, m. 14.
74. *SR* 27 Henry VIII, c. 38, s. 13; PRO SC12/23/29, fo. 4ʳ; LR12/21/636.
75. PRO SP1/232, fo. 81ʳ (*LP* Add. i. 216); CP40/1016, rot. 527, 1017, rot. 137; KB27/ 1076, rot. 22ᵛ; 1054, rot. 25, 65ᵛ; *LP* IV. ii. 2395, 4229 (7, ii).
76. SRO Tl/2/1.4, mm 9ᵛ, 11ʳ, 12ʳ, Tl/2/5.1.
77. PRO LR12/21/636; SRO HA18/DB1/2, m. 10.
78. SRO HE10/1/6, mm 3, 5ᵛ.
79. W. R. B. Robinson, 'Patronage and Hospitality in Early Tudor Wales: the Role of Henry, Earl of Worcester, 1526–49', *Bulletin of the Institute of Historical Research*, 51 (1978), 25; M. E. James, 'Two Tudor Funerals', in his *Society, Politics and Culture* (Cambridge, 1986), p. 185.
80. M. Cherry, 'The Courtenay Earls of Devon: the Formation and Disintegration of a Late Medieval Aristocratic Affinity', *Southern History* 1 (1979), 76–7; I. Rowney, 'Resources and Retaining in Yorkist England: William, Lord Hastings and the Honour of Tutbury', in *Property and Politics: Essays in Later Medieval English History*, ed. A. J. Pollard (Gloucester, 1984), p. 145.
81. *LP* II. i. 297, 331, 367, 468, 665, 740.
82. Bodl. MS DD All Souls Coll. Arch. *c.* 280; *LP* II. i. 1861; ii. p. 1478; PRO SP1/232, fo. 81 (*LP* Add. i. 216).
83. Bindoff, *Commons* iii. 640–1; *Report on the Manuscripts of the Earl of Ancaster* (HMC 66, 1907), pp. 488, 496; PRO CP25 (2)/25/155/42, 28/189/47, 39/257/31, 36, 57, 39/ 258/40, 39/259/22, 50, 39/260/2, 18, 51/362/6; STAC2/26/254.
84. F. Metzger, *Das Englische Kanzleigericht unter Kardinal Wolsey 1515–1529* (Inaugural- Dissertation, Friedrich-Alexander-Universität, Erlangen-Nürnberg, 1977), p. 355; An *Inventory of the Historical Monuments in London* (5 vols, Royal Commission on Historical Monuments, 1924–30), ii. 53 (I am grateful to Mr Henry James for this reference); *The Register of Admissions to Gray's Inn 1521–1889*, ed. J. Foster (London, 1889), cols 2, 5, 9 (Robert Wingfield: PRO SC12/37/16, m. 5; William Naunton: Bodl. MS Ashmole 1109, fo. 143ᵛ; Richard Welby: PRO Cl/917/23); *The Reports of Sir John Spelman*, ed. J. H. Baker (Selden Soc. 93–4, 1975–6), i. ix (John Spelman: PRO LR12/21/636).
85. *LP* II. i. 2170; PRO CP25 (2)/39/258/34, 28/190/22, 39/260/3, 5, 39/257/5, 43, 61; E41/32; *CAD* v. A12241.

86. PRO CP40/1027, rot. 140; BL Harl. Ch. 47A46.
87. PRO CP25 (2)/39/257/5, 43, 61, 39/258/34, 39/260/3, 5, 28/190/22; E36/215, fo. 342ʳ.
88. SRO HE10/1/6, mm 11ʳ, 23ʳ, 25ᵛ; PRO LR12/27/922; SC6/Addenda/3482/94, m. 3ᵛ.
89. NRO Bulwer NRS 2567, m. 4ʳ; 2568, m. 2ᵛ; SRO HA18/DB1/2, mm 6ᵛ, 8; HA18/ DF1/2, mm 3, 7; HE10/1/6, mm 5–9, 11, 14, 16–21, 24–5.
90. PRO E36/214, fo. 239ᵛ; E36/215, p. 662.
91. PRO C54/384, m. 2; CP40/1040, rot. 421; PROB11/23/13; Bindoff, *Commons* ii. 140.
92. PRO E179/69/4; W. St J. Hope, 'The Last Testament and Inventory of John de Veer, thirteenth Earl of Oxford', *Archaeologia*, 66 (1915), 319; *LP* IV. ii. 3324 (3); PRO C54/384, m. 2; Bindoff, *Commons* iii. 182–4.
93. Hope, 'Last Testament', pp. 318–19.
94. PRO C54/384, m. 2.
95. PRO C54/388, m. 26; PROB11/21/3; NRO Bishops' Register 14, fo. 60ᵛ.
96. PRO CP40/1037, rot. 433; J. M. Wingfield, *Some Records of the Wingfield Family* (London, 1925), p. 125.
97. PRO PROB11/20/9; NRO NCC Briggs 73–5; C. Rawcliffe, *The Staffords, Earls of Stafford and Dukes of Buckingham, 1394–1521* (Cambridge, 1978), p. 229; *LP* II. ii. 2970.
98. *LP* II. i. 242, 1397; IV. iii, App. 155; PRO C54/385, m. 21.
99. e.g Robert Dukett, SRO HA18/DF1/2, m. 4; *Suffolk in 1524*, ed. S. H. A. Hervey (Suffolk Green Books 10, 1910), p. 100.
100. PRO LR12/21/636; E179/69/4, 5.
101. W. R. B. Robinson, 'The Officers and Household of Henry, Earl of Worcester, 1526–49', *Welsh Hist. Rev.* 8 (1976–7), 31–3.
102. *Suffolk in 1524*, p. 268; 'Norfolk Subsidy Roll', p. 409.
103. PRO E137/42/3/3–5; D. N. J. MacCulloch, *Suffolk and the Tudors* (Oxford, 1986), pp. 108, 356–72.
104. Ibid., p. 415.
105. PRO LR12/21/636.
106. *LP* II. i. 2347; III. i. 455; Wingfield, *Wingfield Family*, p. 36; see tables 2.2 and 2.3. It is often impossible to date with precision an individual's marriage or entry into ducal service, and this leaves it unclear whether Brandon was recruiting relatives or rewarding servants with good matches in the family. He was probably doing both.
107. *CAD* ii. A3355, v. A10952; SRO HE10/1/6, m. 2; T4374/Box 9, no. 5.
108. *CAD* v. A10951–3, 10957.
109. E. K. Chambers, *The Medieval Stage* (2 vols, Oxford, 1913), ii. 252; BL MS Egerton 2092, fos 297ʳ, 376ʳ, 486ʳ (*LP* IV. iii, App. 89); HMC *Third Report*, p. 323; HMC *Fifth Report* (1876), pp. 551, 553; HMC *Rutland*, iv. 322, 324; HMC *Middleton*, pp. 334, 360–1, 378; *Report on the Manuscripts of the Corporation of Beverley* (HMC 54, 1900), p. 174; PRO LR12/21/636.

110. *Records of Plays and Players in Norfolk and Suffolk 1330–1642*, ed. G. R. Proudfoot (Malone Society Collections 11, 1980), pp. 221–2, 225–6. I owe this reference to Dr J. Maule.
111. PRO LR12/21/636; *The Visitation of Shropshire*, ed. G. Glazebrook, J. P. Rylands (Harl. Soc. 28–9, 1889), ii. 509.
112. NRO Jerningham 1 T176B1; J. Foster, *Penningtoniana* (London, 1878), p. 46; PRO E179/69/5.
113. *LP* IV. ii. 3772.
114. ERO D/B3/3/228, 3/3/69, 3/3/230; NRO Norwich 7g 1514–15, m. 24; 1518–19, mm 15, 16; 1522–3, m. 20; 1523–4, mm 18, 19; KLBRO KL/C39/71, m. 1ʳ; 73, m. 2ᵛ.
115. 'Ely Episcopal Registers', *Ely Diocesan Remembrancer*, 305 (1910), p. 181, 307 (1910), p. 216, 312 (1911), p. 87; Bodl. MS Tanner 141, fo. 77ʳ.
116. SBT DR5/2023, 2024, 2028; PRO SC12/37/16, mm 9–11.
117. *The Cartulary of Oseney Abbey*, vi, ed. H. E. Salter (Oxford Historical Society 101, 1936), p. 280.
118. PRO CP25 (2)/42/285/21; *LP* III. i. 365, ii. 3197; IV. i. 1082; Add. i. 430–2.
119. M. Howard, 'Power and the Early-Tudor Courtier's House', *History Today* 37. 5 (1987), 47–8; S. J. Gunn and P. Lindley, 'Charles Brandon's Westhorpe, an Early Tudor Courtyard-House in Suffolk, *Archaeological Journal*, 145 (1988), 272–89.
120. *CSPV* iii. 88, 466. Brandenburg had married the widow of Ferdinand of Aragon.
121. Richardson, *Mary Tudor*, p. 166.
122. D. Gurney, 'Extracts from the Household and Privy Purse Accounts of the Lestranges of Hunstanton, from A.D. 1519 to A.D. 1578', *Archaeologia*, 35 (1834), 435–6, 447.
123. BL MS Add. 33748, fo. 30ʳ.
124. H. A Tipping, *English Homes* (9 vols, London, 1920–37), ii. 202.
125. AN KK349, fo. 69ᵛ; BL MS Cotton Titus BI, fo. 71 (*LP* II. i. 1605).
126. BL Harl. Ch. 43F23; MS Egerton 985, fos 61ᵛ–64ʳ (*LP* II. i. 1652; ii. 3489).
127. *LP* II. ii. 3487.
128. *SR* 1 Henry VIII, c. 8; *LP* III. i. 684.
129. PRO LR12/21/636. Some of the wards' revenues must have been spent on their upkeep. Cash liveries in 1523, some of them to Mary in Suffolk's absence, totalled £974 5s. 8 3/4d., but various payments were made directly by the receivers.
130. *LP* II. ii, pp. 1465, 1467, 1470; PRO E36/215, p. 613 (*LP* II. ii, p. 1482); *LP* II. i. 1861; ii. 3487; Gunn, 'North Wales', p. 487.
131. *LP* III. i. 220; ii. 2074 (18), 2648 (22), 3162; PRO E36/150 p. 31; SC12/37/16, m. 15.
132. *LP* II. i. 80, 468; ii, App. 7; ULC MS Add. 4875, fos 54–5.
133. BL MS Cotton Caligula DVI, fo. 319 (*LP* II. ii. 3367); PRO E179/69/4, 5.
134. *LP* I. i. 1365 (6); ii. 2861 (20), 3344; II. i. 792; *CAF* viii. 32241, 32291.
135. PRO SP1/10, fos 50, 158 (*LP* ii. i. 144, 370); *LP* II. ii. 4567; *CAF* v. 16761.
136. *LP* II. ii. 4388; III. ii. 2076, 2446; College of Arms MS R36, fos 38ʳ–40ʳ.
137. *CSPV* ii. 679; *LP* III. i. 1239.
138. *LP* II. i. 180, 197; J. de Iongh, *Margaret of Austria* (London, 1954), p. 167; BL MS Add. 14840, fo. 2 (*LP* II. i. 529); ADN B18871/31875.
139. *LP* II. i. 45, 522, 828.
140. Ibid., pp. xlviii-ix (1113).
141. *CSPV* ii. 638, 730; *LP* II. i. 1244.
142. *LP* II. i. 834, 913, 1025, 1026, 1030.
143. *LP* II. i. 1959; ii. 2925; *CSPV* ii. 750.
144. HL MS El. 2655, fos 9ᵛ, 10ʳ, El. 2654; *LP* II. i. 2347; ii. 3093; PRO IND10217/1, fo. 2ᵛ; Bindoff, *Commons* ii. 482.
145. *LP* II. ii. 3973, 4057, 4060, 4161; III. i. 1; B. J. Harris, *Edward Stafford, Third Duke of Buckingham, 1478–1521* (Stanford, 1986), p. 205. I have also drawn on Mr P. J. Gwyn's reconstruction of these events.
146. *LP* II. i. 1605, ii. 4043, 4061, 4124; PRO SP1/16, fo. 182 (*LP* II. ii. 4035).
147. *LP* II. ii. 4061, 4134; Add. i. 210.
148. PRO SP1/232, fo. 75 (*LP* Add. i. 210).
149. *LP* II. ii. 4035, 4308, 4334; Add. i. 216.
150. PRO SP1/232, fo. 81 (*LP* Add. i. 216).
151. PRO SP1/17, fos 7–8 (*LP* II. ii. 4334).
152. *LP* II. ii. 4303, 4346; PRO SP1/232, fo. 81ʳ.
153. *LP* II. ii. 4346; III. i. 779 (25); ii, pp. 1537, 1544; Add. i. 269.
154. PRO SP1/17, fo. 12 (*LP* II. ii. 4355).
155. SP1/17, fo. 67 (*LP* II. ii. 4448); *LP* II. ii. 4388.
156. *LP* II. ii. 4469, 4475, 4481, 4504; *CSPV* ii. 1085, 1095.
157. HL MS El. 2655, fo. 13ʳ.
158. *LP* III. i. 14, 15.
159. AN KK349, *passim*.
160. *LP* I. ii. 3344; *CAF* v. 16103.
161. *Le Journal de Jean Barrillon*, ed. P. de Vaissière (2 vols, Société de l'Histoire de France, 1897–9), i. 56; *LP* II, ii, App. 43*; III. i. 488, 1174, 1441.
162. *LP* III. i. 488; BN MS Dupuy 486, fos 180ʳ, 181ʳ.
163. PRO SP1/12, fo. 72 (*LP* II. i. 1397); *LP* II. i. 1547. There are problems in dating all these letters, but the few places named by Suffolk would fit his probable itinerary in 1516.
164. SP1/13, fo. 27 (*LP* II. i. 1604).
165. *Polydore Vergil...1485–1537*, p. 233; *LP* II. i. 1605–6; PRO SP1/17, fo. 7 (*LP* II. ii. 4334).
166. PRO SP1/232, fos 6–8 (*LP* Add. i. 171).
167. PRO C54/385, mm 26–7; SP1/235, fo. 32; LAO 2Anc 3/B/2 (the original signed by Henry).
168. *LP* III. i. 1153.
169. *LP* II, ii, pp. 1478, 1480; PRO C54/385, m. 26.
170. *LP* II, ii, p. 1534.
171. *LP* III. i. 1395, 2288; *CSPS* FS, p. 73; *Rutland Papers*, pp. 72, 81; Hall, p. 641.
172. Richardson, *Mary Tudor*, p. 211.
173. BL Harl. Ch.43Bl.
174. PRO SP1/24, fo. 188 (*LP* III. ii. 2288 (4));

BL MS Cotton Galba BVI, fo. 211 (*LP* III. i. 926); *LP* I. ii. 2575; II. i. 256.
175. *Analectes Historiques*, p. 194; *LP* III. i. 174, 180.
176. *LP* II. ii. 1902, 2105, 2472, 2487; *CSPV* ii. 875, 901, 942.
177. PRO SP1/14, fo. 215ᵛ (*LP* II. ii. 2826).
178. *LP* II. ii. 3872; III. ii. 3064.
179. PRO C24/28, 29, Haworth and Powis v. Suffolk, *passim*.
180. PRO E179/69/4 (*LP* IV. ii. 2972); Longleat House Misc. Vol. 11, fos 126–35.
181. *LP* III. i. 702 (2. i).
182. PRO LR12/21/636; *LP* II. ii. 4448, p. 1501.
183. Bodl. MS Wood F33, fo. 45ᵛ; PRO E179/69/4, 5; *Chronicle of Calais*, pp. 76–7; BL MS Egerton 985, fos 61ᵛ–64ʳ (*LP* II. i. 1652, ii. 3489); *LP* Add. i. 269.
184. *LP* I. ii. 3348 (3), 3357; II. ii. 3489; *Test. Vet.* ii. 658.
185. BL MS Egerton 985, fo. 62ʳ; *GEC* xi. 303.
186. Bindoff, *Commons* ii. 545; BL MS Egerton 985; fos 61ᵛ–64ʳ; PRO PROB11/16/2; *LP* XIV. i. 1211; PRO SP1/15, fo. 33 (*LP* II. ii. 3018).
187. PRO E179/69/4, 5; SC12/23/29, fo. 3ᵛ; LAO LMR16/7/29.
188. C. Carpenter, 'The Beauchamp Affinity: a study of Bastard Feudalism at work', *EHR* 95 (1980), 514–18; B. Coward, *The Stanleys, Lords Stanley and Earls of Derby, 1385-1672* (Chetham Society, 3rd ser. 30, 1983), pp. 85–6; R. B. Smith, *Land and Politics in the England of Henry VIII: the West Riding of Yorkshire, 1530–46* (Oxford, 1970), p. 138; PRO E179/69/4–6; E150/237/9; *LP* I. ii, App. 26; XI. 522; *The Visitation of Yorkshire in the years 1563 and 1564*, ed. C. B. Norcliffe (Harl. Soc. 16, 1881), pp. 339–40. For evidence that Suffolk's vice-chamberlain was Sir Thomas Wentworth of West Bretton and not the future Lord Wentworth (as in Bindoff, *Commons* iii. 583) see *LP* X. 1063 (5); F. Ford, *Mary Tudor, a Retrospective Sketch* (Bury St Edmunds, 1882), p. 42.
189. LAO lAnc 7/A/l; J. M. W. Bean, *The Estates of the Percy Family, 1416–1537* (Oxford, 1958), pp. 137–9; Harris, *Buckingham*, pp. 101–2, 130.
190. *LP* II. i. 1292; ii. 4423; Add. i. 269.
191. Ford, *Mary Tudor*, p. 39; PRO E179/69/4; SC6/Henry VIII/2573, mm 4ᵛ, 6ᵛ; Cl/1130/79; LR12/21/636; SC6/Addenda/3482/94, m. 4ᵛ; Bodl. MS Tanner 135, fos 120–2.
192. PRO E179/69/4, 5; *Lincolnshire Pedigrees*, ed. A. R. Maddison (Harl. Soc. 50-2, 55, 1902–6), iii. 794; M. E. Wingfield, *Muniments of the Ancient Saxon Family of Wingfield* (London, 1894), p. 18.
193. *Suffolk 1561* ii. 328; *Lincs. Peds.* i. 5.
194. PRO SP1/15, fo. 33 (*LP* II. ii. 3018).
195. College of Arms MS R36, fo. 1ᵛ.
196. Bindoff, *Commons* ii. 564; *LP* Add. i. 269; BL MS Add. 12462, fos. 4–5; *HMC Rutland* iv. 563; *Calendar of the Manuscripts of the Most Hon. the Marquis of Salisbury*, xiii (HMC 9, 1915), 10; *Test. Vet.* ii. 642; *LP* III. i. 1186 (8); IV. i. 366.

197. Bindoff, *Commons* ii. 283; LAO lAnc 7/A/l; *LP* IV. ii. 3264; A. B. Emden, *A Biographical Register of the University of Oxford to A.D. 1500* (3 vols, Oxford, 1957–9), ii. 781; Harris, *Buckingham*, p. 218.
198. Rawcliffe, *Staffords*, p. 229; R. A. Griffiths, *The Principality of Wales in the Later Middle Ages*, i (University of Wales, Board of Celtic Studies, History and Law ser. 26, 1972), 556–7; PRO LR12/21/636.
199. De la Pole papers survive among the Ancaster deposit in the LAO. *SR* 11 Henry VII, c. 39; BL Egerton Roll 8779; PRO SC12/37/16, m. 5.
200. PRO SP1/10, fo. 50 (*LP* II. i. 144); *LP* II. i. 1397, 1861; IV. iii, App. 155.
201. Bodl. MS Top. Berks. b2, fo. 13; PRO LR12/21/636.
202. PRO SP1/13, fo. 7 (*LP* II. i. 1547); SRO EE2/Ll/4t; Tl/2/1.4, m. 14ʳ.
203. PRO SP1/13, fo. 249 (*LP* II. i. 2170).
204. BL MS Cotton Titus BI, fo. 320ʳ (*LP* II. i. 1606).
205. *LP* II. ii, pp. 1506–7; III. ii, pp. 1552–3; Hall, p. 622.
206. *LP* II. ii, p. 1510; Starkey, 'King's Privy Chamber', pp. 89–90.
207. *LP* II. ii, pp. 1507–9; Anglo, *Great Tournament Roll* i. 63–4.
208. C. Ffoulkes, 'Jousting Cheques of the Sixteenth Century', *Archaeologia*, 63 (1912), 8, fig. 1; S. Anglo, 'Archives of the English Tournament', *Journal of the Society of Archivists*, 2 (1961), 153–62.
209. E. Lodge, *Illustrations of British History* (3 vols, London, 1791), i. 17 (*LP* II. i. 1935).
210. *LP* II. ii, p. 1510.
211. D. R. Starkey, *The Reign of Henry VIII, Personalities and Politics* (London, 1985), pp. 71–2; *CSPV* ii. 918; *LP* II. ii, p. 1510; BL MS Add. 30543, fo. 85ᵛ.
212. *CSPV* ii. 918, 920; *LP* II. ii. 3462.
213. *CSPV* ii. 918; Malory, *Works* ii. 568–70; *The Manuscripts of the Earl of Dartmouth*, iii (HMC 15, 1, 1896), 1–50.
214. *LP* II. ii, pp. 1515–17; III. ii. 2305, pp. 1556–8; Hall, p. 635.
215. B. de Montfaucon, *Les Monumens de la monarchie françoise* (5 vols, Paris, 1729–33), iv. 182–91.
216. *LP* III. i, p. 311; Bodl. MS Ashmole 1116, fo. 102ʳ.
217. *LP* III. ii. 2305, p. 1554; Hall, pp. 595, 597, 599, 635; *CSPV* ii. 1085; Starkey, *Reign of Henry VIII*, p. 81.
218. Hall, pp. 595, 597; *LP* II. i. 1861, ii. 3446; III. i. 491, 528, 577, ii. 2305, pp. 1558–9; *CSPV* iii. 50; *CSPS* FS, p. 250.
219. Hall, p. 597; Starkey, *Reign of Henry VIII*, pp. 77–8.
220. Richardson, *Mary Tudor*, p. 277; V. Leroquais, *Bibliothèque de la ville de Lyon, Exposition de Manuscrits à Peintures du VI au XVII Siècle, Catalogue descriptif* (Lyons, 1920) pp. 39–40; BN MS Fr. 6622, fo. 5; *LP* V, pp. 750, 758.
221. R. Strong, *The English Renaissance Miniature* (London, 1983), pp. 36–7; BL Add. Ch. 73511.

222. Gunn and Lindley, 'Charles Brandon's Westhorpe'.
223. MacCulloch, *Suffolk*, pp. 146–7; J. Palsgrave, *The Comedy of Acolastus*, ed. P. L. Carver (EETS 202, 1937), pp. xiv–xvi, xxix–xxx.
224. J. G. Russell, *The Field of Cloth of Gold* (London, 1969), p. 104; *LP* III. i, pp. 499, 505.
225. Bodl. MS Ashmole 1109, fo. 127ʳ.
226. *LP* I. ii. 3357; III. i. 152.
227. *LP* III. ii. 2395; PRO C142/35/32; D. R. Starkey, 'From Feud to Faction', *History Today*, 32. 11 (1982), 19; D. M. Loades, *The Tudor Court* (London, 1986), p. 47.
228. *LP* III. i. 684; IV. i. 400; Add. i. 269; Bindoff, *Commons* i. 575.
229. *LP* I. ii. 3324 (34); III. i. 246, 704, 999; *Rutland Papers*, p. 101.
230. *LP* III. ii, p. 1543; Add. i. 269.
231. *LP* I. i. 546 (67); III. i. 1115.
232. Anstis, *Garter* i. 278, 283–4, 287–8, 290–2, 358–60.
233. Ibid., pp. 278–90, 358–60, 361–3; *LP* II. i. 138.
234. *LP* II. i. 1114, ii. p. 1503.
235. *LP* I. i. 1661 (1, 4), ii. 1844, 2304 (3), II. i. 510; III. ii. 3139; PRO PROB11/23/13; CP25 (2)/7/32/4.
236. PRO KB27/1032, rot. 28; 1040, rots 26, 85; SP46/163, fo. 32.
237. PRO CP40/1034, rot. 576; 1035, rot. 334; *LP* Add. i. 269.
238. *LP* III. i. 55 (28); PRO C54/386, m. 22; CP40/1024, rot. 135.
239. PRO Cl/519/53; STAC2/18/83, 29/72.
240. *LP* II. i. 1436, ii. 4423; III. i. 455, 602, 854 (6), 1324 (6); E. W. Ives, 'Crime, Sanctuary and Royal Authority under Henry VIII: the exemplary sufferings of the Savage family', in *Of the Laws and Customs of England*, ed. M. S. Arnold et al. (Chapel Hill, 1981).
241. PRO IND4, 1330, 1331, 6649; Rawcliffe, *Staffords*, p. 175.
242. PRO CP 40/1006, rot, 599; 1037, rot. 793; 1038, rot. 121.
243. SBT DR5/2915, 2917–20, 2922.
244. *The Domesday of Inclosures*, ed. I. S. Leadam (2 vols, London, 1897), i. 129–46; PRO C 54/388, m. 7.
245. *LP* II. i. 630; ii. 3093; III. i. 185; ii. 3161, 3162.
246. PRO WARD9/147, fo. 31ʳ.
247. *LP* Add. i. 196; PRO SP1/30, fo. 260 (*LP* IV. i. 182).
248. *LP* II. i. 80, ii. 4308; IV. iii, p. 2766; 'King Henry VIII's Jewel Book', ed. E. Trollope, *Reports and Papers of the Associated Architectural Societies*, 17 (1884), 163, 171.
249. *LP* II. i. 1153, ii. 3437 (6,8); III. i. 906; Hall, pp. 591, 594,599, 629, 640; PRO LC2/ 1, fo. 146ʳ; *CSPV* iii. 50.
250. S. Anglo, *Spectacle, Pageantry, and Early Tudor Policy* (Oxford, 1969), p. 146; *CSPV* iii. 50.
251. *LP* II. i. 666, 673, 716; *CSPV* ii. 653, 659, 667.
252. *LP* II. i. 1335; *CSPV* ii. 682, 844.
253. BL MS Lansdowne 1, fo. 108ʳ; HL MS El.

254. *CSPV* ii. 878; PRO SP1/19, fo. 228 (*LP* III. i. 684).
255. *LP* III. ii, pp. 1538–9; P. Heath, 'The Treason of Geoffrey Blythe', *Bull. Inst. Hist. Res.* 42 (1969), 109; PRO KB9/475/2/16.
256. Hall, pp. 623–4; LJ i. 46, 54; *LP* III. ii. 2956. On the triers, see Miller, *English Nobility*, p. 122.
257. Ibid., p. 103.
258. *LP* II. ii. 2733, App. 48; *HMC Ninth Report* ii. 282; BL Harl. Ch. 43F9; *LP* XIV. i. 181 (iii).
259. R. Whittinton, *Libellus Epygrammaton* (London, 1519).
260. *LP* III. ii. 1440, 1462; *CSPS* FS, p. 182.
261. *CSPS* FS, pp. 182, 197, 208, 211–13.

3 Power in the Counties, Power at Court: 1523–1529

1. S. J. Gunn, 'The Duke of Suffolk's March on Paris in 1523', *EHR* 101 (1986), 596–634.
2. G. W. Bernard, *War, Taxation and Rebellion in Early Tudor England. Henry VIII, Wolsey and the Amicable Grant of 1525* (Brighton, 1986), pp. 18–40; Haus-, Hof-, und Staatsarchiv, Vienna, PA 14/3, fos 25ʳ, 76ᵛ; 15/1, fos 64ʳ, 184ʳ; Archives Générales du Royaume, Brussels, État et Audience 39, fo. 92ʳ; *LP* IV. i. 456, 605; *CSPS* FS, p. 384.
3. *CSPS* FS, p. 342; *LP* IV. i. 680, 841.
4. *LP* IV. i. 605, 648, 653 (3), 684; *CSPS* FS, pp. 390–1.
5. Haus-, Hof-, und Staatsarchiv PA 15/1, fo. 67ᵛ; *CSPS* FS, pp. 388–9.
6. PRO SP1/32, fo. 39 (*LP* IV. i. 619).
7. *LP* IV. i. 1261, 1265.
8. *CSPS* III. i. 1012; *LP* IV. ii. 2638, 2948, 3518.
9. *CSPS* III. i. 315, FS, pp. 304, 348.
10. *CSPS* III. i. 20, 39, 111, 160, 341; FS, p. 438; *CSPV* iii. 1037,1150,1169,1201,1231.
11. *LP* IV. i. 895, 961, 1049, 1136, 1377, 1610, 2002.
12. *LP* IV. i. 1253.
13. 'Inventory of the Wardrobe, Plate & c. of Henry Fitzroy, Duke of Richmond and Somerset', ed. J. G. Nichols, in *The Camden Miscellany*, 3 (Cam. Soc. 61, 1855), pp. lxxxiv–v; College of Arms MS R 36, fo. 55v.
14. PRO CP40/1006, rot. 599; BL MS Add. 6113, fos 57v, 59r.
15. LAO 2Anc 3/B/4; *LP* IV. i. 1431.
16. NRO Register 14, fos 135ᵛ, 186ᵛ, 210ʳ, 212ʳ (my translations).
17. *Six Town Chronicles of England*, ed. R. Flenley (Oxford, 1911), p. 195; *The Manuscripts of the Corporations of Southampton and King's Lynn* (HMC 11.3, 1887), p. 173.
18. *Butley Register*, pp. 51–5.
19. *LP* IV. i. 1235, 1241.
20. PRO SP1/34, fos 143–4 (*LP* IV. i. 1260); Hall, p. 699. Much of this account is dependent on Bernard, *War, Taxation and Rebellion*.

21. Hall, pp. 699–700; *Report on Manuscripts in the Welsh Language*, i (HMC 48, 1898), p. ii.
22. HMC *Welsh Language* i. ii-iv; *LP* IV. i. 1319, 1323.
23. PRO SP1/34, fo. 196ʳ (*LP* IV. i. 1329); BL MS Cotton Appendix L, fo. 12 (*LP* IV. i. 1324).
24. PRO SP1/34, fo. 209 (*LP* IV. i. 1343).
25. *LP* IV. ii. 4045; Anstis, *Garter* i. 383; PRO SP1/47, fo. 223 (*LP* IV. ii. 4183).
26. MacCulloch, *Suffolk*, p. 298.
27. *LP* IV. ii. 3649, 3664, 3702, 3703, 3760, 3811, 3883 (1), 4192.
28. PRO SP1/46, fos 220–1 (*LP* IV. ii. 3883).
29. *LP* IV. ii. 3811, 4012; F. Blomefield, C. Parkin, *An Essay towards a Topographical History of the County of Norfolk* (11 vols, London, 1805–18), iii. 198; *Butley Register*, p. 54.
30. PRO SP1/46, fo. 218 (*LP* IV. ii. 3883 (1)); SP1/53, fo. 165 (*LP* IV. iii. 5415); HL MS El. 2652, fo. 7ᵛ.
31. *LP* IV. ii. 4129, 4141, 4145, 4188, 4310; iii, App. 163.
32. *LP* IV. ii. 3663; PRO SP1/53, fo. 165 (*LP* IV. iii. 5415).
33. PRO SP1/46, fos 122–3 (*LP* IV. ii. 3811).
34. E. M. Richardson, *The Lion and the Rose* (London, 1922) i. 82 (citing MS household accounts).
35. MacCulloch, *Suffolk*, pp. 58–9; R. Virgoe, 'The Recovery of the Howards in East Anglia, 1485–1529', in *Wealth and Power in Tudor England*, ed. E. W. Ives et al. (London, 1978), p. 18; PRO LR12/21/636.
36. *LP* IV. ii. 4399; iii, App. 270.
37. *LP* XII. ii. 304; BL Egerton Roll 8796; *Six Town Chronicles*, pp. 193–4.
38. KLBRO KL/C39/75, m. 2ᵛ; NRO Norwich 7g 1522–3, m. 20; 1523–4, m. 18; 18a 1531–2, fo. 34.
39. *LP* IV. ii. 3760; iii, App. 12; KLBRO KL/C43/3.
40. RO KB27/1061, rot. 30v; CP40/1045, rot. 330. Peers' creditors often sued the sureties rather than the debtor because peers could not be arrested for debt: Harris, *Buckingham*, p. 133.
41. CP40/1051, rot. 338; 1055, rot. 422.
42. *LP* II. ii. 3018; IV. i. 1260, 1298, 1543, 1642; ii. 3760, 3811, 3884, 3997, 4183, 4616, 4620; iii, App. 12, 270; XIII. i. 642; PRO SC12/37/16, m. 8.
43. PRO SP1/40, fo. 216 (*LP* IV. ii. 2807).
44. BN MS Dupuy 462, fo. 33; *LP* II. i. 1436, 1547; IV. i. 1615, ii. 4324.
45. SRO HE10/1/6, mm 16–18; HA18/DF1/2, m. 7ʳ; *Suffolk in 1524*, pp. 100, 330.
46. SRO HE10/1/6, mm 18–20; *Suffolk in 1524*, p. 277; N. Bacon, *The Annalls of Ipswiche*, ed. W. H. Richardson (Ipswich, 1884), p. 222.
47. *LP* IV. i. 737; *CAD* v. A12465, 12848, 12859; *Suffolk in 1524*, pp. 359,426; Rawcliffe, *Staffords*, p. 93.
48. *LP* IV. iii, App. 12; PRO SC12/37/16, m. 4; E150/627/18; CP25(2)/29/194/12, 39/259/1; LAO 2Anc 3/B/3.
49. LAO 2Anc 3/B/3; PRO CP25(2)/39/261/32; Cl/585/42–7.
50. PRO CP25(2)/39/261/33, 51/362/6; Bod. MS Wood F33, fo. 27ʳ.
51. BL Cotton Ch. V7; *LP* II. ii. 4404, 4423; PRO CP25(2)/51/365/5; Cl/519/53; *The Visitations of Essex*, ed. W. C. Metcalfe (Harl. Soc. 13–14, 1878–9), i. 114.
52. *GEC* x. 244–5; PRO C54/394, m. 17.
53. *LP* IV. i. 106 (4), ii. 2372; PRO C54/394, m. 17.
54. *LP* IV. i. 2311; ii. 3324 (3).
55. *LP* IV. i. 106 (5), 1377 (16); ii. 3324 (3).
56. *LP* IV. i. 106 (5, 6); ii. 4586; ULC MS Mm 1.45, p. 302; PRO SP1/30, fo. 130 (*LP* IV. i. 106 (5)).
57. PRO SP1/39, fo. 90 (*LP* IV. ii. 2427).
58. *LP* IV. i. 106 (7); ii. 4586, 4588; PRO STAC2/27/113, 28/2.
59. PRO E41/209, 220; *SR* 23 Henry VIII *c.* 32.
60. PRO SP1/32, fo. 133ʳ(*LP* IV. i. 737); NRO Register 15, fo. 29ᵛ.
61. For what follows, see PRO Cl/498/7; SP1/132, fos 132–3.
62. PRO E150/80/6, 1183/3; C142/47/46.
63. PRO IND1331; KB27/1046, rot. 29; 1047, rot. 31; 1050, rot. 61; 1051, rot. 65; 1052, rot. 72ᵛ.
64. *The Records of the Honourable Society of Lincoln's Inn* (2 vols, London, 1896), i. 40.
65. NRO Register 14, fo. 161ᵛ.
66. PRO SP1/32, fo. 131 (LPIV. i. 736). For similar behaviour in arbitration, see M. A. Hicks, 'Restraint, Mediation and Private Justice: George, duke of Clarence as "Good Lord"', *Journal of Legal History*, 4 (1983), 62–9.
67. PRO Cl/498/7, dorse.
68. PRO E150/80/6, 1183/3; C142/47/46; see below Ch. 4.
69. PRO KB27/1061, rot. 30; Cl/585/45; STAC2/24/427/1; *LP* IV. i. 183.
70. *LP* IV. ii. 5125; Emden, *Oxford to 1500* ii. 1279; *Valor Ecclesiasticus* (6 vols, London, 1810–34), ii. 59, 63; PRO C24/29, Haworth and Powis v. Suffolk, deposition of Christopher Lynham.
71. *LP* Add. i. 477; PRO SC2/292/14, 18; C54/389, m. 14; PROB11/23/2.
72. PRO CP25(2)/39/260/35; *GEC* ii. 16.
73. *LP* IV. i. 1136 (16); PRO CP25(2)/7/32/4; LR12/21/636; LAO lAnc 11/C/lb.
74. PRO CP40/1043, rot. 566.
75. PRO E315/464, fos 72ʳ, 79ᵛ, 87ʳ, 95ʳ, 96ᵛ, 97ʳ.
76. PRO E313/11/116; E315/464, fo. 72ʳ; E405/479, fo. 17ʳ; Bodl. MS Top Berks b2, fo. 13.
77. *LP* IV. ii. 4573; iii. 5285, 6490 (20), 6751 (24), p. 3066, App. 103.
78. Berkshire Record Office WI Fac 1, *passim*.
79. Gunn, 'North Wales', pp. 477–92.
80. *LP* IV. i, pp. 864–5.
81. Starkey, *Reign of Henry VIII*, pp. 88–9; *LP* IV. ii. 2911, 4468; HL MS El. 2655, fo. 18ʳ.
82. PRO SP1/36, fos 236–7 (*LP* IV. i. 1854); E30/1446 (*LP* IV. ii. 2744 (1)); C54/395, mm 12–14. Neither copy is dated beyond the regnal year 18 Henry VIII.

Notes

83. *CSPS* FS, p. 232; *LP* IV. i. 186, 586, 1250, 1378, 1421.
84. G. Jacqueton, *La Politique extérieure de Louise de Savoie* (Bibliothèque de l'École des Hautes Etudes 88, 1892), p. 126; PRO SP1/35, fo. 235 (*LP* IV. i. 1543).
85. PRO SP1/35, fos 234–5 (*LP* IV. i. 1542–3).
86. Jacqueton, *Politique extérieure*, p. 352; *LP* IV. i. 1595, 1600; AN J966, no. 40/6.
87. *LP* IV. i. 1617; Jacqueton, *Politique extérieure*, pp. 144, 352.
88. PRO SP1/36, fos 4, 36 (*LP* IV. i. 1615, 1641).
89. *LP* IV. i. 1641; DNB v. 828–9.
90. BN MS Fr. 12158, *passim*; MS Fr. 2997, fo. 54 (*LP* IV. ii. 3619); AN J922, no. 7 *bis*; J923, no. 8, 8/2, 8/3; *LP* IV. iii. 5891.
91. BN MS Fr. 12158, fos 40ᵛ, 49ᵛ, 59ᵛ.
92. *LP* IV. i. 1705.
93. AN KK349, fo. 69ᵛ; BN MS Fr. 3087, fo. 148.
94. BL MS Cotton Caligula DIX, fo. 325 (*LP* IV. i. 2047).
95. BL MS Cotton Caligula EII, fo. 62 (*LP* IV. i. 2064); *LP* IV. ii. 2891 (2); *CAF* v. 17632.
96. BL MS Cotton Caligula DIX, fo. 233 (*LP* IV. i. 2256); *LP* IV. ii. 4392, 4615, 5064.
97. PRO SP1/30, fos 42–3 (*LP* IV. i. 57); *LP* III. ii. 3535.
98. *LP* IV. ii. 4015, 4023, 4064, 4848.
99. *LP* IV. i. 57; ii. 4660, 5049, 5068.
100. *LP* IV. ii. 4023, 4615, 4848, 5049; iii. 5950.
101. *LP* IV. ii. 2980, 4615, 4616; R. J. Knecht, *Francis I* (Cambridge, 1982), pp. 90, 194, 203.
102. BN MS Fr. 3015, fo. 20; MS Fr. 2932, fos 11, 13 (*LP* IV. ii. 4392).
103. BN MS Fr. 2932, fo. 3; Richardson, *Mary Tudor*, pp. 23, 88.
104. BN MS Fr. 3014, fo. 28 (*LP* IV. ii. 5064); AN KK99, fos 14ᵛ, 27ᵛ.
105. *LP* IV. i. 1641; ii. 2981 (2); V, p. 313; *CCJB* i. 88.
106. Gunn and Lindley, 'Charles Brandon's Westhorpe'.
107. W. R. B. Robinson, 'Edward Grey, lord Powys; the last Medieval lord of Powys', *The Montgomeryshire Collections*, 67 (1979), 125; Gunn, 'North Wales', p. 463; PRO WARD9/147, fo. 31ʳ.
108. Their livery indentures give their revenues as £409 19s 4d for Lord Powys, and £604 19f. Ad. for Lord Monteagle (PRO C54/392, m. 26; 398, m. 14).
109. *LP* III. ii. 2927, 2944, 2960, 3276; IV. i. 48, 120.
110. *LP* IV. i. 13, 634, 880, 958 (3), 1125, 1608, 2130 (2); ii. 2989, 5105 (1); Add. i. 434.
111. *LP* IV. i. 221, 880; iii, App. 109.
112. PRO DL10/403; C54/398, mm. 13–14; *Butley Register*, p. 55; *LP* IV. ii. 5815 (13).
113. *LP* IV. ii. 4350; Add. i. 653.
114. *LP* III. ii. 3288; IV. ii. 4246, 4257; PRO SP1/55, fo. 64 (*LP* IV. iii. 5859).
115. *GEC* xii, pt. ii, pp. 671–3; PRO WARD9/148; LAO 2Anc 3/A/49.
116. PRO C24/29, Haworth and Powys v. Suffolk, deposition of Christopher

Lynham; LAO 2Anc 3/A/35, 38, 39; PRO CP25(2)/51/362/9.
117. PRO WARD9/148; LAO 2Anc 3/A/48.
118. PRO WARD9/149, fo. 7ᵛ, LAO 2Anc 3/A/46.
119. *LP* IV. iii. 5336 (12).
120. M. E. James, 'Obedience and Dissent in Henrician England: the Lincolnshire rebellion 1536', *Past and Present*, 48 (1970), 42–5, reprinted in *Society, Politics, and Culture*; *LP* VII. i. 223; PRO SP1/47, fo. 38 (*LP* IV. ii. 3997).
121. PRO SP1/47, fo. 224 (*LP* IV. ii. 4184); James, 'Obedience and Dissent' pp. 44–5.
122. MacCulloch, *Suffolk*, pp. 62–3.
123. Hall, p. 674.
124. *LP* IV. i. 965; Hall, p. 689; College of Arms MS Tournament Cheques 1j.
125. *CSPV* iv. 105; *LP* IV. ii. 3098 (2–3); *CSPM* 803–4; Hall, p. 719.
126. *LP* IV. i. 965, ii. 4896 (2); Hall, p. 688.
127. Hall, pp. 707, 719; *LP* IV. i. 1792; *HMC Rutland* iv. 267.
128. LAO 1Anc 11/C/lb; 8Anc 9, fo. 155ʳ; *LP* III. i. 750, 852; ii. 3517; IV. ii, p. 1395; V, pp. 314, 320, 324; PRO LR12/21/636.
129. Hall, pp. 689–90; *LP* IV. ii. 3564.
130. G. Wyatt, 'The Life of Queen Anne Boleigne', in *The Life of Cardinal Wolsey by George Cavendish*, ed. S. W. Singer (2 vols, London, 1827), ii. 186–7; *LP* IV, ii, p. 1412; *CSPV* iv. 105.
131. Anstis, *Garter* i. 365–84.
132. PRO C24/29, Haworth and Powys v. Suffolk, deposition of Thomas duke of Norfolk; *LP* XXI. ii. 554. Both are of course unreliable for various reasons: in the first a very aged Norfolk was demonstrating the plausibility of his evidence, in the second a very distressed Norfolk was bewailing the multiplicity of his enemies.
133. MacCulloch, *Suffolk*, pp. 55–8.
134. PRO SP1/59, fo. 53 (*LP* IV. iii, App. 11); SP1/48, fo. 98 (*LP* IV. ii. 4324).
135. PRO SP1/46, fo. 222 (*LP* IV. ii. 3884); *LP* IV. ii. 3997. She did not in the end marry Freston (PRO C1/610/2).
136. R. Somerville, *History of the Duchy of Lancaster*, i, 1265–1603 (London, 1953), p. 423; PRO DL28/6/24, fo. 5ᵛ; *LP* IV. ii. 3747 (3); iii. 5815 (6).
137. PRO PROB11/22/28; E122/53/22.
138. For what follows, see BL MS Stowe 141, fos 43–4.
139. *LP* IV. ii. 3254, 3276–7.
140. PRO E404/1101, m. 20; E150/639/13.
141. J. Palsgrave, *L'Éclaircissement de la langue française*, ed. F. Génin (Documents Inédits sur l'Histoire de France, 1852), pp. iv, vii; *LP* XIII. i. 1449.
142. PRO SP1/55, fos 16–17 (*LP* IV. iii. 5808); NRO Register 14 (ii), fo. 29ᵛ; 16, fos 89ᵛ–90ʳ.
143. PRO SP1/39, fo. 75 (*LP* IV. ii. 2407).
144. *LP* IV. i. 1785; ii. 2608, 3748.
145. HLMS El. 2655; J. A. Guy, *The Cardinal's Court: the Impact of Cardinal Wolsey in Star Chamber* (Hassocks, 1977), pp. 133, 177.

257

146. HL MS El. 2652, fo. 12ʳ; Cherry, 'Courtenay Earls of Devon', pp. 75–6; Wright, *Derbyshire Gentry*, pp. 111–12; A. H. Smith, *County and Court: Government and Politics in Norfolk, 1558–1603* (Oxford, 1974), p. 35.

147. *LP* IV. i. 1511, 2159; Jacqueton, *Politique extérieure*, p. 405; College of Arms MS R36, fos 33ʳ–35ᵛ.

148. BN MS Dupuy 462, fos 32–3.

149. *CSPS* III. ii. 37; *LP* IV. ii. 3080, pp. 1399–1407, 1411.

150. *LP* IV. ii. 2974, pp. 1400–5; *CSPS* III. ii. 69; BN MS Fr. 20994, fo. 206ᵛ (*LP* IV. ii, App. 106).

151. *LP* IV. ii, pp. 1410–12; *CSPM* 800, 809; *CSPV* iv. 97; BN MS Fr. 20994, fo. 206ᵛ.

152. *LP* IV. ii. 3142, 3420; iii. 6248 (12); Bodl. MS Jesus College 74, fo. 101ᵛ *StP* vii. 67- 8; Hall, p. 739; PRO WARD9/148/2.

153. *LP* IV. ii. 4036, 4037; Hall, p. 748.

154. Hall, p. 749; BN MS Fr. 5499, fos 11–12 (*LP* IV. iii, App. 173).

155. Hall, p. 749; *LP* IV. ii. 4376; *AAJB*, p. 259.

156. Ives, *Anne Boleyn*, pp. 129–30; *CSPS* III. ii. 69; *AAJB*, pp. 38–41; *Clifford Letters of the Sixteenth Century*, ed. A. G. Dickens (Surtees Society 172, 1962), p. 106; PRO PR031/ 18/2/1, fo. 283 (*CSPS* III. ii. 224). Fitzwalter, Rochford, the duchess of Norfolk, and the dowager countess of Oxford were all at court (*LP* IV. ii. 3318).

157. PRO SP1/42, fo. 255 (*LP* IV. ii. 3318); PR031/18/2/1, fo. 283ᵛ *StP* i. 194–5, 261.

158. Ives, *Anne Boleyn*, pp. 129–32; *LP* IV. i. 2151 (2); ii. 4229 (9), 4706, 4778.

159. *LP* IV. ii. 3537 (ii), 4778; iii. 5186; PRO C54/397, m. 37; SC12/18/58, fo. 6; SC6/ Henry VIII/3402, m. 4; *CAD* iii. A4754–5.

160. *LP* IV. iii. 5594, 5639.

161. Ives, *Anne Boleyn*, p. 141; *LP* IV. iii. 5750; PRO C54/396, m. 31; Palsgrave, *Acolastus*, pp. xxxv-xlii.

162. J. A. Guy, *The Public Career of Sir Thomas More* (Brighton, 1980), pp. 30, 107, 109. Much of this view is based on the unfortunate rendering of Chapuys's very vague 'si cela se demene', following Suffolk's words at the legatine court, as 'if these sentiments of the duke gain ground' (PRO PR031/18/2/1, fo. 41v; *CSPS* IV. i. 160).

163. e.g. PRO SP1/46, fo. 222 (*LP* IV. ii. 3884); MacCulloch, *Suffolk*, pp. 158–9; BL MS Harl. 1664, fo. 22ᵛ.

164. Sotheby & Co., *Bibliotheca Phillippica Sale Catalogue, 11 November 1946* (London, 1946), p. 27; T. Paynel, *The Assaute and Co[n]quest of Heven tra[n]slated out of Frenche into Englishe* (London, 1530); D. Erasmus, trans. T. Paynel, *De Contemptu Mundi* (London, 1533); J. K. McConica, *English Humanists and Reformation Politics* (Oxford, 1965), pp. 138–9; PRO SP1/34, fo. 143 (*LP* IV. i. 1260).

165. J. J. Muskett, 'The recantation of Anthony Yaxley', *The East Anglian*, NS 3 (1897), 380–1; *Suffolk 1561* i. 141; PRO El79/69/4, 5; C24/28, 29, Haworth and Powis v. Suffolk, *passim.*; *Test. Vet.* ii. 497;

MacCulloch, *Suffolk*, p. 150; NRO Register 14, fo. 210ʳ.

166. Palsgrave, *L'Éclaircissement*, p. vii; J. and J. A. Venn, *Alumni Cantabrigienses; pt i to 1751* (4 vols, Cambridge, 1921–7), iv. 293; *LP* VIII. 618.

167. NRO Register 14 (ii), fo. 20ʳ; 17, fo. 5ᵛ; G. Baskerville, 'Married Clergy and Pensioned Religious in Norwich Diocese, 1555', *EHR* 48 (1933), 58–9.

168. NRO Register 16, fos 23ʳ, 58ᵛ–59ʳ, 60ʳ; ACT4/4b, fo. 138ᵛ; NCC Heyward, fo. 91ᵛ; Briggs, fo. 229ʳ; Mingaye, fo. 297ʳ; Wymer, fos 20ʳ–21ʳ.

169. *LP* IV. ii. 3264; iii, App. 11; *Val. Eccles.* iii. 301–483. He made sixteen, she fourteen (NRO Registers 14–16).

170. NRO Register 14 (ii), fo. 150ʳ; 17, fos 2ᵛ, 232ʳ; PRO E179/69/5; LAO Register 27, fo. 183v.

171. NRO Register 14 (ii), fo. 15ᵛ; 16, fos 89ᵛ–90ʳ; *Val. Eccles.* ii. 63, iii. 356, 440.

172. NRO Register 14, fo. 210ʳ; *CAD* iii. A4755; Foster, *Penningtoniana*, p. 50.

173. NRO Register 14, fo. 186ᵛ, 14 (ii), fo. 30ʳ; J. J. Muskett, *Suffolk Manorial Families* (3 vols, Exeter, 1900–14), ii. 284–5; KLBRO KL/C38/29; *LP* I. i. 438 (3, m. 4).

174. NRO Register 16, fo. 74ʳ; 17, fo. 232ʳ.

175. NRO Register 14 (ii), fo. 17ᵛ; 16, fo. 81ᵛ; *Visitations of the Diocese of Norwich A.D. 1492–1532*, ed. A. Jessopp (Cam. Soc. NS 43, 1898), p. 223.

176. LAO Register 27, fo. 191ᵛ; B. Willis, *The History and Antiquities of the Town, Hundred and Deanry of Buckingham* (London, 1755), p. 243.

177. NRO Register 14, fo. 226ᵛ; 17, fo. 47ᵛ; *Suffolk 1561* ii. 244; PRO Cl/1050/17.

178. Ives, *Anne Boleyn*, pp. 161–3; M. Dowling, 'Anne Boleyn and Reform', *Journal of Ecclesiastical History*, 35 (1984), 35–7; Guy, *Sir Thomas More*, p. 107; S. Ehses, *Römische Dokumente zur Geschichte der Ehescheidung Heinrichs VIII von England, 1527–1534* (Paderborn, 1893), pp. 76–8, 105–6; *LP* IV. ii. 4167, 4251, 4288, 4290, 4881; iii. 5417, 5428.

179. W. Ullmann, 'This Realm of England is an Empire', *Jnl. Eccles. Hist.* 30 (1979), 175–203; C. A. Haigh, 'Anticlericalism in the English Reformation', *History*, 68 (1983), 391–407; J. A. Guy, 'Thomas Cromwell and the Intellectual Origins of the Henrician Reformation', in A. Fox, J. A. Guy, *Reassessing the Henrician Age* (Oxford, 1986), pp. 151- 79. I have also benefited from Peter Gwyn's views on the subject.

180. PRO SP1/46, fo. 122ᵛ (*LP* IV. ii. 3811).

181. *LP* IV. ii. 4820, 4851, 4857; V, p. 307; *CSPV* iv. 385.

182. Ives, *Anne Boleyn*, pp. 136–7; *LP* IV. ii. 3992, 3993; *StP* i. 332.

183. BL MS Add. 28578, fos 16–18 (*CSPS* III. ii. 621); *CSPS* III. ii. 614.

184. *CSPS* III, ii. 600; *AAJB*, p. 543.

185. *CSPS* III. ii. 81, 621, FS, p. 438; *CSPV* iv. 461; N. Harpsfield, *The Pretended*

Divorce between Henry VIII and Catherine of Aragon, ed. N. Pocock (Cam. Soc. NS 21,1878), p. 184.
186. Guy, *Sir Thomas More*, p. 107.
187. PRO PR031/18/2/1, fo. 391ʳ (*CSPS* IV. i. 135).
188. *AAJB*, p. 542.
189. BL MS Cotton Caligula BVI, fo. 132 (*LP* IV. iii. 5258).
190. *LP* IV. iii. 5482, 5535. They replaced Sir John Russell at the last moment before he was due to depart, and Du Bellay (six weeks after the event) attributed Suffolk's appointment to Anne's influence working against Wolsey (Ives, *Anne Boleyn*, p. 140). But Fitzwilliam's inclusion and the obvious military significance of sending Suffolk render this interpretation rather improbable.
191. *LP* IV. iii. 5572, 5588; V, p. 311; *CCJB* i. 15–16.
192. *CCJB* i. 16–17; Ehses, *Römische Dokumente*, pp. 80–1; *CSPS* IV. i. 16.
193. PRO SP1/54, to. 30 (*LP* IV. iii. 5585); *LP* IV. iii. 5597, 5598; *CAF* vii. 28668; *I diarii di Marino Sanuto*, 50, ed. F. Stefani et al. (Venice, 1897), col. 517; *StP* vii. 179–82.
194. *LP* IV. iii. 5599, 5647, 5648; *StP* vii. 181; *CCJB* i. 32.
195. *CSPV* iv. 471; *CSPS* IV. i. 44; *CCJB* i. 25, 37–8.
196. *LP* IV. iii. 5675; AN KK100, fos 51ᵛ, 76ʳ, 80ʳ; *CCJB* i. 39.
197. *CCJB* i. 43–5, 50; *LP* IV. ii. 5704, 5723.
198. *Chronicle of Calais*, p. 41; *LP* IV. iii. 5645, 5713, 5733, 5752.
199. *CCJB* i. 51; *LP* IV. iii. 5713, 5733.
200. *CSPV* iv. 484; *CCJB* i. 58, 62; *LP* IV. iii. 5771.
201. *StP* vii. 182–4.
202. *CCJB* i. 19, 22, 24, 107; *LP* IV. iii, App. 163, 193.
203. *CCJB* i. 22; BL MS Cotton Caligula DXI, fo. 61ᵛ (*LP* IV. iii. 5562).
204. *LP* IV. iii. 5597, 5635, 5646, 5647, 5675, 5696; *StP* vii. 179–82.
205. BL MS Cotton Caligula DXI, fo. 26 (*LP* IV. iii. 5598).
206. *LP* IV. iii. 5719, 5747; *StP* i. 261; *CCJB* i. 110.
207. *CCJB* i. 64–5, 72.
208. *CCJB* i. 58. Suffolk reached Calais on 29 June (*Chronicle of Calais*, p. 41). The first witnesses testified in the legatine court on 28 June (H. A. Kelly, *The Matrimonial Trials of Henry VIII* (Stanford, 1976), p. 95).
209. *LP* IV. iii. 5749; XII. ii. 186 (38).
210. *LP* IV. iii. 5774 (10); Kelly, *Matrimonial Trials*, pp. 101, 112, 119, 122; *CSPS* IV. i. 28.
211. For a fuller discussion of the court's suspension, see P. J. Gwyn, *The King's Cardinal* (London, 1990), pp. 525–30; Cavendish, *Wolsey*, p. 90; Harpsfield, *Pretended Divorce*, pp. 183–4; *The Life of Fisher*, ed. R. Bayne (EETS, extra ser. 117,1921), p. 66; *Chronicle of King Henry VIII of England*, ed. M. A. S. Hume (London, 1889), p. 9; PRO PR031/18/2/1,

fo. 411ᵛ (poorly rendered in *CSPS* IV. i. 160).
212. Hall, p. 758; *CSPS* IV. i. 83.
213. *CSPS* IV. i. 43; *LP* IV. iii. 5687; *CAF* i. 3445, 3450, vi. 19861; *CCJB* i. 88.
214. *StP* i. 339, 342; *LP* IV. iii. 5802; *CSPS* IV. i. 160.
215. *LP* IV. iii. 5850, 5851; *CSPS* IV. i. 160; *StP* i. 339.
216. *CCJB* i. 65; *StP* i. 338–9.
217. *CCJB* i. 72; PRO PR031/18/2/1, fo. 391ʳ (*CSPS* IV. i. 135).
218. Ives, *Anne Boleyn*, pp. 144–50; *StP* i. 347–8.
219. PRO PR031/18/2/1, fo. 410v (*CSPS* IV. i. 160); Cavendish, *Wolsey*, p. 93; *LP* IV. iii. 5953.
220. *LP* IV. iii. 5953; Hall, pp. 759–60; PRO PR031/18/2/1, fos 426ᵛ, 428ʳ (*CSPS* IV. i. 182).
221. *LP* IV. iii. 5953; *CCJB* i. 83.
222. *LP* IV. iii. 6000; *CCJB* i. 94, 104–5.
223. *CSPV* iv. 514.
224. *CCJB* i. 103, 116, 117.
225. *CSPS* IV. i. 211; Guy, *Sir Thomas More*, p. 32.
226. PRO PR031/18/2/1, fo. 434r (*CSPS* IV. i. 194).
222. Cavendish, *Wolsey*, p. 98; *LP* IV. iii. 6025; *CCJB* i. 117.
228. *CSPS* IV. i. 194; *CCJB* i. 113; BL MS Lansdowne 1, fo. 108ᵛ.
229. *CCJB* i. 113; *CSPS* IV. i. 194; *LP* IV. iii. 6025; Hall, p. 761.
230. *CCJB* i. 115; PRO E192/2, account book, fo. 37ᵛ; *SR* 27 Henry VIII, c. 38, s. 1.
231. Guy, *Sir Thomas More*, p. 116; *Select Cases in the Council of Henry VII*, ed. C. G. Bayne, W. H. Dunham (Selden Soc. 75, 1958), pp. xxxviii-xl.
232. PRO PR031/18/2/1, fo. 432ᵛ (*CSPS* IV. i. 194); *CCJB* i. 117.
233. *CCJB* i. 108, 117.
234. *CCJB* i. 110.
235. *CSPS* IV. i. 160; Dowling, 'Anne Boleyn', pp. 35–7; *LP* IV. iii. 5749.
236. Guy, *Sir Thomas More*, pp. 115—17.
237. For what follows, see Bindoff, *Commons*, *passim*.
238. On the Cornewalls, see Gunn, 'North Wales', p. 464.
239. PRO PROB11/24/3.
240. S. E. Lehmberg, *The Reformation Parliament 1529–36* (Cambridge, 1970), pp. 17–18.

4 Years of Eclipse: 1529–1536

1. *CSPV* iv. 694.
2. *CSPS* IV. i. 257; *SR* 21 Henry VIII, c. 20; Miller, *English Nobility*, p. 206.
3. *LP* IV. iii. 6075, 6085; *SR* 21 Henry VIII, c. 23; PRO C54/398, m. 28.
4. LAO Register 27, fo. 172ʳ; *CSPS* IV. i. 241, 249, 250.
5. PRO PR031/18/2/1, fo. 536ʳ (*CSPS* IV. i. 250).
6. Guy, *Sir Thomas More*, p. 128.
7. *LP* IV. iii. 6225, 6262, 6436, 6575, 6738; *StP* i. 352, 355; *CSPS* IV. i. 373; Cavendish,

Wolsey, pp. 114–17, 124, 127; *SR* 22 Henry VIII, c. 22.

8. *LP* IV. iii. 6395, 6720; *CSPS* IV. i. 302, 445; Guy, *Sir Thomas More*, p. 146.
9. C. A. Haigh, *The Last Days of the Lancashire Monasteries and the Pilgrimage of Grace* (Chetham Society, 3rd ser. 17, 1969), p. 18; Guildhall Library, MS 7086/1, fo. 16ʳ (I owe this reference to Ian Archer).
10. *CSPV* iv. 601, 616, 617.
11. Guy, *Sir Thomas More*, pp. 126–74; *CSPS* IV. i. 481; *LP* V. 112,148, 850,1013; Ives, *Anne Boleyn*, p. 172.
12. *CSPS* IV. i. 445; *LP* V. 755, 1025; VIII. 174; Add. i. 752.
13. LAO Register 27, fo. 193ᵛ; *LP* XIII. ii. 191; PRO PROB11/36/14; A. B. Emden, *A Biographical Register of the University of Oxford A. D. 1501 to 1540* (Oxford, 1974), pp. 25–6.
14. LAO lAnc 10/A2.
15. *LP* V. 40, 45, 70, 564, 864, 932; VI. 212, 296, 465, 556, 1018; VII. 690; IX. 1036; *CSPV* iv. 802.
16. *LP* V. 712, 1075, 1207 (39); VI. 73, 197; VII. 1332; *LJ* i. 58–82; Miller, *English Nobility*, p. 111.
17. *LP* V. 171; Hall, pp. 785–6.
18. *CSPS* IV. ii. 1047, 1053.
19. *LP* V. 1705; VI. 661; VII. 5, 6; Lehmberg, *Reformation Parliament*, p. 199.
20. *LP* VIII. 815, 886, 974.
21. *CSPS* IV. i. 270; *LP* IV. iii. 6303 (ii), App. 254 (iv).
22. A. Wood, *The History and Antiquities of the University of Oxford*, ed. J. Gutch (3 vols, Oxford, 1792–6), ii. 53–4; *Selections from the Records of the City of Oxford*, ed. W. H. Turner (Oxford, 1880), pp. 110, 115; *LP* V, 1332, VI. 1017.
23. *LP* VIII. 207, 247, 263, 276, 278, 330, 350, 356, 365, 386.
24. *CSPS* V. i. 86, 90; *LP* IX. 720.
25. *LP* VII. 296, VIII. 342.
26. *LP* V, p. 317, 686; VI. 32; VIII. 9; *LL* iii. 671.
27. *LP* V. 392 (9), 1370 (10, 16), pp. 748, 753, 755, 759, VIII. 989; *CSPV* iv. 792.
28. *LP* V. 216.
29. *LP* VI, App. 7; VII. 337, App. 13; XIII. i. 1029.
30. *CSPS* IV. ii. 739. The case for Suffolk's consistent opposition has been lucidly made in Ives, *Anne Boleyn*.
31. *LP* VI. 693, 1193; *Chronicle of King Henry VIII*, p. 135.
32. *LP* VI. 1522, 1558; X. 28, 141, 284.
33. *CSPS* IV. ii. 739, 1165; *LP* VI. 324, 1486, 1541–3; VII. 83; *StP* i. 415–17.
34. PRO PR031/18/2/1, fo. 1032 (*CSPS* IV. ii. 1164); Ford, *Mary Tudor*, p. 43.
35. LAO 8Anc 9, fo. 155ʳ; PRO E163/11/18.
36. Anstis, *Garter* i. 386–7, 394; *LP* VI. 613.
37. *LP* IV. iii. 6199, 6738; Add. i. 730; Hall, p. 812; *SR* 25 Henry VIII, c. 12; Ives, *Anne Boleyn*, pp. 171–6, 195, 206.
38. *CSPS* IV. i. 302; *Life of Cardinal Wolsey*, ed. Singer, ii. 190–3.

39. *CSPS* IV. ii. 765; *CSPS* iv. 761; Ives, *Anne Boleyn*, p. 35.
40. *LP* X. 782, 792, 834, 848, 876, 896; W. Cobbett et al., *State Trials*, i (5th edn, London, 1809), col. 410. The evidence for any involvement by Suffolk in Anne's fall is tenuous in the extreme: Ives, *Anne Boleyn* pp. 379–80.
41. PRO SP1/68, fo. 92 (*LP* V. 576); SP1/67, fo. 103 (*LP* V. 431).
42. SP1/67, fo. 103; *LP* V. 521; VIII. 149 (53).
43. *LP* IV. iii. 5285, App. 103.
44. *LP* VII. 882; IX. 1168.
45. PRO SP1/85, fo. 32 (*LP* VII. 942).
46. *LP* IX. 178, 301, 341.
47. *LP* V. 1183; VI. 1372.
48. *LP* V. 1403,1598 (10); VI. 1481 (29); VII. 1498 (13); IX. 914 (22); XI. 1217 (23); *LL* i, pp. 680–4; ii, pp. 177–8.
49. *LL* i. 5, p. 683; *LP* VII. 1658.
50. *LP* VI. 45, 76, 209, 672, 1007; Add. i. 1037.
51. *LP* IX. 1111; B. H. St J. O'Neil, 'Stefan von Haschenperg, an engineer to King Henry VIII and his work', *Archaeologia*, 91 (1945), 137–55.
52. *LP* VI. 666, 942, 1440; X. 1068, 1077; Add. i. 857.
53. *LP* V. 1274(3); VI. 1111,1510; VII. 1297; C. Wriothesley, *A Chronicle of England*, ed. W. D. Hamilton, i (Cam. Soc. NS 11, 1875), 34–5, 41; Anstis, *Garter* i. 385, 392, 395–8.
54. PRO SP1/75, fo. 245ʳ (*LP* VI. 415). Suffolk had been earl marshal since the death of Norfolk's father in 1524.
55. *LP* VII. 1498 (37); PRO SP1/75, fo. 245ᵛ; SP1/76, fo. 195 (*LP* VI. 613).
56. Hall, pp. 798, 800, 804; Wriothesley, *Chronicle* i. 19–20; *LP* VI. 578 (50), 584, 601.
57. *CSPS* IV. i. 211; *LP* V. 445. There were other profits: C. Howard, *Historical Anecdotes of some of the Howard Family* (London, 1769), pp. 141–3, 160–1.
58. BL MS Add. 33376, fo. 26ᵛ; College of Arms MS R36, fo. 1ʳ.
59. PRO SP1/76, fo. 195 (*LP* VI. 613); College of Arms MS R36, fos 1ʳ, 267ʳ.
60. College of Arms MS M6 bis, fos 26ᵛ–30ᵛ, 94, 100ᵛ–101ʳ; MS M9, fo. 120; MS R36, fos 1ᵛ 38ʳ–40ʳ, 55ᵛ, 267ᵛ.
61. College of Arms MS M9, *passim*; MS R36, fos 245ʳ–247ʳ.
62. G. D. Squibb, *The High Court of Chivalry* (Oxford, 1959), p. 31; A. R. Wagner, *Heralds of England* (London, 1967), p. 69.
63. *LP* IV. ii. 3991 (12), 4313 (6), 4801 (1); iii. 6314; V. 1232; Bodl. MS Wood F33, fo. 22ᵛ.
64. Bodl. MS Wood F33, fo. 27ʳ; *LP* IV. ii. 5130.
65. BL MS Add. 33376, fo. 26ᵛ; College of Arms MS R36, fos 140–3; Hall, p. 745; *LP* VI. 560.
66. Bodl. MS Ashmole 857, p. 517; NRO Register 14, fos 210ʳ, 212ᵛ; PRO C54/397, m. 37; C82/660/1 (*LP* V. 1370 (2)); SP1/235, fo. 31 (*LP* Add. i. 477).

67. BL MS Harl. 283, fo. 126 (*LP* VI. 877); MS Cotton Faustina EI, fo. 252ʳ; *LP* VII. 671.
68. Bodl. MS Wood F33, fo. 23ʳ; *LP* IV. i. 787 (24).
69. BL MS Add. 6297, fo. 12ᵛ.
70. Wagner, *Heralds of England*, pp. 98, 100–1; Bodl. MS Ashmole 857, pp. 510–6. The much-sued Barker never tried to claim immunity: PRO KB27/1036, rot. 37; 1060, rot. 38; STAC2/32/9; Cl/464/51.
71. Wagner, *Heralds of England*, p. 167; idem, *Heralds and Heraldry in the Middle Ages* (London, 1939), pp. 9–10, 83–99; BL MS Add. 6297, fos 12ᵛ–13ʳ.
72. BL MS Cotton Faustina EI, fos 248ᵛ, 254ʳ, 257ᵛ; MS Add. 6297, fos 61ᵛ–71ᵛ; College of Arms MS Heralds V, fos 126–9; *LP* XIII. i. 1127.
73. PRO SP1/75, fo. 245ᵛ (*LP* VI. 415).
74. PRO LR12/21/636; SC12/37/6/2. See map 4.1.
75. Virgoe, 'Recovery of the Howards', pp. 18–20; *LP* V. 1207 (37); VI. 418 (3); IX. 978.
76. *LP* Add. i. 724.
77. *CSPV* iv. 761; Foster, *Penningtoniana*, p. 50; *LP* V. 1139 (11); MacCulloch, *Suffolk*, p. 59.
78. PRO SP1/70, fo. 186 (*LP* V. 1183).
79. LPV. 1139(11), 1336; VII. 923 (vii); *CSPV* iv. 761.
80. PRO KB29/165, rot. 15ᵛ; *LP* V. 657; XIV. i. 904 (15); *CAD* i. A463; iv. A47741; *SR* 25 Henry VIII, c. 32.
81. *LP* VII. 1498(13).
82. *LP* VIII. 1087; NRO Jerningham 1 T176 Bl; PRO Cl/625/27; Blomefield, *Norfolk* viii. 236; x. 277, 423, 455; xi. 91, 94, 217, 250.
83. 'Norfolk Subsidy Roll', p. 408; Blomefield, *Norfolk* i. 433; *LP* V. 166 (12); *The Manuscripts of the Earl of Westmorland and others* (HMC 10.4, 1885), p. 157; Foster, *Penningtoniana*, p. 54; Cumbria Record Office D/Pen/32/20, 23, 24.
84. Foster, *Penningtoniana*, p. 51; Ford, *Mary Tudor*, p. 40; PRO Cl/868/26.
85. *CSPV* iv. 761.
86. R. Virgoe, 'The Murder of James Andrew: Suffolk Faction in the 1430s', *Proceedings of the Suffolk Institute of Archaeology* 34 (1977–80), 263–8.
87. MacCulloch, *Suffolk*, p. 64; PRO Cl/868/26; *Val. Eccles.* iii. 460; *LP* XI. 659.
88. LAO lAnc 11/c/lb; *LP* II. ii. 2926, 3065; III. ii. 3365, 3381; V. 1183; VIII. 527, 1065; IX. 23.
89. Bacon, *Ipswiche*, pp. 206–7; PRO STAC2/8/200–4, 17/356, 17/133, 19/205.
90. *Suffolk in 1524*, p. 69; LAO 2Anc 3/B/3; Ford, *Mary Tudor*, p. 40.
91. PRO Cl/815/40; *SR* 31 Henry VIII, c. 13, s. 19; NRO Register 17, fo. 41ʳ; LAO Register 27, fos 72ᵛ, 73ᵛ.
92. MacCulloch, *Suffolk*, pp. 228–30.
93. PRO Cl/917/23; CP40/1066, rot. 432ᵛ; 1077, rot. 540; 1081, rot. 525; KB27/11Q0, rot. 27ᵛ.
94. PRO SC6/Henry VIII/2573, 3372, 6899; SC6/Addenda/3482/94; LR12/27/922; M. A. Hicks, *False, Fleeting, Perjured Clarence: George, Duke of Clarence, 1449–78* (Gloucester, 1980), p. 185; C. Carpenter, 'The Duke of Clarence and the Midlands: a Study in the Interplay of Local and National Politics', *Midland History* 11 (1986), 23–48; Smith, *Land and Politics*, pp. 137–8; Robinson, 'Officers and Household', pp. 31–2.
95. PRO KB9/519/132, 520/55, 57, 521/18, 23, 25, 151, 522/6, 8, 14, 40, 58, 523/83, 84. Western Suffolk, where the duke held virtually no land, comprised the liberty of St Edmunds Abbey.
96. KB9/519/20, 520/22, 84, 521/149, 522/17, 523/81; KB27/1080 Rex, m. 3; SP2/Fol M, fo. 142ᵛ. The Woodbridge sessions were those of the Liberty of St Audrey, whose officials were mostly Howard followers (MacCulloch, *Suffolk*, p. 20). On the quorum, see M. L. Zell, 'Early Tudor JPs at Work', *Archaeologia Cantiana* 93 (1977), 141.
97. *LP* VI. 142; VII. 1237; X. 571; SRO HE10/1/6, mm 23ʳ, 25ᵛ.
98. MacCulloch, *Suffolk*, pp. 106–7.
99. NRO Norwich 18a, fos 62ʳ, 101ʳ, 130ᵛ, 132ᵛ, 150ᵛ; *Butley Register*, pp. 53, 55; *Val. Eccles* iii. 437; LAO lAnc 11/C/lb; PRO SP5/1, fo. 157ᵛ; R. Horrox, 'Urban Patronage and Patrons in the Fifteenth Century', in *Patronage, the Crown and the Provinces in Later Medieval England*, ed. R. A. Griffiths (Gloucester, 1980), p. 148.
100. MacCulloch, *Suffolk*, pp. 65–6; PRO SC6/ Henry VIII/6305; SRO T4373/103 (Phillipps 28585).
101. Virgoe, 'Recovery of the Howards', p. 16; Foster, *Penningtoniana*, p. 50; *LP* VII. 1237.
102. PRO CP40/1052, rot. 433; CP25(2)/39/263/24; Cl/712/17.
103. Ford, *Mary Tudor*, p. 39; PRO SC12/37/16, m. 5; C54/401, mm 26, 37.
104. PRO CP25(2)/40/267/18, 37. Wingfield was an auditor by 1523 (PRO LR12/21/ 636).
105. PRO E179/69/4; PROB11/25/16.
106. PRO Cl/840/16.
107. Wright, *Derbyshire Gentry*, pp. 79–80.
108. PRO Cl/792/14, 796/12, 13; LR3/62/1; SRO HA18/DB1/2, m. 6; HE10/1/6, mm 25ᵛ, 26ᵛ.
109. PRO CP25(2)/39/257/5,39/264/17, 40/267/7; Bacon, *Ipswiche*, pp. 179, 196, 222.
110. PRO C54/404, m. 13.
111. Ford, *Mary Tudor*, p. 42; PRO LR12/27/922; CP25(2)/25/161/5.
112. Carpenter, 'Beauchamp Affinity', pp. 517–18; S. K. Walker, 'John of Gaunt and his Retainers, 1361–1399' (Oxford Univ. D. Phil. thesis, 1986), pp. 116–26; PRO E321/ 40/82; *Val. Eccles.* iii. 420, 423, 437.
113. Carpenter, 'Beauchamp Affinity', pp. 515–16; Walker, 'John of Gaunt', pp. 196–224; MacCulloch, *Suffolk*, p. 117; C. F. Richmond, *John Hopton, a Fifteenth Century Suffolk Gentleman* (Cambridge, 1981).

114. Ford, *Mary Tudor*, p. 39; PRO E179/69/4; LAO 2Anc 3/B/25; 3Anc 8/1/3.
115. For what follows, see Ford, *Mary Tudor*, pp. 38–45.
116. Heydon held a court at Cawston in 1523: NRO Bulwer NRS 2567, m. 14^v.
117. Lord Edward Grey (senior) was involved in the christening of Henry Brandon in 1516: BL MS Add. 6113, fo. 118^v.
118. T. Martin, *The History of the Town of Thetford, in the Counties of Norfolk and Suffolk, from the Earliest Accounts to the Present Time* (London, 1779), App., pp. 38–9.
119. Ford, *Mary Tudor*, p. 40.
120. BL Harl. Ch. 47A49 (*LP* VIII. 894).
121. *Butley Register*, pp. 60–1, 68.
122. Anstis, *Garter* i. 390, 394; PRO CP40/1068, rot. 428^v; 1070, rot. 421, 437^v; Robinson, 'Edward Grey, Lord Powis', p. 125.
123. LAO lAnc 11/C/la; 2Anc 3/B/6.
124. LAO lAnc 11/C/la; 2Anc 3/B/6.
125. BL Harl. Ch. 47A48 (*LP* VII. 1187).
126. *CSPS* IV. i. 373.
127. *LP* V. 1139(26).
128. PRO SP1/82, fo. 158^v (*LP* VII. 153); WARD9/149, fo. 40^v; *LP* V. 1557; VI. 300 (20).
129. *LP* V. 926; VII. 153, 153 (2); XIII, i. 1519 (47).
130. *Clifford Letters*, p. 24; H. Coleridge, *Lives of Northern Worthies* (London, 1825), p. 25.
131. Letters of the Cliffords, Lords Clifford and Earls of Cumberland, c.1500–1565', ed. R. W. Hoyle, *Camden Miscellany*, 31 (Cam. Soc. 4th Series, 44, 1991), no.39. *SR* 27 Henry VIII, c. 36; *FOR*, p. 28; *Clifford Letters*, p. 141.
132. College of Arms MS R36, fo. 81^v; *LP* VI. 1069; *GEC* xii, pt. ii, p. 673.
133. College of Arms MS R36, fo. 55^v; *LP* VII. 281.
134. Blomefield, *Norfolk* v. 282–3; Ford, *Mary Tudor*, pp. 39, 42; *LP* VII. 224.
135. Guy, *Sir Thomas More*, p. 60; PRO STAC2/17/399, 19/241; Cl/589/38, 595/53.
136. PRO STAC2/18/182, 21/22, 30; Cl/691/26, 712/13.
137. PRO C1/665/40, 691/26, 712/13; STAC2/17/321.
138. PRO REQ2/4/141/3.
139. James, 'Obedience and Dissent', pp. 42–4; LAO lAnc 5/B/ld; PRO STAC2/17/ 399; SP1/68, fos 68^v–69^r (*LP* V. 554); *Test. Vet.* ii. 620–2.
140. *SR* 27 Henry VIII, c. 40; *LP* X. 635.
141. LAO lAnc 5/B/lj; PRO STAC2/21/30/II.
142. *SR* 27 Henry VIII, c. 40; LAO lAnc 5/B/la; PRO Cl/1392/35.
143. *GEC* xii, pt. ii, p. 703.
144. *LP* IV. iii. 6490 (20); *Val. Eccles.* iii. 281–488; *SR* 27 Henry VIII, *c.* 45, s. 12; LAO Register 26, fo. 170^r.
145. PRO E36/104, fos 10^r–13^r (*LP* IV. iii. 6788); SP1/82, fos 217^v 220^r, (*LP* VII. 243); *LP* VII. 1676.
146. *LP* XIII. ii. 246; S. E. Lehmberg, *Sir Thomas Elyot, Tudor Humanist* (Austin, 1960), pp. 33–4.

147. BL Add. Ch. 24182; PRO SC6/Henry VIII/5911, 5913; *LP* VI. 1689.
148. *LP* V. 119 (54); PRO LR12/21/636; LAO lAnc 7/A/l.
149. LAO 2Anc 3/B/5; H. A. Napier, *Historical Notices of the Parishes of Swyncombe and Ewelme in the County of Oxford* (Oxford, 1858), p. 202; PRO PROB11/34/29.
150. *LP* VI. 1481 (29); VII. 1498 (13); VIII. 149 (52); IX. 914 (22).
151. *LP* IV. iii. 6438; VII. 56.
152. *FOR*, p. 83; *Registra Stephani Gardiner et Johannis Poynet* (Canterbury and York Soc. 37, 1929–30), p. 182; PRO C54/431, m. 29; Cl/1159/30–1; KB27/1131, rot. 67^r; 1140, rot. 148^r.
153. PRO Cl/601/27.
154. PRO C24/28, Haworth and Powis v. Suffolk, deposition of David Johns; *Acts of Court of the Mercers Company 1453–1527*, ed. L. Lyell, F. D. Watney (Cambridge, 1936), p. 768; *LP* IX. 1168; PRO KB27/1080, rot. 66^v.
155. *LP* V. 1715; VI. 299 (ix, G), 736,1056; VII. 257, 923 (xxviii, xxxv); PRO SP1/85, fos 103^v–4^r (*LP* VII. 1657).
156. *SR* 27 Henry VIII, c. 38; LAO 2Anc 3/B/5.
157. PRO LR1/310, fo. 8^v.
158. For what follows, see PRO SP1/94, fos 37, 142–3 (*LP* VIII. 1101, 1130).
159. PRO SP1/95, fos 13–14 (*LP* IX. 21); *LP* VIII. 1061, 1101.
160. PRO E313/11/49–52; LAO lAnc 2A/18/35; *SR* 27 Henry VIII, c. 38, s. 4, 8.
161. LAO 2Anc 3/B/7; *LP* IX. 1063 (5–7).
162. *SR* 27 Henry VIII, c. 39; LAO lAnc 10/A/2.
163. *LP* X. 804, 850, 891; LAO Register 26, fos 263^r, 267^v.
164. Miller, *English Nobility*, pp. 219–20, 231–2, 248–9.
165. LAO 8Anc 9, fos 154–5; *LP* VII. 1637–8.
166. Gunn, 'North Wales', p. 487.
167. LAO 8Anc 9, fo. 156^r. This would suggest that the profits of office, plus estate casualties (entry fines, wood sales, and so on), made up less than a third of Suffolk's regular income, since the clear revenues of all his estates before the 1535 exchange, less the annuity to Norfolk but plus the French pension, totalled some £1,800. Such a calculation can of course have no pretensions to accuracy, especially since it is unclear what Suffolk did or did not include in his reckoning.
168. *LP* XI. 139; *SR* 26 Henry VIII, c. 19, s. 3.
169. J. Strieder, *Aus Antwerpene Notariatsarchiven* (Deutsche Handelsakten des Mittelalters und der Neuzeit 4, 1930), pp. 58–9, 64, 72.
170. PRO CP25(2)/29/194; CP40/1063, rot. 430.
171. LAO 2Anc 3/A/52; PRO CP25(2)/40/266/57; Copinger, *Suffolk Manors*, ii. 81–2; Bodl. MS Suffolk Ch. 229; Blomefield, *Norfolk* v. 375.
172. BL Cotton Ch. XII 24; Add. Roll 23637.
173. PRO LR12/21/636; SC12/37/6/2; Bean, *Percy Family*, p. 67; Heal, *Prelates and Princes*, pp. 55, 61–2.
174. *LP* XIII. ii. 1193; PRO KB9/357/175.

175. *LP* V. 653; PRO LR12/21/636; C54/407, m. 10.
176. PRO C1/934/17.
177. *LP* VI. 924, 1382; VII. 48.
178. LAO lAnc 10/A/2.
179. *LP* V, pp. 325, 748; VI. 736; *CAF* ii. 5202.
180. BN MS Fr. 3014, fo. 79ʳ; 3021, fo. 70 (*LP* V. 199); *CAF* ii. 4657, 5088; vii. 26766.
181. BN MS Fr. 3021, fo. 70; MS Dupuy 726, fo. 71; *CSPS* IV. ii. 775.
182. *CSPS* IV. ii. 775,778; *CSPV* iv. 860; *LP* V. 212, 1450, 1453, 1463; VI. 172, 405, 649, 788, 1076.
183. Ford, *Mary Tudor*, p. 36; *CAF* ii. 6074; vii. 29115, 29203.
184. *CSPS* IV. ii. 1123; *LP* VI. 1382 may support this. The Ely vacancy revenues totalled £2,033 (Heal, *Prelates and Princes*, p. 108).
185. *LP* VI. 1434; *CAF* ii. 6426, 6604, 6618.
186. *LP* IX. 437; PRO PROB10/5; SP1/97, fo. 6ʳ (*LP* IX. 437).
187. BN MS Dupuy 726, fo. 71; AN J923, no. 115; J966, no. 46.
188. An J966, no. 46. This was one six-monthly payment, worth some £800–900 sterling.
189. *LP* VI. 1303; College of Arms MS R36, fo. 98ᵛ.
190. LAO lAnc 11/C/la.
191. *CSPV* iv. 802; CS'Rs'lV. ii. 993, 995; *LP* V. 1231, 1292.
192. *LP* V. 1373, 1484, p. 760; *CSPV* iv. 822, 824; *CAF* ii. 4993–4, 5211.
193. *CSPS* V. i. 114; *LP* X. 351, 1070; Ives, *Anne Boleyn*, p. 207.
194. *LP* X. 351; Ives, *Anne Boleyn*, pp. 350–5.
195. *CSPS* V. ii. 61, 71.
196. *CSPS* IV. i. 216, 224; ii. 897; V. ii. 29.
197. *CSPS* V. ii. 71; *LP* X. 888, 1069, 1070.
198. PRO PR031/18/2/1, fo. 968ʳ (*LP* VI. 1125).
199. *LL* iv, p. 164, n. 1; *LP* IX. 217, 386.
200. *LP* X. 601.
201. PRO DL30/735/59, mm 36–7; SC12/37/16, mm 3, 5.
202. *LP* XI. 7, 40, 45, 233; Wriothesley, *Chronicle* i. 46, 50; *LJ* i. 84–101.
203. *LP* X. 1256 (12); Ford, *Mary Tudor*, p. 46; *The Visitations of Norfolk*, ed. W. Rye (Harl. Soc. 32, 1891), p. 229; see above p. 64.
204. M. L. Bush, 'The Rise to Power of Edward Seymour, Protector Somerset, 1500- 1547' (Cambridge Univ. Ph. D. thesis, 1964), pp. 114–15; PRO E326/5761.

5 The Move to Lincolnshire: 1536–1540

1. PRO LR12/21/636; *LP* VI. 710.
2. PRO SC6/Henry VIII/6899; SC12/23/29.
3. LAO lAnc 3/7/17, 18, 3/10/84, 3/14/84, 3/17/58; 2Anc 2/21/16.
4. *Test. Vet.* ii. 621–2; LAO lAnc 5/B/lc; PRO Cl/818/13; STAC2/17/321; *LP* XIII. i, p. 578.
5. S. J. Gunn, 'Peers, Commons and Gentry in the Lincolnshire Revolt of 1536', *Past and Present*, 123 (1989), 52–79.
6. BL MS Add. 25114, fo. 215ᵛ (*LP* XI. 656). The fullest treatments of the revolt are James, 'Obedience and Dissent' and A. Ward, *The Lincolnshire Rising 1536* (Nottingham, 1986).
7. *LP* XI. 559, 601, 615, 617, 625, 807.
8. M. H. and R. Dodds, *The Pilgrimage of Grace 1536–1537 and the Exeter Conspiracy 1538* (2 vols, Cambridge, 1915), i. 119–20; PRO SP1/107, fo. 100ʳ (*LP* XI. 615).
9. *LP* XI. 603; PRO SP1/107, fo. 104ʳ (*LP* XI. 616).
10. Ibid.
11. *LP* XI. 567, 852; PRO SP1/107, fos 100ʳ, 101ʳ (*LP* XI. 615).
12. Ibid., fo. 101; *LP* XI. 580 (2, 5), 642.
13. *LP* XI. 615, 621, 658, 808.
14. *LP* XI. 600, 661, 680, 808.
15. James, 'Obedience and Dissent', pp. 66–8; G. W. Bernard, *The Power of the Early Tudor Nobility: a Study of the Fourth and Fifth Earls of Shrewsbury* (Brighton, 1985), p. 34; Ward, *Lincolnshire Rising*, p. 30; *LP* XI. 691.
16. Ibid. 680.
17. Ibid. 789.
18. James, 'Obedience and Dissent', p. 52.
19. *CCJB* ii. 503; *LP* XI. 571, 585, 587 (3), 650.
20. R. W. Hoyle, 'Thomas Master's Narrative of the Pilgrimage of Grace', *Northern History* 21 (1985), 65; PRO SP1/110, fo. 171ᵛ (*LP* XI. 971).
21. *LP* XI. 665, 728; PRO SP1/108, fo. 3 (*LP* XI. 672); Hoyle, 'Master's Narrative', p. 67.
22. *LP* XI. 716, 756, 773, 808.
23. Ibid. 717, 756.
24. *LP* XI. 728; XII. i. 380.
25. Hoyle, 'Master's Narrative', pp. 67, 69; *LP* XI. 728, 764, 829, 950, 958.
26. *LP* XI. 773–4, 800; *StP* i. 489.
27. *LP* XI. 765, 768, 788–9, 803, 823–4, 833, 836, 845.
28. Hoyle, 'Master's Narrative', p. 67.
29. College of Arms MS M16*bis*, fo. 13ʳ.
30. *LP* XI. 559, 764, 789.
31. Ibid. 764, 780, 789, 833, 843, 850, 866; PRO E36/121, fo. 52ʳ (*LP* XI. 780).
32. *LP* XI. 756, 854 (i); PRO SP1/110, fo. 12 (*LP* XI. 913); LAO PAR St James Louth 7/2, fo. 41ᵛ (I am grateful to Anne Ward for drawing my attention to this document).
33. *LP* XI. 850, 913.
34. BL MS Cotton Appendix L, fo. 66 (*LP* XI. 838); Hoyle, 'Master's Narrative', p. 69; *LP* XI. 838.
35. 'Hagworthingham Church Book', *Lincolnshire Notes and Queries* 1 (1888–9), 8.
36. *LP* XI. 789, 843, 865–6, 883, 888.
37. PRO E36/121, fo. 61 (*LP* XI. 843); *LP* XI. 658, 780.
38. *LP* XI. 833, 838, 842 (3).
39. *LP* XII. i. 70 (vii); PRO SP1/110, fo. 81 (*LP* XI. 938 (2)).
40. *LP* XI. 828, 838, 888, 938 (2); XII. i. 70 (vii).
41. *LP* XI. 843, 880, 888.
42. Ibid. 967, 972, 974–5.
43. Ibid. 1015, 1018.
44. Ibid. 838, 850, 909.
45. Ibid. 1016, 1034, 1036, 1087, 1094.
46. Ibid. 1061, 1095, 1103.
47. Ibid. 1155 (5. ii), 1169–70; PRO SP1/111, fo. 131 (*LP* XI. 1077).

48. *LP* XI. 1017, 1086, 1128.
49. Ibid. 1006, 1103, 1166, 1170.
50. Ibid. 966, 1017, 1026, 1086.
51. Ibid. 883, 989, 1004–5, 1103, 1106, 1115, 1128, 1162, 1207, 1221.
52. Smith, *Land and Politics*, pp. 181, 183; *LP* XI. 1077, 1166, 1176, 1197, 1236.
53. Ibid. 998, 1075, 1078, 1095, 1169, 1176.
54. Ibid. 1126, 1197, 1207, 1224, 1227.
55. *LP* XI. 1061, 1086, 1103; XII. i. 1036 (4).
56. *StP* i. 522.
57. J. W. F. Hill, *Tudor and Stuart Lincoln* (Cambridge, 1956), p. 47; *LP* XI. 1169,1176; PRO SP1/112, fo. 128ʳ (*LP* XI. 1239).
58. *LP* XI. 1084, 1176, 1236.
59. PRO SP1/112, fo. 21 (*LP* XI. 1180); *LP* XI. 1268.
60. PRO SP1/112, fo. 74ʳ (*LP* XI. 1224).
61. PRO SP1/112, fo. 128ʳ (*LP* XI. 1239).
62. PRO SP1/112, fo. 130 (*LP* XI. 1240).
63. PRO SP1/112, fo. 180 (*LP* XI. 1267).
64. *LP* XI. 1093, 1163, 1179–80, 1283, 1288; XII. i. 19, 148.
65. *LP* XI. 1410 (3); XII. i. 201 (iv), 228; *LL* iv, p. 268.
66. *LP* XII. i. 636, 1284.
67. *LP* VIII. 149 (45–7); XII. i. 590, 1207 (5); PRO KB9/539/1, 542/12–15.
68. *LP* XII. i. 590–1, 608, 639, 677, 700, 768, 1193, 1213; ii. 8, 489, 657; XIII. i. 65, 887 (17).
69. *LP* XI. 959, 1104–6; XII. i. 581; PRO KB9/542/15.
70. *LP* XIII. i. 190 (22), 646 (10, 37), 1309 (8).
71. *LP* XII, ii. 156, 228.
72. *LP* XII, i. 591, 639; ii. 57, 75, App. 31; Dodds, *Pilgrimage of Grace* ii. 151.
73. PRO KB9/542/12.
74. PRO KB9/542/3.
75. *LP* XV. 592; PRO KB9/557/11–13.
76. G. R. Elton, *Policy and Police: the Enforcement of the Reformation in the Age of Thomas Cromwell* (Cambridge, 1972), pp. 67–71.
77. *LP* XIV. i. 398; PRO WARD9/149, 151, 187; *LP* XIII. ii. 328; E. B. Tempest, 'Tattershall', *Lincs. Notes and Queries* 15 (1918–19), 72.
78. *LP* XIII. ii. 528, 613, 649.
79. LAO PAR St James Louth 7/2, fos 42ᵛ, 46ʳ, 50ʳ.
80. BL Harl. Ch. 4412.
81. Hill, *Lincoln*, p. 47; LAO lAnc 3/3/22, mm 1–5, 3/14/84; 2Anc 2/25/20, fo. 28ᵛ.
82. Tempest, 'Tattershall', pp. 71—2; N. E. Saul, *Knights and Esquires: the Gloucestershire Gentry in the Fourteenth Century* (Oxford, 1981), p. 70. Only Thomas Derby of Benington lived more than 11 miles from Eresby, and he was close to the Willoughby manors of Skirbeck and Fishtoft.
83. PRO E179/137/370/18, 21, 28; El79/238/81; WARD9/151.
84. PRO STAC2/27/169; Cl/689/32; Gunn, 'Peers, Commons and Gentry'.
85. PRO PROB11/26/8.

86. PRO STAC2/5/124, 15/67; KB9/540/48; *LP* V. 119(14, 64, 69); *Val. Eccles.* iv. 38, 45; *Lincs. Peds* ii. 403.
87. Bindoff, *Commons* ii. 607; PRO E179/137/370/13; Cl/803/9, 841/33; *LP* VIII. 962 (28); *Val. Eccles.* iv. 34, 43, 67, 74, 99.
88. PRO SP2/Fol. M, fo. 136ᵛ; KB9/540/48, 545/64, 67,71; LAO lAnc 3/3/22, mm 1–5; 2Anc 1/5/6, 2/2.5/2.
89. LAO LCl/1/1/1, fos 259ᵛ, 261ʳ, 273ʳ, 274ᵛ, 275ʳ.
90. Bindoff, *Commons* ii. 607–8.
91. See table 5.1.
92. James, 'Obedience and Dissent', p. 45; *Lincolnshire Wills, 1500–1600*, ed. A. R. Maddison (Lincoln, 1888), i. 34; PRO PROB11/26/16; ERO D/DRg1/105.
93. Bindoff, *Commons* iii. 260; *LP* VIII. 149 (44); XVI. 714; *Val. Eccles.* iv. 67, 74–5, 84, 98, 137; PRO STAC2/2/279; KB9/545/64, 71.
94. PRO KB9/540/48, 541/161; E137/20/4/1/1–2.
95. PRO KB9/545/69; ERO D/DRg1/105.
96. *LP* XIV. i. 749, 1348; ii. 4.
97. PRO SP1/123, fo. 121 (misdated, *LP* XII. ii. 364); SP1/130, fo. 108 (misdated, *LP* XIII. i. 566); LAO Register 27, fo. 67ᵛ.
98. *LP* XV. 942 (52); LAO 2Anc 1/5/6, 3/A/48, 49. Some expenditure was still needed to fulfil the late lord's will.
99. *Val. Eccles.* iv. 87, 139; PRO E315/209, fos 36ʳ–37ʳ, 70ᵛ; LAO Register 27, fos 83ʳ, 86.
100. *LP* XIII. i. 384 (85), p. 581; PRO CP25(2)/25/167/11.
101. *GEC* xi. 661; PRO C54/420, m. 22; 425, m. 7; *LP* XIII. i. 1519 (49); XIV. i, p. 605; XV. 733 (44); XVI. 1395 (22); XVIII. i, p. 556; *The Itinerary of John Leland*, ed. L. T. Smith (5 vols, London, 1907–10), i. 38.
102. PRO E179/137/404/7ᵛ, 137/422/3ʳ; PROB11/37/11; *LP* XIV. i, p. 276.
103. *LP* XIV. i. 1192 (16); Bindoff, *Commons* iii. 2–3.
104. *LP* XIII. ii. 142.
105. *LP* XI. 1267; XIV. i. 878, 923, 951, 1075, 1145.
106. *LP* XIV. i. 295; D. Wilson, *A Tudor Tapestry: Men, Women and Society in Reformation England* (London, 1972), pp. 22–3, 156–61.
107. PRO C1/918/11–14.
108. PRO C1/1061/35; BL MS Add. 29549, fo. 4.
109. *LP* XIII. ii. 52, 57; XIV. i. 1348; PRO SP1/123, fo. 131 (*LP* XII. ii. 364).
110. *LP* XII. ii. 364,771; *TRP* i. 138; G. R. Elton, *Reform and Renewal: Thomas Cromwell and the Common Weal* (Cambridge, 1973), p. 165.
111. PRO SP1/150, fo. 121 (*LP* XIV. i. 749).
112. PRO SP1/153, fo. 159 (*LP* XIV. ii. 214). William Leach led the Horncastle rebels in 1536.
113. M. Bowker, *The Henrician Reformation: the Diocese of Lincoln under John Longland 1521–1547* (Cambridge, 1981), pp. 158–80.
114. PRO SP1/153, fo. 2 (*LP* XIV. ii. 4).
115. Wilson, *Tudor Tapestry*, pp. 166–7; Hill,

Notes

Lincoln, p. 61; for similar behaviour by Norfolk, see Baskerville, 'Married Clergy', p. 203.

116. ERO D/Drg1/103; *FOR*, p. 128; LAO Register 27, fos 67, 69ᵛ, 71ᵛ, 75ᵛ, 79ᵛ.

117. *FOR*, pp. 66, 73, 128; NRO Register 16, fo. 23ʳ; 17, fos 33ᵛ, 40ᵛ, 42ᵛ, 47ᵛ.

118. Baskerville, 'Married Clergy', p. 61; PRO PROB11/31/38; NRO NCC Mingaye 297ʳ; LAO LCC Wills 1545–6&C. ii, fo. 198; 1578, fo. 213ᵛ.

119. *FOR*, pp. 88, 95; LAO Register 27, fos 66ᵛ–67ʳ; LCC Wills 1541, fo. 188ᵛ; NRO Register 16, fos 16ʳ, 118ʳ; 17, fos 30ʳ, 31ᵛ; NCC Goldingham 314—15; PRO PROB11/30/ 41, 31/10.

120. *LP* XIII. i. 1129; H. Cotton, *Fasti Ecclesiae Hibernicae* (6 vols, Dublin, 1845–78), ii. 152.

121. PRO SP1/126, fo. 35 (*LP* XII. ii. 998); *LP* XV. 585; Hennessy, *Novum Repertorium*, p. 248.

122. Bowker, *Henrician Reformation*, p. 140; Emden, *Oxford 1501–40*, p. 82; LAO 5Anc 1/1/44.

123. PRO C1/1170/16; E179/69/4, 5; NRO Register 17, fos 2ᵛ, 44ᵛ; Bowker, *Henrician Reformation*, p. 118.

124. *LP* XIII. i. 704.

125. J. Knox, *Works*, ed. D. Laing (6 vols, Edinburgh, 1846–64), i. 45–8, 532; LAO Register 27, fo. 69ᵛ; *LP* XIV. i. 1192 (46); J. Foxe, *Acts and Monuments*, ed. S. R. Cattley, G. Townsend (8 vols, London, 1837–41), v. 449.

126. S. E. Brigden, 'Popular Disturbance and the Fall of Thomas Cromwell and the Reformers, 1539–40', *Historical Journal*, 24 (1981), 266; *LP* Add. ii. 1463; J. Bale, *Scriptorum Illustrium Maioris Brytannie ... Catalogus* (Basle, 1557–9), Cent. xiv, p. 224; Foxe, *Acts and Monuments* v. 449–51.

127. *The Declaracio[n] made at Poules Crosse in the cytye of London, the fourth sonday of Advent by A. Seyton, and Mayster W. Tolwyn, in MDXLI* (London, 1542); J. Bale, 'The Image of Both Churches', *Select Works*, ed. H. Christmas (Parker Society 36, 1849), p. 433.

128. LAO Register 27, fos 78ʳ, 79ᵛ; Bale, *Scriptorum Catalogus*, p. 224.

129. Wriothesley, *Chronicle* i. 132.

130. *LP* XIV. i. 403 (19); *FOR*, pp. 40, 125; NRO Register 17, fo. 37ʳ; Longleat House Misc. Vol. 18, fos 48ᵛ, 59ᵛ, 90ʳ; LL v. 1526; Cranmer, Cromwell, and Catherine Parr all seem to have avoided dating by saints' day. On Luther and the assumption see W. Tappolet, *Das Marienlob der Reformatoren* (Tübingen, 1962), p. 56.

131. *FOR*, p. 214; Emden, *Oxford 1501–40*, p. 345; *Narratives of the Days of the Reformation*, ed. J. G. Nichols (Cam. Soc. 77, 1859), pp. 276–8.

132. *LP* VIII. 387; XII. i. 1095; LAO 1Anc 7/A/l; PRO E179/69/4, 5; LR12/21/636; PROB11/30/34.

133. PRO SP1/130, fo. 9 (*LP* XIII. i. 476); Bodl. MS Ashmole 1109, fo. 145ᵛ.

134. *Lincs. Peds.* ii. 637; J. Stow, *A Survey of London*, ed. C. L. Kingsford, 2nd edn (2 vols, Oxford, 1971), i. 261; Hennessy, *Novum Repertorium*, p. 311; *FOR*, p. 243.

135. PRO PROB11/36/18.

136. MacCulloch, *Suffolk*, pp. 157, 160.

137. Ibid., pp. 159, 176–80; PRO DL30/735/59, mm 36–8.

138. H. McCusker, *John Bale, Dramatist and Antiquary* (Bryn Mawr, 1942), pp. 7–8; *LP* III. i, p. 499; PRO LR12/21/636.

139. For what follows, see Bale's deposition, printed in McCusker, *Bale*, pp. 8–12.

140. PRO E326/12522; SP1/114, fo. 54 (*LP* XII. i. 40).

141. PRO C54/407, m. 17; Ford, *Mary Tudor*, p. 39.

142. PRO SP1/114, fo. 54; C54/407, m. 17; SC6/ Henry VIII/3372, m. 6.

143. NRO Register 16, fo. 26ʳ; PRO SP1/130, fo. 9 (*LP* XIII. i. 476).

144. *Letters Relating to the Suppression of Monasteries*, ed. T. Wright (Cam. Soc. 26, 1843), p. 160 (*LP* XII. ii. 81).

145. *LP* IV. ii. 3884; PRO LR12/27/922.

146. MacCulloch, *Suffolk*, p. 159; *LP* XIII. ii. 554, 571, 964; PRO Cl/1170/16; PROB11/37/20; NRO Register 14 (ii), fo. 17ᵛ; 16, fo. 23ʳ; NCC Mingaye, fo. 297ʳ (Righton's will, including a bequest to Tyrrell).

147. Blomefield, *Norfolk* v. 378; MacCulloch, *Suffolk*, p. 67; SRO T4373/428; Bodl. MS Tanner 137, fo. 46; ULC MS Hengrave 3, fo. 25. I owe the last two references to Dr MacCulloch.

148. PRO E314/82.

149. Robinson, 'Officers and Household', pp. 27–8; Rawcliffe, *Staffords*, p. 91; V. F. Snow, *Essex the Rebel: the Life of Robert Devereux, the Third Earl of Essex 1591–1646* (Lincoln, Nebraska, 1970), pp. 85–6.

150. CAD iii. A4755; LAO 1Anc 7/A/1; PRO E179/69/6.

151. PRO SC6/Henry VIII/6899; BL Harl. Ch. 49A46; *LP* XIII. i. 1129; XIV. ii. p. 322.

152. PRO SP1/150, fo. 121 (*LP* XIV. i. 749); *LP* XV. 925; XVII. 428.

153. PRO E101/148/22; LAO 1Anc 2/22/7; 3/27/6, 7.

154. PRO DL30/735/59, m. 38ᵛ; PROB11/26/8; SC6/Add./3482/94, m. 4ᵛ; SC6/ Henry VIII/3372, m. 13ʳ; SRO HE10/1/6, m. 26ᵛ; *LP* XIII. i. 1115 (67); XIV. i. 1056 (51).

155. PRO SP1/115, fos 38, 175 (*LP* XII. i. 216, 318); *LP* XII. i. 252.

156. *LP* VII. 800; XII. i. 917; XIII. ii. 6, 57, 554; Add. ii. 1318; PRO STAC2/8/201.

157. PRO SP1/115, fo. 38 (*LP* XII. i. 216).

158. *LP* XI. 659; McCusker, *Bale*, p. 8; *LP* XII. i. 711, 836.

159. PRO C54/407, m. 14; 408, m. 21; 419, m. 32; CP25/(2)/40/267/7.

160. MacCulloch, *Suffolk*, pp. 358, 373.

161. PRO SC12/37/16, m. 5; REQ2/4/358; *Suffolk in 1524*, p. 121; *LP* XIII. i, p. 580.

162. MacCulloch, *Suffolk*, p. 59; R. A. Houlbrooke, *Church Courts and the People during the English Reformation 1520—1570* (Oxford, 1979), pp. 193–4.

163. MacCulloch, *Suffolk*, p. 59; see table 2.3.
164. PRO LR12/27/922; SRO HE10/1/6, mm 25ᵛ, 26ᵛ; HA18/DB1/2, m. 6; PRO DL30/735/59; LR3/62/1; SC6/Henry VIII/3372, 6899.
165. Smith, *Land and Politics*, p. 156; Bindoff, *Commons* ii. 302; Suffolk 1561 i. 107; MacCulloch, *Suffolk*, pp. 70, 364–5.
166. *LP* V. 653; XIII. i. 1519 (20); PRO LR12/27/922; NRO Bulwer NRS 2567, mm 4, 6, 13; SRO HE10/1/6, m. 17ᵛ.
167. *Butley Register*, p. 71; *LP* XI. ii. 304.
168. *LP* XII. i. 1125; XIII. i. 1209 (misdated); PRO SP1/120, fos 100ʳ–101ʳ (*LP* XII. i. 1212).
169. PRO SP1/120, fo. 202 (*LP* XII. i. 1284); NRO Norwich 18a, fo. 150*ᵛ.
170. *SR* 28 Henry VIII, *c*. 51.
171. PRO E315/209, fos lʳ–2ʳ (*LP* XIII. ii. 1520 (iv)). The rent was £214 8s 11d.
172. *LP* XI.1377; Miller, *English Nobility*, pp. 232–5. Though Brandon secured more Suffolk monasteries than Howard, Howard's grants of Coxford and Castleacre in Norfolk balanced these successes (cf. MacCulloch, *Suffolk*, pp. 66–7).
173. MacCulloch, *Suffolk*, pp. 69–71 places more stress on the needs of East Anglia than on those of Lincolnshire.
174. PRO SP1/141, fos 192–3 (*LP* XIII. ii. 1269); SRO HA11/C2/3, 18/DES/2.
175. PRO SC6/Henry VIII/3372, mm 4ᵛ, 9ᵛ, 10, 12ᵛ, 13ᵛ, 15ᵛ, 17ᵛ, 6899; E211/61.
176. *LP* XI. 385 (17); H. W. Aldred, *The History of the Manor of Benhall* (Camberwell, 1887), p. 10; BL Add. Ch. 909 (*LP* XII. ii. 246); Add. Ch. 10225 (*LP* XIII. i. 391); MS Egerton 2713, fo. 13.
177. BL Harl. Ch. 55H44 (*LP* XIII. i. 1058).
178. *LP* XIII. i. 1115 (51); PRO C54/411, m. 4.
179. PRO SC6/Henry VIII/3372, m. 9ᵛ; *LP* XIII. i. 393.
180. BL Harl. Ch. 55H43 (*LP* XIII. i. 553); *LP* XIV. i. 651 (57); BL Harl. Ch. 47A52 (*LP* XIV. ii. 442); NRO Register 17, fo. 56ʳ.
181. *HMC Eighth Report* ii (1881), fo. 24ᵇ; *LP* Add. ii. 1311; PRO SC12/37/16, printed in part in Gunn and Lindley, 'Charles Brandon's Westhorpe'.
182. PRO E315/208a, fos 11–13; *LP* VIII. 800; XIII. ii, p. 533.
183. PRO SC 12/23/63; *HMC Eighth Report* ii. 24b, 25b.
184. PRO SP1/130, fo. 220 (*LP* XIII. i. 642).
185. PRO C54/411, m. 4; *LP* XIII. i. 1349.
186. In March and April 1538 he was still commuting Leiston pensions with benefices: *FOR*, p. 73; NRO Register 17, fo. 40ᵛ.
187. PRO SP1/130, fo. 220.
188. PRO C54/411, mm 15–16 (*LP* XIII. i. 1329); E326/12901; E323/1 pt. 1, m. 11ʳ (*LP* III. i. 457); SC12/37/16.
189. PRO E318/20/1076, 1081; C54/411, m. 10.
190. PRO C54/412, mm 43–4; SC6/Henry VIII/6899; SC12/37/6/1, 2, 37/16.
191. PRO SC6/Henry VIII/6899; Bindoff, *Commons* i. 524–5, 744.
192. PRO C54/413, m. 10; CP25(2)/30/203/77; Blomefield, *Norfolk* v. 215.
193. PRO SC12/37/6/2; LR3/62/1; LR12/22/688;

DL30/735/59, m.40; REQ2/2/78; SRO HA18/DB1/2, m. 5; HE10/1/6, m. 28ᵛ; TI/2/1.4, m. 4.
194. *LP* XIII. ii. 1182 (18); XIV. i. 651 (45).
195. PRO SC12/23/29.
196. *LP* XIII. i. 642, 1118; ii. 1119, 1182 (20–2, 27), XIV. i. 191 (27, 28), 359, 651 (48), 1018; PRO C54/413, mm 38–9; E326/12414; LAO 2Anc 3/B/14.
197. BL Harl. Ch. 47A53 (*LP* XV. 895).
198. *LP* XIV. i. 651 (38); L. Binyon, *Catalogue of Drawings by British Artists and Artists of Foreign Origin working in Great Britain preserved in the Department of Prints and Drawings in the British Museum*, ii (London, 1900), 335–6.
199. LAO 2Anc 3/A/50, 3/B/13; BL Harl. Ch. 47A51 (*LP* XV. 236).
200. LAO 1Anc 11/C/1a, 1b; PRO Cl/950/85,972/42 show that Compagna was active in London by 1541.
201. *LP* XIV. i. 651 (58); PRO SC12/32/29; SC6/ Henry VIII/1928, mm 4ʳ, 5ʳ; C1/ 1034/67. See map 5.2.
202. *LP* XV. 831 (46); LAO 1Anc 11/C/1b.
203. *LP* XIV. i. 651 (17); *Lincs. Wills* i. 139.
204. *LP* XI. 531; XV. 831 (19); *Lincs. Peds*. ii. 421; PRO E179/136/337/1.
205. LAO 3Anc 8/1/3 pp. 34–6; PRO E305/2/ A51; E318/20/1080; *LP* XVI. 678 (9).
206. PRO E323/1, pt. 1, mm 6ᵛ–7ʳ (*LP* XIII. ii. 457); BL Harl. Ch. 47A50 (*LP* XIV. i. 71); Harl. Ch. 49A46.
207. G. A. J. Hodgett, *Tudor Lincolnshire* (History of Lincolnshire 6, 1975), pp. 52–4; *LP* XI. 1217 (1); XIII. i. 1115 (1), pp. 578, 581; XIV. i. 651 (49).
208. *LP* XII. i. 41; ii. 411 (29); Longleat House Misc. Vol. 18 *passim*.
209. *Chronicle of King Henry VIII*, p. 136.
210. PRO SP1/121, fo. 193 (*LP* XII. ii. 171).
211. *LP* XIV. ii, p. 342; Add. ii. 1414; PRO C54/413, m. 36; Longleat House Misc. Vol. 18, fos 11ᵛ, 27ᵛ, 83ᵛ, 127ᵛ; LAO 1Anc 11/C/1b.
212. PRO SP1/157, fo. 140 (*LP* XV. 163); BL Harl. Ch. 51H24; LAO 2Anc 3/B/ll.
213. PRO C54/425, m. 40; LAO lAnc 11/C/la.
214. BL MS Cotton Vespasian FXIII, fo. 219 (*LP* XIII. i. 486).
215. *LP* XIV. ii. 4; Letters of the Cliffords, nos 37, 38.
216. Ibid., nos 40, 47, 48.
217. *LL* iv. 854a, 874–5, 880, 901, pp. 131, 133; v. 1396a, 1441, 1526.
218. *LL* iv. 854a, 887, 895, 901; v. 1525–6.
219. *LP* XIV. i. 1312; *HMC Rutland* iv. 293.
220. W. M. Brady, *The Episcopal Succession in England, Scotland and Ireland AD 1400 to 1875* (3 vols, Rome, 1877), iii. 493.
221. *LP* XII. i. 291, 332–3, 636; XIII. i. 628, 671, 756; ii. 968; XIV. i. 1153; XV. i. 791, 966; *Reports of Sir John Spelman* ii. 352; *LL* vi, p. 118.
222. *LP* XII. ii. 1155; *TRP* i. 170; *SR* 23 Henry VIII, c. 7, s. 4.
223. *LP* XII. ii, App. 7; XIII. ii. 979 (5), 986 (1); XIV. i. 290 (9); XV. 652, 697; Wriothesley, *Chronicle* i. 80, 96.

224. *LJ* i. 103–63; S. E. Lehmberg, *The Later Parliaments of Henry VIII* (Cambridge, 1977), p. 89.
225. *LJ* i. 105, 107–9,115–19, 122–4, 126, 130, 145–7, 150, 155–6.
226. Lehmberg, *Later Parliaments*, p. 55; *LP* XII. ii. 911, 1060; Wriothesley, *Chronicle* i. 98.
227. College of Arms MS M6, fo. 15ᵛ; *LP* XIII. i. 5, 579; ii, p. 538; XIV. i. 5.
228. *LP* XIV. i. 1026; Longleat House Misc. Vol. 18, *passim*.
229. *LP* XIII. i. 583; ii. 833, 884; Anstis, *Garter* i. 403–16.
230. *LP* XII. ii. 329, 437–8; XIV. ii, pp. 321, 325.
231. *LP* XI. 1445; XII. ii. 1226; PRO SP1/112, fo. 202 (*LP* XI. 1281).
232. *LP* XV. 190, 296; XVI. 220 (2), 503 (5), p. 717; XIX. i. 812 (17); PRO SP1/158, fo. 46 (*LP* XV. 340).
233. *LP* XI. 1417 (17); XII. i. 795 (43); XIII. i. 646 (15); XIV. ii. 435 (41); XV. 282 (68), 1027 (9), p. 565.
234. *LP* I. ii. 3324 (18); XIII. ii. 243, 843; XIV. i. 652 (M6); ii. 68; PRO Cl/1080/61; *Letters and Papers of the Verney Family*, ed. J. Bruce (Cam. Soc. 56, 1853), p. 49.
235. *LP* XIV. i. 505; PRO STAC2/28/77.
236. *LP* XX. i. 717; *Records of the City of Oxford*, p. 159.
237. PRO E101/148/22, mm 1–3, 149/33; *SR* 33 Henry VIII, c. 39, s. 18–26.
238. PRO LR1/310, fo. 39ᵛ; *LP* XIII. i. 1168.
239. *LP* XII. i. 898; XIV. ii. 494; XV. 1016; *LJ* i. 158–9; *SR* 32 Henry VIII, c. 35.
240. HMC *Salisbury* ii. 146; *LP* XII. ii. 191 (36); XIII. ii. 5; G. R. Elton, *The Tudor Revolution in Government* (Cambridge, 1953), pp. 382–5; Miller, *English Nobility*, p. 173; Somerville, *Duchy of Lancaster*, p. 423.
241. *SR* 31 Henry VIII, c. 8, s. 4; c. 10, s. 4; 32 Henry VIII, c. 39; Elton, *Tudor Revolution*, p. 384.
242. Ibid., pp. 389–92, 394–6, 402; *Household Ordinances*, pp. 208–27.
243. PRO KB9/544/38.
244. *LP* XIV. ii. 783; XV. 14.
245. BL MS Add. 45716, fo. 6ᵛ; *LP* XV. 381. The second may have been the son of Lewis Wingfield, brought up in Calais by Sir Robert (*LP* XII. i. 440; XIX. ii. 414).
246. PRO PROB11/20/9; P. Sidney, *Memoirs of the Sidney Family* (London, 1899), p. 3; LAO 1Anc 11/C/1a.
247. Bindoff, *Commons* i. 572; *LP* XI. 1104; XIX. i, p. 161; XX. ii. 707 (13); *Report on the Manuscripts of the Most Honourable the Marquess of Bath*, iv (HMC 58, 1968), 31, 67.
248. *LP* XIV. ii. 751; College of Arms MS Tournament Cheques Id.
249. *LP* XIV. i. 1348; ii. 183, 217, 286.
250. *LP* XIV. ii. 572, 754; XV. 21; Add. i. 269.
251. *LP* XV. 719, 767, 804; *Chronicle of King Henry VIII*, pp. 99–100.
252. *LP* XV. 823, 850 (3–9, 12–13).
253. Ibid. 860, 872, 874, 883, 898, 908, 925; *LJ* i. 153.
254. *LP* XV. 883, 925, 991.
255. PRO CP40/1094, rot. 138; 1095, rot. 531; LAO 1Anc 11/C/1a.
256. *LP* XV. 588, 959.
257. D. Potter, 'International Politics and Naval Jurisdiction in the Sixteenth Century: the case of François de Montmorency', *European Studies Review*, 7 (1977), 6, 13–14; *LP* XII. i. 626; XIV. i. 445; ii. 779 (8); *Correspondance politique de MM. de Castillon et de Marillac*, ed. J. Kaulek (Paris, 1885), pp. 146, 176–7, 199, 204–5.
258. *LP* XIII. i. 1449.

6 The King's Lieutenant: 1540–1545

1. *LP* XVI. 269, 311; XVII. 654.
2. *LP* XX. i. 1023, 1218; ii. 14, 209.
3. *LP* XVI. 212–628.
4. *LP* XVI. 1381–1480; XVII. 1–233.
5. *LP* XIX. i. 227–781; ii. 653–777; XX. i. 35–1320; ii. 23–188, 952.
6. *Castillon et Marillac*, p. 243.
7. *LJ* i. 164; *LP* XVII. 957.
8. PRO SP1/226, fo. 122ᵛ (*LP* XXI. ii. 417).
9. *LP* XX. i. 426–7; ii. 178, 197.
10. PRO E179/69/5; SC12/23/29, fo. 3ᵛ; *LP* XVIII. i. 623 (19); LAO 1Anc 11/C/1b; 2Anc 3/B/25.
11. *StP* v. 306.
12. *York Civic Records* iv, ed. A. Raine (Yorkshire Archaeological Society, Record Series 108, 1945), pp. 97–8; *LP* XVIII. i. 775; ii. 519; XIX. i. 162.
13. *LP* XVIII. i. 884; ii. 287.
14. *LP* XVIII. i. 161, 214, 237, 291, 432, 692; ii. 63, 74; XXI. ii. 543.
15. *LP* XVIII. ii. 475, 518; XIX. ii. 34.
16. *LP* XVIII. 1006; XVIII. i. 546.
17. Bernard, *Early Tudor Nobility*, p. 119; PRO E315/248, fo. 55ᵛ; *LP* XVIII. ii. 57, 90, 361, 408.
18. *York Civic Records* iv. 103.
19. *LP* XVIII. i. 962; Add. ii. 1566.
20. *LP* XX. i. 481–2, 1157, 1236; ii. 118,169; PRO SP1/204, fo. 192 (*LP* XX. i. 1326).
21. *LP* XIX. i. 178.
22. *LP* XVIII. i. 497, 498, 981 (52, 58), ii. 74; PRO SP1/177, fos 69ᵛ–70ᵛ (*LP* XVIII. i. 432).
23. *LP* XVIII. i. 548, 909; ii. 120.
24. *LP* XVIII. ii. 332; Bindoff, *Commons* i. 488–9.
25. *LP* XVIII. i. 53, 123, 138, 192, 342; ii. 36, 93, 118, 239; XIX. i. 99; *York Civic Records* iv. 100, 102–3.
26. *StP* v. 317.
27. HMC *Bath* iv. 32; Bindoff, *Commons* iii. 500–1.
28. *LP* XVIII. ii. 193; PRO SP1/178, fos 152–7 (*LP* XVIII. i. 649); STAC2/3/65–7, 15/245, 17/340; E314/39/43; KB27/1115, 1116.
29. HMC *Bath* iv. 58; *LP* XX. i. 100.
30. *LP* XVII. 957, 982, 994, 996, 1025, 1036, 1051.
31. *LP* XVIII. i. 80, 127, 289, 378.
32. *LP* XVIII. i. 64, 72, 96, 109, 152, 172, 186–8; *The Scottish Correspondence of Mary of Lorraine*, ed. A. I. Cameron (Scottish History Society, 3rd ser. 10, 1927), pp. 5, 7.

33. *LP* XVIII. i. 132, 140, 158, 173; A. J. Slavin, *Politics and Profit: A Study of Sir Ralph Sadler 1507–1547* (Cambridge, 1966), pp. 94–131.
34. *LP* XVIII. ii. 461; *The Hamilton Papers*, ed. J. Bain (Edinburgh, 1890–2), ii. 285.
35. *LP* XVIII. ii. 377, 387, 450, 461.
36. *LP* XVIII. ii. 394, 407, 417, 423, 433, 443–4, 451, 496, 510; XIX. i. 58.
37. *LP* XVIII. ii. 424, 434, 487; XIX. i. 92.
38. *LP* XVIII. i. 764.
39. *LP* XVIII. ii. 127, 131, 146; XIX. i. 41; ii. 33.
40. *HMC Bath* iv. 85; *LP* XVIII. ii. 295, 297.
41. *LP* XVIII. i. 88, 104, 117, 129, 156–7, 161, 174, 186, 191, 228, 286, 316; ii. 110, 118, 319.
42. *LP* XVIII. i. 536, 549, 567, 580, 670, 694, 695, 937, 958–9, 978; ii. 103, 110.
43. *LP* XVIII. i. 592, 627, 741, 761, 768, 827; *StP* v. 307.
44. *LP* XVIII. i. 809, 957, 964; PRO SP1/178, fos 20, 53 (*LP* XVIII. i. 536, 567).
45. Bodl. MS Ashmole 1109, fo. 144ᵛ.
46. *LP* XVIII. i. 937; ii. 173; XIX. i. 122; M. E. James, 'Change and Continuity in the Tudor North: The Rise of Thomas First Lord Wharton', in *Society, Politics and Culture*, pp. 103–41.
47. *LP* XVIII. i. 691; ii. 137, 209, 263, 339, 340, 422, 469, 487; *Hamilton Papers* ii. 256.
48. Ibid. 64.
49. Ibid. 266.
50. *LP* XVII. 982, 994, 1037; *HMC Bath* iv. 31; Bodl. MS Ashmole 1109, fo. 143ʳ; PRO E179/137/370/19.
51. Bernard, *Early Tudor Nobility*, p. 118; *LP* XVIII. i. 104, 123, 686; ii. 11, 93,119, 145, 192, 287.
52. *LP* XVIII. i. 139, 162, 686; ii. 71, 120, 195.
53. *LP* XVIII. i. 123; ii. 192, 414, 468.
54. *LP* XVIII. ii. 119, 192, 195–6, 207.
55. *LP* XVIII. i. 455; ii. 9, 234.
56. *LP* XVIII. i. 146–7, 151; XIX. i. 24, 59, 92.
57. *LP* XIX. i. 95, 103, 107, 109, 114–17, 136, 189, 254; Bush, 'Edward Seymour', pp. 335–8.
58. *LP* XVIII. i. 90, 409, 460, 466; ii. 72, 237; XIX. i. 71, 103, 140.
59. *Hamilton Papers* ii. 269.
60. *LP* XVIII. i. 64, 741, 768; ii. 9, 170, 184, 192, 195–6, 198, 234, 236, 237 (2).
61. *LP* XVIII. ii. 236; XIX. i. 59, 71, 83, 95, 103, 136.
62. *LP* XVIII. i. 799; ii. 540.
63. *LP* XVII. 1029; XVIII. i. 567, 571, 691, 694; ii. 119, 171, 318, 319, 417, 433, 521; XIX. i. 83; XX. i. 758; BL Harl. Ch. 43B20.
64. *Hamilton Papers* i. 446.
65. *LP* XVIII. ii. 412; XIX. i. 71.
66. Gunn, 'March on Paris', p. 629; U. Fulwell, *The Flower of Fame* (London, 1575), fos 34ʳ–35ʳ; but see *LP* XIX. i. 872.
67. D. Willen, *John Russell, First Earl of Bedford* (London, 1981), pp. 47–8; G. J. Millar, *Tudor Mercenaries and Auxiliaries, 1485–1547* (Charlottesville, 1980), pp.

98–100; M. B. Davies, 'The "Enterprises" of Paris and Boulogne', *Fouad I University, Bulletin of the Faculty of Arts*, 11 (1949), Brussels, Archives Générales du Royaume, État et Audience 99, fo. 410ᵛ.
68. PRO SP1/194, fo. 64 (*LP* XIX. ii. 483).
69. PRO SP1/191, fo. 46 (*LP* XIX. ii. 36).
70. *LP* XIX. ii. 182.
71. *LP* XIX. i. 694, 835 (2); Arch. Gén. État Aud. 1630/3/271, unnumbered (Suffolk-Mary, July).
72. *LP* XVIII. ii. 217, 221, 236, 244, 262; XIX. i. 814–15, 835, 847, 872, 875, 932, 940, 947, 970; LAO 3Anc 8/1/1, pp. 28–9.
73. Bodl. MS Ashmole 1109, fo. 144ᵛ; *LP* XIX. ii. 424; XX. ii. 209; W. A. J. Archbold, 'A Diary of the Expedition of 1544', *EHR* 16 (1901), 504.
74. Arch. Gén. État Aud. 1630/3/164ʳ; Davies, 'Paris and Boulogne', p. 84; *LP* XVIII. ii. 118; XIX. i. 86.
75. Arch. Gén État Aud. 1630/3/164ᵛ; Gunn, 'March on Paris', p. 616; *LP* XVIII. i. 80, 237; ii. 63, 118, 170, 236, 519; XIX. i. 136.
76. PRO SP1/192, fo. 69ᵛ (*LP* XIX. ii. 221).
77. *LP* XIX. i. 949; ii. 424.
78. *LP* XIX. i. 273 (1), 275; ii. 334, 524 (I. ii. 13, 19); Archbold, 'Expedition of 1544', pp. 505–6; *HMC Bath* iv. 30.
79. Archbold, 'Expedition of 1544', pp. 505–6; Davies, 'Paris and Boulogne', p. 57; *LP* XIX. i. 949, 964; ii. 424, 526 (II. 4).
80. *LP* XIX. i. 903; *Chronicle of King Henry VIII*, pp. 114–15; BN MS Fr 20521, fos 25, 28ʳ, 72ʳ.
81. *LP* XIX. i. 1003; ii. 116,424; PRO SP1/192, fo. 70ᵛ (*LP* XIX. ii. 221); Davies, 'Paris and Boulogne', pp. 74–5.
82. *LP* XIX. ii. 5, 222, 236, 276, 424.
83. *LP* XIX. ii. 236–7, 258, 280, 285, 304, 307, 317–18.
84. PRO SP1/193, fo. 62 (*LP* XIX. ii. 378); *LP* XIX. ii. 347.
85. *LP* XIX. ii. 352–3, 424; Davies, 'Paris and Boulogne', p. 85.
86. Millar, *Tudor Mercenaries*, p. 119; ADN B2442, fo. 488ᵛ; Arch. Gén. État Aud. 1661/ 2/f/113, 115, 116.
87. *LP* XIX. ii. 353, 424; Millar, *Tudor Mercenaries*, pp. 119–20.
88. *LP* XIX. ii. 353, 374, 383.
89. *LP* XIX. ii. 365, 377, 395, 402, 415.
90. PRO SP1/193, fo. 62 (*LP* XIX. ii. 378).
91. *LP* XIX. ii. 383, 432, 436, 479, 484; PRO SP1/194, fos 64–5 (*LP* XIX. ii. 483).
92. *LP* XIX. ii. 505, 515, 542, 555–6, 623 (2).
93. *LP* XIX. ii. 582, 595, 604, 612, 653.
94. *LP* XIX. ii. 337 (2), 423; XX. i. 530.
95. PRO E318/20/1077, m. 1; E323/2B, pt. 1, m. 30ʳ.
96. PRO E318/20/1079, mm 3–5.
97. *LP* XX. i. 846 (92).
98. *LP* XX. i. 986, 1174, 1297; ii. 25, App. 19.
99. *LP* XX. i. 814, 958, 1166, 1220; ii. 66.
100. *LP* XX. i. 846 (13), 1275, 1314; ii. 24, 62; Bodl. MS Ashmole 1109, fo. 144ᵛ.
101. *LP* XX. ii. 25, 38, 51, 61, 71, 82.
102. *LP* XX. i. 1174, 1255; *HMC Bath* iv. 103–4.
103. *LP* XIX. i. 215, 234; XX. i. 181, 187, 468.

Notes

104. *LP* XX. i. 43, 188, 426, 689.
105. *LP* XIX. i. 630, 725, 733, 659, 779.
106. *LP* XIX. ii. 800 (30); Wriothesley, *Chronicle* i. 151; *Chronicle of the Grey Friars of London*, ed. J. G. Nichols (Cam. Soc. 53, 1852), p. 48.
107. *LP* XIX. i. 293; XX. i. 859, 1195; ii. 418 (73).
108. *LP* XVII. 957; XVIII. i. 894; Wriothesley, *Chronicle* i. 154.
109. D. Hoak, *The King's Council in the Reign of Edward VI* (Cambridge, 1976), pp. 242–58; A. J. Slavin, 'The Fall of Lord Chancellor Wriothesley', *Albion*, 7 (1975), 284; A. D. Tucker, 'The Commons in the Parliament of 1545' (Oxford Univ. D.Phil. thesis 1966), p. 655.
110. *LP* XXI. ii. 555 (4).
111. *LJ* i. 166–97; Lehmberg, *Later Parliaments*, pp. 141, 155.
112. *LP* XVI. 1126, 1253, 1482; XVII, p. 721; XIX. i. 462.
113. *LP* XVI. 660, 1332, 1426; XVII. 124; *LJ* i. 171, 176.
114. *LP* XIX. ii. 800 (27); XX. i. 1081 (50); PRO LR15/147.
115. Foxe, *Acts and Monuments* v. 690; G. Redworth, 'The Political and Diplomatic Career of Stephen Gardiner', 1538–1551' (Oxford Univ. D.Phil. thesis 1985), pp. 151–2.
116. *LP* XX. ii. 63; Willen, *John Russell*, p. 48; Redworth, 'Career of Gardiner', pp. 150–2, 156–60, 170, 176–7.
117. Ibid., pp. 120–1, 198; *LP* XIX. ii. 423; XX. i. 1315; *HMC Bath* iv. 103.
118. *LP* XVII. 982, 996, 1025–6; *HMC Bath* iv. 84–5.
119. *LP* XVI. 436; *Privy Purse Expenses of the Princess Mary*, ed. F. Madden (London, 1831), pp. 50–143.
120. *LP* XVIII. i. 873; XIX. i. 620 (ii); ii. 688; Longleat House Misc. Vol. 19; *HMC Bath* iv. 99. Lady Herbert was the queen's sister.
121. Foxe, *Acts and Monuments* viii. 570; *Chronicle of King Henry VIII*, p. 136.
122. *LP* XX. ii. 899; Add. ii. 1572.
123. PRO WARD9/149, fo. 136ʳ; E179/69/48, m. 1; Starkey, *Reign of Henry VIII*, pp. 136–7, 141, 154, 156.
124. Foxe, *Acts and Monuments* v. 547, 557; *LP* XXI. i. 1384 (2); ii. 756; PRO E179/69/41, m. 1; McConica, *English Humanists*, p. 227; E. Read, *Catherine, Duchess of Suffolk* (London, 1962).
125. MacCulloch, *Suffolk*, p. 159.
126. Bodl. MS Ashmole 1109, fo. 143ᵛ; PRO C24/29, Haworth and Powis v. Suffolk, deposition of Christopher Lynham; O. Manning, W. Bray, *The History and Antiquities of the County of Surrey* (3 vols, London, 1804–14), iii. 645.
127. *SR* 21 Henry VIII, c. 13, s. 11; Bodl. MS Ashmole 1109, fos 142ᵛ–3ʳ; Emden, *Oxford 1501–40*, pp. 35, 530.
128. PRO PROB11/38/21; C1/1169/36–8; Borthwick Inst. Adm. 1542/4; *VCH East Riding Yorks*, iii (1976), 10.
129. PRO PROB 11/35/30; LAO 3Anc 8/1/3, pp. 6, 19, 20; Gunn, 'North Wales', p. 491.
130. *CPR 1553–4*, p. 384. I have been unable to identify the sixth chaplain.
131. *FOR*, pp. 231, 254; Baskerville, 'Married Clergy', p. 59; NRO NCC 278 Cowlles; PRO PROB11/42B/1.
132. *FOR*, p. 128; LAO Register 27, fos 62ʳ, 75ᵛ, 77ᶜ, 78ʳ, 79ʳ, 79ᵛ; 1Anc 3/1c/25, m. 23; 3/12/9, m. 16; 5/B/1e; 2Anc 2/6/26, 3/A/45; PRO C1/1392/35; STAC2/27/169.
133. Baskerville, 'Married Clergy', p. 217; LAO LCC Wills 1544–5&C ii, fo. 198; Borthwick Inst. Adm. 1544/5; A. G. Dickens, 'The Marian Reaction in the Diocese of York, part I', in his *Reformation Studies* (London, 1982), p. 107.
134. C. Garrett, *The Marian Exiles* (Cambridge, 1938), pp. 87–8, 244–5; Emden, *Oxford 1501–40*, p. 433; *LP* XIV. i. 684; *The Letter-Book of John Parkhurst*, ed. R. A. Houlbrooke (Norfolk Record Society 43, 1975), pp. 20–1.
135. Ibid., p. 21; J. Parkhurst, *Ludicra sive Epigrammata Iuvenilia* (London, 1573), pp. 11–12, 37–8.
136. Ibid., pp. 11–12, 72, 138; PRO PROB11/59/10.
137. Parkhurst, *Ludicra*, pp. 18, 19, 138.
138. M. Dowling, *Humanism in the Age of Henry VIII* (London, 1986), p. 237; LAO 3ANC 8/1/1, pp. 30–1.
139. LAO 3Anc 8/1/1, pp. 2–5.
140. *LP* XXI. i. 369, 1459; *SR* 33 Henry VIII, c. 25; O. de Smedt, *De engelse natie te Antwerpen in de 16e eeuw* (2 vols, Antwerp, 1950–4), ii. 116, 459, 563.
141. *LP* I. ii, p. 1511; II. i. 1510, 2296; ii, 3978; XIV. i. 535.
142. *LP* XIV. ii, pp. 333, 338, 340; XX. ii, 342, 602; XXI. i. 1491.
143. I. Blanchard, 'English lead and the International Bullion Crisis of the 1550s', in *Trade, Government and Economy in Pre-Industrial England*, ed. D. C. Coleman, A. H. John (London, 1976), p. 22.
144. LAO 1Anc 11/C/1a. For what follows, see *Kölner Inventar*, ed. K. Höhlbaum, H. Keussen, i (Verein für Hansische Geschichte, Inventare Hansischer Archive des Sechszehnten Jahrhunderts 1, 1896), 15–20.
145. De Smedt, *Engelse natie* ii. 564; *LP* XX. i. 1055, 1240, 1247.
146. *LP* XVI. 220 (31); XX. ii. 259, 343, 598, 602.
147. PRO LR12/20/627; E318/20/1078.
148. Bodl. MS Ashmole 1109, fo. 143ʳ; *LP* XX. ii. 598.
149. *LP* XX. i. 250, 315, 322, 587, 634, 643.
150. H. Junius, *Epistolae* (Dordrecht, 1662), pp. 21–3, 36–8, 42–4, 144–6.
151. *Kölner Inventar*, p. 20; J. Roberts, *Holbein* (London, 1979), p. 15; P. Ganz, *The Paintings Of Hans Holbein* (London, 1950), no. 87.
152. Roberts, *Holbein*, p. 100; *LP* VII. 800; LAO 1Anc 11/C/1a.
153. Roberts, *Holbein*, p. 96; P. Ganz, 'A rediscovered Portrait of Charles Brandon, Duke of Suffolk, by Holbein', *Burlington Magazine*, 57 (1930), 59–60. The

authenticity of one of these portraits is now in doubt: J. Rowlands, *Holbein* (Oxford, 1985), p. 234.

154. *LP* XIX. i. 828, 1035 (111).
155. *LP* XX. i. 375; XXI ii. 648 *(36); Chronicle of King Henry VIII*, p. 139; Bodl. MS Ashmole 1109, fo. 143ʳ; PRO PROB11/35/18.
156. *LP* XVI. 36, 82, 350; XVIII. i. 163.
157. PRO C24/29, Haworth and Powis v. Suffolk, deposition of Sir William Sidney; PROB11/30/7.
158. Bindoff, *Commons* ii. 545; *LP* XX. i. 530, 1183, 1220.
159. Gunn, 'North Wales', p. 492; PRO WARD9/152.
160. *LP* XX. ii. 1067 (29); XXI i. 717 (1).
161. Gunn, 'North Wales', p. 464; *LP* V. 431, 1334; *Visitation of Shropshire* i. 147.
162. LAO Register 27, fo. 101ᵛ; *LP* XIX. i, p. 153.
163. *LP* XVI. 580 (11); XVII. 881 (25); *Records of the City of Oxford*, pp. 161, 168–9, 174.
164. PRO KB9/561/41.
165. *Visitations of Norfolk*, p. 15; Bodl. MS Ashmole 1109, fo. 144ʳ; LAO 1Anc 11/C/1b.
166. PRO CP40/1112, rot. 122ᵛ; 1121, rot. 334ʳ; *Great Yarmouth Assembly Minutes 1538–1545*, ed. P. Rutledge (Norfolk Record Society 39, 1970), pp. 58–9.
167. *LP* XIII. i. 646 (49). On the funeral see Bodl. MS Ashmole 1109, fos 143–5.
168. Bindoff, *Commons* iii. 2–3; PRO SC6/Add./3482/94, m. 4ʳ.
169. PRO LR12/27/922; *HMC Bath* iv. 32; *Suffolk 1561* i. 201, 205.
170. *Suffolk 1561* ii. 220.
171. LAO 2Anc 3/B/25; PRO WARD7/2/181–2.
172. *HMC Bath* iv. 30–1; PRO PROB11/27/33; *LP* XII. i. 440.
173. *LP* IX. 459; XX. i. 884, 1218; PRO PROB11/27/33; Foxe, *Acts and Monuments* v. 509.
174. *HMC Rutland* iv. 305, 316–17, 321, 338–9, 346.
175. *GEC* xi. 256; xii, pt. ii, p. 557; *LP* XXI. ii. 417, 419.
176. *LP* XVI. 961.
177. Smith, *Land and Politics*, p. 245; *LP* XVIII. ii. 118; *Visitation of Yorkshire*, p. 93; *HMC Bath* iv. 31.
178. *Lincs. Peds.* ii. 669; *HMC Bath* iv. 30–1.
179. *LP* XVI. 947 (74); *Yorkshire Fines*, i (Yorks. Arch. Soc. Rec. Ser. 2, 1887), 109.
180. Smith, *Land and Politics*, pp. 102, 227, 237.
181. PRO SC 12/23/29, fos 2ᵛ, 4ʳ.
182. *LP* XIII. i. 646 (27); XXI. i. 963 (41), p. 320.
183. *LP* XVI. 1266, 1272; XVII. 1079.
184. LAO 3Anc 8/1/3, p. 80.
185. F. Haslewood, *The Genealogy of the Family of Haslewood: Wickwarren, Belton and Maidwell Branches* (London, 1875), p. 8; *LP* XI. 1217 (23); XII. ii. 1150 (18); XIII. ii. 967 (26); XIV. i, p. 608; ii. 619 (38); XVI. 305 (80); XVIII. ii. 449 (79); XX. i. 282 (52), 620 (55); ii. 910 (52); PRO CP25(2)/26/172/46.
186. PRO CP25(2)/26/173/22; BL MS Add. 29549, fo. 6; *LP* XVI. 164.

187. *HMC Bath* iv. 31.
188. *LP* XX. i. p. 673; W. C. Richardson, *The History of the Court of Augmentations* (Baton Rouge, 1961), pp. 222–3.
189. *LP* XVIII. i. 135; XX. ii, App. 7; BL MS Add. 46501, fo. 3.
190. Bindoff, *Commons* i. 518; ii. 179; iii. 72, 638.
191. PRO KB9/557/63, 561/25; *LP* XIX. i. 837, 1023; ii. 317.
192. BL MS Add. 45716A, fos 50ʳ–53ʳ; PRO E101/423/1, 423/4, 423/7, 424/6; *LP* XVI. 1488 (4, 25).
193. PRO E210/8284; *LP* XX. ii. 427.
194. PRO SP1/209, fo. 33ᵛ (*LP* XX. ii. 598).
195. *LP* XX. i, pp. 269–70; PRO E318/20/1082, m. 2ᵛ.
196. PRO E318/20/1082, dated by Richardson, *Court of Augmentations*, p. 66.
197. *LP* XVII. 274; PRO E323/2B, pt. 1, m. 13ᵛ.
198. PRO E318/20/1078, 1082, m. 2ʳ; LR12/20/627.
199. PRO E163/15/23.
200. PRO SC12/23/29, fo. 3ʳ; LAO 1Anc 11/C/1a, fos 1ʳ–2ʳ; 3Anc 8/1/1, pp. 20–2, 46–7.
201. PRO E179/69/54; WARD9/149, fos 64ᵛ–65ᵛ.
202. L Stone, *Family and Fortune: Studies in Aristocratic Finance in the Sixteenth and Seventeenth Centuries* (Oxford, 1973), pp. 167, 212–13; PRO E163/15/23; *Report on the Manuscripts of Lord De L'Isle and Dudley*, i (HMC 77, 1925), 178, 202, 299.
203. PRO SC12/23/29, fos 4ᵛ–5ʳ; LAO 2Anc 3/A/49.
204. PRO WARD7/2/175–84; PROB11/31/29.
205. BL MS Add. 29549, fos 1, 3 (*LP* XVI. 164, 714); PRO E210/8284.
206. Penshurst, De L'Isle and Dudley papers 1198 (BL Film M 772 (54)); LAO 3Anc 8/1/3, pp. 21–4, 31a, 34–6, 101–2.
207. PRO KB27/1123, rot. 22.
208. PRO E318/20/1077, m. 1; C54/426, mm 34–5; *LP* XVII. 137 (22).
209. *LP* XVII. 137 (34, 57), 362 (53).
210. LAO 2Anc 3/B/17, 19; PRO C1/1151/11; C54/431, mm 48–9.
211. *LP* XIII. ii. 1182 (18, m, n); LAO 2Anc 3/B/20; PRO C54/442, m. 31.
212. PRO E210/8284.
213. *LP* XVI. 580 (9); PRO C54/439, mm 6–7.
214. LAO 2Anc 3/A/51; PRO CP25(2)/26/174/32.
215. House of Lords Record Office, Original Acts, 37 Henry VIII, c. 26.
216. *LP* XIX. i, p. 506.
217. *HMC Bath* iv. 67, 84–5; *LP* XVII. 1031.
218. PRO E179/380/15–17.
219. *Lincs. Peds.* i. 217; *LP* XX. i, p. 316.
220. PRO WARD7/2/181–2; *LP* XV. 942 (12).
221. *Lincs. Peds.* i. 176; *LP* V. 838 (27); PRO WARD7/2/173–4.
222. Walker, 'John of Gaunt', p. 83; Cherry, 'Courtenay Earls of Devon', p. 75; Smith, *County and Court*, p. 32.
223. *LP* XVI. 305 (67); XX. i, pp. 316–17.
224. PRO KB9/554/35, 556/19, 557/99, 560/136, 140, 564/49–51, 52, 54; C67/74, m. 17; C193/12/1, fos 20ᵛ–21ʳ.
225. PRO KB9/550/140, 563/5; *The Records of the Commissioners of Sewers in the Parts

of Holland 1547–1603, i, ed. A. M. Kirkus (Lincoln Record Soc. 54, 1959), pp. 59–60.

226. *LP* XXI. ii. 472; PRO Cl/1034/67; STAC2/4/52; Bindoff, *Commons* ii. 278–9, 607–8; iii. 2–3, 260–1.

227. PRO E179/137/404/2; *LP* XV. 381; LAO 3Anc 8/1/3, pp. 5–6.

228. LAO 3Anc 8/1/3 pp. 1, 33, 101–2; Bodl. MS Ashmole 1109, fo. 145^v; PRO PROB11/36/18; De L'Isle and Dudley Papers 1198; *Suffolk 1561* ii. 220; Leland, *Itinerary* v. 34.

229. LAO LCC Wills 1589, fo. 31.

230. W. Dugdale, *Monasticon Anglicanum*, ed. J. Caley, H. Ellis, B. Bandinel (8 vols, London, 1817–30), iv. 474; PRO PROB11/31/29.

231. LAO 3Anc 8/1/3, pp. 29–31, 38–40; LCC Wills 1543–5, fo. 386^r; 1545–6 i, fo. 239^v.

232. *Val. Eccles.* iv. 43; PRO CP25(2)/26/174/14; De L'Isle and Dudley Papers 1198; 37 Henry VIII, c. 26; Bodl. MS Ashmole 1109, fo. 145^r.

233. PRO C1/1006/7,1034/67; LAO 3Anc 8/1/3, pp. 40–2; LCC Wills 1569 i, fo. 211^v; *Lincs. Wills* i. 22, 34; *Lincs. Peds.* iii. 1116–18; PRO PROB11/41/72.

234. PRO E179/137/370/19, 28, 404/5, 421/5, 426/6; LAO 1Anc 3/25/51; 3 Anc 8/1/ 3, pp. 12–14; PRO PROB11/31/40; *Lincs. Peds.* ii. 447.

235. PRO CP25(2)/26/172/43; *Lincs. Peds.* i. 115; Bodl. MS Ashmole 1109, fo. 143^r; LAO 3Anc 8/1/3, pp. 49–57, 103.

236. PRO C1/1006/7, 1127/1; CP40/1118, rot. 537^r; 1122, rot. 422^r; PROB11/36/26; STAC2/13/248.

237. PRO PROB11/34/22; *Lincs. Wills* i. 49; *CAD* v. A12403.

238. PRO PROB11/36/26, 37/11; STAC2/10/140; CP25/(2)/26/174/42.

239. *LP* XVIII. ii. 449 (28); XIX. ii. 166 (28); XXI. ii. 648 (22); *Lincs. Peds.* i. 176; PRO CP25(2)/26/173/16, 26/174/50, 51.

240. Tempest, 'Tattershall', p. 72; PRO PROB11/36/26; REQ2/3/278; *Lincs. Peds.* ii. 421; Bodl. MS Ashmole 1109, fo. 144^r.

241. *Lincs. Peds.* i. 135; iii. 849; Bindoff, *Commons* i. 488.

242. *Lincs. Peds.* ii. 403; *LP* XVIII. i. 623 (28); PRO Cl/1111/131; El79/137/404/7; KB9/546/51; PROB11/27/13.

243. LAO 2Anc 3/A/42; 3Anc 8/1/3 pp. 31a, 87; PRO CP40/1121, rot. 334^r; Harris, *Buckingham*, p. 138; M. E. James, 'A Tudor Magnate and the Tudor State: Henry, fifth earl of Northumberland', in *Society, Politics and Culture*, p. 53.

244. Cherry, 'Courtenay Earls of Devon', p. 79.

245. PRO PROB11/31/29; LAO LCC Wills 1545–6 i, fo. 239^v; 3Anc 8/1/3 p. 27.

246. Rowney, 'Resources and Retaining in Yorkist England', pp. 144–50.

247. PRO PROB11/26/8, 11, 14, 16, 27/13.

248. PRO PROB11/31/29, 40, 32/9; LAO LCC Wills 1541, fo. 9^r; 1541–3, fo. 48^v; 1543–5, fo. 386^r; 1545–6 i, fo. 239^v.

249. Bindoff, *Commons* i. 488; PRO PROB11/34/22, 35/18, 36/18, 26, 37/11.

250. PRO PROB11/39/54, 41/72; LAO LCC

Wills 1553–5 & 6, fo. 208; 1558 iv, fos 41, 226; 1565, fo. 103^v; 1569 i, fo. 211^v; Bindoff, *Commons* iii. 261.

251. Wilson, *Tudor Tapestry*, p. 167.

252. Starkey, *Reign of Henry VIII*, p. 156; James, 'Obedience and Dissent', p. 45; *LP* Add. ii. 1477; PRO E192/2 Account book, fos 41^r, 43^r.

253. *Lincs. Peds.* ii. 472, 481–3; iii. 895; *LP* XIII. i. 795; XVI. 379 (46), 947 (34); XVII. 1154 (37); XVIII. i. 226 (72); XIX. i, p. 386; PRO WARD9/152; E192/2 Early draft will, m. 3; Account book, fo. 46^r.

254. *LP* XIII. i. 1115 (1); PRO CP25(2)/26/173/18; E179/137/370/19; Leland, *Itinerary* v. 37; *Lincs. Peds.* iii. 889. Willoughby was knighted in 1542.

255. Starkey, *Reign of Henry VIII*, p. 156; *LP* XIII. i. 795; *Test. Vet.* ii. 709; PRO E192/2 Later draft will, m. 1; E315/161/11, 12, 14, 25^v; P. W. Hasler, *The History of Parliament: The House of Commons 1558–1603* (London, 1981), iii. 537–8. Tyrwhit was knighted in 1543.

256. PRO WARD9/152; *LP* XVI, 580 (93); *Lincs. Peds.* i. 136.

257. *LP* XVI. 379 (59); XVII, p. 698.

258. PRO WARD9/152.

259. *Lincs. Peds.* iii. 1019; LAO MM1/16/12; *HMC Bath* iv. 32.

260. PRO WARD9/149, fo. 145^v; Bindoff, *Commons* ii. 278.

261. PRO E179/137/370: the Heneages, Dymokes, Tyrwhits, Skipwiths, and Willoughbys.

262. e.g. Sir Edward Madison, Sir Thomas Missenden, and Sir Thomas Massingberd.

263. LAO 1Anc 3/12/9, m. 12; 13/19, m. 22.

264. LAO 3Anc 8/1/3, pp. 15–16; PRO CP40/1123, rot. 331^r.

265. LAO 1Anc 3/25/25/3, 25/31/4; PRO Cl/1034/67.

266. PRO C1/1006/6–7, 1034/67.

267. *Lincs. Peds.* ii. 680–1; *LP* XIII. i. 623 (4, 13); PRO STAC2/2/103.

268. *Lincs. Peds.* iii. 946–7; PRO C1/1156/14; REQ2/3/278.

269. PRO C1/1123/90–1; STAC2/11/101; WARD9/152.

270. Walker, 'John of Gaunt', pp. 139–54.

271. LAO Mon 7/7, fos 29–33; LC1/1/1/1, fos 231–59; PRO CP40/1091, rot. 432; 1094, rot. 137^r.

272. PRO STAC2/13/257, 16/220; CP25(2)/25/166/98, 25/167/38, 26/174/29, 26/ 175/3; E179/137/422/27.

273. PRO STAC2/13/265.

274. PRO STAC2/13/248–9, 257–66.

275. LAO LC1/1/1/2, fo. 34^v; PRO STAC2/32/71.

276. LAO 1Anc 3/1C/25, mm 19, 21,23; 7/19; 12/9, mm. 14,16; 16/24, m. 17; 21/103; 2Anc 2/6/26.

277. *HMC Salisbury* i. 80–1; *HMC Rutland* i. 56.

278. Hill, *Lincoln*, p. 52; LAO LC1/1/1/2, fos 24^r, 26^r, 33^v.

279. PRO C1/1116/71; STAC2/11/12.

280. PRO CP25(2)/26/172/3, 26/174/35, 26/175/1; Cl/1076/26–7; KB27/1131, rot.

71ʳ; *Records of Lincoln's Inn* i. 39, 41; PRO E179/137/404/2b, 3.

281. PRO STAC2/10/22–3, 25.

282. PRO C1/1161/8; KB27/1136, rot. 153ʳ.

283. Bodl. MS Ashmole 1109, fo. 143ʳ; LAO 2Anc 2/6/26; 3Anc 8/1/3 pp. 1, 37.

284. *LP* IV. i. 970 (2) (misdated); XVI. 1090, 1126; XVII. 312 (2); LAO LC1/1/1/2, fo. 32ʳ.

285. LAO LC1/1/1/2, fos 4ʳ, 16ᵛ, 25ʳ, 35ᵛ–36ʳ; the phrase was Sir Robert Tyrwhit jun.'s.

286. Bindoff, *Commons* i. 133.

287. PRO E179/137/370/19; E318/20/1079, m. 2; Bodl. MS Ashmole 1109 fo. 143ʳ.

288. MacCulloch, *Suffolk*, p. 68; LAO 3Anc 8/1/3 pp. 34–6; Leland, *Itinerary* v. 37.

289. Ibid. i. 23; T. Fuller, *The History of the Worthies of England*, ed. P. A. Nuttall (London, 1840), ii. 266.

290. LAO 1Anc 7/A/l, fos 17ᵛ–41ʳ

291. LAO 3Anc 8/1/1, p. 51.

292. Anstis, *Garter* i. 419–20; *LP* XIX. ii. 690 (37); LAO 3Anc 8/1/1, pp. 16–19.

293. LAO 3Anc 8/1/1, pp. 7–8; P. Ganz, *Die Handzeichnungen des Hans Holbein D.J.* (Berlin, 1937), no. 100; HMC *Bath* iv. 67; *Test. Vet.* ii. 652.

294. HMC *Rutland* i. 32; *LP* XXL ii. 61; Bindoff, *Commons* iii. 260–1.

295. *LP* XX. ii. 849, 1067 (47), 1068 (34).

296. *LP* XXI. i. 289, 504 (20); ii. 475 ('04–5).

297. LAO 3Anc 8/1/1, p. 5; Dowling, *Humanism*, p. 212.

298. T. Wilson, *The Arte of Rhetorique* (London, 1553), fos 8ᵛ–9ʳ; Wriothesley, *Chronicle* i. 160.

299. M. B. Davies, 'Boulogne and Calais from 1545 to 1550', *Fouad I Univ. Bull. Faculty of Arts* 12 (1950), 25.

300. Hall, p. 863.

301. Read, *Catherine, Duchess of Suffolk*, p. 49; Bodl. MS Ashmole 1109, fo. 145ᵛ.

302. LAO 1Anc 10/A/3, fos 1–3; HMC *Ancaster*, pp. 453–6.

303. *Lincs. Wills* i. 36; Tempest, 'Tattershall', p. 72.

304. W. H. Dunham, *Lord Hastings' Indentured Retainers, 1461–1483* (Transactions of the Connecticut Academy of Arts and Sciences 39, 1955), p. 18; LAO 3Anc 8/1/1, p. 30.

305. PRO C24/28, Haworth and Powis v. Suffolk, deposition of John Gedge.

7 Conclusion

1. Ives, *Anne Boleyn*, pp. 207, 218, 231. Henry's sudden visit of late July 1532, though, rests only on information reaching the Venetian ambassador at London. Would the king really have travelled from Ampthill (Beds.) to Grafton (Northants.) via Ewelme (Oxon.)? See *LP* V. 1207, 1270.

2. J. Lydgate, *The Fall of Princes*, ed. H. Bergen (4 vols, EETS extra ser. 121–4, 1924–7), ii. 441–2, iv. 55.

3. *Medieval English Lyrics*, ed. R. T. Davies (London, 1963), p. 154; R. F. Green, *Poets and Princepleasers, Literature and the English Court in the Late Middle Ages* (Toronto, 1980), p. 29.

4. W. R. B. Robinson, 'Early Tudor Policy towards Wales Part 2: The Welsh Offices held by Henry Earl of Worcester (1526–1549)', *Bulletin of the Board of Celtic Studies* 21 (1964–6), 45–7; E. W. Ives, 'Patronage at the Court of Henry VIII: the Case of Sir Ralph Egerton of Ridley', *Bulletin of the John Rylands Library* 52 (1969–70), 365–6.

5. Coward, *Stanleys*, p. 25; Virgoe, 'Recovery of the Howards', p. 20.

6. Harris, *Buckingham*, pp. 133–4; L. Stone, *The Crisis of the Aristocracy, 1558–1641* (Oxford, 1965), pp. 273–334, 542.

7. Harris, *Buckingham*, pp. 104, 282.

8. J. Hurstfield, *The Queen's Wards* (London, 1958), pp. 280–1; idem, 'Corruption and Reform under Edward VI and Mary: the example of Wardship', in his *Freedom, Corruption and Government in Elizabethan England* (London, 1973), pp. 166–8; C. Cross, *The Puritan Earl: the Life of Henry Hastings, Third Earl of Huntingdon 1536–1595* (London, 1966), pp. 99–105.

9. Miller, *English Nobility*, p. 255.

10. Willen, *John Russell*, pp. 73–81.

11. Walker, 'John of Gaunt', pp. 190–3, 244–9; Carpenter, 'Clarence and the Midlands', pp. 34–5; James, 'Change and Continuity in the Tudor North', pp. 100–1.

12. Loades, *Tudor Court*, p. 142.

13. Ibid., pp. 144, 187–8; M. E. James, 'At a Crossroads of the Political Culture: the Essex Revolt, 1601', in *Society, Politics and Culture.*

14. Stone, *Crisis*, pp. 210–11; S. L. Adams, 'Eliza Enthroned: the Court and its Politics', in *The Reign of Elizabeth I*, ed. C. A. Haigh (London, 1984); D. Wilson, *Sweet Robin: a Biography of Robert Dudley, Earl of Leicester, 1533–1588* (London, 1981), pp. 158- 62; W. Hunt, *The Puritan Moment: the Coming of Revolution in an English County* (Cambridge, Mass., 1983), pp. 160–72.

15. P. Clark, *English Provincial Society from the Reformation to the Revolution: Religion, Politics and Society in Kent, 1500–1640* (Hassocks, 1977), pp. 49–57.

16. Willen, *John Russell*, pp. 23, 32–3, 41–3.

17. BL MS Cotton Caligula DVI, fo. 184ᵛ (*LP* II. i. 80); MS Cotton Vespasian FXIII, fo. 153 (*LP* II. i. 367).

18. K. Muir, *The Life and Letters of Sir Thomas Wyatt* (Liverpool, 1963), p. 201.

19. e.g. annuities to Dorothy Verney (PRO LR12/21/636), Elizabeth Hall and Margaret Blakeborne (WARD7/2/179–80), and Anne Kyng, late nurse to Lady Frances (LAO 2Anc 3/B/25).

20. Christopher Jenny: PRO Cl/934/17; LAO 1Anc 11/C/la, b. Francis Monford: Bindoff, *Commons* ii. 611; PRO CP40/1063, rot. 430, Cf. C. Rawcliffe, S. Flower, 'English Noblemen and their Advisers: Consultation and Collaboration in the Later Middle Ages', *Journal of British Studies* 25 (1986), 165–8.

Bibliography

This is intended as a bibliography of manuscripts and printed primary sources and is not intended to cover any secondary works.

Manuscript sources
Bangor, University College of North Wales
Library
    Penrhyn MSS
    Brussels, Archives Generates du Royaume
    Conseil d'État et Audience 39
(Correspondence of Margaret of Austria)
    Conseil d'État et Audience 99, 1630,
1661 (Correspondence of Mary of Hungary)
Cambridge, University Library
    Additional MS 4875 (Acton transcripts)
    MS Hengrave 3
    MSS Mm 1.41, 1.45 (Baker MSS)
Carlisle, Cumbria Record Office
    D/Pen/32 (Muncaster Deposit, Pennington
Deeds)
Chelmsford, Essex Record Office
    D/B 3 (Maldon Borough Chamberlain's
Accounts)
    D/DRg (Birch Hall Estate Papers)
Coventry, City Record Office
    A 79/26 (Letter from Henry VIII, 1513)
Hawarden, Clwyd Record Office
    D/PT (Plas Teg MSS)
Ipswich, East Suffolk Record Office
    EE 2 (Eye Borough Records)
    HA 11 (Rous Papers)
    HA 18 (Long Papers)
    HE 10/1 (Benhall Manorial Court Rolls)
    T 1 (Kettlebaston Estate Records)
    T4373 (Iveagh Papers)
    T4374 (Cornwallis Papers)
King's Lynn, Borough Record Office
    KL/C (Chamberlain's accounts)
Lille, Archives Departementales du Nord
    B 2442 (Accounts of Treasurer-General of
War, 1544)
    B 3345 (Household Accounts of Archduke
Charles, 1513)
    B 18864, 18871 (Correspondence of

Margaret of Austria) Lincoln, Lincolnshire
Archives Office
    1–8 Anc (Ancaster Deposits)
    Episcopal Registers
    Lincoln Consistory Court Wills
    LC 1/1/1 (City Council minutes)
    LMR (Lindsey Manorial Records)
    Mon (Monson Deposit)
    MM 1 (Montgomery Massingberd Deposit)
    PAR St James Louth 7/2 (Churchwardens'
Accounts)
London British Library
    Additional Charters and Rolls
    Additional MSS 6113, 6297, 12462, 14840,
21480, 25114, 28578, 29549, 30543, 33376,
33748, 45716A, 46501
    Cotton Charters
    Cotton MSS Caligula B VI, D VI, DIX,
D XI, EII; Claudius C III; Faustina E I, E
VII; Galba B VI; Titus B I; Vespasian F XIII;
Appendix L
    Egerton MSS 985, 2092, 2713, 3025
    Egerton Roll 8796
    Harleian Charters
    Harleian MSS 283, 1664
    Lansdowne MSS 1, 818
    Stowe MSS 141, 146
    Film M 772 (54) (Penshurst, De L'Isle and
Dudley Papers 1198)
London College of Arms
    Heralds' MSS
    M Series MSS
    R Series MSS
    Tournament Cheques
London Guildhall Library
    MS 7086/1 (Pewterers' Company, Wardens'
Accounts)
London House of Lords Record Office
    Original Acts
London Lambeth Palace Library

Registers of the Archbishops of Canterbury
London Public Record Office, Chancery Lane
C 1 (Early Chancery Proceedings)
C 24 (Town Depositions)
C 43 (Pleadings in Chancery, Common Law Side)
C 47 (Chancery Miscellanea)
C 54 (Close Rolls)
C 66 (Patent Rolls)
C 82 (Warrants for the Great Seal)
C 142 (Inquisitions Post Mortem)
C 244 (Tower and Rolls Chapel, Corpus cum Causa)
C 260 (Tower and Rolls Chapel, Recorda)
CP 25 (2) (Feet of Fines)
CP 40 (Common Pleas, Plea Rolls)
DL 10 (Duchy of Lancaster, Royal Charters)
DL 28 (Duchy of Lancaster, Receiver-General's Accounts)
DL 30 (Court Rolls)
E 30 (Diplomatic Documents)
E 36 (Treasury of Receipt, Miscellaneous Books)
E 41 (Original Deeds)
E 101 (Accounts, Various)
E 122 (Customs Accounts)
E 137 (Estreat Rolls)
E 150 (Inquisitions Post Mortem)
E 163 (Exchequer Miscellanea)
E 179 (Lay Subsidy Rolls)
E 192/2 (Heneage Papers)
E 198 (Returns of Knights' Fees)
E 305 (Augmentations Office, Deeds of Purchase and Exchange)
E 313 (Letters Patent)
E 314 (Augmentations Office, Miscellanea)
E 315 (Augmentations Office, Miscellaneous Books)
E 318 (Particulars for Grants)
E 321 (Proceedings in the Court of Augmentations)
E 323 (Court of Augmentations, Treasurer's Accounts)
E 326 (Augmentations Office, Ancient Deeds)
E 404 (Writs and Warrants for Issues)
E 405 (Rolls of Receipts and Issues)
IND (Index Volumes and Rolls)
KB 9 (King's Bench, Ancient Indictments)
KB 27 (King's Bench, De Banco Rolls)
KB 29 (King's Bench, Controlment Rolls)
LC 2 (Records of Special Events)
LR 1 (Auditors of Land Revenue, Enrolments)
LR 3 (Court Rolls)
LR 12 (Receivers' Accounts)
LR 15 (Ancient Deeds)
PRO 31/18 (Vienna Transcripts)
PROB 10 (Prerogative Court of Canterbury, Filed Wills)
PROB 11 (Prerogative Court of Canterbury, Registered Copy Wills)
REQ 2 (Court of Requests Proceedings)
SC 2 (Court Rolls)
SC 6 (Ministers' Accounts)
SC 11 (Rentals and Surveys)
SC 12 (Rentals and Surveys)
SP 1 (State Papers, Henry VIII)
SP 2 (State Papers, Henry VIII, Folios)
SP 5 (Suppression Papers)
SP 46 (State Papers Domestic, Supplementary)
STAC 2 (Star Chamber Proceedings)
WARD 7 (Inquisitions Post Mortem)
WARD 9 (Court of Wards, Miscellaneous Books)
Longleat House
Miscellaneous Volume 11 (Household Account of John, Earl of Oxford)
Miscellaneous Volumes 18, 19 (Kitchen Accounts of Edward, Earl of Hertford)
Norwich, Norfolk Record Office
Act 4 (Episcopal Act Books)
Bishops' Registers
Bulwer MSS
Jerningham MSS
Norwich City Records
Norwich Consistory Court Will Registers
Oxford, Bodleian Library
Ashmole MSS 852, 857, 862, 1109, 1115, 1116
MS DD All Souls College Archive c.280 (Bursars' Accounts)
MS Jesus College 74 (Thomas Master's Collections)
MS Suffolk Charters 229
Tanner MSS 135, 137, 141
MSS Topographical Berkshire
MSS Topographical Suffolk Wood MS F33
Paris Archives Nationales
J 922, 923, 966 (Trésor des chartes, mélanges)
K 80 (Cartons des rois)
KK 99, 100, (Comptes royaux)
KK 349 (Comptes particuliers et divers)
Paris Bibliotheque Nationale
MSS Dupuy 462, 486, 726
MSS Français (Anciens fonds) 2932, 2997, 3014–5, 3021, 3087, 5499, 6622, 12158, 20521, 20994
Reading, Berkshire Record Office
WI/Fac 1 (New Windsor Chamberlains' Accounts)
San Marino, Henry E. Huntington Library
Ellesmere MSS 2652, 2654—5 (extracts from lost Privy Council Registers)
Stratford-upon-Avon, Shakespeare's Birthplace Trust Record Office
DR 5 (Throckmorton MSS)
Vienna, Haus-, Hof-, und Staatsarchiv
PA 14, 15 (Correspondence of Margaret of Austria and Mary of Hungary)
York, Borthwick Institute of Historical Research
Admissions to Benefices, Diocese of York

Printed primary sources

Acts of Court of the Mercers Company, 1453–1527, ed. L. Lyell, F. D. Watney (Cambridge, 1936).
Ambassades en Angleterre de Jean du Bellay, ed. V.-L. Bourrilly, P. de Vaissière (Archives de l'histoire religieuse de la France, 1905).
Analectes historiques, ed. A. J. G. Le Glay (Paris, 1838).
The Anglica Historia of Polydore Vergil A.D.

1485–1537, ed. D. Hay (Cam. Soc. 3rd ser. 74, 1950).

Anglo, S., *The Great Tournament Roll of Westminster* (2 vols, Oxford, 1968).

Anstis, J., *The Register of the Most Noble Order of the Garter* (2 vols, London, 1724).

The Antiquarian Repertory, ed. F. Grose, T. Astle (new edn, 4 vols, London, 1807–9).

Archbold, W. A. J., 'A Diary of the Expedition of 1544', *EHR* 16 (1901).

Bacon, N., *The Annalls of Ipswiche*, ed. W. H. Richardson (Ipswich, 1884).

Bale, J., 'The Image of Both Churches', *Select Works*, ed. H. Christmas (Parker Soc. 36, 1849).

Bale, J., *Scriptorum Illustrium Maioris Brytannie ....Catalogus* (Basle, 1557–9).

Baskerville, G., 'Married Clergy and Pensioned Religious in Norwich Diocese, 1555', *EHR* 48 (1933).

Calendar of Inquisitions Post Mortem, Henry VII (3 vols, London, 1898–1955).

Calendar of State Papers, Milan (1385–1618), ed. A. B. Hinds (London, 1912).

Calendar of State Papers, Spanish, ed. G. A. Bergenroth, P. de Gayangos, M. A. S. Hume, G. Mattingly (15 vols, London, 1862–1954).

Calendar of State Papers, Venetian, ed. R. Brown, C. Bentinck, H. Brown (9 vols, London, 1864–98).

Calendar of the Close Rolls, Henry VII (2 vols, London, 1953–63).

Calendar of the Manuscripts of the Most Hon. the Marquis of Salisbury, ii, xiii (HMC 9, 1888, 1915).

Calendar of the Patent Rolls, Henry VI–Philip and Mary (21 vols, London, 1901–39).

The Cartulary of Oseney Abbey, vi, ed. H. E. Salter (Oxford Historical Society 101, 1936).

Catalogue des actes de François Ier (10 vols, Academie des Sciences Morales et Politiques, Collection des Ordonnances des Rois de France, 1887–1908).

Cavendish, G., *The Life and Death of Cardinal Wolsey*, ed. R. S. Sylvester (EETS 243, 1959).

The Chronicle of Calais, ed. J. G. Nichols (Cam. Soc. 35, 1846).

Chronicle of the Grey Friars of London, ed. J. G. Nichols (Cam. Soc. 53, 1852).

Chronicle of King Henry VIII of England, ed M. A. S. Hume (London, 1889).

Clifford Letters of the Sixteenth Century, ed. A. G. Dickens (Surtees Soc. 172, 1962).

Cobbett, W., et al., *State Trials*, i (5th edn, London, 1809).

A Collection of Ordinances and Regulations for the Government of the Royal Household (London, Society of Antiquaries, 1790).

Correspondance du Cardinal Jean du Bellay, ed. R. Scheurer (2 vols, Société de l'Histoire de France, 1969–73).

Correspondance politique de MM. de Castillon et de Marillac, ed. J. Kaulek (Paris, 1888).

Davies, M. B., 'The "Enterprises" of Paris and Boulogne', *Fouad I University, Bulletin of the Faculty of Arts*, 11 (1949).

—— 'Boulogne and Calais from 1545 to 1550', ibid. 12 (1950).

The Declaracio[n] made at Poules Crosse in the cytye of London, the fourth sonday of Advent, by A. Seyton, and mayster W. Tolwyn, in MDXLI (London, 1542).

Descriptive Catalogue of Ancient Deeds in the Public Record Office (6 vols, London, 1890–1915).

I diarii di Marino Sanuto, 50, ed. F. Stefani et al. (Venice, 1897).

The Domesday of Inclosures, ed. I. S. Leadam (2 vols, London, 1897).

Ehses, S., *Römische Dokumente zur Geschichte der Ehescheidung Heinrichs VIII von England, 1527–1534* (Paderborn, 1893).

'Ely Episcopal Registers', *Ely Diocesan Remembrancer*, 305–12 (1910–11).

Excerpta Historica, ed. S. Bentley (London, 1831).

Faculty Office Registers, 1534–1549, ed. D. S. Chambers (Oxford, 1966).

Ffoulkes, C., 'Jousting Cheques of the Sixteenth Century', *Archaeologia*, 63 (1912).

Foxe, J., *Acts and Monuments*, ed. S. R. Cattley, G. Townsend (8 vols, London, 1837–41).

Fulwell, U., *The Flower of Fame* (London, 1575).

Godefroy, T., *Le Cérémonial françois* (2nd edn, Paris, 1649).

The Great Chronicle of London, ed. A. A. Thomas, I. D. Thornley (London, 1938).

Great Yarmouth Assembly Minutes 1538–1545, ed. P. Rutledge (Norfolk Record Soc. 39, 1970).

Gurney, D., 'Extracts from the Household and Privy Purse Accounts of the Lestranges of Hunstanton, from A.D. 1519 to A.D. 1578', *Archaeologia*, 25 (1834).

'Hagworthingham Church Book', Lincolnshire Notes and Queries, 1 (1888–9).

Hall, E., *Hall's Chronicle* (London, 1809 edn).

The Hamilton Papers, ed. J. Bain (2 vols, Edinburgh, 1890–2).

Harpsfield, N., *The Pretended Divorce between Henry VIII and Catherine of Aragon*, ed. N. Pocock (Cam. Soc. NS 21, 1878).

Hazlitt, W. C., *Remains of the Early Popular Poetry of England* (4 vols, London, 1864–6).

Historical Manuscripts Commission, *Third Report* (London, 1872).

Historical Manuscripts Commission, *Fifth Report* (London, 1876).

Historical Manuscripts Commission, *Eighth Report*, ii (London, 1881).

Historical Manuscripts Commission, *Ninth Report*, i, ii (London, 1883–4).

Hope, W. St. J., 'The Last Testament and Inventory of John de Veer, thirteenth Earl of Oxford', *Archaeologia*, 66 (1915).

Hoyle, R. W., 'Thomas Master's Narrative of the Pilgrimage of Grace', *Northern History*, 21 (1985).

'Inventory of the Wardrobe, Plate, & c. of Henry Fitzroy, Duke of Richmond and Somerset',

ed. J. G. Nichols, *The Camden Miscellany*, 3 (Cam. Soc. 61, 1855).
The Itinerary of John Leland, ed. L. T. Smith (5 vols, London, 1907–10).

Jeayes, I. H., *Descriptive Catalogue of the Charters and Muniments at Berkeley Castle* (Bristol, 1892).
Le Journal de Jean Barrillon, ed. P. de Vaissière (2 vols, Soc. de l'Hist. de France, 1897–9).
Journal de Louise de Savoie, ed. C. B. Petitot (Collection Complète des Mémoires relatifs a l'Histoire de France 16, 1826).
Journals of the House of Lords (10 vols, London, 1846).
Junius, H., *Epistolae* (Dordrecht, 1662).

'King Henry VIII's Jewel Book', ed. E. Trollope, *Reports and Papers of the Associated Architectural Societies*, 17 (1884).
Knox, J., *Works*, ed. D. Laing (6 vols, Edinburgh, 1846–64).
Kölner Inventar, ed. K. Höhlbaum, H. Keussen, i (Verein für Hansische Geschichte, Inventare Hansischer Archive des Sechszshnten Jahrhunderts, 1, 1896).

The Letter Book of John Parkhurst, ed. R. A. Houlbrooke (Norfolk Record Soc. 43, 1975).
Letters and Papers, Foreign and Domestic, of the Reign of Henry VIII, ed. J. S. Brewer, J. Gairdner, R. H. Brodie (22 vols in 35, London, 1862–1932).
Letters and Papers Illustrative of the Reigns of Richard III and Henry VII, ed. J. Gairdner (2 vols, Rolls Ser. 24, 1861–3).
Letters and Papers of the Verney Family, ed. J. Bruce (Cam. Soc. 56, 1853).
Letters of Richard Fox, 1486–1527, ed. P. S. and H. M. Allen (Oxford, 1929).
Letters Relating to the Suppression of Monasteries, ed. T. Wright (Cam. Soc. 26, 1843).
The Life of Cardinal Wolsey by George Cavendish, ed. S. W. Singer (2 vols, London, 1825).
The Life of Fisher, ed. R. Bayne (EETS extra ser. 117, 1921).
Lincolnshire Pedigrees, ed. A. R. Maddison (4 vols, Harl. Soc. 50–2, 54, 1902—6).
Lincolnshire Wills, 1500–1600, ed. A. R. Maddison (Lincoln, 1888).
The Lisle Letters, ed. M. St. C. Byrne (6 vols, London, 1981).
Lodge, E., *Illustrations of British History* (3 vols, London, 1791).
Lydgate, J., *The Fall of Princes*, ed. H. Bergen (4 vols, EETS extra ser. 121—4, 1924–7).

Macquereau, R., *Traicté et recueil de la Maison de Bourgoigne*, ed. J. A. C. Buchon (Chroniques et Mémoires sur l'Histoire de France 16, 1838).
Malory, T., *The Works of Sir Thomas Malory*, ed. E. Vinaver (3 vols, Oxford, 1947).
Manners and Meals in Olden Time, ed. F. J. Furnivall (EETS 32, 1868).
The Manuscripts of the Corporations of Southampton and King's Lynn (HMC 11.3, 1887).
The Manuscripts of the Earl of Dartmouth, iii (HMC 15.1, 1896).
The Manuscripts of the Earl of Westmorland and others (HMC 10.4, 1885).
Manwood, J., *A Treatise and Discourse of the Lawes of the Forrest* (London, 1598).
Marche, O. de la, *Mémoires*, iv, ed. H. Beaune, J. d'Arbaumont (Soc. de l'Hist. de France, 1888).
Materials for a History of the Reign of Henry VII, ed. W. Campbell (2 vols, Rolls Series 60, 1873–7).
Medieval English Lyrics, ed. R. T. Davies (London, 1963).
Montfaucon, B. de, *Les Monumens de la monarchie françoise* (5 vols, Paris, 1729–33).
Myers, A. R., *The Household of Edward IV* (Manchester, 1959).

Narratives of the Days of the Reformation, ed. J. G. Nichols (Cam. Soc. 77, 1859).
Négociations diplomatiques entre la France et l'Autriche, ed. E. A. J. Le Glay (2 vols, Documents Inédits sur l'Histoire de France, 1845).
Nicolas, N. H., *Testamenta Vetusta* (2 vols, London, 1826).
'Norfolk Subsidy Roll, 15 Hen. VIII', ed. W. Rye, *Norfolk Antiquarian Miscellany*, 2 (1883).

Opus Epistolarum Desiderii Erasmi Roterodami, ed. P. S. Allen (12 vols, Oxford, 1906- 58).

Palsgrave, J., *The Comedy of Acolastus*, ed. P. L. Carver (EETS 202, 1937).
— *L'Éclairassement de la langue française*, ed. F. Génin (Docs. Inédits sur l'Hist. de France, 1852).
Parkhurst, J., *Ludicra sive Epigrammata Iuvenilia* (London, 1573).
Paynel, T., *The Assaute and Co[n]quest of Heven tra[n]slated out of Frenche into Englishe* (London, 1530).
— translated from D. Erasmus, *De Contemptu Mundi* (London, 1533).
Persius, *The Satires*, ed. J. R. Jenkinson (Warminster, 1980).
Privy Purse Expenses of the Princess Mary, ed. F. Madden (London, 1831).

Records of Plays and Players in Norfolk and Suffolk, 1330–1642, ed. G. R. Proudfoot (Malone Soc. Collections 11, 1980).
The Records of the Commissioners of Sewers in the Parts of Holland, i, ed. A. M. Kirkus (Lincoln Record Soc. 54, 1959).
The Records of the Honourable Society of Lincoln's Inn (2 vols, London, 1896).
The Register of Admissions to Gray's Inn, 1521–1889, ed. J. Foster (London, 1889).
The Register or Chronicle of Butley Priory, Suffolk 1510–1535, ed. A. G. Dickens (Winchester, 1951).
Registra Stephani Gardiner et Johannes Poynet (Canterbury and York Soc. 37, 1929–30).
Registrum Ricardi Mayew Episcopi Herefordensis, ed. A. T. Bannister (Canterbury and York Soc. 27, 1921).

The Reports of Sir John Spelman, ed. J. H. Baker (Selden Soc. 93—4, 1975–6).

Report of the Deputy Keeper of the Public Records, 36 (London, 1875).

Report on Manuscripts in the Welsh Language, i (HMC 48, 1898).

Report on the Manuscripts of His Grace the Duke of Rutland, i, iv (HMC 12.4, 1888; 24, 1908).

Report on the Manuscripts of Lord De L'Isle and Dudley, i (HMC 77, 1925).

Report on the Manuscripts of Lord Middleton (HMC 69, 1911).

Report on the Manuscripts of the Corporation of Beverley (HMC 54, 1900).

Report on the Manuscripts of the Earl of Ancaster (HMC 66, 1907).

Report on the Manuscripts of the Most Honourable the Marquess of Bath, iv (HMC 58, 1968).

Rotuli Parliamentorum (7 vols, London, 1832).

Rutland Papers, ed. W. Jerdan (Cam. Soc. 21, 1842).

Rymer, T., Foedera, Conventiones, Literae et cujuscunque generis Acta Publica (3rd edn, 10 vols, The Hague, 1739–45).

The Scottish Correspondence of Mary of Lorraine, ed. A. I. Cameron (Scottish History Soc., 3rd ser. 10, 1927).

Select Cases in the Council of Henry VII, ed. C. G. Bayne, W. H. Dunham (Selden Soc. 75, 1958).

Selections from the Records of the City of Oxford, ed. W. H. Turner (Oxford, 1880).

Six Town Chronicles of England, ed. R. Flenley (Oxford, 1911).

State Papers, King Henry the Eighth (11 vols, London, 1830–52).

Statutes of the Realm, ed. A. Luders, T. E. Tomlins, J. Raithby, et al. (11 vols, London, 1810–28).

Stow, J., A Survey of London, ed. C. L. Kingsford (2nd edn, 2 vols, Oxford, 1971).

Strieder, J., Aus Antwerpener Notariatsarchiven (Deutsche Handelsakten des Mittelalters und der Neuzeit 4, 1930).

Suffolk in 1524, ed. S. H. A. Hervey (Suffolk Green Books 10, 1910).

Tempest, E. B., 'Tattershall', Lincs. Notes and Queries, 15 (1918–19).

Thorpe, T., A Catalogue of the most Splendid, Interesting and Truly Important Collection of Autograph Letters ever offered for Sale (London, 1840).

Trevelyan Papers iii, ed. W. C. Trevelyan, C. E. Trevelyan (Cam. Soc. 105, 1872).

Two Tudor Interludes: The Interlude of Youth, Hick Scorner, ed. I. Lancashire (The Revels Plays, 1980).

Tudor Royal Proclamations, ed. P. L. Hughes, J. F. Larkin (3 vols, New Haven and London, 1964–9).

Valor Ecclesiasticus, ed. J. Caley, J. Hunter (6 vols, London, 1810–34).

The Visitation of Shropshire, ed. G. Glazebrook, J. P. Rylands (2 vols, Harl. Soc. 28–9, 1889).

The Visitation of Suffolk, 1561, ed. J. Corder (2 vols, Harl. Soc. NS 2–3, 1981–4).

The Visitation of Yorkshire in the years 1563 and 1564, ed. C. B. Norcliffe (Harl. Soc. 16, 1881).

The Visitations of Essex, ed. W. C. Metcalfe (2 vols, Harl. Soc. 13–14, 1878–9).

The Visitations of Norfolk, ed. W. Rye (Harl. Soc. 33, 1891).

Visitations of the Diocese of Norwich A.D. 1492–1532, ed. A. Jessopp (Cam. Soc. NS 43, 1888).

Whittinton, R., Libellus Epygrammaton (London, 1519).

Wilson, T., The Arte of Rhetorique (London, 1553).

Wreyland Documents, ed. C. Torr (Cambridge, 1910).

Wriothesley, C., A Chronicle of England, i, ed. W. D. Hamilton (Cam. Soc. NS 11, 1875).

York Civic Records, iv, ed. A. Raine (Yorkshire Archaeological Soc., Record Series 108, 1945).

Yorkshire Fines, i (Yorks. Arch. Soc., rec. ser. 2, 1887).

Index

Places in England and Wales are located in their sixteenth-century, rather than their modern, counties. Places and persons mentioned only in the maps and genealogical tables are not included in the index, nor are all references to Charles Brandon and to Henry VIII. Dates following titles of nobility or offices are those of the creation or succession to the dignity of the individual concerned.

Fulstow, Lincs. 147, 170, 232
Furness Abbey, Lancs. 131
Furniture 86, 93

Gage, Sir John 206, 209, 210, 220
Gainsborough, Lincs. 161, 163
Gambling 75, 82, 83, 112, 122, 132, 133, 156
Gapton Hall, Suff. 184
Gardiner, Stephen, bishop of Winchester (1531) 126, 154, 190, 194, 204, 211, 212, 215, 235
Garter, Order of the 23, 32, 83, 94, 112, 133, 135, 144, 173, 191, 233
Garter king of arms 35, 137
Gates, John 212
Gayton le Marsh, Lincs. 187, 225, 229
Gedney, John 186
Geldeston, Norf. 120
gentlemen pensioners 193–4
Germany and Germans 28, 30–1, 48, 89, 91, 152, 155, 213, 215–6
Gildon, Katherine 172, 173, 219
  Thomas 169, 172, 173, 219, 226
  Thomas jun. 172, 226
Girlington family 229
  Nicholas 224, 226
Glemham, Christopher 63, 144, 178, 217
  Edward 63, 144, 178, 181
  Francis 63, 120
  Sir John 19, 60, 66, 93, 96, 140, 158–9, 178, 248ⁿ
Glentworth, Lincs. 224
Gloucester, Humphrey, duke of 210
  Richard, duke of, see Richard III Gloucestershire 37
Godparents 69, 110, 155, 190, 210, 212
Golde, John 79
Gosberton, Lincs. 170, 193
Gouffier, Artus, seigneur de Boisy 73
Guillaume, seigneur de Bonnivet 48, 49, 69, 73, 82, 105
Grafton, Northants. 126, 270ⁿ
Granado, Jacques 235
Grantham, Hugh 169, 172, 186, 221, 224, 226, 230, 231, 242
  Vincent 172, 186
Gray's Inn 60
Greatford, Lincs. 191
Greatham, Durh. 202
great mastership of the household 190, 192–4, 220
Great Yarmouth, Norf. 53–4, 60, 95, 96, 128, 192
Greenwich, Kent 52, 206
Gresham, Sir Richard 191
Grevyn, Francis 198

Grey, Anne (née Brandon), Lady Powis 42, 44, 70, 108–9, 134, 188
  Lady Anne 77, 78
  Edward, Lord Powis 86, 108–9, 134, 142, 143, 144, 188, 233
  Lord Edward, brother of Thomas, marquis of Dorset 144
  Lord Edward, brother of Henry, marquis of Dorset 194, 234
  Lady Elizabeth 77
  Elizabeth, Baroness Lisle 32–4, 36, 42–44, 52, 69, 104
  Frances (née Brandon), marchioness of Dorset 75, 109–10, 145–6, 152, 190, 212, 233, 270ⁿ
  Henry, marquis of Dorset (1530), duke of Suffolk (1551) 109, 145–6, 149, 182, 189, 206, 209, 233
  John, Viscount Lisle 36–7
  Lord Leonard 112
  Margaret (née Wotton), marchioness of Dorset 145–6
  Lord Richard 189
  Roger 226, 227
  Thomas, marquis of Dorset (1501) 30, 39, 47, 52, 81, 99, 108, 146, 152
Griffith, Sir William 38
Grimsby, Lincs. 163
Grimsthorpe, Lincs. 170, 171, 185, 213, 218–9, 232–3
Grimston, Edward sen. 55
  Edward jun. 55, 144, 177, 179, 193
Gruffydd, Elis 234
Guildford, Sir Edward 20–1, 54, 75, 83, 112
  Sir Henry 20–2, 34, 46, 52, 80, 83, 84, 108, 112, 131
  Lady Jane 18, 47
  Sir Richard 18
  Richard 75
Guines 117, 207
Gunby, Anthony 230
Gurney family 63, 78
Guyenne 29
Gwynello, Syrres 142

Hagnaby Abbey, Lincs. 187, 213
Hagworthingham, Lincs. 162, 223, 226
Hainton, Lincs. 186, 233
Halesworth, Suff. 232
Hall, Edmund 64, 191, 206, 218, 225, 227, 229
  Edward 52
  Elizabeth 270ⁿ
  Francis 61, 64, 76, 79, 105, 143, 149, 151, 152, 191, 243

Robert 48, 225, 226, 227
Haltham, Lincs. 225
Hamilton, James, earl of Arran 200–2
Hampshire 209, 220
Hampton, George 70, 73, 104, 106, 153–4, 216, 243
  James 106
Harman, John 180
Harrington, John 158
Haselwood, John 219
Hasilwode, Joan 85
Hastings, Sir Brian 163
Henry, earl of Huntingdon 239
  John 225
  William, Lord Hastings 142, 197, 214, 222
Hatton, Sir Christopher 239
Haughley, Suff. 55, 58
Haydor, Lincs. 224
Hector 81
Heneage family 186, 228
  George, dean of Lincoln 165
  Robert 228
  Sir Thomas 186, 228–9, 230, 233, 240
Henham, Suff. 58, 97, 152, 182
Henry V 91
Henry VI 16
Henry VII 15–20, 23, 25, 26, 32, 74, 127
Henry VIII, duke of York (1494), prince of Wales (1503): before 1509 19–21, 25; divorce from Catherine of Aragon 102, 106, 108–11, 117–18; relationship with Brandon 15, 20–25, 27, 30, 44, 46, 48–52, 71–73, 79–83, 86, 90, 110, 111–2, 114–5, 124–5, 127, 132–3, 135, 137–8, 138, 150–1, 154–6, 161, 165, 182–3, 190–1, 203, 207–8, 234–5, 237–8, 242–4
heralds, kings of arms and pursuivants 17, 28, 30, 35, 39, 55, 70, 97, 135–7, 154, 159, 243
Herbert, Sir William and Anne (née Parr) 212
  Lord, see Somerset
Hertford, earl of, see Seymour
Heveningham, George 62, 77, 78
Heydon, Sir Christopher 62, 144
high marshalcy of the army 30–31, 33, 40–1
high stewardship and constableship of England 136
Hoby, Sir Philip 212
Hogsthorpe, Lincs. 226
Holbeach, Henry, bishop of Rochester (1544) 235
Holbein, Hans 185, 216, 234, 243